BE A MASTER® OF PSYCHIC ENERGY

YOUR KEY TO TRULY MASTERING YOUR PERSONAL POWER

Dr. Theodoros Kousouli

A Personal Empowerment Book

Kousouli Enterprises
Los Angeles, CA

Copyright © 2018 by Theodoros Kousouli D.C., CHt.

All rights reserved. No part of this book may be reproduced or utilized in any form or by any means, electronic or mechanical including photocopying, recording, or by any information storage and retrieval system, without permission in writing from the author and publisher, except for the inclusion of brief quotations in a review with proper credit cited.

The BE A MASTER® BOOK SERIES (http://www.BEAMASTER.com) trademarked brand and work is Copyright of Dr. Theodoros Kousouli.

The KOUSOULI® mark and the Kousouli® Method 4R Intervention health system are registered trademarks of Theodoros D. Kousouli D.C., CHt. and Kousouli Enterprises.

Heartfelt gratitude to the following for their contributions:
Editor: Essence Chandler
Co-Editor: Latasha Doyle
Research & data assistance: Arindam Chaudhury, PhD
Cover and internal photography: Matthew A. Cooke
Freehand sketch illustrations: Eric Vasquez
Layout coordinator: Gustavo Martinez

ISBN: 978-0997328530   Softcover
ISBN: 978-0997328547   Epub
ISBN: 978-0997328554   Kindle

Library of Congress Control Number: 2016909169

Kousouli Enterprises
P.O. Box 360494
Los Angeles, CA 90036

Printed in the United States of America

CONTENTS

Foreword xi
Disclaimers xiii
Acknowledgements xvii
Preface xix

PART I: INTRODUCTION 1

PART II: AWAKENING – Understanding the Game 5

Chapter 1: Spiritual, but not Religious? 15
1.1 When No One Else Can Help 17
1.2 Emotionally Believing in the Healing 19
1.3 The Antenna Between the Physical and the Spiritual 21
1.4 That Magnificent Mind Power 22

Chapter 2: Energetics Rule Your World 25
2.1 It is What it is - There is No "Could Have Been" 25
2.2 The Reality of Energetic Sensitives 26
2.3 Kinds of Energy - Invisible and Imaginary? 26
2.4 Energy Development of the Unseen 28
2.5 Mentally Ill vs. Energetically Sensitive 29
2.6 Graduating with a Spiritual Diploma 31

Chapter 3: Everything and Everyone is Connected 33
3.1 Understanding Parallel Realities 33
3.2 Understanding Dimensions 35
3.3 Talking about God 37
3.4 How Do I Know What is From God or 'Real'? 38

Chapter 4: The Original Church: What Happened to Christianity? 41
4.1 Religious Hypocrisy 41
4.2 Consider This... 42
4.3 Know Your Religious Beginnings 43
4.4 Was Original Christianity Jewish? 44
4.5 The Roman Catholic Church Decides to Change the Rules 45
4.6 Summary of the Great Schism 47
4.7 Did God Himself Write the Religious Texts? 47
4.8 Who Are "The Father," "The Son," and "The Holy Spirit"? 48

    4.9 The First Great Question of Life is…"Why am I Here?" 49
    4.10 The Second Great Question of Life Is… "Do I Matter? Is My Life of Value?" . . 50
    4.11 The Lord's Prayer 52

Chapter 5: What is a Soul? - The Original You 55
    5.1 Limiting the Limitless Soul 56
    5.2 Past, Future, and Current Lives 57
    5.3 The Soul's Progression. 59
    5.4 When You Were Born. 59
    5.5 Death - A Naturally Safe or Unsafe Process? 61

Chapter 6: S.I.N. – Self-Inflicted Negativity 63
    6.1 What is Right and What is Wrong? 63
    6.2 What is SIN?. 63
    6.3 Where Did the Idea of Hell Come From, and Who is Satan? 64
    6.4 What Does Misunderstanding SIN do to My Well-Being? 67
    6.5 Planet Earth - The Grand Stage 67
    6.6 Regulating Human Thought – What You See is not What You Get 69
    6.7 Desensitizing People - Everyone is a Salesman. 70
    6.8 Hidden Communication of the Occult in Plain Sight 72
    6.9 Mother, Father, Teacher, and Preacher Programming 73

PART III: EMPOWERMENT – Tapping into Your Spinal Power 75

Chapter 7: The Kousouli® Method – Healthy Living in Today's World 77
    7.1 Is Your Mind Really Involved in the Dis-ease Process? 77
    7.2 Retracing Your Recovery Pathway 78
    7.3 How Does Emotion Affect Your Health?. 80
    7.4 The Kousouli® Method 4R Intervention System. 82

Chapter 8: The Nervous System: Gateway for Turning Your Life Around 89
    8.1 The Neuron. 89
    8.2 Body Communication Via the CNS and PNS. 91
    8.3 The Autonomic Nervous System (ANS) and Peripheral Nervous
        System (PNS). 91
    8.4 The Spinal Connection Further Explored 93

Chapter 9: Chiropractic Care and Kousouli® Spinal Stretches (KSS™)
       for Well-Being 95
    9.1 How Does Spinal Degeneration Affect You?. 95

    9.2 Vertebral Subluxation and Neurological Compression Syndrome 97
    9.3 The Importance of Scar Tissue Removal in Supporting the Spine 99
    9.4 Relief and Corrective Care 100
    9.5 Corrective Care of Chronic Pain 101
    9.6 The Kousouli® Method Spinal Stretches (KSS™) 101
    9.7 Sleep Well to Reenergize the Mind and Improve Body Chi 111
    9.8 Sleeping Ergonomics 112

Chapter 10: Nutrition Guidelines for Increasing Chi Energy **115**
    10.1 Acidosis - Starting Grounds for Dis-ease 115
    10.2 Does Negative Emotional Energy Contribute to Acidosis? 115
    10.3 Cleansing and Detoxification 116
    10.4 Home Detox Tips to Get Rid of Acidosis and Raise Chi Energy 116
    10.5 Overcoming the Deficiencies 118
    10.6 Chlorophyll – The Green Blood 121
    10.7 Nutritional and Habitual Tips *to Grow Your Natural Chi* 121

PART IV: TRANSFORMATION – 'Awe'-Waken your Power **129**

✶**VISUALIZATION AND MANIFESTATION**✶

Chapter 11: Spiritual Wisdom and Laws that Allow Your Abundance **131**
    11.1 About Confidence 131
    11.2 About Courage 133
    11.3 Overcoming Confusion 135
    11.4 Overcoming Discouragement or Fear 136
    11.5 About Love 139
    11.6 About Perseverance 143
    11.7 About Success and Prosperity 144
    11.8 About Money 147
    11.9 Gaining Financial Power 151
    11.10 Why Isn't My Wealth Here Yet? 153
    11.11 Know These Universal Laws for Creating Abundance 154

Chapter 12: Exercises for Visualizing and Manifesting Abundance **163**
    12.1 Manifestation Method - Your Personal Valet Angel 163
    12.2 Manifestation Method - The 'In-Vision Board' 164
    12.3 Manifestation Method - The 'Never-Ending Gratitude List' 166
    12.4 Manifestation Method - The 'Big-Money Multiplier' 167

12.5 Manifestation Method - The 'Journal of (I AM) Praise' 169
12.6 Manifestation Method - The 'This was Your Life Biography' 169
12.7 Manifestation Method - The 'Things To Do Before I Leave List' 170
12.8 Manifestation Method - '365 Days of Calendar Power' 170
12.9 Manifestation Method - The 'Universal To-Do List' 171
12.10 Manifestation Method - The '4-D Experience' 172
12.11 Manifestation Method - 'Chalk on Glass or Mirror' 172
12.12 Manifestation Method - The 'Previously Manifested List' 174
12.13 Manifestation Method - 'Big Brother Benjamin' 175
12.14 Formula for Successful Manifestation 176
12.15 The Key is FOCUS 177

Chapter 13: The Chakra System - Healing Through the Unseen 179
13.1 Remedy Through the Invisible 179
13.2 Hypnosis 180
13.3 Hypnotherapy and the Mind-Body Problem 181
13.4 The Influence of Mind-Body Theory on Medicine 181
13.5 States of Brain Wave Activity 182
13.6 Covert Hypnosis Is All Around Us 182
13.7 Common Myths About Hypnosis Exposed! 183
13.8 Dreams 185
13.9 Astral Projection 186
13.10 Understanding the Third Eye 187
13.11 Love, Sex, Relationships and Auric Spaces 189
13.12 Attracting the Right Mate for a Lasting Relationship 193
13.13 Relationship Misunderstandings 194
13.14 You're In Charge of Your Own Life 195
13.15 Take the Lead Role In Your Play 196
13.16 Changing Who You Are To Who You Can Be 196
13.17 A Loner Maybe, But Never Alone 197
13.18 Victim Mentality 198
13.19 Sex and the Creative Forces of the Lower Chakras 198
13.20 Sexual Consciousness 199
13.21 Clear the Mind and Heart of Burdened Thoughts 200
13.22 Angels in the Auric Field 202
13.23 Common Angels 204
13.24 Angel Numbers and Their Sequence Meanings 205

  13.25 The Chakras 207
  13.26 Color and Possible Frequency Interpretations in the Auric Field and
     Energy Healing 209
  13.27 The Chakras and Auric Field 211
  13.28 Energy Channels 211
  13.29 Trifecta Palm Chakra Energy Exercise 213

✶ENERGY HEALING✶

Chapter 14: Prayer, Meditation and Aura Healing Basics 215
  14.1 Just Get Out of Your Way 215
  14.2 We Are All Healers 216
  14.3 The Path of a Healer 218
  14.4 The Healer's Tool Belt 219
  14.5 The Healer's Wardrobe 219
  14.6 Creating and Respecting the Healing Container (Healing Space) 220
  14.7 Know There's Healing Happening 220
  14.8 How to View Aura Energy 221
  14.9 Your Spiritual DNA and Aura 222
  14.10 Pelvic Adjustment Pre & Post Treatment 224
  14.11 Cervical Adjustment Pre & Post Treatment 224
  14.12 How to Meditate 225
  14.13 How to Pray 227
  14.14 How to Scan and Prepare the Aura for Healing 228

Chapter 15: Energetic Healing of the Patient using the Kousouli® Method 233
  15.1 The Crux of Energy Healing 233
  15.2 Understanding Yin and Yang for Healing 234
  15.3 Kousouli® Method Energy Healing Case Studies 235
  15.4 Kousouli® Method Master Chart 243

✶PSYCHIC AWARENESS✶

Chapter 16: Performing a Clairvoyant Reading 245
  16.1 Energy Potentials, Not Prophecy or 'Future Telling' 245
  16.2 Clairvoyant Terminology 248
  16.3 Psychic Visualization and Meditation Tools to Move and Clear Energy 255
  16.4 Performing a Clairvoyant Reading Session 258

Chapter 17: Performing a Group Manifestation Meditation 269
  17.1 Power in numbers 269

17.2 How to Perform a Group Manifestation Meditation 270

Chapter 18: Remotely Viewing Universal Information 275
18.1 Communicating with God 275
18.2 Can I Talk to God? 276
18.3 Remote Viewing: Using the God Eye to View Faraway Places 278
18.4 What Do You Want to Know? 278
18.5 The Elusive Aspect of Time 278
18.6 The Program A Template 279
18.7 The Program B and C Templates 290
18.8 Troubleshooting the Program 295

Chapter 19: Spiritual Warfare - Neutralizing Negative Energies 297
19.1 The Thoughts in Our Heads 297
19.2 The Vibrations of Darkness 298
19.3 How Do I Break Away From Serious Negative Energy, Sorcery, or
 Possession? 300
19.4 How Do You Know if the Negativity Means You Need a Psychiatrist, or
 If It Is Possession? 301
19.5 How Does One Fall Prey to Being Possessed by Negativity? 301
19.6 Sleep Paralysis 302
19.7 Do Not Trust Plural or Negative Voices 304
19.8 A Simple Prayer for Protection 304
19.9 Commanding Negative Energy Away From Another 305
19.10 Seeing the Good in All 305
19.11 Unpure Thoughts are Wild 306
19.12 What Do I Do When a Client Is So Overwhelmed With a Negative
 Situation? 306
19.13 Change the Programming and End Suffering 307
19.14 Negative Subliminal Messages and Commands in Music 307
19.15 Is Your Self-Esteem Low From Negative Self-Talk? 308
19.16 Recognize Your Negative Thought Patterns 309
19.17 Get Out of Negative Vibrations ASAP 310
19.18 Keeping Your Attitude Positive 311
19.19 Dumping Negativity 312
19.20 Self-Appreciation, Not Selfishness 313

Chapter 20: Becoming a Spiritual Super-Human ... 315
- 20.1 Building Awareness ... 316
- 20.2 Don't Lie to Yourself ... 316
- 20.3 Balancing Your Life ... 317
- 20.4 Be Malleable but Decisive ... 319
- 20.5 Fanaticism Weakens Your GOD Power ... 320
- 20.6 Going Hunting for Lost Energy in the Home ... 320
- 20.7 Things and Spaces: Taking Energy Back ... 322
- 20.8 Bringing Old Thoughts to Physical Form and Deleting Them ... 324
- 20.9 Get Off the Pain Train Immediately ... 325
- 20.10 Rejection Isn't Personal; It's a Process ... 326
- 20.11 Get Up Like a Winner ... 327
- 20.12 Starting and Ending Your Day ... 327
- 20.13 Apply a New Routine ... 328
- 20.14 Come On, Laugh a Little ... 328
- 20.15 Twenty Minutes to Changing the 'Real' ... 328
- 20.16 Free Will and Choosing Not to See ... 329
- 20.17 The Importance of Judging and Timing ... 329
- 20.18 Living Longer – The Secret to Anti-Aging ... 330
- 20.19 Tips on Living Longer, Healthier, and Abundantly ... 331
- 20.20 Remaining Young with Natural Aging ... 333
- 20.21 Live Fully By Leaving Earth Without Regrets ... 335
- 20.22 Materialism ... 336
- 20.23 Claiming It and Seeing It ... 338
- 20.24 Develop Your Board of Directors ... 339
- 20.25 How Do We Clean This Planet Up? ... 339

Chapter 21: Conclusion ... 341
- 21.1 A Gift of Visions ... 341
- 21.2 Closing Thoughts ... 345

About the Author ... 349

References ... 351

Be a Master® of Psychic Energy

Life Changing Products · Books · Seminars · Empowerment Audios · Get on the Newsletter!

Connect with Dr. Kousouli, www.DrKousouli.com and on all Social Media Platforms
@DrKousouli #DrKousouli #KousouliMethod

You Will Also Enjoy Dr. Kousouli's Other Published Works Available Now from Major Retailers:

BE A MASTER® OF MAXIMUM HEALING
How to Lead a Healthy Life Without Limits
- Holistic Solutions for over 60 Diseases to Help You and Your Loved Ones Heal!

BE A MASTER® OF SEX ENERGY
Hypnotize Your Partner for Love and Great Sex
- Build a Stronger Bond with Your Lover(s) Using Subconscious Science!

BE A MASTER® OF SUCCESS
Dr.Kousouli's 33 Master Secrets to Achieving Your Dreams
- Solid Success Principles You can Apply Right Now to Empower Your Life!

BE A MASTER® OF SELF IMAGE
Dr.Kousouli's 33 Master Secrets to Living Healthier, Happier and Hotter
- Simple Holistic Tips & Tricks for More Weight Loss and Body Benefit to You!

BE A MASTER® OF SELF LOVE
Dr.Kousouli's 33 Master Secrets to Loving Your Extraordinary Life
- Overcome Bullying, Abuse, Depression and Build Massive Self-Esteem & Self-Love!

BE A MASTER® OF YOUR REALITY
Authentically Manifest Your Desires
- Use the Law of Attraction to Radically Transform Your Life!

If you would like to share your story of how Dr. Kousouli's books, audios or seminars have impacted your life for the better, we would love to hear from you! (Messages are screened by staff and forwarded when appropriate.)

For A Free Gift from Dr. Theo Kousouli visit www.FreeGiftFromDrTheo.com

Foreword

By Elena Gabor CMHt, CI

"Truth has no special time of its own. Its hour is now - always."
~ Albert Schweitzer

Why do you think you picked up this specific book? Do you think it was chance, destiny, or just plain luck? You picked up this book because deep inside, you are looking for answers, and something drew you to the contents within. Perhaps you have been asking deep questions and intuitively know there's more than what you see with your physical eyes; you want to know how it all *really* works. We have an inner yearning to discover and reconnect with our true identity, where we come from, and what we can do to heal ourselves and live happy and prosperous lives.

In all my university, medical, and dental training, or during postgraduate studies, I was not instructed on the subconscious power of the mind, benefits of positive thinking, or the power of the mind-body connection. I had to step out of the classical, medical, and limited belief that the mind and body are separate, and the idea that consciousness is the byproduct of brain activity. I had to enter into a holistic perspective in order to discover the secrets of consciousness and healing. Now, as a medical hypnotherapist in the holistic field, I have learned how amazing and incredible each one of us is singularly, as well as a collective consciousness. We have just scratched the surface in understanding our true nature and the nature of true reality.

I see people every day experiencing amazing transformations that far exceed their expectations. Some of the most fascinating cases of recovery attained by involving all of our levels of consciousness in healing were presented in my book, *Home at the Tree of Life*. Over the years, I have helped thousands of people improve their health and overcome their life challenges by teaching them the power of positive thinking and reconnection with their higher levels of consciousness. That's how I met Dr. Theo Kousouli. I had the privilege to be his hypnotherapist, to help him explore his subconscious universe and to discover other amazing aspects of his greater-self. Through our work, he discovered that his abilities as a leader, teacher, and healer have been surfacing many times throughout his journey of evolution as eternal consciousness.

Dr. Kousouli is a remarkable chiropractor, hypnotherapist, healer, and teacher who has developed exciting, innovating techniques for healing that he incorporated in a unique healing technique, *The Kousouli® Method*. This is a powerful system that helps relax and de-stress both the mind and body. I've experienced his methods of healing myself with magnificent results. This method helps people become more aware by **expanding their healing skills and psychic intuition** so that they can function from a **higher level of perception**.

BE A MASTER® OF PSYCHIC ENERGY is an illuminating book that will truly open your mind toward understanding the amazing power of healing and its mind-body relationship. In this book, Dr. Kousouli describes his philosophy and method of healing, presents wonderful meditations and exercises to expand your body's chi energy flow, and teaches practical techniques to unlock your untapped psychic ability! This book also breaks the mundane rules of religious dogma, the teachings of our parent's generation of conformist mediocrity, gives you practical steps to neutralize negativity in your life, and explores the modern healing of this century utilizing age-old wisdom. You will further find answers to questions such as how you can focus your energy for abundance manifestation, how your nervous system is connected to healing, and how history's great healers, such as Jesus Christ, were able to heal.

If you would like to tap into the unlimited abilities of your mind and activate your inner healing potential, read this extraordinary book! Dr. Kousouli will teach you how to not only keep healthy and expand your thinking, but he will give you a concrete plan to live everyday as if it were magic. Take his course and dive into the beginning of the rest of your life!

Elena Gabor CMHt, CI
Medical Hypnotherapist and Author of *'Home at the Tree of Life'*

After ten years of practicing as a Doctor of Dental Medicine, Dr. ELENA GABOR redirected her focus toward researching a new field of study - subconscious medicine - the science of the subconscious universe. As a medical hypnotherapist and expert in subconscious science, she helps her clients overcome their health and emotional challenges, and explore their immortality. She is the author of the groundbreaking book entitled "Home at the Tree of Life," which sheds light on the mysteries of consciousness, life, past lives, death, afterlife, and the underlying causes of physical and mental conditions. For more information please visit www.drgabor.com

DISCLAIMER

In a land where being politically correct seems more 'right' than standing for the 'truth,' or more desired than expressing an honest opinion, it's sad that I must digress and add the following legal disclaimer to remind you, the reader, that ***you must think for yourself***.

This book is a collection of experiences and research that form my thoughts, opinions, and conclusions as a board certified Doctor of Chiropractic (D.C.) and Hypnotherapist (CHt); not a Doctor of Medicine (M.D.). The content herein is controversial as it presents an alternate view to the status quo. There are establishments who may disagree with certain contents of this book, and would have preferred that this information never found your eyes. However, this book is not intended for them; it was written for the countless individuals yearning for better health and well-being amongst a society that has lost its way.

The writings in this book are based on my personal research, experience, interpretations and beliefs. Your personal beliefs will affect your ability to review this material, as you will put it through your own filters. I intend to guide you in developing your own ability to use your personal energy in a healthy manner, and this book is a guide for you to grow, but is not by any means the final word on the subject.

I encourage you, the reader, to research, analyze and develop your own opinions on the subject matters discussed. As a holistic health care provider, I express the truth as I have come to know it. It is my duty to aid in the growth of my beloved patients, family, and friends with this love so they too may reach the heights of what their Creator made possible for them to be.

Theodoros Kousouli D.C., CHt.

LEGAL DISCLAIMER

This publication is for informational purposes only. The material presented herein denotes the views of the author as of the date of press. The material and ideas provided herein are believed to be truthful and complete, based on the author's best judgment and experience, formed from the available data at the time of publication. Because of the speed by which conditions and information change, the author reserves the right to amend and update his opinions at any time based upon the new data and circumstances. While every effort has been made to provide complete, accurate, current, and reliable information within this publication, no warranties of any kind are expressed or implied. The publisher, author, and all associated parties involved with this publication assume no responsibility for errors, inaccuracies, oversights or conflicting interpretation of the content herein. The author and publisher do not accept any responsibility for any liabilities resulting from the use of this information. Readers acknowledge that the author is not engaging in rendering guarantees of income or outcome of any kind in connection with using any methods, techniques, or information stated or implied. Any perceived results of the material's use can vary greatly per case and individual circumstance. Mention of any persons or companies in this book does not imply that they endorse this book, its content, or the author, and similarly the author does not endorse them. Any supposed slights of specific establishments, corporations, organizations, peoples, or persons are unintended.

You should consult your own chiropractor, acupuncturist, herbalist, naturopath, hypnotherapist or other holistic doctor(s) in combination with sound medical advice. Readers are cautioned to first consult with proper health professionals about their individual circumstances on any matter relating to their health and personal well-being prior to taking any course of action. The author is not a licensed medical doctor or psychiatrist and the ***information provided in this book should not be construed as personal, medical, or psychiatric advice or instruction.*** All readers or users of the information herein, who fail to consult proper health experts, assume the risk of any and all injuries.

The contents of this book and the information herein have not been evaluated or approved by the Food and Drug Administration for the treatment or cure of any disease, disorder, syndrome, or ailment mentioned herein.

Dedicated to my friend and late mentor, Dr. Scott Lewis, and the many souls of light that work tirelessly in bringing more love to this planet so humanity can be that which it was destined to be.

"Empty your mind. Be formless; shapeless. Like water…

Now you put water into a cup; it becomes the cup.
You put water into a bottle; it becomes the bottle.
Put it into the teapot; it becomes the teapot.
Now water can flow or it can crash…

Be water my friend."

~ Bruce Lee

Acknowledgements

*"Feeling gratitude and not expressing it is like
wrapping a present and not giving it."*
~ William Arthur Ward

I would like to thank all those who waited patiently for this book to be completed, and who aided with encouragement as the months turned to years. Gratitude goes to my parents for the early life lessons taught to me and for sacrificing their own comforts to make sure my siblings and I had the necessities to thrive. Thankful for my brother, Nicholas, and sister, Chrisa, both who also serve to better the health care system in America; I love you. My appreciation also for my close friends: Peter Lamas, Elina Loukas, Angela Pond, Alek Romanoff, and Essence Chandler who are used to hearing the words, "I am working on the book," when calling to see if I am still breathing. Further gratitude to my spiritual mentors, colleagues, and teachers: Dr. Scott Brown, Dr. Michael Kostas, Dr. Hari Bhajan Singh Khalsa, Dr. Scott Lewis, Dr. Elena Gabor, Marisa Marinos, and Racquel Moore. I am grateful for having been touched by your evolved presence and humbled by your vast knowledge. I am thankful also for the loving teachings of Lee Carroll, Darryl Anka, and Ester and Jerry Hicks. Through their astounding contribution to humanity, I am constantly reminded to give bountiful service to my neighbor and lead by example.

Thanks to all my amazing patients who allow me the ability to serve my purpose and be a part of their world in this incarnation. Special thanks goes to Alki David, Ana T. Salazar, Michael Littenberg, Mark Weiss, and Jill Abrams.

Lastly, but definitely not least, I thank the Almighty Creator of all things visible and invisible, great and small, explainable and unexplainable. I stand in awe of your pure magnificence as you lead and sustain me through your playground day by day.

This list deserves to be far longer than it reads. If I have forgotten your name in these writings of ink, kindly forgive me - and know that I am in gratitude to you from the depths of my heart.

Preface

"The greatest wealth is health."
~ Virgil

I had the best of two dogmatic worlds; a military father and a very religious mother. I grew up in a Greek American Eastern Orthodox home, in a very traditional setting, consisting of the rare 'nuclear' family, with my wonderful two younger siblings who are fraternal twins. My father, a strict ex-merchant marine for the Greek Navy, became a restaurant owner when he immigrated to the U.S. in the 70's, whereas my mother was a traditional stay-at-home mom who took care of three highly energetic kids. We lived in Deptford, NJ, a quiet middle-income suburban town barely on the map. My father always provided the tough love, practical work ethic, food, clothing, and roof over our heads. My mother provided the religious law needed to live a structured life within society.

I never understood why my parents chose each other as mates. It seemed that they derived more pleasure from their arguments than enjoying the pleasant presence of peace. As children we rarely saw our parents treat each other with unconditional love or kindness. Both had their parenting strengths, and opposing weaknesses, but we loved them both equally. In the end, as with all parents, they did the best they could with what they derived from their own experiences. My parents lived through post World War 2 as children, and my father remembered vividly the Nazi occupation coming through his village in Elika, Greece as a young child. These experiences would later shape his thought process, belief system, and the way he would raise his own family. My parents raised three wonderful children, by society's standards, as everyone who meets us affirms this, which makes them even more proud. However, all may have looked happy on the outside, but I was hurting on the inside. It was not until I wasn't living under my father's roof that I would understand the sacrifices and reasons for their parenting wins and failures. After going out on my own and heading to college, I would begin to forgive the emotional programming impressed upon on me, and also begin to see the world from their eyes as an adult. I also wouldn't see, until I left the family nest, how the emotional energy I received from that suburban South Jersey home environment would shape how I would attract or repel my experiences and creation in my future world.

I never liked public school. It reminded me exactly of a prison system, where the principal was the warden and the teachers controlled the classrooms and patrolled the hallways; always on the lookout for escapees. I felt confined behind the brick walls of the compound and felt that no matter how hard I tried, I could not do well enough to meet teacher expectations, nor be cool enough to avoid the bullies on the recess fields. In my grade school years I was perceived as a tiny, odd, and quiet kid. I was the smallest person in the class, often bullied for nothing more than looking like an easy target for others to release their day-to-day insecurities and stress upon. However, deep down inside myself I felt like a giant, multitalented, genius and more powerful than a king. I felt this way throughout my childhood, though the feeling was suppressed daily by negative people in my immediate environment.

In those years, the school system didn't fully challenge us, nor did it encourage identifying and growing our individual innate abilities. Instead, school would be the same mundane cycle day in and day out; and as long as you did not think for yourself and stayed subordinate, you got the grade. I never felt school was about actual learning, just rote memorization and regurgitating it back in time for the test, only to forget the material and never use most of it again. How many of us have ever used the Pythagorean Theorem as adults anyways?! The bell would ring, we would have to switch books, and report to the next class like good little prisoners. I detested the system for not tapping into my more profound abilities, or recognizing that I was someone who had more than just rote memorization to offer the world. I wanted to be free to create and express myself without repression. Being the oldest of the siblings, I was by nature a very rebellious free thinker with high energy. I excelled without effort in courses such as English, Science, Art, and Music, but I did not take well to authoritative suppression of my childhood freedoms and liberties. When some of my other assignments came home with C, D, and F grades, my father disciplined with anger. I remember sitting at home, scratching my head over a rough math problem on my desk that looked more like Chinese than Greek or English to me. We would dread his visits to our rooms, especially me. It meant that if I did anything wrong I would be slapped or hit with a leather belt, no matter how trivial. Periodically, during television commercial breaks from the dreaded nightly news, my father would leave the couch to visit our rooms and suppress his boredom by 'checking up' on us while we did our homework. His words were like thunder when he looked down at my paper and saw I answered incorrectly. "No it's not correct, stupid!" he yelled as his hand grabbed a chunk full of my hair, pulling me sharply sideways, making me fall right off of my chair. As children, we feared our father but did not have much respect. It would be over a decade later that I would understand the rationale behind his internal programming concerning gaining respect and authority by forceful deeds, and then learn how to reverse the pain it created by beginning the healing process for this and other life circumstances.

Naturally, after that incident, anything involving math got terribly difficult for me. From that teary-eyed moment forward, my subconscious had associated math and numbers with pain and punishment. I ended up failing math that quarter and a parent teacher conference was scheduled. My father was not happy with his little "Spartan." He always disciplined by tough love, and fear was his weapon. The short walk to the school for the conference felt like a mile. I vividly remember his words to my teacher: "If he misbehaves or gets another F, you have my permission to lock him in the janitor's closet, and leave him there," as he laughed along with the teacher. You can imagine what that felt like as a young child, having the only person in the world that you want to make proud, along with another authority figure, your teacher, put you in a dark place of seclusion; exiling you to some closet away from your sense of belonging to life, friends, and the growth of the classroom. As a child, I did not understand sarcasm or disciplining by fear, though that incident, along with many others, would mount through the coming years, re-enforcing the emotional pain within my life experiences and my perception of a cruel world.

Going through college was an interesting time in my life. I was able to leave my small town long enough to mix my mind with more seasoned, interesting people. Like all young men and women moving along toward adulthood, I questioned many times what scholastic concentration to focus on, and what career path to take. I knew I wanted to decide on a pre-medical major and entertained the idea of a general medical family practice, dentistry, podiatry, or dermatology. If not the medical option, then it would be either an engineer or politician; my father's choices for me – not mine.

Thanks to our religious mother, some form of spirituality was alive in our household. I would pray at night before bed, and I remember asking God to help me find the work I could do that would help others, and provide me peace of mind so that I would enjoy my life. I was confused with who I was, or if I had a purpose, and questioned why I even existed. I asked God to make the answer very clear for me, so I would know without a doubt what He wanted me to do with this life. I witnessed how difficult my father's life was as he slaved in the restaurant business to provide for us, yet came home and hardly had any time to spend with us as a family. I really think he wanted to enjoy his life with us, but there was no more energy in him after the long 12-hour shifts he endured. From a young age I could see that this was not healthy. The stress from slacking employees, rude customers, and day-to-day operations was unfortunately taken out on my mother, siblings, and I whenever he did have the time to spend with us. I was more interested in going into life utilizing my talents as an artist; making large projects and sculptures for museums, collectors, and art galleries. However, I always had a fondness for the magnificent work of art that the human body is, and its workings continue to leave me in awe every day. Little to my understanding at that time, God was soon about to put my life together for me, in ways that helped it all make sense.

Didn't Fit In

I remember being a joyful nerdy little child who loved everyone. I would go up to everyone and hug and kiss them on the cheek without second-guessing my actions. I was full of love and the thoughts of anger, hate, jealousy, etc. were not in my nature or vocabulary. My mother could not stop my impulsiveness and would sternly reprimand me that it was not good to kiss strangers even on the cheek. I asked, "But why Mom?" and she laughingly said, "It is just not what you do." I again asked, "But why mom? I love them." I remember her face as she smiled and slowed down to explain it in terms my ten-year-old mind would understand. "Big Boy (the nickname I earned since I was the oldest of three), you can hug them or shake their hand but no more kissing OK?" I was puzzled and sad about that, but I obeyed my mother and fell into line like everyone else in society, as I shook hands and remained socially acceptable.

Between the ages of four and twelve, I believed I had extra sensory abilities; one of them being that I could fly. I later found out that while asleep, I was doing a phenomenon called astral traveling, where your soul leaves the body and vividly explores the wonders of all creation. A feeling of lifting and flying is common with this phenomenon as you cannot tell the difference between the physical world and the astral world. I would seriously feel as if this was an ability I could do without hesitation and was confident it was possible for me anytime I wished. I told my mother and father about this, and they kept telling me it was a dream and that it would go away. I never questioned it. However, to my disappointment and frustration it became less frequent, happening only 50% of the time. As I got older, it did not happen much past 14 years of age. I thought everyone knew about this ability. I was confused and wanted to get answers from my parents. "Leave me alone, I'm watching the news," or, "Get out of the way, I can't see the T.V.," was a common response from my father when I tried to share my thoughts or concerns.

As I was growing up through my youth and teens, classmates and my siblings would ask me, "Why are you talking to yourself?" They'd laugh and tease me, wiggling their lips and making funny faces. In reality, what was going on was I was talking to someone - be it my guide, or God, or higher power. I would see colors vividly and I felt as if I was multitasking in two worlds. As mumbling would occur, sounds and thoughts would often come in a very fast manner. I hardly noticed it happening as I was in a dialogue in my brain, in what seemed like a daydream state, though still conscious about the happenings in the world around me. My sister would tease and say, "Mom, Theo's talking to himself again!" I would pretend to laugh and hide it within a joke, so as to not explain what I was experiencing or humiliate myself trying to.

At the age of thirteen, I can recall being in my room at my desk doing homework, and blacking out into a vision of a man in a uniform touching someone lying lifeless on a table. I saw people crowded in a room overlooking the body on the table. The man who sat at the top end of the table touched the still body's neck, releasing a bright light (resembling an electric blue flame), which then flowed down the body and around the table. Instantaneously, the body then became animated as I awakened out of the vision. When I came back, my hands were pulsing, sweating, and very warm. I was in shock of what had just occurred. I was waving my hands as you would if you just realized you touched a hot stove fanning them out to cool them down. However, I soon realized that I was alright and my hands were not burned. I immediately left my books and ran downstairs, flew out the door and went 3 houses down to my younger brother and sister who were over at our friend Kelsie's house (our usual hangout after school and where we would go to escape boredom). Out of breath and still high from excitement, I started huffing and puffing as I ran up to my brother and sister who were in the back yard swing set. Looking at my hands I said, "Something happened, there was a blue light!," I blurted out in a squeaky huff and puff. "What? You're crazy," said my sister followed by the laughter of my brother and Kelsie. I started to clam up to avoid further humiliation, so I just decided it would be best to leave. Between the bully beatings in school for being different, and the lack of support in my own house, I crawled inside myself - deep inside.

I continued having many dreams, even seeing what I believe was an angel, resembling the Virgin Mary, looking and smiling at me while sitting at the table with my mother one morning. My mother would be the only one who would even entertain the possibility of me seeing anything like that. Mothers are inherently powerful psychics by nature; the protective instinct for their children is often aided by their sixth sense. Throughout my life, my mother was the most supportive when I reported sightings and had dreams, as she herself was used to her own events of dream premonitions and psychic phenomenon.

On our refrigerator door there was a photo my mother particularly liked of us as kids. My sister would tease, "Look at your pointed ears, you're an alien, you're an alien! Theo's adopted from another planet!" to which I replied, "I am not an alien, I am not adopted, and I am not from another planet." I would get really upset, because I wanted to fit in so badly. In many ways, however, I did feel very alien. By the time I was 15, the bullying at school was overwhelming. I had tolerated it since 1st grade and now I was going into middle school. Tormented by bullies in class, unable to decipher the dreams and visions, and the emotional abuse at home, I became convinced that I was too crazy and too different to fit in. One day after school, beat up and emotionally lifeless, drowning in tears, I'd decided to end my life by cutting my wrists with a razor. Just as I was about to slice my wrists, a voice inside sternly said "NO!" It echoed so loudly it vibrated through me like lightning and I couldn't bring myself to take the razor across my wrists; my grip on the razor went limp. An overwhelming peace and calm came over me, as I felt comforted by a feeling unlike any other. I somehow internally understood at that moment that I was not meant to end my life and that it was the environment that was sick, not me. I knew I was here for a reason and believed there was something grander that needed to be done, but was yet unfinished. I knew not where this instant clarity came from, but it was very much welcomed.

Incidental Blessings

One summer break, we went to Greece to visit our grandmother. During our stay, we would visit a summer camp for teens to get out of busy Athens. Getting a little mountain air is what my mother thought would be best, since it allowed us American children to make some Greek friends at the camp, and enjoy our summer a little more.

Boys will be boys, and we played games of "Chicken" as we wrestled in the pool to see who would be victorious. That's where two people would hoist a person on their shoulders, and see who could knock the other pair down first. In a round that did not go our way, my partner on my shoulders lost the wrestling match and as he fell, his legs took my head and neck with him. There was a violent turn to the right, and I felt an immediate sharp searing pain deep in my neck and chest. It felt as if someone lodged a dagger deep into me. My left arm felt limp as I gave all my effort to move it, and I was suddenly having difficulty breathing. There were no positions I could move to escape the pain, and even swallowing was a difficult task. My heart and lungs slowed down, labored in their function, as if someone hit the slow motion button. It was frightening to feel that way; so vulnerable, fragile, as if I could die at any moment. At the same time, any head movement felt as if hot liquid tar was running down my neck, back, and chest even at the slightest quiver of motion. After I was pulled out of the pool, I calmed down. My condition stabilized slightly, but could hardly be called 'improved' during our remaining time in Greece, until we headed back to the States to get proper care. My mother would do all she could to comfort me and tell me it will get better, although even she felt helpless to offer thoughts on how. My father, being ex-military, told me to bear the pain, and even teased me about it; telling me to just tough it out like a Spartan. It could've been easy for anyone to give such advice, since I looked perfectly normal on the outside, but I felt like I was dying slowly on the inside. My mother's voice of reason pressured my father to take me to our family medical doctor. My father routinely looked at the overall expenses and costs of a medical visit rather than its benefits, but after weighing the options of not having to hear me whine anymore from the pain, he reluctantly took me to get checked. The medical doctor took my medical history, x-rays, did a small evaluation and then brushed it off as a strain sprain of the neck. I merely received a prescription for painkillers from the M.D., and he told us it would soon go away.

A little ice, pain pills, and rest, then my problems would be a thing of the past, right?! Wrong! Two weeks later I felt the same pain without any relief. On the follow up visit, the doctor suggested an MRI, with the possibility of surgery if nothing else worked. They were not the options that any of us even wanted to entertain, and my father cringed at the $2,000+ costs for an MRI back then, so we waited it out to see if my pain would at least lessen in severity by the next week. When the 'kink' in my neck didn't improve much, I slowly managed to drive myself to a massage therapist for a treatment. With clenched teeth, I held back screams of pain as the masseuse pushed on my neck trying to relieve the knot. Next, I found myself in a physical therapist's office that was also unable to get their treatment in properly; hindered by all the moaning and pain, as I felt worsening irritation with every movement. After many sleepless nights and many tears shed, one day I passed by a local chiropractor's office in town. The office was busy and there were many cars outside, but from the things my father had said about chiropractors I was afraid to even try walking through the door. He felt they were not to be trusted, with their 'pseudo–science' back and neck popping wrestling maneuvers. He said we would just be wasting more money. Of course, as with most things misunderstood, my father spoke about what he heard from rumors and mass media, not from what he'd experienced with a chiropractor for himself. Yet, thoughts of voodoo, chanting, lotions, and potions ran through my mind when I heard the word chiropractor, thanks to my father, and also my own naïve understanding and lack of research at that time.

I figured since nothing else had worked to cure my arm, chest pain, and semi-paralysis, maybe some voodoo magic would bring me relief! I was ready to try anything! Somehow I convinced my father to take me to the chiropractor. I remember that day clearly, as I lied down on the table staring at the light on the ceiling, waiting to be seen next. I was motionless and hopeful, but mostly fearful. When the doctor came into the room he looked nothing like the witchdoctor I had envisioned in my mind, but was a very professional, youthful, energetic gentleman in his early 40's who seemed very confident that he could help my condition with what he saw on my x-rays. I'd went to specialists within the medical field who looked much more knowledgeable and were also much older than this guy, but he was telling me he was sure he could fix me up?! He continued telling me how he was going to help get me back to normal. I relaxed the best I could, but my doubt turned to fear again as he took hold of my head, felt my neck muscles and pushed to feel my bone alignment that he'd viewed on the x-rays. He instructed me to breathe and I found my thoughts wandering as I closed my eyes. "God please don't let him further paralyze or kill me," I remember saying to myself. Others had tried to move my neck and nothing good came out of it other than more pain and moaning. Then, just as I ended my pleading thoughts, in one fast effortless swoop of his hands and tilt of my neck, I heard an audible noise and a current of power surged into my body. I started to gasp at what felt like ten thousand waterfalls overtaking me in a rush of relief. I had such a moment of peaceful serenity from the sudden release of pain that I was now in tears, laying on my back in this voodoo witchdoctor's room, totally amazed at what had just taken place within a fraction of a second. My arm started to tingle and re-animate as my heart and lungs were going back to full speed and regulating. A great deal of the pain lifted, and I was speechless and in awe of every feeling that I was feeling! My life force was coming back; it was once again flowing through me and being expressed with vitality! Still speechless and with my mouth wide open, I sat up and started moving again. What a miracle! I remember wiping back tears as I asked the doctor, "What happened!? What did you do to me? What did you do differently that no one else could do? What are you? You cured me!! I can't understand why I didn't come here first!" I had so many questions. He said, "I removed the interference (subluxation) from your neck, and your brain was able to reconnect again to your body through your nervous system, allowing the full expression of your life to flow again." With total amazement, wonder, respect and gratitude I uttered the words that began everything I am today: "I want to do this for others, just like you did it for me. I want to free people like you freed me!" Soon after I registered for school to learn the healing manual therapeutic art and science that is called **CHIROPRACTIC** (Greek "Chiro," meaning "hand"; "Praktikos," meaning "done by/practiced by").

    When I told my father how life-changing the experience was and that I wanted to now be a chiropractor myself, my father could not understand how much I valued the work I had seen with my own eyes and experienced firsthand. He even feared the shame that my decision to go into chiropractic might bring upon the family. His limited knowledge of what chiropractic healing really was (and is) overrode what this science and art could do, as the public did not recognize it as widely then as it does today.

Fast Forward to Age 28: Valuable Lessons in Health - Round 2

October 5, 2005. I will never forget that day. I remember it vividly, as anyone in my position would. *"You have about eight months to live if we don't get your aortic valve replaced. Your heart will give out and then you'll internally bleed to death."*

It does not sink in - at first - when you're told that you might die soon.

Time speeds up, as if racing you to see if you can catch up.

Life was stressful with relationships, board exams, and mounting bills. After passing out at my desk twice within a week for no reason, I got concerned and started getting full blood work, a physical, EKG's, and echocardiograms to find out why I was blacking out for no reason. Up until then, when I felt any chest pains, I had the typical macho tough guy mentality: Stick it out as long as possible and deny everything, even if it kills you. Thank God common sense prevailed as I worried that I might black out while driving, so I submitted to more tests and follow up visits. It was just like the movies - I would be fully alert and then all of a sudden it was if someone turned the lights out; only this time there was no beautiful vision or premonition seen like in my teens. How ironic that my mother had always told me I was special because I had a big heart; *literally, I did!* The cardiologist called it cardiomegaly: a condition of an enlarged heart caused by the stress of pumping blood out to the body. My aortic valve was malformed since birth with two cusps (bicuspid) instead of the normal three (tricuspid). Instead of pumping blood away from my heart towards my head and neck, where it should have travelled, my aortic valve's two leaflets had become overstressed, and were leaking blood (regurgitating) backwards towards the heart. As a result, I blacked out because of the lack of oxygen and nutrients to my brain.

Terror once again gripped me as my mind remembered the swimming pool accident years earlier. My fears worsened as I inherently wondered if the heart murmur that I was diagnosed with as a child had suddenly suffered enough stress. Now that innocent little heart murmur I was born with, that gave me three heartbeats instead of two, was about to go on permanent strike. I was still too young for my heart to be taking a final lap around the track, when I had not done all the things in life I wanted to do yet. You can say that my "lack of" life started to flash before my eyes, as I began to see my uncertain future, and all of the things I'd said I would get to later. "Later" was suddenly sooner than anyone could have expected - Especially to 28 year old me!

As I stared at the clock wishing the second hand would not move so fast, I began to resent myself for not traveling more, wasting away days, not saying "I love you" more to my family, and not spending enough quality time with friends. As my lack of life became crystal clear, I wasn't happy with what I saw.

I was at my cardiologist's office for my final appointment, before scheduling my surgery, and I argued with the doctor. "But there has to be another way to fix it without having to be on Coumadin for the rest of my life. That's like a death sentence!" I raged on: "It's like rat poison. That stuff is a slow death. In addition, I have to monitor my blood levels every day? No…no way. Not me. How can this be modern medicine? Hasn't something more progressive been invented by now?"

I was upset that the only options I had were a metal valve that needed Coumadin (blood thinners to keep the metal joints of the valve from clotting with possibilities of stroke), or an animal valve that might eventually fail and then need to be replaced with another surgery in the future. I had two not-so-fabulous choices, but was grateful that I still had choices that could keep me alive. I chose the natural cow-bovine valve, knowing it would only be a matter of time that I might be going through the same fate again in the future, when the valve degenerated. However, unlike the metal valve's need for blood thinners, with a natural cow's valve I would at least have a chance at a more normal life.

I was snarling at the doctor for not having better solutions, and felt angry with God that I was in this position. I felt there had to be another way. The cardiologist tried to calm me down, stoically touching my shoulder, but his forehead was wrinkled with worry.

After many exhausting nights of deep thought, I finally made peace with the fact I had to go through with the surgery. Before I knew it, the surgery date came and I was prepped and put into my requisite gown. I kissed my family goodbye and watched them disappear into the waiting room, as my mortality was becoming clearer by the second. "*I might never see them again,*" I thought to myself as I was wheeled down the cold hospital hallway to the operating room for what seemed like forever. I quietly started to pray. In desperation and mounting anger I was beginning to lose my faith, but like most folks facing possible death, I decided to make a deal with God.

Up to this point in my life, I realized that I'd lived too selfishly and egotistically. I took too much for granted - my family, my friends, my time, my purpose - my whole life. What a waste it would be to let this life go without making something more of the gifts and talents I'd been given. I remember praying, "*God If you want me to come back – And yes*

I do want to come back - I will dedicate my time to serving you through helping others. Let me know you are with me when I ask, and when people ask for help, let me be able to give it to them through your grace. But please, if you want me to open my eyes and come back to continue this life, please make it easier for me so that I don't have to struggle like I used to. God, I want to feel love. I want to know what love is - real Love. If you agree to all this, then I want to live and fulfill the highest purpose you have for me here." With those last words in my mind, I saw the anesthesiologist's hand place the mask over my face as I dropped into rest. I had finally let go and surrendered myself, as I allowed my soul much needed inner peace.

The surgery was rough; the surgeon had to open me up again a second time after they believed they were done - I bled internally and they raced to re-stabilize me. My folks in the waiting room were very worried, and my mother went into super-prayer mode. The surgeon's second attempt, although completed later than planned, was a success. As I came in and out of consciousness, I could see things coming into focus. I was on machines, unable to breathe for myself, and in a strange bed with tubes everywhere. I saw what looked like a white lab coat come into focus. Then I saw a doctor or technician in front of me doing his routine business. I made noises of distress and finally caught his attention; he turned to me, saw I was awake, flipped a few switches, and I was able to breathe again. I frantically took many deep breaths, and I was out again - back to a deep sleep. It was such a freaky moment. It was what I now remember as my second chance – my rebirth in the Intensive Care Unit.

Post ICU, nurses used me as a human pincushion as they jabbed both my arms for blood every few hours. They missed my highly visible veins several times, to the point that I angrily yelled at the staff for no more blood withdrawals. I would listen to the small talk of nurses as they came into my room during their routine checks, and I could tell who truly had their heart in their work and who was there just to pass the shift. The unappetizing processed meals including wheat, milk, and cheese products given to patients were too unhealthy for recovery or proper body nutrition. The television helped stimulate our brains, but they had it on negative news castings. I would get myself out of the bed and take walks around the hospital since there was no rehab program that encouraged body movement or stretching there. As I passed others' rooms in the hallway and peeked in, I would witness people in agony and with a stoic trance of desperation evident in their eyes, some would stare at me while lying motionless in their hospital beds. I had an eerie feeling that it didn't matter to the staff If I got better or if they kept me there as long as possible; there was no actual push or healthy incentive to get better soon after surgery - just their job to monitor me. I started realizing how hospitals were a big business; with many holding cells of the sick for their profit making. Post-surgery, the majority of my real healing was to happen outside those walls, not within them. As I came to the conclusion that only I could get myself back to 100% from here, I asked to be released as soon as possible and decided to take recovery further into my own hands.

In subsequent visits, the cardiologist told me that full recovery would take 4-6 months. I was impatient and wanted to get on with my new life; there was too much to do. I always knew from my hypnosis and mind-body studies how powerful suggestions were, and that the mind can speed up my recovery. I went into meditation every chance I got while in the hospital and after being released. I must have meditated for 14 hours a day. I would envision cells healthy, my heart repairing itself, and reinforcing tissues around the new valve. I would see myself in the gym, running, in the pool swimming, jumping rope, etc., seeing myself as normal, healthy, and free. I was alive, my heart was beating, and amazed at what I'd just experienced. A cow's valve is now functioning as my own heart valve! I was extremely grateful for my surgeon's knowledge and skill.

Back home, I enjoyed my mom's fine Greek cooking, took my vitamins, supplements, herbs, drank plenty of fluids, watched many funny movies, and only discussed positive things with positive people. I neglected to take my pain meds though; I didn't like how they slowed down my digestive system, giving me horrid constipation and unbearable pain in my abdomen. I focused on the benefits of not taking the pills because I knew from my chiropractic studies how painkillers and other drug neurotoxins can affect the nervous system - prohibiting healing instead of aiding it. With constant meditation, my mind quickly dealt with the pain as if I had taken the painkillers anyway. When I gained the strength to get around, I immediately scheduled a treatment with the same "voodoo" chiropractor who had healed me from semi-paralysis years earlier. The trauma of the operation and bad positioning in the hospital bed had my neck and body misaligned. Now that the surgeon did his amazing job of replacing the valve, it was my job to give my body what it needed to recover the wounds. I knew when the chiropractor properly adjusted my neck it would take away all internal neurological stress, and I would start to heal much quicker, as my body's energy would focus completely on the heart again. Since the neck is the pathway to the rest of the body (especially the chest, heart and lungs), this would open vital pathways and my brain could begin fixing and sending proper nutrients to their respective places for repair without hindrance. The combo of good nutrition, meditation, rest, visualization, self-hypnosis, a loving environment, and chiropractic care allowed me to super heal completely in about 45 days post-surgery! I remember finishing a bench-press set upon returning to the gym in awe and gratitude to God that I was able to get back to life so quickly after such a major surgery. The steps I took post-op helped heal my heart so that I could quickly resume living with purpose!

My personal experiences, clinical successes, and research in various Eastern healing arts has led me to the development of my method of healing, the Kousouli® Method, which I've taught to help thousands of patients achieve phenomenal results in my private practice. I am now sharing it with you and millions of people all over the world.

In my previous book, *BE A MASTER® OF MAXIMUM HEALING*, you learned about regaining control of your body's health through the Kousouli® Method by: **Removing** toxins from the tissues, **Reviving** the brain-body spinal connection, and **Rebuilding** your body with proper nutrition. Here, in *BE A MASTER® OF PSYCHIC ENERGY*, we will review these concepts with special emphasis on the 4th part of the Kousouli® Method: **Resetting** the internal programming and reconditioning of the conscious and subconscious mind, along with exploring extrasensory abilities, or what is commonly referred to as the sixth sense.

Thank you for allowing me to present you with this vital information. When you begin to remove the body discomforts of dis-ease, you can then start to focus on the more important internal self and reach a new level of awareness, consciousness, and vibration you never felt before. You can then live your life with more passion and zest. It begins with proper care of your spinal column – the direct link of your neural impulse to your body, which allows the expression of your life to manifest in this physical plane we call our world. I sincerely welcome you to this exploration, by the end of which you will find a new YOU!

PART I:
INTRODUCTION

"I searched for God and found only myself. I searched for myself and found only God."
~ Sufi proverb

If you had told me in 1995 as I graduated high school in New Jersey that I would become a doctor in Beverly Hills, one of the most prestigious cities in the United States, that I would be in charge of the health of America's high society, celebrities, and elites, that I would have friends who are millionaires or even famous, or that I would be invited to dine in their mansions, and that by my mid-thirties I'd be sharing my knowledge of health and abundance with the world, I might've said to you, "I'd like to help you find some professional help." Now, here I am giving the professional help; what a beautifully divine irony!

"I wish I knew then, what I know now." We've all heard this said by others, or we ourselves have uttered these exact words. What if you did know then what you know now? How would your life be different and how would it be the same? Would you be better off or worse? What if there was a way to know instantly more now than you ever knew prior? What if you could use this information to better yourself faster and gain ground on your goals quicker? Imagine if you could be a better you right NOW. I tell you with certainty: <u>This Is Possible</u>!

I have gone through the transformation myself, analyzed its procedure, researched what works, interviewed people who apply the principles, and have been teaching this to those who want to awaken themselves to a higher level of perception. The journey is not without its challenges and definitely not without its lessons however. These experiences of growth that you would miss out on help you rise to your next level of being. What thoughts or pre-programming would you have to let go of to get new results? And if you did let go of old thoughts, what new thoughts would shape your new paradigm of thinking? How would you disconnect from pain and focus on healing?

Healer consciousness in the last few decades has switched focus from healing others to showing one how to heal "the self." Various energy treatment methods have exploded in the West, like Reiki, Healing Touch and bodywork, intertwined with visualization, chanting, and breathing, which stimulates our personal chi (energy). We are learning from past healers and shamans, who showed us how to project chi to open the energy capacity of the patient so that healings are quick, long lasting, pain free, and confirmed by medical examination with no other therapy needed afterwards!

Recent healers such as Edgar Cayce, Olga Worrall, Gordon Turner, Harry Edwards, Bruno Groening, Agnes Sanford, and many others, laid out the groundwork for many of the energy healers today.

Edgar Cayce (1877 - 1945) was known as the "sleeping prophet" because he could see visions as a child and throughout his adult life. He would enter a self-induced sleep state, which opened his mind and placed him in contact with all knowingness. He helped people for over forty-three years by giving amazing detailed readings to those who sought his aid. The help for his clients ranged from knowing the correct diet for their body, to curing life-threatening illness and understanding how to connect stronger with God.

Olga Worrall (1906 - 1985) demonstrated healing capabilities and clairaudience (hearing messages from another realm) from the age of three. She was quite a popular spiritual healer of the 20th century. Olga firmly stressed the importance of intention, while remaining neutral for God to allow energy to flow through her. Mainly using prayer and "laying of hands," she also had visions that allowed her to see friends and family members who had passed through the veil we call death. She repeatedly expressed the importance of active prayer for those in our thoughts.

Gordon Turner (1950's - 70's) was a British healer who would preach about endless energy and a power with unlimited resources that ran through all of us. He would test his local and remote patients for results after his healings. He recorded that many reported color sensations and feelings of cold, heat, tingling, sharpness or pinching occurring during his healings. People who went to see him often recovered from serious illnesses and circumstances unable to be helped by conventional methods at that time.

Harry Edwards (1893 - 1976) would do multiple simultaneous healings, treating many serious illnesses with multitudes or singularly just by placing his hands on individuals for ten to thirty seconds at his Religious Treatment Haven in Surrey, Britain. He was also known to project healings across great distances to those who had written in to him for support.

Bruno Groening (1906 - 1959) was a faith healer in the post-WWII era in Germany. News of his healings included treating muscular atrophy, deafness, the crippled, and terminally ill. People would line up from all over the world to receive healings. Bruno was well known for being so close with plants, nature, and animals that even wild animals would follow him for healings! Groening believed that to remain pure for receiving the energy of God, one must focus on the Godly aspects of life and reject evil and sin.

Agnes Sanford (1897 - 1982), a well-known healer from the US, would recite the original Orthodox prayer during her healings, and miracles would occur. She claimed, "Learning to live in the Kingdom of Heaven is learning to turn on the light of God within. There is more in the Bible than mere information. A spiritual energy we call faith seems to connect with the very book itself."

These miraculous healers understood their abilities as God's gift and knew they could be taught and learned, but their paramount understanding of their actual workings came through a personal experience with God. Their focus was on healing others by teaching them to understand God's love for themselves. Spiritual awakening is more than just words; it is an experience YOU should aspire to live. You can implement spiritual healing without religious dogma and you DO NOT need any special magic crystal wands or capes to realize healing and inner abilities - only a rational mix of logic and faith, both in yourself and the power that animates the living you.

BE A MASTER® OF PSYCHIC ENERGY was developed from the workings in my personal and professional experiences, and written to introduce the mind to a spiritual, rather than a religious, perspective for understanding and applying a higher human potential through energy healing. ***Although the terminology and examples used are Christian in context, the underlying message of love's connection can be applied universally to help yourself and your neighbor, <u>regardless of religious upbringing</u>.*** *Applying these universal truths can bring you deep inner personal expansion, as it has for me and countless numbers of my clients. Open your heart and mind, and receive.*

PART II:
AWAKENING – Understanding the Game

"Impersonal forces, over which we have almost no control, seem to be pushing us all in the direction of the Brave New Worldian nightmare; and this impersonal pushing is being consciously accelerated by representatives of commercial and political organizations who have developed a number of new techniques for manipulating, in the interest of some minority, the thoughts and feelings of the masses."
~ *Aldous Huxley*

It seems as if the world has finally gone insane. People feel lost now more than ever, always harboring a feeling of being involved in a chaotic rush to nowhere. Most people are now unsure of themselves and their own abilities, have stopped thinking rationally, and are more intent on trusting what the "truth" is from other 3rd parties, such as the skewed nightly news, radio, gossipy friends, biased newspapers, or total strangers. Our teachers, preachers, and parents all continue to run old programming that is obsolete and cannot guide the new youth. Slaves themselves to debts and the banking cartels, they can only teach the same principles of "lack mentality" to the newborn generation. Just step back for a moment and consider that, even though we work so hard to attain some goals or a positive livelihood, no one actually owns anything. It is all loaned or bought from the banks: your car, home, education, and even the furniture you may be sitting on may be leased - with no money down, pay later, or zero percent interest until 2099! It's essentially a "gratification now, pain and debt later" mentality.

American students who hold massive educational debts also seem to be the least educated among the world's countries. Pharmaceutical drugs sedate the public, and big media uses covert hypnosis (hidden messages) in magazines and billboards, as television attempts to sway or control people into thinking only about satisfying their tangential whims, all of which are never beneficial to the individual citizen in the long run. The three real superpowers within both the United States and the world are: Big Pharma (pharmaceutical companies), the Church Empire, and the Mass Media. All are doing their part to control their segment of the people, which now feel powerless on their own.

Toxic drug dependency, bad living habits, and chemicals in our air, food, and water supply slowly limit our inborn natural powers and abilities - so much so that we have almost forgotten that a fully functioning and well-adjusted nervous system and spine are the central key to everyone's personal power. Re-claiming your spine, brain, and nervous system from chemicals and stimulants can give you the control needed to change your life and serve you beneficially, as it moves you to more function, higher awareness, and personal freedom. However, those are just the first steps. For this to happen, we also have to stop being slaves to our self-defeating attachments to popular coffee brands, latest cell phone gadgets, mindless TV shows, celebrity gossip columns, designer label handbags, or other materialistic hoarding, and instead start listening to our innate identities as we re-tune our body and mind to what they are meant to be used for. This in turn will help us expand our knowingness and collective consciousness - our awareness to what we are capable of doing or being as a powerful humanity.

Spiritual Awakening

Spiritual awakening has been an integral part of traditions and practices of many religions throughout history. Spiritual awakening is the experience where an individual has had an enlightening interaction with the supernatural or divine. The definition of "enlightenment" is personal, since it is based on an individual's perception and understanding of divinity. Others who do not believe in the same views, or who may not have had the same personal experience, could perceive the experience differently, or possibly as terrifying. Even though different religions and traditions have a diverse appreciation of the divine and "supreme beings," they do appear to have some unities.

Those in prayer or meditation find themselves separating from this world to seek closeness with God, as they discover what God personally means to them. After the awakening experience, the person has a deeper connection to the unseen world. They achieve select understanding of humanity and innate knowledge of our physical world - sometimes seemingly overnight.

Those of spiritual awakening experience enhanced emotion as their senses are heightened, and can be extra-sensitive during spiritual experiences. Becoming more energy-sensitive equates to a lower tolerance level to some frequency vibrations, especially in situations that passed prior to the experience.

Enlightened people report an ability to see vivid colors and glittery particles around anything alive. Some can see colors, forms, and shapes with their eyes closed. Others feel swift blasts of power without warning. Hearing also seems sharper, and soft whispers sound like thunder. Smell, taste, and touch are also seem grander, which is why some have extreme sensitivity to certain foods and smells. Some people say that they experience heat from the top of their head to the soles of their feet, while others say the feeling is colder and pulsating, twitching, pushing, or pulling.

To be certain, the revolution one undergoes via a spiritual awakening depends on how they see themselves and understand their connection to divinity or God. In some religions, some of the transformational methods are not acceptable, while other religious traditions would consider certain transformations vital in order to claim the event as legitimate and complete.

Religious activities however, are not the only path to experiencing spiritual awakenings; they can also be experienced through dreaming, paranormal or psychic activity, near death phenomenon, or medicinal herbs used for divinatory and healing purposes. Shaman natives in South America routinely drink Ayahuasca tea which has *N,N*-Dimethyltryptamine or DMT, a naturally occurring psychedelic in plants that is also found in trace amounts in mammals, including humans. Profound visions leading to inventions, discoveries, music, and artwork have been achieved using Ayahuasca and other herbs, like Salvia Divinorum, or drugs like LSD. Francis Harry Compton Crick (1916 –2004), co-discoverer of the structure of the DNA molecule in 1953 and winner of the Nobel Prize, is rumored to have confessed prior to dying that he learned about the composition of the double helix in a vision while experimenting with LSD.

Those who have experienced their spiritual awakening say that even though it may have been physically, emotionally, mentally, and spiritually draining and difficult to deal with the darkest deepest side of themselves - their ego - it was totally worth it. Some even describe their experience as blissfully humbling. Once awakened, life's little moments tend to mean a lot more, as the compassionate changes of their attitude, character, and habits start to show in their daily life.

As one begins to "knock on the door" and seek truth, they will be given the answers as they go along the path of knowledge. Many come to their spiritual enlightenment after experiencing relaxation techniques like hypnosis, or mind body techniques like reiki. Whatever is used, the removal of the non-self and awakening of the real self occurs. For Christians, this awareness is that they have fallen short of the perfection of God, or they have sinned. For others, they may bring a bad circumstance to themselves (like a health crisis or abusive relationship) that requires them to make a large personal sacrifice so they can find their spirituality or connection with God.

However, simply knowing you need to connect closer to spiritual enlightenment is the beginning. Development of one's spiritual attention to mind and actions, arising from their day-to-day actions, needs to be accomplished if one ever wishes to go beyond only simple awareness that they need to move to the next level.

People with an awakened spirit seem to maintain a level of self-control in mannerisms while pursuing their goals. They seem to have reached a degree of calmness where current problems, issues, past experiences, and even tempting desires no longer cause misperception and disruptions. It's as if every distraction has been removed, resulting in a clear path. When reaching this level of spiritual enlightenment, one knows what self-defeating habits need to be deleted, free will is used correctly, and the desire to move towards better wisdom and judgment deepens. The new awareness helps further one's purpose faster, while it becomes easier to dodge temptation in excessive worldly pleasures, which often leads to suffering in the long run.

Practicing non-attachment, and improving one's intuition and inner happiness are also signs of an awakened soul. Awakened spirits tend to live in harmony with nature, animals, and people, with compassion for everyone regardless of culture, race, or nationality. An awakened soul is patient, slow to anger, practices humility and selfless love for others, and evicts arrogance and pride from their character. Part of having an awakened spirit is the enthusiasm to work towards the well-being of not only one's self, but for the community as a whole.

You may have noticed successful connection to your higher self, the God-Power, or the awakening experience if any of the above is true for you after a session of meditation and prayer. Continued soul awakening and self-development will lead to a balanced and more productive life, which will bring more happiness and abundance in time. Spiritual healing can be a bit of a challenge to articulate in this age of modern medicine and technology where much is hidden by greed and profit. However, it is difficult to ignore the fact that there is a Supreme Being, behind our very existence. All around evidence of intelligence design abounds.

"Anyone who becomes seriously involved in the pursuit of science becomes convinced that there is a spirit manifest in the laws of the universe, a spirit vastly superior to that of man."
~ Albert Einstein

In an Associated Press poll in 2011, it was found that 77% of Americans believe in angels. In addition to 3 out of 4 Americans believing that angels do exist, 4 out of 10 of those polled never attend religious services. From this statistic, we can see that the belief and acceptance of spirituality is alive and well for many, regardless of their "religion" or lack thereof.

It is widely believed that our physical healing relies heavily on how the spirit of the individual heals. Spiritual healing has power because it heals not just the body, but also the emotions, spirit, and the mind. Spiritual healing performed through visualization, prayer, concentration, and focus has helped many patients slow-down or reverse illnesses.

Believing in Energetic Healing

The spirit and mind are incredibly powerful as they shape and form our physical existence. Energy healing is invaluable to those who have energy leaks in areas of their physical being, directly impacted by healing in the spiritual, mental, or emotional realm. However, healings may have lesser impact if the individual seeking healing has chronic depletion of their energy vortices, manifested as a firm internal way of life for them. They would need more time convincing or developing belief in their new healthy state and living as their new fact or reality in order for the healing to occur and remain permanent. When someone has a major illness such as diabetes, heart disease, or multiple sclerosis, for instance, there have been long standing attacks on the energy centers of that being. Reversing the leaks of energy in those chakra vortices around the physical body (aura) can allow the being to maintain and refill their energy levels to a healthy homeostatic state. However, the patient with the dis-ease must detach themselves from the belief that they are sick and only maintain the feelings and thoughts of what it feels like to be healthy; only then will the care of competent holistic-minded doctors help the body of the inflicted regain energy from the unstable leaky centers. It would be foolish to attempt to use an old skeleton key on a modern combination lock, just as it would be foolish to attempt energy healing on a patient who is either uninterested in changing their beliefs on their situation, is a highly negative skeptic, or uncooperative in stopping negative lifestyle habits. Consider even that all those whom energy healers healed had the common sense to desire healing in the first place. They were open to receiving healing with no doubt in their heart or mind. However, those opposed to it, who doubted and did not believe or have faith in the process of healing, did not receive healings. For example, those who sought out the healer Jesus of Nazareth were so ready to allow their healing that simply being in his presence shifted their perspective from disallowing to allowing their ability to believe healing was possible. This shifted their existing reality to another parallel universe - from one where they were disallowing health to one that made possible a new version of themselves, which was healed. Spiritual, mental, and emotional energy is discharged into the body as a manifestation of the creative process of thought. This is the mind-body connection. Some channel their negative feelings or stress into their heart, creating arrhythmias, chest pains, or heart attacks. Others channel it into their stomach causing ulcers, while some hold it in their reproductive organs and cause malfunction, such as infertility. My success as a healer is based on these fundamental truths of non-linear thinking when it comes to healing.

Energy Transference is a Real Thing

We are multi-dimensional electromagnetic beings. Have you ever touched an antenna and the radio signal improved? Or have you walked by a radio receiver only to hear the signal clearer than previously heard? Our reality and ability to attract what we desire in our lives is related to the signal we send out into the Universe. I have found that patients routinely manifest their abundance when their nervous system is properly cared for, by simply adjusting the spine. As their health improves, so does their confidence in their body's healing control, and the way they use their energetics to manifest.

Psychics, Qi Gong practitioners, and holistic healers have cultivated heightened sensitive energies compared to those who don't exercise their innate abilities. Patients or clients of the aforementioned can feel their energy, as the contrast between their energy and the healer's energy flow can be vast. If the healer projects their energy and the patient accepts to match the energy state, it can upgrade or higher the bio level of the patient, leading to a healing or sense of health empowerment. Many of my patients reported getting promotions at work, receiving financial abundance, lost loves returning, colleague communications at work improving, diseases quickly eliminated, pains vanished, and other such phenomenon consistently occurred around the time spinal improvement began. This was found to be even more frequent with clients who not only began treatment to reconnect their nervous system and stop neural energy leaks, but also learned new techniques of meditation and prayer mentioned later in this book and taught at our live seminars.

Measuring Extrasensory Energy

It's easy for disbelievers to write off the unseen energy healing that happens because it is exactly that - unseen with the physical eyes. This energy is in the non-physical realms and thus we cannot calculate it (yet) in our current dimension. But maybe we can try? Electrical energy is everywhere in your body and all cells are communicating with each other. This energy can also be detected for several meters around the body, when seen and felt by sensitive energy intuitives. Let us consider our important electromagnetic pump - the heart. This bioelectrical energy can even be detected and measured using magnetometers outside the body. Using a basic voltage meter we can even see the reading of someone's surface energy in millivolts (equal to one thousandth (10^{-3}) of a volt), which fluctuates during good and bad health, as well as in times of meditation and prayer. So this energy is something real, and can be measured. Imagine being the most powerful supercomputer you could be. Now imagine that over time, viruses were either allowed consciously or unconsciously into your programming, keeping you from performing at your highest levels possible. This is the case when someone feels powerless in their life, overridden with negative emotions of pain, terror, and hurt rather than harmony, love, and peace - the attributes of higher-level consciousness.

According to Dr. Bruce Lipton, author of *Biology of Belief and The Wisdom of your Cells*, the intelligence of a cell is not in the nucleus of a cell, but in the membrane of the cell. The membrane receives information from our consciousness and writes the new version. If we want to change what we see, the energy we send out will bring about a new appearance or message about who we are according to our environment, which means we are reprogrammable as needed.

The heart is the strongest generator of this invisible electromagnetic power, followed second by the brain. The umbilical area, incidentally also where the umbilical cord nourishes the unborn child, is the area believed that clairsentience (innate feeling), energetically interacts with the physical reality. These places of the energy body send out vibrations to the universal matrix, where one can find and connect with another person of the same vibratory level. Even when a lover, spouse, or family member is hurt on another continent, their loved one can feel a shift in their personal energy halfway around the world. This energy travels in real time, without lag, as it is manifested. In the same way, healing can be sent to anyone in the world and they can feel the effects, no matter where they are on the planet.

The experiences we attract in our lives are not by chance. Whether it's the energies you connect with on the road that cause car accidents, or it's the energy you find in someone you consider a soul mate, it's all related to the signal being sent out by your personal antenna. This is where the prominence of the Kousouli® Method comes in. It can help to close off the energy leaks, process of dis-ease, and aids in replenishing the body's innate ability to generate and maintain its personal power for higher-level manifestation. Many of my clients have reported to me that there is nothing more important to them than their attention and assimilation of learning this process of directing their energy for their personal empowerment. To them, their results speak for themselves and I whole - heartedly agree.

Getting Clarity

You must learn who you are or everything around you will remain chaotic and painful. Nothing will make sense. Relationships will always be in turmoil, family pressures will persist, and these problems may even send you into depression. It may seem that the world kicks you around and there's nothing you can do about it. However, the truth is that the wool has been swept over your eyes since birth to keep you from asking the important questions: "Who is God to me? And who am I to God?" Religion is often described as man-made thought control through manipulation - not the Godly spiritual Divine essence of truth. Religion is a collective manipulation of tradition, ritual, culture, and beliefs over thousands of years' time. It is a system of living via instruction passed down by rulers or spiritual gurus who wanted the masses to believe what they wanted people to believe about God. Ultimately, our true inherent identification to God has been left out, or at least not examined thoroughly with an open mind. Most have been born into a manipulated system of religion handed down to them by their parents. If one does not know that they come from a royal bloodline (God Source), they will live their life as a lost pauper (removed from all abundance that is truly God Source). Similarly, if you are not aware of your true abilities and power, you would not know how to exercise and develop them to their fullest potential!

"But you are a chosen race, a royal priesthood, a holy nation, a people for his own possession, that you may proclaim the excellencies of him who called you out of darkness into his marvelous light."
~ 1 Peter 2:9

Evolved spiritual information was known in the old world, but conveniently left out, or de-emphasized in scholastic institutions, in order to control the modern masses. Even though you would get some progress on your own over time, you may not get the real metamorphosis your soul seeks to attain without fully realizing who you are truly are. Are we finite or infinite beings? We are eternally infinite. There are no limits to the spirit - unless the limits are self-imposed. Success in spiritual awakening begins with knowing you are part of or connected to God as an heir to the Kingdom, without the false pride associated with claiming you are 'the' God. The fulfillment of your soul is much larger than the fulfillment of the ego or physical self. Knowing your purpose here will be answered when you remove the obsolete filters and programming you were instilled with by others during your youth, at a time when you began to forget who and what God really is, and why you came here to do what it is you will do. Until you understand all this, you'll continue to live your life with frustration, dissatisfaction, and with emptiness in your heart, while knowing that there has to be more to life than what you are currently experiencing.

Chapter 1:
Spiritual, but not Religious?

"I believe in God, but not as one thing, not as an old man in the sky. I believe that what people call God is something in all of us. I believe that what Jesus and Mohammed and Buddha and all the rest said was right. It's just that the translations have gone wrong."
~ John Lennon

Many people are putting in their hours in church but are feeling unfulfilled inside. They've been reminded that they're missing the mark and sinning too much. They know in their soul that love governs all things, and that they should feel good about God, but that's not what they are getting from their religious institutions. Why are so many now proclaiming themselves as spiritual but not religious? Why is it so confusing these days to decipher one's true beliefs? The word "Christian" these days has so many different implications that it makes it difficult to know exactly what that stands for anymore. Ask a Protestant, Methodist, Catholic, Orthodox, and Baptist Christian what they believe and you will get different answers about how you should pray and whether or not you're going to be punished for every less-than-pure thought you think. Something about current organized religion just isn't ringing true in people's hearts anymore, and the trend is growing.

Many who see the difficulties of what religion has brought into the world, whether it's war, dis-unity, and pain, don't want to participate any longer. In addition, some find the practices of some religions too constrictive to be applicable to today's lifestyles, or they have rules for going to heaven, claiming all others as excluded for believing in other religious teachings. Hearing you are going to hell because you are not of a particular religious denomination is beginning to vibrate as a false doctrine to many. There is an awakening among the people to trust what feels truthful in their heart.

Some may be quick to throw the whole God thing out the window and even say that there is no God if he allows bad things to happen. But if we take God totally out of the equation, then we take the solution out of the problem! Many find ways of dealing with their rationalization of their existence. For instance, different philosophies can give humans a reason to stay here on Earth. Those that embrace the *naturalistic* philosophy say that humans are only a product of the random natural processes, and are simply here on Earth for biological reasons: giving purpose to life to just continue its cycle. Those enthralled in the *hedonistic* philosophy say that our only purpose in life is to experience as much pleasure as possible and party it up. But we know that by itself pleasure is empty, and real pleasure from material or emotional gain is satisfying when it is attained by honest work, creative hobby, or via meaningful relationships with others. When those philosophies make no sense, the *materialistic* philosophy attracts many who believe in putting physical material possessions as the primary value of life, before any spiritual empowerment. For materialists, the more toys and things you have, the happier, bigger, and more important you are in society. Their sole belief is that those who have the most are the most important. We all know however, that the harder you work to attain material things the faster you lose your health, and you alienate loved ones in an effort to focus on things rather than loving relationships with other people. In the end, they may die lonely, as no one can take any material or monetary gains with them to the afterlife. Lastly, if nature, hedonism, or materialism doesn't appeal, there is always the *spiritual* philosophy, which preaches that our purpose is deep within us and adds ancient ideas with modern practicality to make a new form of religion. In America, especially the West Coast, you can now find bookstore after bookstore with countless titles that remove God from the equation and serve a cookie cutter cultish recipe on how to become your own God.

The Kousouli® Method of Living

As a young man I searched to understand the laws that governed my environment, my world, my life, and defined my success or failure. I knew early on of my intuitive ability, but could not quite understand at that time how to cultivate and grow it quickly in order to better serve my mission here on earth. As I searched for guidance and training in understanding my purpose, it became frustrating to me that those I was turning to (teachers, preachers, parents, and friends) were even more stuck in their life troubles than I was in mine. Looking around I noticed many didn't enjoy their life, and thought that we all live in a cruel, negative, scary, and harsh world. These individuals continuously took the path of least resistance as they lost their ability to grow, and seemed doomed to constant depression without seeing any of life's beauty.

As I grew older and wiser, I never stopped having an unquenchable thirst for knowledge, and sought answers to that which the mundane textbooks of school could not answer. Eventually struggles with self-esteem in my youth, semi paralysis, physical and emotional pain, and heart valve failure led me to ask the right questions about my health and eventually understand the systems that govern it. I also studied, through chiropractic, the innate power of the nervous system and its marvels, which led me to more mind healing and Qi Gong principles of working with energy empowerment through hypnosis. Along with my greatest trials and misery came my grandest journey into the development of my sixth sense and finding, once again, the precious power that had been sitting idle inside of me for so long. I set forth to continue to understand, trust, and develop these extra sensory experiences beyond the five senses. I found that, when I called on this part of me, that I was able to accomplish things much easier than when I didn't acknowledge its presence. What you hold in your hands is this information gathered from over 30 years of personal experience and what I understand as truth at this time of my life.

The Kousouli® Method 4R intervention system was developed to explain to my patients and students the cycle of health, dis-ease, and maintenance of a balanced happy life. Understanding and implementing the four parts of the Kousouli® Method (Remove, Revive, Rebuild, and Reset) can open new areas of personal expansion for you as it has for many. It also helps align with the understanding of energy and healing, as it sets you up for great success in all realms of your life. May it serve you as it has served me in health and abundance.

"What we really need in health care is a total paradigm shift, where energy is seen as primary and the physical body is seen as secondary . . . We're energy bodies as well as physical bodies, and the two work synergistically."
~ *Joan Borysenko, Ph.D.*

1.1 When No One Else Can Help

There are cases where people who feel pain or hold illness are dismissed as healthy by their doctors. The exams, imaging, and laboratory tests can't find what is actually wrong with the patient. However, when you ask the patient how they feel, they tell you they know that something is off and they don't feel well. Sometimes, the patient will spontaneously feel body pains without any direct physical impact to the area of injury. What are the doctors missing from their tests, diagnoses, and prognoses? There are countless cases where a patient is sent home and then the doctor hears that the patient suddenly had a heart attack or has been re-admitted to the hospital. Many traditional "old school" doctors are too quick to dismiss something as "just stress," or write a few prescriptions to numb the pain, although that rarely fixes the root of the problem. So what is it, if it is not a physical pain that later manifests itself as a physical health problem? Or what of those countless terminally ill patients who are miraculously "cured" by an unknown phenomenon that the medical establishment just shrugs off as "luck" or takes false credit for it by terming it a "spontaneous medical remission"?

After suffering from recurrent depression for many years, Agnes Mary White Sanford, founder of the Inner Healing Movement, found healing with a faithful Protestant clergyman. In her autobiography she claims that this man laid his hands on her head while reciting a prayer. Over the course of the next several months she repeated the prayer: "Lord have mercy on me, and fill me with Your Holy Spirit." Her depression started to lift and she was finally free of it. Until that time, nothing else helped her. She says, "I believe imagination is one of the most important keys to effective praying. God touches me through my imagination. Imagination is one of the keys to the relationship of prayer with God. Prayer happens through the imagination by picturing the healing."

She believed Jesus had become part of the human race's collective subconscious and would work through both the living and the dead spirits, using any energy to be anywhere needed. She called God "primal energy," and "the very life-force existing in a radiation of an energy ... from which all things evolved." Her book, *Healing Light*, outlines many examples of miraculous events and states: "The first step in seeking to produce results by any power is to contact that power. The second step is to turn it on. The third step is to believe that this power is coming in to be utilized, and to accept it by faith. No matter how much we ask for something it becomes ours only as we accept it and give thanks for it."

Extrasensory energy healing works through laws made by the highest order of law. Agnes claimed, "If one thinks of a miracle not as the breaking of God's laws but as His own using of His laws, then the world is full of miracles." Sanford further goes on to compare wonderfully the power of God with electricity: "The whole universe is full of it, but only the amount of it that flows through...will work."

No one probably understands the above statements better than Dr. Daniel David Palmer, a student of metaphysics, science, magnetics, and the founder of Chiropractic healing. His theory was that the electrical circuitry of the nervous system, if not correctly flowing because of misaligned spinal joints, would eventually lead to dis-ease. He stated in his book, *Text-Book of the Science, Art, and Philosophy of Chiropractic*, "A subluxated vertebra ... is the cause of 95 percent of all diseases ... The other five percent is caused by displaced joints other than those of the vertebral column." Dr. Palmer helped his janitor, Harvey Lillard, by restoring his hearing. He freed him from deafness by administering what is now described as the first chiropractic spinal adjustment. Similarly to Agnes Sanford, Dr. Palmer was involved in energy healing; although he was not considered a spiritual faith healer like Agnes Sanford was. What Dr. Palmer did for his patients was to allow electrical energy to flow, unblocked, through the spinal system via physical means, as opposed to Sanford who taught allowing energy in by spiritual means. Dr. Palmer performed energy healing by unleashing the patient's inborn electrical energy potential through adjustment of the spinal system, to allow the healing flow to be fully expressed. According to both these healers, we can allow this power to work through us and direct it to heal what we wish.

Practicing both as a chiropractor and hypnotherapist, I wholeheartedly believe that the mind has power beyond our current understanding and it shapes the physical world we experience. Agnes Sanford clearly explains how healing occurs on the physical body, and mentions that much of this healing is done in the mind through imaginative thought, along with the powers of God's Law, that supersedes the limited known physical law. I believe that prior to becoming a physical problem, the root issue begins on other levels of subconscious awareness and ends up in the physical plane, as a signal to us that we may not be focusing or using our energy correctly. I believe there is usually first an intrusion (or obstruction) in the spiritual plane, which affects the mental plane (becoming a chronic thought), and this affects the emotional plane (the mood in day-to-day life of the patient), and then this embodies the physical plane (harboring itself into the physical organ or body as an illness manifestation). Healing the negative vibrational frequency within the first three areas, prior to fully manifesting in the physical realm, usually reverses the illness issue and brings about healing.

1.2 Emotionally Believing in the Healing

When we ride the rollercoaster of life we have highs and we have lows. When we are low, we seek to get back up and stay there. If we can maintain some kind of level ground, we consider ourselves well. We will often visit a doctor when we are ill, and seek to reconnect to our wellness homeostasis. The doctor will give us their treatment according to their school of thought and philosophy that their institution instilled in them. If they are medically based, they will usually seek to give an external remedy along with exercise and dietary advice. If they are holistically based, their treatment will consist of a nature-based regimen of correcting the internal conflict using diet, exercise, and herbal remedy.

Remembering that doctors cannot cure dis-ease, and only the mind and body of the patient itself can cure dis-ease, we ask ourselves, "Then what does a doctor provide a patient if they do not cure dis-ease?" The doctor is the bridge for the patient to attain knowledge, skill, and empathy for allowing their healing. The very important thing the doctor is paid their fee for is their ability to transform the frequency of illness to one of hope and health through a system of healing best suited to connecting with the frequency the patient needs at that time. Healing is defined as being created whole again, whereas treating a symptom involves covering it up temporarily so that it is not active.

A significant aspect of healing is allowance and acceptance. By seeking a healer, this step usually completes itself when the patient agrees to undergo a treatment plan or procedure. Once the patient has allowed this, they must emotionally accept the treatment as being able to help them transform their current state of illness. Once accepting, they believe the healing is coming to them. Our society usually promotes emotional trust in doctors who have degrees, diplomas, and social proof through media that they are "the best." Patients who seek out these doctors may not know anything about them, other than what they choose to believe and emotionally accept, which still allows their healing to occur. This can be acceptable if the patient feels absolutely comfortable with their decision. The steps to healing are different for everyone, and many paths can lead to the right experience for those who seek healing. A patient may pray for healing also, which puts forward the asking aspects and moves the energy of creation in their favor, thus bringing them the healing they asked for. They may mentally think about their health and envision their function back to full capacity. They can emotionally feel how wonderful it will be to once again do the things they miss doing. As the physical starts to improve, the belief strengthens, and the faith that their health can be restored becomes even more solid.

You get on the path of healing when you agree to new truths about your situation and what may be possible for you. You must feel that you are connected to "all that is" so that all – including your healing, is possible. With new truth comes a new potential outcome towards a new way of life. Many who have been spontaneously cured from an illness were healed because they decided to release the thoughts in their minds that were negatively constrictive and held as "the only truth." The dis-ease had to remain present until they recalculated the perception that they were holding onto, and allow unwanted thought energy to dissolve. In turn, this gave them a lesson on how to become more open to love and dissolve resistance. Racism and sexism are examples of such energies that people hold onto as old thoughts that separate and divide the human race instead of unite it. As centuries continue forward, the thoughts parents and grandparents pass on may be limiting the youth, instead of helping it thrive. Children are not born racists - it is a learned behavior that continues to persist in society. The thoughts that vibrate the frequency of racism are put into the reptilian brain of the child's neurology. As the child grows, emotions will be fired up as various experiences test the belief system that is held as truth. Our emotions help make us aware when we are in connection to love and God, or if we are creating an upward or downward spiral in our health. If we align our thoughts properly in the spiritual, mental, and emotional planes, we see healing in the physical self as well. Thus, what is important is that the illness is cleared in all the unseen realms before it is to be actualized in the current perceived reality.

Emotions should not be internalized. Emotions are meant to be expressed and then neutralized. A repressed emotion is energy not in motion. If it is not in motion, it is stored or transferred to be stored. When someone advises that you put something that is bothering you in the back of your mind so you can forget about it, they are not giving you sound advice. Over time, this storing of energy will cause an explosion of emotion, pain, or dis-ease if not correctly moved for neutralization. This is why it is so important to hold a happy mind set free of negativity. Not only is it healthy for you, but also for others around you, as energy is contagious.

1.3 The Antenna Between the Physical and the Spiritual

"But the fruit of the Spirit is love, joy, peace, patience, kindness, goodness, faithfulness, gentleness, and self-control. Against such things there is no law."
~ Galatians 5:22-23

Right now, you are floating through space on a large piece of rock. Right now, you are being bombarded with radio waves. Right now, microbial organisms and bacteria are crawling all over and inside of you. Right now, the opposite side of the earth is probably sleeping while you are awake. These are real statements outside your immediate perception. Until you focus on them and put them into perspective, you don't acknowledge their presence or reality in your life.

Similarly, you are most likely unaware of the power your spinal system holds, or the reality that is the link between your physical world and your unseen spiritual world. Your spine is a highly sophisticated broadcasting station, and it is always on the job, even if your present perception is unaware of its workings. You constantly absorb or discharge frequencies that you hold as beliefs. Over time, these frequencies become your core beliefs. These core beliefs become your actions. These actions become your character. Your character then becomes your personality, which defines who you are perceived as to yourself and others.

In the practice and development of my healing method, I have come to a clear understanding of the relationship that exists between the physical and the non-physical. The importance of the spiritual aspect of the human body must be taken into consideration when a healer is seeking answers to a patient's physical problem. The attack to the physical body can be coming from an emotional complaint, or a problem with the emotional guiding system itself. However, this is generally associated with how the person has been programmed to think and react to stress from many previous experiences since youth, or even previous incarnations. The mental is not a physical thing we can touch or perceive in a third or fourth dimensional reality, and is believed to exist in the fifth dimensional space, which is considered a divine aspect of the human being. Thus the answers to physical ailments can be attributed to surface in any level outside just physical, but ultimately all connect to the energies which we are made up of on higher dimensional planes. It would be wise to understand the unseen work that goes on behind the scenes of the nervous system. The Kousouli® Method, works through the understanding and application of these energies.

1.4 That Magnificent Mind Power

With an average of seventy thousand plus thoughts a day, it's amazing we manage to stay sane. Most of these thoughts get filtered by our subconscious mind as they trigger our already programmed neural pathways, and either repeat what we already have installed, or grow new synapses to make new pathways occur. Learning to listen to your emotions can help you monitor the effects of what is being programmed into you. This inner guiding system - that exists in everyone - is the key to adding more of the same patterns or building a new belief pattern. When signals coming in are not in agreement with our inner joyful self, we get a feeling in our body that is not good and this usually makes us feel weak or sick. When we re-focus our thoughts and remove ourselves from low vibration by re-reconnecting to a higher frequency, we regain our feeling of happiness. Without being impulsive to feelings or allowing ourselves to be thrown around by a crying fit or rage, we must stop once we notice our feelings astray and ask ourselves at that very moment: "Do I want more of the same, or something different?" And if the answer is that you want to have a different experience, then by becoming aware, you will be able to direct your actions towards being proactive for change instead of reactive for more of the same. Reactive action is usually the work of your reptilian brain, the ingrained "old school" or "old brain" programming that runs survival. The limbic system of our brain gives rise to the emotions and our ability to feel. The neo-cortex is the "new brain," and the part of the brain that can enact the amazing power of imagination, learning, and higher consciousness. In our evolution as humans the survival needs of sex, food, and aggression have taken a backseat to the higher levels of the neo-cortex so that humans now thrive instead of just survive.

In our current society, those who are flexing their power over the people are knowledgeable of the reptilian brain's impulsiveness. They use advertisements and popular fads to enslave the mass thought of the populace. Using this programming instilled in us all, they lure customers through triggering vibrational thoughts of sex, fear, and violence in people's deep-seated programming. By triggering this reptilian brain aspect of the human nervous system, advertisers hope people automatically react without thinking rationally when buying products or taking an action which may not be in the best interest of the targeted consumer. Without discriminating the feelings you are having, and allowing the reptilian brain to make the decision, you don't second-guess what you are doing. Your ability to choose wisely in your best interest to thrive is substituted so that all you do is survive. When you "get wise" to this and choose to monitor your thoughts and feelings, you will start to distinguish energies and ideas that are projected at you. This will shift your perception and create for you a new reality that brings you back into your power. All that is needed in man's mass consciousness to bring us out of war, famine, and fear is the activation of our higher minds and the constant triggering of the problem solving neo-cortex.

"You cannot solve a problem from the same consciousness that created it. You must learn to see the world anew."
~ Albert Einstein

Chapter 2:
Energetics Rule Your World

"Any method through which you can stimulate the power of God to flow into your mind is legitimate and usable."
~ Norman Vincent Peale

2.1 It is What it is - There is No "Could Have Been"

Our entire environment consists of vibrational energy, which is continuously experienced through our five senses: seeing, hearing, touching, smelling, and tasting. All vibrational energy is also always in motion and travels fast or slow. Every second of every moment, we change the way our reality unfolds for us, as well as how we co-create with our neighbors.

Upon waking up, we can choose our breakfast of ham and eggs instead of waffles or pancakes, and then our next reality changes; the food we digest changes, the vitamins and minerals we metabolize change, the way we change that energy into flesh and express our physical body changes. Perhaps we decide to speak to someone we usually don't at work, and then our mood changes, as does theirs; the conversation could lead to another meeting or connection with that person, which moves into a building or breakdown of a relationship, and so on. Every action in your reality (from your thoughts and mind) changes the scenario of your reality, millisecond by millisecond. Even the body you are in now is different from the body you had as a child, as the atoms and molecules are manifestations of thoughts and energies that you are made up of now as opposed to then. You continue to create, in every moment of every second, and it changes as your will freely changes. The choices you have and make, are limitless. What each of us creates is our own version of energetic reality, and we can also share this reality. The observer is always controlling the experience. Thus, the explanation is the observer's. What they experience is the way it is - there may have been other opportunities and potentials, but those were not chosen. The present is what it is. This is why someone can see the same event and express it differently from different vantage points, as is often the case in an auto accident, where witnesses are asked to recall events in court. Everyone sees the same event but interprets it differently and gives a different version of the same incident, according to their perception and free will to choose what they believe they experienced as truth and their reality.

2.2 The Reality of Energetic Sensitives

Many energetically sensitive people, or "energy sensitives," usually develop their intuition again later in life, even though they may have forgotten they had it. They usually reawaken their abilities in their late twenties to early thirties when some other life information, understanding, or experiences have been attained without knowingly using this "ability." Some, however, turn it off after age six due to peer pressure to fit in with other children who have submitted to concepts of what is right and wrong within their tradition, culture, or society at that time. They then don't again reactivate their intuition until it is safe to do so after the scrutinizing years of high school and college are completed. The abilities of hearing, feeling, and seeing things others cannot, permeates the energetic sensitive with confusion, frustration, and shame, believing that they are different and cannot fit in. They may fear that they could be branded as "crazy" or a "mutant." Instead of seeing it as a blessing, it's viewed as a curse.

Energetic sensitives, who yearn to be guided by a teacher that knows what they are going through, must understand that doctors and counsellors who are termed professionals or "the best" by the psychiatric or medical establishment are not necessarily the best or most proficient in understanding energetic ability or energy power themselves. Some experts believe those who are gifted with abilities should be studied and examined like a lab rat, or may even decide to enroll them into a drug and research program which would disrupt the psychic development. Worse yet, the doctor could be so out of touch with the energetic sensitive that they may brand the energetic sensitive as insane or crazy, which would be most detrimental to any attained progress. Any energetic or psychic phenomenon should of course be met with question, critique, and analysis for genuine validation. However, it is important that the correct individuals are chosen to provide needed assistance to the energetically sensitive and encourage growth, not hinder it.

2.3 Kinds of Energy - Invisible and Imaginary?

> *"Reality is merely an illusion, albeit a very persistent one."*
> ~ Albert Einstein

The better you leverage your thought energy, the better you can move in this society and the faster you can accomplish your goals. Let's take a quick look at common forms of energy we were taught in school: kinetic, potential, and manifested, and its impact on Aether (or ether), as it pertains to the things we see in our world via mental to material manifestation.

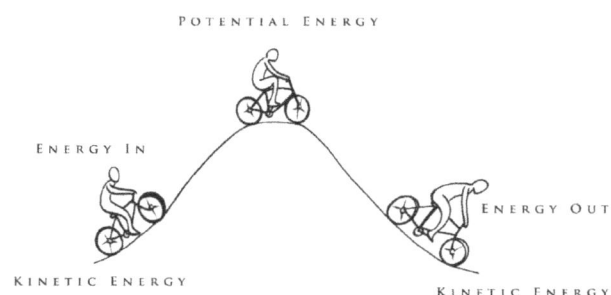

Potential Energy: E.g. Possible thoughts.

Kinetic Energy: E.g. Thoughts combined with action.

Manifested Energy: E.g. The world as we see it; the end product of collective consciousness at any precise moment.

Aether (Ether): Einstein's definition was that ether is a medium, which is itself devoid of all mechanical and kinematical qualities. Aether is also referred to the unseen or dark matter around the seen matter. It is a theoretical substance that permeates all solid matter, our body, the sky, air, fire, water, rock, the oceans, planets, and our entire universe. It is in us as well as all around us. Aether can be any color, shape, density, or texture. It is unseen but believed to hold the very planets together. It is also a force like wind and breath, can be molded like clay by thought, and although invisible to people it can be seen by mentalists, psychics, and spiritually evolved individuals. This is the energy believed to be used during meditation, clairvoyance, telekinesis, and other extrasensory activities. This type of energy has recently sparked large excitement in the scientific community and is being studied and researched for deeper understanding.

Simplified Examples of (+/-) potential, kinetic, and manifested energy:

Positive energy movement: A talented person feels the need to turn talent into money: *Potential Energy*. Singer writes new songs for record company: *Kinetic Energy*. Singer sings his/her new songs passionately; millions purchase singer's CD or attend their concert: *Manifested Energy*.

Negative energy movement: Someone cuts you off while driving. Thoughts say you have been harmed or dishonored: *Potential Energy*. You make an unpleasant gesture while yelling out your window: *Kinetic Energy*. Traffic jam created and drivers around you are all annoyed, or worse, an accident or personal assault occurs: *Manifested Energy*.

2.4 Energy Development of the Unseen

When a student travels the path of understanding exactly what intuitive and energetic power they possess, they may expect their siblings, friends, or colleagues to develop their ability at the same rate and way that they do. This is untrue, as no one has the same set of abilities or energetic powers. Neither are they at the same level of skill as another. There is great variety in all aspects of intuition, power, ability, skill, and understanding of potentials. Similarly, there is no one set way of learning them or developing them. Each is as individual as a snowflake or a fingerprint. We all incarnate at different levels.

Another common mistake energetic sensitives commit, especially in early training, is to choose incorrect systems that do not fit their purposes. They may travel the world going to various unrelated seminars looking for the next popular guru, mantra, magic pill, amulet, or gizmo bracelet that will give them instant powers, rather than focusing on developing the small ability they have in the comfort of their own home through simple meditation. Also, new students to the discipline will expect to levitate or move objects with their minds within a week of starting a course or mediation program. This is just not so. Some spend lifetimes developing their psychic abilities. Much of the time needed to gather this information has been cut down and put into this book so that you can fast-forward your progress in this field of study.

New recruits also fall victim to 'guru' worship mentality, thinking they must follow a special guru around and give constant donation from their finances for their spiritual nourishment or awakening. In the end, these individuals are always taken advantage of by the guru who may, at times, seem to have supernatural powers and ability. However, a student must understand that their own ability to connect to the Divine is just as powerful, and total devotion or enslavement to another human being is not only anti-God, but also contraindicative to being productive in reaching higher levels of enlightenment. No matter what a guru, priest, or rabbi promises or offers you, you can attain spiritual nirvana yourself through connecting to God without a middleman.

If a student of energy is frustrated in the process of learning about their ability and trying to get back their power, they should rest assured that eventually the correct path into awareness will open if they are diligent. Sometimes your higher self will lead you into what seems to be a turbulent and difficult path prior to giving you the key. The challenge may seem at first as misfortune, but can turn out to be the blessing you needed to see towards your spiritual awakening. Just ask, be patient, and in Divine time it will be given to you. Know that sooner or later, you will find the answers to your questions along the way, and they will make sense. There are many paths and various obstacles for everyone individually. Allow the journey, and trust that you are moving forward without looking back, no matter how much you may be feeling lost or side-tracked. The road to enlightenment is always rewarding, no matter the costs paid to attain it.

2.5 Mentally Ill vs. Energetically Sensitive

Why is it that when a child tells us they see angels, beings, entities, or can talk to something invisible, we humor them? We do not call them crazy, and do not check them into a mental institution, but when someone older says this, we immediately call them insane and treat them like an outcast? A child's world is full of possibilities, and there is no doubt in their minds that magical things, spirits, and a vastness of creativity exists. Why is it that as we age into adulthood, we lose these beliefs of wonder and second-guess our power, only to spend the rest of our lives looking to re-connect to the knowingness of this information? Perhaps we all have been put into a system that slowly deteriorates this knowingness? Perhaps the public school system is to blame for making everyone fit a certain "mold" in society? For instance, the American school system puts pressure to conform through standardized testing, requiring this of students from almost day one, while Japanese schools hold off on testing until after age 10, or 4th grade. Similarly, in Australia, most students don't have the pressure of significant exams until 11th grade, or the age of 16. This allows the child some time to create and enjoy their individuality, develop their character, and allow their mind to better differentiate who they are in their environment.

Standardization of thought, and branding improper thought as "diseased," comes from a book psychiatrists use to diagnose what could be a seemingly normal behavior. This nearly 1,000-page book is called the "DSM," or *Diagnostic and Statistical Manual of Mental Disorders*." It is a manual that consists of mental disorders, including anxiety and borderline personality disorders. This manual is compiled by the American Psychiatric Association, updated periodically, and is so broad in its description of symptoms that literally anyone reading this book can find a mental or personality disorder they could have. The American mental health field has conveniently also provided specific drugs that help you if you are so unlucky as to be diagnosed in anything mentioned in this book. However, psychologists will admit they cannot cure anyone with the poisonous psychoactive drugs they prescribe, and that the drugs they give out may even cause more issues than what you went to them to get help for.

The main difference between a mentally ill patient and one who is energetically sensitive, such as an empath (sensitive to the feelings of people or world around them), clairaudient (hears voices that inform), or clairvoyant (sees images or future potentials of what will occur) is that the mentally ill individual cannot maintain their sense of self during a psychic or supernatural event. The energy in the body is not the same person who is being controlled by the action; it's a foreign energy. This is called a "walk in," as if someone walked into the body and controlled it. In this event, the body becomes ungrounded and can lunge forward, go into spasm, yell incoherent or obscene things, shake, or try to cause harm to itself or others. If one does not understand psychic or energy phenomena, and they believe only in what is seen by the physical eyes, then every problem they come in contact with will be dealt with a hammer, when they may need to use a screwdriver.

People we look at as scholars or leaders hear thoughts that sound like voices all the time and are considered sane. The Greek philosopher Socrates claimed that, through his whole life, he was guided by a voice, which he described as "the voice of God." Psychologist Carl Jung even spoke of his spirit guide, Philemon, and claimed to see him in visions as a bearded older gentleman, possibly as an extension of his own psyche - seeing himself as an older wiser man. Insanity can happen whenever voices or psychic involvement becomes so overwhelming that the personal self-identity is totally lost, or has given up this dimensional reality. Those who are energetically sensitive, not mentally ill, can lead healthy and productive lives; they are in control of their body and mind. They are present even if they are engaged fully in a psychic, or out-of-this-world, experience. The energetically sensitive person is secure in who they are and what is occurring, without feeling the need to prove or defend their ability to others because they know they are genuine. These individuals can find much solace and understanding in other individuals that are like them through Internet support forums, meet-ups, and holistic centers that teach the natural understanding, and use of, their body and mind. Thankfully, as we expand our human awareness, the discovery of people's abilities is becoming more and more common and accepted.

To make sure acceptance is widespread, doctors must be responsible in differentiating between those who are seriously mentally ill and those who are energetically sensitive (within every varying degree of medical possibility). They shouldn't be quick to label someone as ill or medicate him or her. If you have been medically cleared of hormonal and neurological imbalances, and still believe you may be energetically sensitive, it would be advisable to also seek out professionals who are involved daily in the psychic or energy-healing establishment. Energetic sensitives should explore all options and research everything before accepting a regimen of drugs and mind-altering chemicals, which may dull out their natural abilities.

2.6 Graduating with a Spiritual Diploma

A pupil of energy sensitivity is one who wishes to further their abilities in this lifetime. They understand that in order to express their highest level of potential, they must decide to change the energy focus within priorities of their daily material world. They must drop the ego, substitute it with unconditional love, and understand their place in the galaxy as a part of the whole system. They begin making other's lives better, and focus on the community, rather than self-serving acts. They become sensitive to people's feelings and help comfort them. They trust in becoming guided by God's forces that bless them with peace and abundance in their lives. They take into account their body, and nurture it correctly with wholesome, clean food energy. Toxins such as caffeine, sugar, drugs, alcohol, and nicotine are limited, and then eliminated. They remove the influence of negative outer electromagnetic stimuli such as television, radio, and movie propaganda. Their habits change and become only focused on priorities that further their soul work here. They do not have to exclude themselves and join a monastery, but they should find the monastery and God within themselves, where they can quiet the mind and connect the heart. At the end of the lifetime, the energy and lessons amassed help the soul become an even more powerful ambassador, and more ascended soul in successive incarnations.

Chapter 3:
Everything and Everyone is Connected

"A dream you dream alone is only a dream.
A dream you dream together is reality."
~ John Lennon

Our lives are bound to others, both in the past and the present, as we cannot exist without each other. We work with others to bring about our experiences, beliefs, mistakes, successes, choices, and potentials. Each thought brings a new potential of an illusion we each hold dear to us, as our story that we call our reality. We cross and re-cross previous tracks through life's future, present, and past, hoping to change things as we experience new versions of who we believe we are, in various ways, and in various lifetimes with various people. Birth, life, death are part of a cycle that repeats for everyone many times. Love, hope, courage, fear, belief, and kindness are forces that move the course of life, and are there long before we come to the planet, and will be present long after we leave this realm.

3.1 Understanding Parallel Realities

Some may have a hard time thinking that another universal reality (or multiverse reality), other than the one they are living in and currently experiencing, exists. They understand they have a past, a present, and can contemplate their future. They can't understand that there are parallel universes that are different versions of them depending on their choices, and if in a difficult position in life, they can change their situation. Let me explain: You are like a book, similar to the one you are holding. You have a life, this incarnation, which has a starting birth, middle, and finishing end. You have your life story. Similarly, the book also has a beginning, middle, and end. Your life has its cast of characters, plot, climaxes, drama, comedy, etc., just as a book does. Our left-sided analytical brain allows us to order this life in a linear, one-by-one fashion (If this, then that). We each have our own set path we follow, in order to enjoy the details in this book of our life. We pick it up and read from left to right, and in sequential order. However, this depends on the reader (or observer), as some cultures or ethnicities read from right to left – but that's neither here nor there.

Furthermore, we could skip around in the book, read the jacket of the book, or the back cover to get an idea of what is in store for us. Some like to skip around in the book, while others don't. Some read the book once, some many times over, while some stop half way through and jump to another book that may be more interesting. Our life, and parallel universes, can be compared to books. Think of a book as one life, and then a library with many books as all of your lives.

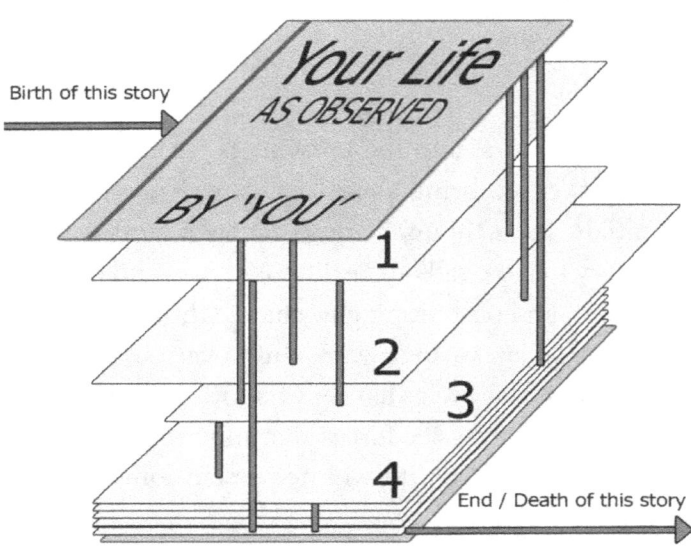

Each life has other parallel stories that become reality when your eyes read the pages. They come to life, and they become real to you as you observe them. Move your eyes to another book, but the book you just read does not simply vanish or become non-existent; it's just not real to you at that moment, while you focus your attention on another one of your books or stories. Likewise, your life is a continual story of many books, of which you are the writer or creator, and as such, you get to experience what you want to experience by what you *focus* on. Are you in the mood for a drama or action story, a comedy, or a suspense thriller perhaps? Or are you content reading about a love story set in a tropical location? With each change of story, the scenes, the cast of characters, and the locations all change to suit the creator's (your) imagination, thoughts, and expectations. When you want to change the story, you simply pick up another book or continue to the next chapter. Take a look at the photo of the dissected book. You can see the usual sequence of pages 1, 2, 3, 4 and so on. You may be on page 130 of your current story, which seems to be a horror story full of pain and misery, and all you need to do is change the characters, scenes, location, and stage to experience another story – your new reality.

How do you do this? You stop focusing on what you do not want, or do not desire to experience any longer, and you immediately put down that book. You stop that story by not discussing, observing, or thinking anything more about that topic. Instead, you pick up another book, or another version of your life. It may be the same plot, but a different, more pleasurable story, and so you continue on that path. You may have loved the story written so far, all the way up to page 130 on the previous book, and now want to skip to page 28 of a similar parallel book to continue the story as another, more pleasurable adventure. When you finish the story of that book and come to the end, it is similar in death in an incarnated lifetime, except it is a reincarnation of a new story or lifetime. You may even decide not to pick up another book immediately, and instead roam the library, enjoying the break in between the stories or lifetimes you create. Remember what the teacher Christ taught: We are eternal beings, and thus the spirit (soul) inside us never dies, it can simply recreate itself in a new light. This is the spirit of God, which lives inside us all. You are part of the whole incredible creation, which never ends.

3.2 Understanding Dimensions

Think of a piece of paper. It has length and width that can be measured, but there is no height. This represents a 2-dimensional world (also referred to 2D, or 2nd density consciousness). We can change its dimensions by cutting and folding the paper into a physical cube. The cube now has length, width, and height. Our movie theaters used to only project 2D movies, until society's collective consciousness fully accepted 3D films. We can now allow our minds to transform the experience of 2D into a more real environment through the use of 3D projection. 3D (or 3rd Density) is where we are all consciously experiencing ourselves at the present physical level, mixed with the next higher level, the fourth dimension, or fourth density consciousness, where time and energy blend. 5D can be explained as a non-physical reality; where thoughts and intentions can manifest through to lower dimensions, and our collective consciousness exists. The limitation of the $3/4^{th}$ dimension or density consciousness is that our thoughts are still very linear in their application. This, then that occurs; one, two, and three o' clock; A, B, C, D... etc. in consequential order. A filmstrip of film has many frames on the film. Each dimension is a frame in the film, but as the projectionist you can look at all the frames at one time. All dimensions exist right now; it is just the method of attention we use to experience the dimension(s). There are many non-linear thoughts and ideas; far more than what we may be consciously experiencing. Currently there are many radio waves flying

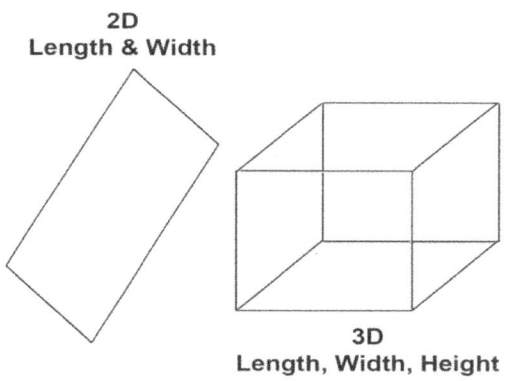

around us but we do not pick them up or focus attention to them, unless we get a device that can do so. Our understanding of our current third and fourth dimensions allows us inquisitive exploration of the fifth dimension also, where movement in any direction is possible. This will happen when enough of society has accepted and allowed for the possibility of relaxing the consciousness so that bending and molding space and time can happen. By living in the now, we depend less on the past and future ideas of reality; when this occurs, our perception of extrasensory information increases. The use of hypnosis can bring us clearer understandings of 5th density by allowing us to experience things like lucid dreaming, astral or past life traveling, and heightened clairvoyant ability, even though we may be currently living in a dense lower linear 3D/4D dimension.

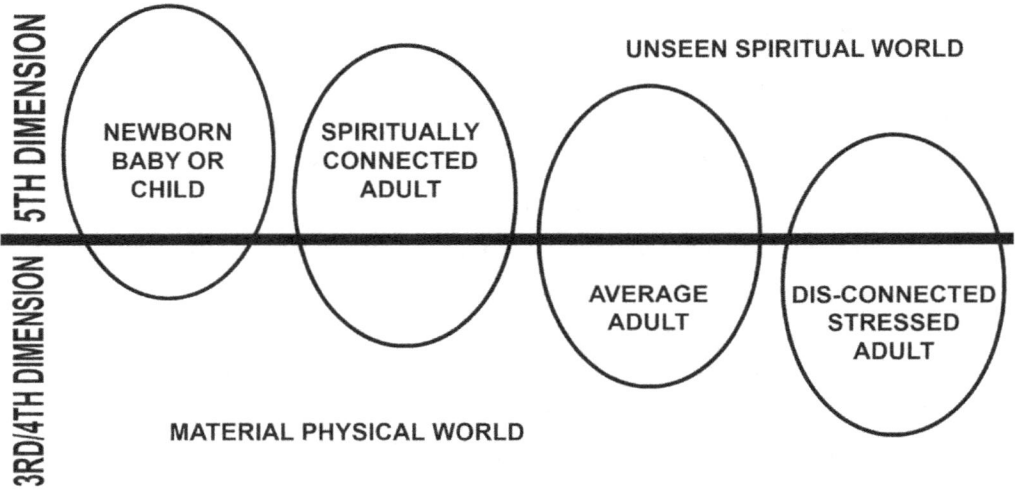

The 3RD, 4TH, and 5TH dimension diagram shows an example of how much of our spiritual energy we may have invested in the realms. A newborn child through approximately age eight is still fresh from the 5th dimensional space, and most of their energy and focus is still in 5th dimension, as they try to understand life here in this reality. A spiritually connected adult that has worked on themselves, or who never lost connection with the spiritual essence they had as a child, is also working in higher consciousness. An adult that does not meditate or clear the mind of this 4th dimension's co-created issues or challenges, which are held in belief as real, can get so focused and involved in strife that they become less connected to their higher self, and may even doubt or disbelieve their higher self, extrasensory perceptions, or God. However, you do not need to be spiritual, religious, or even believe in God to still be connected to God. Everyone (even those who deny his or her connection), is still connected to God. If they choose to do so, through their own free will, they can choose to limit their connection consciously. However, at some point, we all eventually return to our Creator.

When you awaken each morning, you leave the 5th dimensional space and experience the 3RD dimension existence of height, width, and length, along with the 4th dimension, which includes the idea of time. When we sleep we experience our reconnection to our true home and the place where all things are possible; where we may meet with other souls we know in our dreams. You may have had someone say that you visited him or her in his or her dream last night, or they saw you doing something in their dream. Since you are an eternal spirit connected to your maker, you have the ability to move your energy as your soul pleases. However, you cannot have 100% of your full spiritual energy expressed here on Earth. You would vanish in a flash of light and disintegrate the physical body, like the prophet Elijah did as told in the Old Testament. Elijah was seen being taken up to the sky by what was best explained at that time as a "fiery chariot." Even the masters like Jesus, while on Earth, had high percentages of their being expressed about 80-90% of the time, but never 100%. It would be too much for the physical body to accept in this limited dimension, making it difficult to operate and relate to other human beings. When your spiritual energy diminishes in this realm and the soul returns to its origin, you will leave on Earth a small part of you with your loved ones, and another part, the organic physical material you are made of, returns to Earth as a record that you were here.

This raises the question, "What dimension is God in?" The simple answer is: *all of them*. In the next sections, we will be discussing God as an all-powerful energy, and also evaluating the human influence that reduces Him from an all-dimensional power to a human interpretation of power.

3.3 Talking about God

Through time, cultures and religions have always worshipped the Divine. The ancient Mayans, Romans, Greeks, and Africans asked favor from many gods. Buddhists believe there is no God, aside from nature and our own manifested power that flows through each of us. Hindus worship multiple forms of God and claim that God is one in many. However, some religions, particularly Christianity, believe in and worship one absolute God as omnipotent, omnipresent, understanding, approachable, and loving. Muslims also believe there is a powerful God but he/she/it is unknowable, except as ALLAH, whose prophet was Muhammad. New Age followers believe that they themselves are God-like. In the *Sikh Religion*, there is only One, Hari, who has many names and many forms. No matter where humanity existed, you will also find within them the belief in a higher power, or God. When we look at the world's religions and their thoughts about God, it is very much diverse, and there are confusing or contradictive teachings and belief systems within their variant views of God. In the next chapter we explore the history of the Christian church, the connection between the words of Christ in the Bible, and what it means for us to connect through the Holy Spirit in terms of health, and furthering our understanding of abundance and prosperity on Planet Earth. This is in no way a religious book, nor do I intend to sway you towards any particular religion or path. I merely present this information, and make certain points to you, as I have researched and experienced them myself.

In the *Christian Religion*, there is only One God, who is comprised of the Trinity: the Father, Son and Holy Spirit. These are three of one, or one of the same. In life and nature, the Trinity phenomenon exists everywhere. In thermodynamics, ice, water, vapor, or solid, liquid, gas. A triangle has three sides; without any of the sides it cannot be called a triangle. Even the Universe is made up of space, time, and matter; all are 3-way systems that complete their various functions.

3.4 How Do I Know What is From God or 'Real'?

One must experience God personally to understand the connection and meaning of what and who God is. Anything coming from truth and the highest level of love vibration will feel calm, pure, and full of peace. God's truth calms you and gives you a breath of fresh air deep within your soul. Anything other than this feeling is not of the highest vibration, and may be too filtered with human bias, ego or agenda, making it less than pure truth. If a message leaves you fearful, paranoid, grieving, or terrified, then the vision or message was not of the highest vibration and its authenticity should be questioned. Miracles and works of amazement with no healing purpose are not by themselves proof of genuine connection to the light and love.

You may be asking yourself, "What does all this talk about religion and God have to do with energy healing?" You see, everyone believes in something. In reality, there are no atheists because everyone puts their mind and energy into something when focusing their innate God Force. This focus can take the form of positivity: peace, love, community, healing, or it can take an egocentric form like money, stocks, fame, narcissism, jealousy, etc. Where you focus your mind you also exercise your worship of God Power.

So if we are going to discuss healing from a spiritual perspective, we must examine the essence and depths of personal belief. We will discuss how one of the world's most popular miracle healers, Jesus Christ, healed the people of his time. By doing so, we examine the faith structure(s) that allow our Divine energy flow. Where our current beliefs are held, within a man-made religious construct, and how we believe we can direct these beliefs, will give us our instructions for what is allowed in healing of ourselves and others.

Chapter 4:
The Original Church: What Happened to Christianity?

"If you say that the history of the Church is a long succession of scandals, you are telling the truth, though if that is all you say, you are distorting the truth."
~ Gerald Vann

4.1 Religious Hypocrisy

If we think about the word "Christianity," we think about many customs and symbolisms introduced to us through the years by mass marketing and faith propaganda. What many people generalize Christianity as resembles nothing that was original Christianity. This then begs the questions: "What happened to original Christianity and the teachings of Jesus and his apostles? Does it still exist, and isn't this what Christians already believe in?"

Many proclaimed Christians don't practice any Christianity as taught by the original Church of Christ and his apostles, and seem to be highly hypocritical when compared to the rules they should be living by. The Catholic Church in particular has been in the crosshairs for child molestation and rape charges for a long time, and has a dark history of behind-the-scenes hypocrisy. The Roman Catholic Archdiocese of Los Angeles paid out a whopping $650 million dollars in 2007 to settle claims from people whose lives have been ruined by pedophile priests. To date, the total rumored to have been paid out by the United States Catholic Church since the 1950's has reached over $3+ billion! All this occurring for decades behind the scenes, as the Vatican covets most of the world's wealth, and as the Pope rides in bulletproof limousines, wearing robes made of the finest silks. We can be pretty sure Jesus Christ did not mean this kind of love, when the greatest commandment received was to love one another.

Jesus never meant to create followers; he sought to create leaders. He was not looking to lead a religion; he was looking to spark knowledge of one's inner power. If Jesus was to come back today, he would likely proclaim, "Why in my Father's good name are you including me in all this junk!?" Most likely, he would be upset about all the wars and pain people have caused for centuries in God's name. He would still be angry with the money-changers who corrupted the Church and use 'God' for fundraisers. He would look at the writings and doctrine that Christians claim to believe, and proclaim they've strayed far from his teachings. However, most shocking to him may be how many different Christian denominations now exist, and how they all think they are "the chosen one."

If the Bible tells us in Hebrews 13:8, that Christ is "the same yesterday, today, and forever," then it must be the people who have changed, not Christ. The change in people happened because over time they did not stick to the Scriptures and commandments. As generations continued, they passed down the best knowledge that was available to them on how to live a good life, but neglected to also pass down the importance of sticking to the parts of Scripture that flourish one's soul prosperity. Many people just accepted what was passed on to them without questioning or testing the material to see if it was still original, or a varied copy of the original. As reported in 2013, 57% of Americans admit to reading their Bible four times or less per year! Only 26% of Americans say they read it more than four times per week. How can people know what they're quoting if they don't actually read the source?

4.2 Consider This...

The rulebook or backbone of belief certainly puts into perspective the path that one will walk. If we want to have the ability to understand how to heal dis-ease, which is a runaway vibration disconnected from its source, or a disconnection from the light or all that is good, then we must understand the parallel between belief and healing. So it becomes clear that one must separate the original truth of what God is, from what God isn't. God isn't religion, as religion is man-made, and the spirit of God is above religion. So clearing up what doctrines of belief we each hold as our 'road map' becomes exponentially important. Many have gone way off track in religion, and they may think it's no big deal. However, this is no small issue when you consider that beliefs you hold dear can make the difference between attaining a prosperous, joyful, and pain-free life, or a confused, anxious, and dis-eased life. Religion as a system can help Man understand God, but unfortunately Man's personification of God and his rules assuredly follow religious-minded people. All great healers possess an unbelievable connection to a faith or belief system that has no obstacle in connecting to God. Wasn't Jesus trying to teach us this very idea through his ministry?

We read in Matthew 7:21-23 that Jesus said, "*Not everyone who says to Me, 'Lord, Lord,' shall enter the kingdom of heaven, but he who does the will of My Father in heaven. Many will say to Me in that day, 'Lord, Lord, have we not prophesied in Your name, cast out demons in Your name, and done many wonders in Your name?' And then I will declare to them, 'I never knew you; depart from Me, you who practice lawlessness!'*"

What exactly is the "will of the Father in heaven" that Jesus speaks about here? It is following his teachings and path of enlightenment through unconditional love for self and others. We also read that many seers, readers, healers, etc. will be able to do amazing feats of trickery and magic, but they will do this in a twisted way that has no real connection to loving or serving God, using God to only satisfy their ego. Jesus says that He never knew them, for they were not aligned in the beliefs and teachings that connect to God.

4.3 Know Your Religious Beginnings

"Church isn't where you meet. Church isn't a building. Church is what you do. Church is who you are. Church is the human outworking of the person of Jesus Christ. Let's not go to Church, let's be the Church."
~ Bridget Willard

Religion is a combination of tradition, symbolism, and metaphors necessary for most people's need for order and organization based on beliefs, or also to fulfill a certain human desire to understand the world around them and give meaning to their lives. However, it is good to answer questions about existence through observations and logic while being open to all possibilities. Few go to church for what it is meant to be: a place of connection with the highest frequency of love and light - with their maker, God. It should be a place of like-minded people who seek to refresh the heart, rebalance the inequity, and heal the soul. Unfortunately for many people, church has become a fashion show, hookup center for meeting Mr. or Mrs. Right, and a who's who of faux good followers. Some drift off to sleep, while others go to keep up on the latest gossip, or show off their latest mink fur.

It would make sense to research the religion you choose to follow before you make it your faith. Without researching your faith's origins, you may end up not knowing how it may have been altered throughout time. Most Christian religions are copies, or copies of copies, of another religious sect. When someone within a religion with influence decides to hold a grudge and take followers away from that religion because of doctrine or a political dispute, it can upset the ranks and cause an uprising into the creation of another sect.

This very example has happened numerous times throughout our history. That's the literal root derivative of a Protestant – protesting something new.

If you joined any of the spiritual establishments known as "Jehovah's Witnesses," "Church of the Nazarene, Pentecostal Gospel," or "Holiness Church," your religion is fairly new in creation and one of the many sects founded within the last 100 years. If you're Christian Scientist, Mary Baker Eddy founded your faith in 1879. If you're with the Salvation Army, your faith was started in 1865 by William Booth in London. Joseph Smith started the Latter Day Saints in Palmyra, New York in 1829. His successor, Brigham Young, called it Mormonism after an angry mob killed Smith in 1844. Methodists believe in the creations of John and Charles Wesley in England in 1774. New York 1628 marks the start of the Dutch Reformed Church, of which Michelis Jones is the founder. Baptists follow the canons of John Smyth, who began the religion in 1606 in Amsterdam. The Protestant Episcopalian faith was a side-shoot of the Church of England, initiated in the 1700's by Samuel Senbury in America's colonies. Robert Brown initiated the Congregationalist faith in 1582 in Holland. If you're Presbyterian, John Knox is your initiator, and your faith started in Scotland in 1560. Belong to the Church of England? If so, your faith was founded by King Henry VIII in 1534 because the Pope would not allow him a divorce so that he could re-marry. In 1517 after disagreeing with the procedures of the Catholic Church, Martin Luther, an ex-monk, decided to start the Lutheran religion. That's the trickle-down effect of the Protestant Reformation; and it continues to reform itself after many other protests, in many other ways.

4.4 Was Original Christianity Jewish?

Christianity, as it is known today, was nothing like it was back in its early beginnings. In the Bible's first chapters, *Acts of the Apostles*, the first Christians were said to be all Jewish, either by conversion or birth. They were Jewish members considered at that time as a sect of Judaism, which was named the Nazarenes. Jewish-Christians followed Jewish law and traditions. After time, this group was later known as the "Christians at Antioch." Even the early Christian doctrine followed the Old Testament traditional writings of those times. The first Christian community was located in Jerusalem with leadership coming from James, John, and Peter. Paul of Tarsus converted to Christianity, and also spread Christian beliefs vastly through the lands. Christianity eventually spread into Greek areas that were around Israel, and another sect called the Gnostics sought specialized study on God and furthered Christianity.

As time went on and Christians established community with each other, the connection between Jewish and new Christian belief severed. By the end of the first century,

Christianity was recognized separate from Rabbinic Judaism. Early Christians very much valued the Jewish Bible as Scripture, (The Talmud was called the "Traditions of the Elders"). Some of Paul's writings also alluded to the breakup of the Jewish and Christian communities. However, Early Christians and Christians today still hold much of Mosaic Law in practice, such as the Golden Rule and Ten Commandments.

4.5 The Roman Catholic Church Decides to Change the Rules

The original twelve apostles spread Christianity until the time of their death, and they did not change Christ's important teachings. Miscommunication in what we call "the divisions" of Christianity comes after a period of time called the Dark Ages. During this rather nasty time of history, Catholic Popes and Bishops changed many of the original teachings of Christ, which separated it from Roman pagan cults of that time. It is believed that there may have been as many as 40 or more authors contributing, over a period of 1,500 years, to what is collectively known today as the Bible. Although the core substance of the Bible is secure in its teachings of prosperity in life, and Jesus undoubtedly walked the Earth and influenced mankind in the ways he did, history shows that the Bible has been manipulated by many men throughout the centuries for personal, political, and economic gain.

The Roman Catholic Church is approximately 1,000 years old. It shared the same humble beginnings for its first thousand years with the Orthodox faith. During the first millennium after Christ, both the Roman and Orthodox Church were the same church. However, in 1054 A.D., Rome's Pope broke away from the other four Apostolic Patriarchates (Alexandria, Jerusalem, Antioch, and Constantinople) by interfering with the original credo of the church, proclaiming himself infallible and God's one messenger for all others to follow. The Pope declared himself supreme; causing what is now known as the Great Schism (Division) of Christianity. Eastern Orthodox Christianity is now almost 2,000 years old. It can be traced back to the original writings of the apostles and teachings of Jesus Christ. Eastern Orthodoxy's message has been about teaching love and forgiveness, not dogmatic practices of fear and damnation. For this reason and its historical solidarity, Orthodoxy, the Church of the Apostles and the Fathers, is considered the true "one Holy Catholic and Apostolic Church." The timeline of events surrounding Christianity's origin is declared in all the history books with undeniable question, though many 'Christian' religious leaders choose not to look at these points of origin as it does not benefit them to tell their followers where and when their faith's beliefs began.

Also widely known is that the Gospels seem to contradict each other in terms of timeline of events, and that the meanings of the teachings were not meant to be taken literally for every situation. Most proclaimed Christians don't even know that Christmas, the sacred day of Jesus Christ's celebrated birth is not actually the birthdate of Christ and is speculated to be more accurate around May, April, or June - not December. The early Christian fathers of the church agreed to hold the celebratory date closer to their winter solstice, celebrating alongside the already established Roman rebirth and renewal celebrations, while taking into account the fitting of their moneymaking and political agendas. However, even after considering the above points, the message of prosperity and healing contained in the Bible still holds keys to our health and happiness today - if correctly understood as the gift that it is.

The diagram maps out some of the breaks of Christian denominations since the schism, but the actual spread today is far grander than what is pictured here.

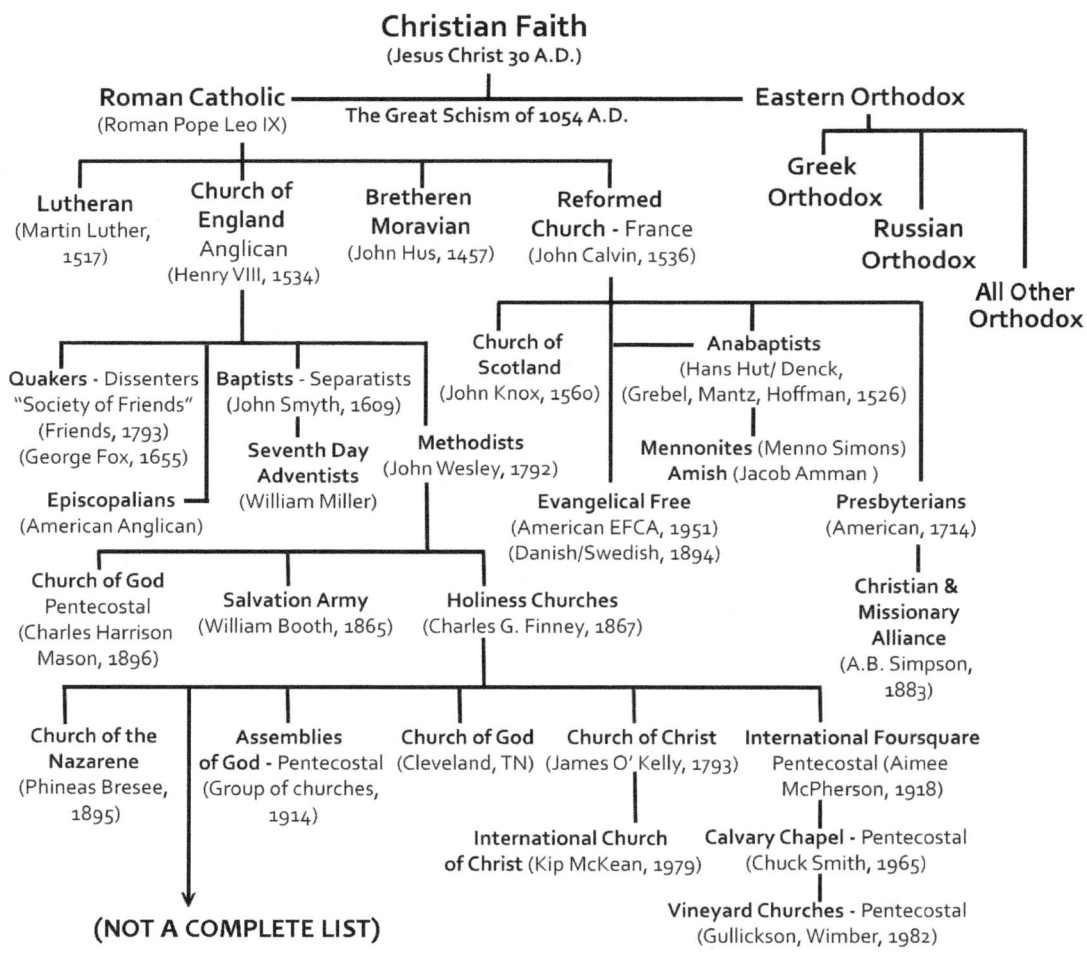

4.6 Summary of the Great Schism

- After the birth of the Church of Jesus Christ, the Apostles made many missions. Over time, five patriarchies were founded at approximately 325 A.D.: Rome, Constantinople, Antioch, Jerusalem, and Alexandria.
- Peter was the first Bishop of Antioch; 12 years later he became first Bishop of Rome. Peter left Paul head of Antioch, and James, brother of Jesus, was the first Bishop of Jerusalem.
- There were disputes between them and how to teach the Old Testament law. James solved the differences that arose by developing ecumenical councils that took care of all doctoral and moral issues. For 1054 years, the church was unified as one. The Council of Jerusalem was the faith of the apostles - the faith of the original Christian Church.
- The Nicene Creed was formed, declaring the faith in 325A.D. at Nicea, Bithynia - now present day Iznik, Turkey. Between 325 and 787A.D. seven ecumenical councils formed to establish the church laws.
- In 1054 A.D., tensions erupted between the Western Roman church and the other Eastern churches. The Roman Bishops declared the Roman Church supreme over the other 4 churches, saying their patriarch was the only true successor of St. Peter. Also in question was the addition of the Pope supremacy, making the Pope a God-like figure on Earth and the changing of the 700-year-old creed. Until this time, everything was unified and there was only one unified Christian religion on Earth.
- A Cardinal was sent by the Roman Bishop who, during a Sunday mass, expelled the Patriarch of Constantinople from the church. The patriarch of Rome then broke off, declaring the Roman Catholic Church independent from the other four Eastern churches.
- This action caused what is now known in history as The Great Schism of the original Christian Church. As of the release of this book, the split remains despite ongoing attempts to connect the churches.

4.7 Did God Himself Write the Religious Texts?

The message itself, which is written in all Scriptures, was written by a human hand, divinely inspired by a higher power, the Holy Spirit, God, or whatever name you want to give 'it,' depending on your personal connection to that which you believe (or were taught to believe) through your tradition or heritage (Jewish, Christian, Muslim, etc.). Storytelling by parable was the most common way of passing important historical or cultural information from generation to generation. Unlike the advancements of current documentation via computers and hard drive back up, it was hard to safeguard coveted sacred writings, which were highly susceptible to fires, flood, theft, or simple degeneration. All the words written throughout time were channeled into being through inspired thought, either by the use of meditation, prayer, fasting, herbal use, or a combination of all four. Our whole society was, and continues to be, shaped by these channeled thoughts and words from Divinity. All things being claimed as 'the word of God' have been transferred, translated, and deciphered by man using personal human filters.

Modern science as we know it from men such as Galileo, Newton, and more recently Einstein, is in no way considered religion, just as religion is in no way considered science even though science and religion are starting to see God 'eye to eye' via the explanation of quantum physics. The occurrences of various religious events on our timeline are so far apart from each other that one cannot explain the other, though people do try to speculate how miraculous religious events may have occurred. Christian Scriptures were based upon 2,000 years before Christ, to about 250+/- years after Christ. As much as we wish we could piece all events together and make it all make perfect sense, the fact remains that there was such sporadic and messy recordkeeping in ancient times that historians will always be baffled with various details. Perhaps it's merely the confusion of many parallel realities existing simultaneously?

4.8 Who Are "The Father," "The Son," and "The Holy Spirit"?

The man called Jesus of Nazareth prayed to his Father, the Creator of all things visible and invisible. We read in Luke 3:21-22, "Jesus was also baptized, and while He was praying heaven was opened, and the Holy Spirit descended upon Him in bodily form like a dove, and a voice came out of heaven, saying 'You are My beloved Son, in You I am well-pleased.'" Here we hear of the Son being baptized, the Holy Spirit descending upon Him, and the Father speaking from the heavens. We all have the same father regardless of religion, upbringing, or tradition, and we all connect to the idea of the "Father" differently. The Father is referred to as many things by various religions; the Universal Intelligence, Allah, Source of all love, highest vibration, or the loving light, just to name a few.

Many Christians today forget that Jesus "The Son" (Yeshua) was not a Christian, but followed the law of the land, which was Judaism. Christianity formed much later from his teachings and sacrificial example. Whoever Jesus Christ was, he was actually not the poor man he was made out to be through the centuries by the Church. He was indeed a humble, wise and gentle man, rebellious against the status quo, though not poor by any means. His Earthly father, Joseph, was a carpenter, which was a noble profession at that time; a skilled trade that was highly in demand and commanded good pay to provide for a family. Jesus was an advanced soul (some New Age teachers speculate he was a Pleiadian, from the Pleiades star cluster about 400 light-years from Earth), which incarnated specifically for the people of Israel, to change the ways of the land there at that time, and to make a historical mark for the development of human consciousness. He was a teacher who came to show humanity how to live a fuller, more spiritually aware and connected life through their Creator, the Father, or God. Jesus was the human messenger and bridge between man and God. In many ways what Jesus did here, as a human form of love, was show us how we can all connect to the Father as sons and daughters of the Father. He repeatedly taught and said we can be like him in our path to God. Just like Jesus, we are also heirs to all the power available through the Father.

Also referred to as the Holy Ghost, internal higher spirit, or collective Christ consciousness, "The Holy Spirit" is said to be the very thing that animates us, gives us breath, and allows us to be more than just a corpse. It's the invisible thing that comforts us, and helps heal our wounds, shrinks the cancer, brings instant clarity or genius, or makes one talk in tongues. We see it pictured in religious paintings as a bright gold energy around the crown chakra of Jesus or as a flame of fire over the head of saints, or anyone who is "enlightened with the light." It is important to remember that we were ALL made in the image and likeness of our Creator. We're given a soul and free will, the ability to choose and create, provided sovereignty; made wiser than other mammals, and given compassion, knowledge, morality, and love.

"Let us make man in our image, in our likeness, and let them rule over the fish of the sea and the birds of the air, over the livestock, over all the earth, and over all the creatures that move along the ground. So God created man in his own image, in the image of God he created him; male and female he created them."
~ *Genesis 1:26-27*

This means we have power that we can enact, or choose not to enact, through our God-given free will.

4.9 The First Great Question of Life Is… "Why am I Here?"

According to Proverbs 16:4 taught in the Bible, "The Lord has made everything for His own purpose." It's for His purpose and there is a perfect divine plan for everything. Every rock has a purpose, every plant and animal have a purpose, and you are no different. His purpose is your purpose, as he has never made anything without a purpose. God knows all the potentials of what you think and the outcomes of what you will pick. However, your gift of free will allows you the ability to create as you please, and this only you know; thus your thoughts are God's thoughts and vice versa, since you are the creation of God and the heir to all your Father (Creator) has and is.

Ephesians 1:4 says, *"Long before he laid down the earth's foundation, he had us in his mind and settled on us as the focus of his love, to be made whole and holy by his love."* You and I are the focus of God's love. We were created to be loved by God. You need to understand that this is what you are here on Earth for. We are here on Earth to be in a loving relationship with God, so that we may create and manifest by and through Him. The feeling of fulfillment when creating with love a piece of music, art, architecture, etc. is the gift of manifesting through creation. God used this process to bring about you, and you use the process to bring about another creation, child, or idea into this world. Our purpose is to continuously create as God does.

4.10 The Second Great Question of Life Is …"Do I Matter? Is My Life of Value?"

The prophet Isaiah asked this same question. *"My work all seems so useless. I've spent my strength for nothing and for no purpose at all"* (Isaiah 49: 4). We were created for meaning. We are destined to mean something to someone. If you don't have meaning and purpose in your life, or don't know *why* God put you here, your life won't make any sense.

Many people are most likely going through life by *just barely surviving*. Those at this level are in survival mode and only a paycheck away from disaster. They're just existing and not really living, controlled by their circumstances and are not creating with awareness for themselves. They put in their time and live for the weekend or some small goal, attaining a false sense of happiness. Others *live only to seek success*; honestly, this is where most are. By the world's ideals, they've got it made. They have comfortable lifestyles compared to the rest of the world, and are considered very wealthy compared to the rest of the world. Freedom, good health, material possessions, job prestige, and success are all there. Yet they still feel unfulfilled, as it takes more than success and status to satisfy the soul. Then there are those who have an *awareness of the magnificent self*. When one knows the meaning of life and understands its mechanisms, knowing how much they are united with God while living their purpose, they become a beacon of light that shines so bright nothing seems to worry or harm them. Others who are lost will seek these people out no matter how much material wealth or status they may possess.

You and I were made to mean something great. It is written, *"I am your Creator. You were in my care even before you were born"* (Isaiah 44v:2). This psalm illuminates how God had us all in mind even before birth. *"You are the one who put me together inside my mother's body, and I praise you because of the wonderful way you created me.... Even before I was born, you had written in your book everything I would do"* (Psalm 139:13-14, 16). These passages hint to our connection with God and our eternal essence and potential. You are intimately connected to God and matter always - even at the point of conception.

Religion is crucial for most people as it brings people to God in some way. Yes there are faults, yes there are issues to work on, and the Church must ascend into what it should be, not what it is today. God's Ten Commandments, which were written down and spoken to the people by Moses, remain strong in Judaism and Christianity. As a rulebook, the Church claims that these commandments can help all people lead a more positive and happy life. These ten guidelines for prosperity, which have been in existence for over two thousand years, are as follows:

The Ten Commandments (Exodus 20:2-17) Explained:

I.) "I am the Lord your God, You shall have no other gods before Me." (Put your Father / Creator as top priority in your life and never substitute Him.)

II.) "You shall not make for yourself a carved image, or any likeness of anything that is in heaven above, or that is in the earth beneath, or that is in the water under the earth; you shall not bow down to them nor serve them." (Nothing or no one is as powerful as the one who you are created from. Do not submit yourself to anything less than God.)

III.) "You shall not take the name of the Lord your God in vain." *(Do not curse the very power you come from; this is self-defeating to your soul as you are one with God.)*

IV.) "Remember the Sabbath day, to keep it holy. Six days you shall labor and do all your work, but the seventh day is the Sabbath of the Lord your God." (Allow time to re-focus all your attention on your Creator; realign mind, body, and soul in truth and gratefulness so you may be replenished.)

V.) "Honor your father and your mother." (Respect those who carried you into this incarnation and will give you challenges to further your soul evolution.)

VI.) "You shall not murder." (Do not end a life, as it goes against another's free will to exist and create as they please.)

VII.) *"You shall not commit adultery."* (Do not act upon evil thoughts to partake in pleasure of the flesh; it distracts from serving your soul's higher purpose.)

VIII.) *"You shall not steal."* (Do not harm another by taking what was not created or manifested by your own efforts.)

IX.) *"You shall not bear false witness against your neighbor."* (Do not speak against your soul's known truth with anything less than love.)

X.) *"You shall not covet your neighbor's house; you shall not covet your neighbor's wife, nor his male servant, nor his female servant, nor his ox, nor his donkey, nor anything that is your neighbor's."* (Do not envy what others have created as you can create your own manifestations.)

Today, just like so many centuries ago, these ten rules are still effective in leading a more peaceful and successful life. Simply ponder the thought that if we all held ourselves to just these ten guidelines, then we just may have the possibility of living in a positive, healthy society with no war, more love, and peace on Earth.

4.11 The Lord's Prayer

The following is the Lord's Prayer and Nicene-Constantinopolitan Creed according to the Greek Orthodox Faith (A.D.381), which is still kept exactly the same today by the Eastern Orthodox faith. These are considered declarations of faith, which followers believe connects them closer to their God power. Many healers regardless of religious upbringing still recite these when giving healings to their patients; they claim the intention of the words holds great power.

Lord's Prayer

English

> Our Father, who art in heaven, hallowed be Thy name.
> Thy kingdom come, Thy will be done, on earth as it is in heaven.
> Give us this day our daily bread; and forgive us our trespasses,
> as we forgive those who trespass against us; and lead us not into temptation,
> but deliver us from evil.

Greek

> Πάτερ ἡμῶν, ὁ ἐν τοῖς οὐρανοῖς ἁγιασθήτω τὸ ὄνομά σου, ἐλθέτω ἡ βασιλεία σου, γενηθήτω τὸ θέλημά σου, ὡς ἐν οὐρανῷ καὶ ἐπὶ τῆς γῆς.

Τὸν ἄρτον ἡμῶν τὸν ἐπιούσιον δὸς ἡμῖν σήμερον.
Καὶ ἄφες ἡμῖν τὰ ὀφειλήματα ἡμῶν, ὡς καὶ ἡμεῖς ἀφίεμεν τοῖς ὀφειλέταις ἡμῶν. Καὶ μὴ εἰσενέγκῃς ἡμᾶς εἰς πειρασμόν,
ἀλλὰ ῥῦσαι ἡμᾶς ἀπὸ τοῦ πονηροῦ.

The Nicene-Constantinopolitan Creed (381 A.D.)

English

We believe in one God, the Father Almighty, Maker of heaven and earth, and of all things visible and invisible; And in one Lord Jesus Christ, the Son of God, the Only-begotten, Begotten of the Father before all ages, Light of Light, True God of True God, Begotten, not made; of one essence with the Father, by whom all things were made: Who for us men and for our salvation came down from heaven, and was incarnate of the Holy Spirit and the Virgin Mary, and was made man; And was crucified also for us under Pontius Pilate, and suffered and was buried; And the third day He rose again, according to the Scriptures; And ascended into heaven, and sits at the right hand of the Father; And He shall come again with glory to judge the living and the dead, Whose kingdom shall have no end. And we believe in the Holy Spirit, the Lord, and Giver of Life, Who proceeds from the Father, Who with the Father and the Son together is worshipped and glorified, who spoke by the Prophets; and we believe in one, holy, catholic (universal), and apostolic Church. We acknowledge one Baptism for the remission of sins. We look for the Resurrection of the dead, And the Life of the age to come. Amen.

Greek

Πιστεύομεν εἰς ἕνα Θεόν, Πατέρα, Παντοκράτορα, ποιητὴν οὐρανοῦ καὶ γῆς, ὁρατῶν τε πάντων καὶ ἀοράτων. Καὶ εἰς ἕνα Κύριον Ἰησοῦν Χριστόν, τὸν Υἱὸν τοῦ Θεοῦ τὸν μονογενῆ, τὸν ἐκ τοῦ Πατρὸς γεννηθέντα πρὸ πάντων τῶν αἰώνων· φῶς ἐκ φωτός, Θεὸν ἀληθινὸν ἐκ Θεοῦ ἀληθινοῦ, γεννηθέντα οὐ ποιηθέντα, ὁμοούσιον τῷ Πατρί, δι' οὗ τὰ πάντα ἐγένετο. Τὸν δι' ἡμᾶς τοὺς ἀνθρώπους καὶ διὰ τὴν ἡμετέραν σωτηρίαν κατελθόντα ἐκ τῶν οὐρανῶν καὶ σαρκωθέντα ἐκ Πνεύματος Ἁγίου καὶ Μαρίας τῆς Παρθένου καὶ ἐνανθρωπήσαντα.
Σταυρωθέντα τε ὑπὲρ ἡμῶν ἐπὶ Ποντίου Πιλάτου, καὶ παθόντα καὶ ταφέντα. Καὶ ἀναστάντα τῇ τρίτῃ ἡμέρᾳ κατὰ τὰς Γραφάς.

Καὶ ἀνελθόντα εἰς τοὺς οὐρανοὺς καὶ καθεζόμενον ἐκ δεξιῶν τοῦ Πατρός. Καὶ πάλιν ἐρχόμενον μετὰ δόξης κρῖναι ζῶντας καὶ νεκρούς, οὗ τῆς βασιλείας οὐκ ἔσται τέλος. Καὶ εἰς τὸ Πνεῦμα τὸ Ἅγιον, τὸ κύριον, τὸ ζωοποιόν, τὸ ἐκ τοῦ Πατρὸς ἐκπορευόμενον, τὸ σὺν Πατρὶ καὶ Υἱῷ συμπροσκυνούμενον καὶ συνδοξαζόμενον, τὸ λαλῆσαν διὰ τῶν προφητῶν. Εἰς μίαν, Ἁγίαν, Καθολικὴν καὶ Ἀποστολικὴν Ἐκκλησίαν. Ὁμολογῶ ἕν βάπτισμα εἰς ἄφεσιν ἁμαρτιῶν. Προσδοκῶ ἀνάστασιν νεκρῶν. Καὶ ζωὴν τοῦ μέλλοντος αἰῶνος. Ἀμήν.

Chapter 5:
What Is a Soul? – The Original You

"And the Lord God proceeded to form the man out of dust from the ground and to blow into his nostrils the breath of life, and the man came to be a living soul."
~ Genesis 2:7

Webster's dictionary describes *"Soul"* (/sōl/) as:

> "The immaterial essence, animating principle, or actuating cause of an individual life; the spiritual principle embodied in human beings, all rational and spiritual beings, or the universe; a person's total self; a person's moral and emotional nature or sense of identity."

When I was in high school, we all believed or were taught to believe that a man has a spirit and mind, and that the body houses both. However, now we know that we are the combination of all experiences, memories, thoughts, accomplishments, and failures up to this point of our existence. There is absolutely no one exactly like you. Alone you made the journey into this life (when you were born), and alone you will leave it (via physical death) when your soul decides your work here is completed. No one is an exception to this. Thus, your understanding of who should influence your experience is *you*, and *only you*.

We are living flesh propelled by divine power - part of Gaea, or Mother Earth. Divine thought manifested Earth's molecules (matter) into you and me. We are souls that take on bodies, not bodies that house a soul, as was contrarily the thought in previous centuries. Therefore, we are truly souls taking on a human experience, and not the other way around. We can prove this by going to any morgue and looking at the cold, life-less meat in the freezers, which were at one point living, breathing, moving, human beings. Attending a funeral of a loved one shows us that the vehicle we are moving around with is only a tool embraced by something truly special - our soul. This is an innate, inborn power both inside and around us, which animates us. This special thing runs without batteries and needs no winding up. A body without a soul is like an immobile car without a driver. The car is the body and the driver is the soul.

5.1 Limiting the Limitless Soul

*"The soul returns to Earth in a body similar to its last one
and has similar talents and inclinations."*
~ Plato

Is there such a thing as past lives? It seems as if Plato believed so. It is indisputable that there is a universal longing for life after physical death. If there is no life after death, then we cannot explain this desire to want to live on. So, what does this universal human desire to live on reveal about our nature and future destiny?

The Buddhists, Hindus, Egyptians, and ancient Greeks all affirmed the survival of the soul and reincarnation. Every religion or spiritual tradition teaches some form of reincarnation, or belief that the soul is eternal and moves on. Today, even Christians believe in a certain form of soul reincarnation; that one day, the dead will rise to be judged. Thoughts from new-age thinking today assert that it may be conceivable that before we are born into this physical reality, we choose the experiences that we desire to have in this earthly incarnation. Prior to leaving the other side of our divine community, our actual "home," we decide a potential path and prepare to enter the tunnel of birth, leading into a human womb, that has been prepared for us. We make agreements, called "contracts," with others who will help us along the way after they reincarnate just before, with, or after us. We may also choose exactly who our parents will be and what type of lifestyle we will experience for maximal soul growth. Just as in your past, in the near future you will meet certain people at the strangest moments of your life that seems serendipitous; you may just think it is a big coincidence or luck. However, the people you are meeting are part of your soul (or karmic) group that now enter your experience for an agreed purpose, and while they go through their own challenges, they may also be helping you with yours.

This may seem unreal to you, especially if you are asking yourself right now, "But why THIS life? I would have surely picked something better than this!" To which the answer is: <u>Because you knew, as an eternal being, that this lifestyle would bring to you the grandest opportunity to grow as a spiritual being.</u> It is providing you contrast to what you may have experienced before in your life. You also learn that you can change things and attract anything you wish to experience to you. So, no matter how good or how bad your life may seem, you already know on a subconscious level, and as an eternal being, that you can improve things here. At your birth, you had a good idea of what you were getting yourself into - just not consciously. When we leave the dimension of limitlessness, we come to a limiting dimension to reinvent ourselves anew. Your personality, skills, talents, character, likes/dislikes, strengths, and weaknesses were already formed from past experiences in other incarnations. Once here, you learn to enjoy the experience of every moment, and grow into a new version of yourself through the constantly changing contrast via your free will. Choose to use your abilities to reach your utmost capacity and further your growth.

5.2 Past, Future, and Current Lives

Technically, lives are not past or present, as all are current happenings in the same time. Metaphysics supports the idea that there are other dimensions and parallel realities happening at the same time. We only place events in linearity here in this three dimensional realm so that we can have a reference point to that which we refer to. In reality, there is no past or future. Only the now - the present moment - is real and exists in the matter(s). This is why we can remember the past and imagine the future, but experience only "the now." The now can bring about a new future, if the now can be seen in a new light, in order to bring about a new reality to your "next now."

One does not need to consciously remember past lives in order to grow the soul. We are the accumulation of the best parts of the whole experience of all that we were or are. When you come into this life, you come with a fresh start to re-experience the world by focusing on a different path of experience. When you have a sense of a past life, you are picking up on the same vibrational tone of where you are in your life right now. There is no point to really worry about past lives because you have instant access to your spiritual DNA through meditation and regression hypnotherapy, which allows you to deal with just about anything you need now. Knowing who you were and what you did in previous incarnations can get in the way of doing your work in this lifetime. Although it is possible to unveil the past lives and gain understanding of them through readers and seers, it can also become distracting to obsessive personality types who would lose focus of the work they are doing here in the present time. Your focus is to live life now in a way that expresses your joy and creates abundantly. Don't concentrate on what was already completed and mastered. <u>You are already the accumulation of all your previous works.</u>

It may seem bizarre or downright wrong by conventional methods to think that in a past life a relative, such as a mother, sister, cousin, or even brother could have been a lover in a previous lifetime. When I first started researching theories like these from various clairvoyants who seemed all too certain that this was the way things were between past lifetimes, I was repulsed. Even suggesting it seemed absurd, at best. However, I kept doing research in the reincarnation theories, and dug into compelling stories of those who have had out of body experiences, near death experiences, and lucid dreams. I seemed to come across the same aspects of the same story all across the board from different cultures, ages, and genders. Further proof of our after-life Divinity was that there was no religious connection. Hindu, Catholic, Orthodox, Jewish - it didn't matter; the stories would match up with similarities from all religious backgrounds. They even had exact descriptions of aspects of their after-life experience, such as the way the River of Life and Tree of Life appear, or the description of the black energy that sweeps anywhere that is void of life, or even the complete peace, love, acceptance, and serenity that was felt when God was experienced. Of the many experiences I researched, never did the individual say he or she was not allowed to participate in the experience because they were not from a certain religion or belief system. They all, regardless of religious or traditional beliefs, were accepted by what they believed was God.

As a non-physical soul, you know all; nothing is new. However, after you take on a physical form, mask, or character, you can re-experience the same things over and over, and things feel anew for a while. Within a lifetime of, say, 50-80 or so years, we have decided to be who we are today, and are here to experience life in this character, this skin, this body, this occupation, this family structure, this mix of events, places, tastes, sights, sounds, etc. We are playing a character in this physical world. The real world is the world we left prior to being born, and we will reenter it when we leave the physical body to experience oneness again with our Creator. The real world is the world of total creation and limitless possibility; the same one we go to when we close our eyes every night only to reawaken in this illusionary world, which we are imagining and creating in daily, through our free-will, thought, and intention in the current moment. Our heaven or hell is our own blockbuster movie, and we are the stars of it. Drama, romance, comedy, science fiction, and all; we make the rules and we break them. Let's say we take on the character of a circle; it reinvents itself if the circle forgets it is a circle, or that it was invented, or that it even existed in the first place. It then will experience what it's like to roll around again, as if it's the first time. It's exciting again, it's fresh, and for a while it is fun - until it's not fun anymore and then a new experience must be done to outdo the last. This happens in the same way that, in our society, dating someone loses its initial mystery and excitement, or the same way eating lasagna for dinner every night loses its appeal (even though lasagna may be your favorite dish), or the way that new car or fancy dress just doesn't look or feel as new as the day you bought it.

5.3 The Soul's Progression

Each and every one of us has our own reasons why we are here on Earth. Souls return for the purification or refinement of the soul through trials and tribulations, to accomplish a specific task, purpose, or mission, to repeat great works, gain talent, or sacred knowledge, learn lessons, or teach other souls the lessons we learned through compassion, empathy, and love. It could be one or a combination of all of these reasons. The soul continues to look for experiences that produce awe, wonder, excitement, or miracles.

A soul can carry unlearned lessons with it in its spiritual DNA, from incarnation to incarnation, until those experiences are learned and graduated from, so new adventures can be had. Talent and abilities move from incarnation to incarnation; some as young as five years of age can pick up a paintbrush and paint as Picasso, where others cannot put a stick figure together. Some may have a phobia or habit in this lifetime that is triggered by fear or frustration because they do not remember it was first brought on in a previous incarnation, which may have involved their death in that lifetime. In certain circumstances, when medical tests and diagnoses can't target the cause of a health issue, one may have to resort to other forms of healing that would be more helpful, such as past life regression hypnosis or other deep shamanic spiritual work.

On the other side of the veil, the soul feels love and compassion for humanity. However, when it comes to this earthly plane, it can just as easily choose to cause mayhem and experience the lifetime as a bad person just as it can experience it as a good person. Most, who are generally good people in current times, may have learned from the lessons of negativity in previous lives. Now, they decide to exude the positive version of self within their reality of their existence here. They could also choose to be a mixture of both good and bad, or simply experience just the negative side of self. We may repeat the old negative self to learn lessons if we have not experienced the love, patience, and compassion needed to finish that incarnation that evolves us to a higher state of being. We should not be judgmental of chosen life paths or lessons, and instead allow each their own way. We're all perfectly imperfect, and we are all loved as we try to find a way to expand more towards what God is, or desires of us to become.

5.4 When You Were Born

Believe it or not, your soul really wanted to be here on Earth. You just have forgotten why you wanted to come. It is made that way. As an eternal being you know all and nothing can be new to you when you know it all. You came back into a limited reality for more awe, and the "wow factor" that comes with every new discovery, or re-discovery, you make. I give the analogy of someone who eats pasta every day, noon and night for a month, with various spices and toppings. Over time they will develop body allergies as the body will become used to pasta and grow tired of the dish and proclaim, "Enough! No more pasta!" The taste buds will know everything about pasta, no matter how it is disguised. At first it's a new flavor, taste, texture, and smell with various spices and dressings. However, over time all there is to know about the pasta, from making it and tasting it, will be known and acquired as experience. New, exciting meals, tastes, and experiences will be desired, and pasta will be avoided. After some time, pasta may be tried again as it becomes forgotten, or when the observer wishes to re-experience its flavor. This is also the way our soul gets to re-visit, re-experience, re-mold, and re-invent itself each time via reincarnation.

The freedom, beauty, and diversity of what was available to you on Earth was very attractive; the physicality and attractiveness of being able to taste, feel, love and live within nature, color, sound; to create new ideas, realities, and new vibrations was all you wanted. Sometimes the soul repeats the same loop, and eventually something changes into a new experience since we are eager to try combinations of life we never had before, or re-experience things we want to do again. The massive contrast available to you through happiness, sadness, love, hate, fear, courage, anger, resentment, etc. is all understood by the soul and is part of the master plan here on this illusionary, co-created plane we call our world.

You did not feel you were coming into the world to perfect it, as you saw it already as perfect. You also saw all beings on it as perfect co-creations of all that is, was, and will be. It is all one big carnival and you wanted to come play in it! You may ask yourself why an all knowing, eternally loving, and all-encompassing being would have such an eagerness to come to such a playground and manifest itself willingly into a limited world. Also, why with such perceived handicaps as a bi-legged animal, which must wake the body daily, feed it, clothe it, and move it around? As we all know, the waking up process every morning seems to be quite a challenge for many.

Your higher self, or inner soul, projected itself into the consciousness wavelength of the physical, and you intermingled with the spiritual and physical DNA (along with your mother's and father's) to give you a new starting point on a new path of soul-discovery. You partly let go of the higher dimension to be born into this realm's density for contrast and further development. The soul knew it as perfect, no matter what challenge or perceived difficulty was to be ahead, because the soul knows its ability to cope, learn, and grow, and it also welcomes the challenges as it did lifetimes before. You are an extension of source power, and thus you are an heir to all abundance, and can bring this abundance from the vibratory wavelengths you wish to bring forth. Your physical body is connected on the other side of the veil or curtain, where you go each night upon sleeping, and ultimately will go again when you leave this world and re-emerge with the energy that is you on the other side. As you experience, and add to your growth, so grows God's entire universe. Our scientists now even claim that the Universe is continually expanding; it's no coincidence.

5.5 Death - A Naturally Safe or Unsafe Process?

"The fear of death follows from the fear of life.
A man who lives fully is prepared to die at any time."
~ Mark Twain

Why are so many afraid of death? What we call a physical death, and the separation of soul from body, is an experience that seems harsh and painful to the living. Except for those who commit suicide for various reasons of escape, most human beings have an intrinsic desire to continue their current life. Every night when we go to bed, we mimic the process of death. Our breathing and heartbeat slow down, our body lies motionless, brain waves slow down, and part of our self goes elsewhere as our body rests. We are barely still alive as we cling to this life while exploring the deepest reaches of the dream world when we're sleeping. Why do we sometimes remember dreams, and other times wake up without remembering what happened to our body during the hours we slept? Do we bring back with us the most vital information from our limitless home realm, or do we intentionally block out that information to deal only with this realm's challenges? If we try to remember dream information, it seems to sift like sand through our fingers as we awaken in the morning. If you were to set up a camera in your bedroom and record yourself sleeping, upon waking up and viewing the tape in fast forward mode you would notice you are in fact very much alive and active. Unbeknownst to you, you might realize you were talking to someone who was not there, or discover you were moving your hands and legs regularly, yawning, scratching your face or nose, and even sleepwalking. During sleep, many have even remembered leaving the body as an energy being and exploring something, and then can report everything clearly upon waking.

This phenomenon is called an OBE, or "out-of-body experience." If the experience happens with trauma and physical death is a possibility, the occurrence is called an NDE, or "near death experience." Both instances can project the soul away from the body, but the soul is still connected to the body and not fully cut off. Upon return and awaking from the experience, the person has amazing insight to the after-life. Many being operated on in surgery, or those involved in serious car accidents vividly report their experience upon coming back from a blackout or being unconscious. Some see angels, God, other deceased relatives, and even bring back important messages for the living.

Have you ever had the feeling of re-experiencing a moment that was eerily familiar to you? This is another extrasensory event called Déjà vu, which in French literally means: "already seen." Déjà vu is the feeling of being in a place or situation you were already in that plays itself out exactly as you remembered it, even if it didn't actually happen already. The moment lasts for a few seconds to minutes, but it is usually just a few seconds before you realize it's happening to you. This phenomenon can be explained as your soul leaving the body during sleep, and preparing you for the experience when your body reunites in the "creative illusive reality" we call this current life incarnation. The life you are living may be a parallel cross with another life, which feels familiar. <u>The reason you wake up every day is because your soul finds value in the body you are operating.</u> The physical body is a vehicle to perform the functions the soul needs to do on this plane for its growth. Déjà vu is also a way for the subconscious to give you reassurance, to let you know you're moving forward correctly on your path, or to prepare you for an upcoming dangerous situation. Your soul is eternal and travels continuously, exploring the realms of our vast Universe; it never needs to sleep. However, your body needs replenishment constantly in this lower realm of existence. Once the body no longer is needed or can no longer serve the soul's mission, the soul leaves it and the very natural process of physical death occurs in this perceived reality by those souls who still co-create their illusion within it.

Souls are always seeking expansion through more truth and happiness. Everything we do is about looking for truth and happiness in life. Even suicide by troubled souls can be seen as seeking happiness or an escape from the real perception of manifested pain. Drug use, sexual anomalies, material addictions - all are *programmed, self-inflicted, negative behaviors of false pretenses or ideas* that the inflicted believes will bring them happiness in this world.

Chapter 6:
SIN – Self-Inflicted Negativity

"He that covereth his sins shall not prosper: but whoso confesseth and forsaketh them shall have mercy."
~ Proverbs 28:13

6.1 What is Right and What is Wrong?

Consider this: A soldier going to war kills many people, comes back as a hero, and is given medals of honor and valor. A man defends his home from an intruder by shooting him, or someone accidentally hits a pedestrian, killing him or her with a car. They are both given murder charges and jailed. Which is right and which is wrong? Who determines what is right and what is wrong? Each era of time and society has its own set of rules as to how it is governed and what is acceptable. In some states, it is acceptable to make a right turn on red, while in another it costs you a ticket and traffic school. To some, another's religious doctrine is considered terrorism and immoral, yet to the believer, it feels as if God himself is commanding certain "faithful" acts for which, if carried out, one will be exalted. In ancient times, stoning was considered just punishment; in some societies it still is. So there seems to be no truly right or wrong standards we can set for all people in all situations or cultures. We can only count on the measure of how far away from love and light we are, while living in a world of duality. So this begs the question: What is right or wrong? And what exactly is sin?

6.2 What is SIN?

I refer to *sin* as "**Self Inflicted Negativity.**" It is our disconnection from our own God power, the Father, or Source of what is good. It is the pinching off of the loving light, and highest vibration of love, which transforms into a perception of negativity, or painful darkness. It is a transgression, or "breaking the law" which takes us backwards, away from progress. It also has whatever negative perception or meaning we give it. Some common sins we commit are greed, sloth, gluttony, and anger. This is truly sin, meaning *Self-Inflicted Negativity*, as the only ones we truly hurt are ourselves. Religious principalities have manipulated this meaning for control of the people through fear of eternal damnation without redemption. Disconnection from God is a scary thing for the soul, and the act of removing yourself from your creator is the most painful thing one could ever do.

Simply put, there is no such thing as a "damning sin," unless we define it as "stopping our growth." Since nothing can do that without your own permission, it is the mental collection of your beliefs that attempt to dictate whether or not you are able to move forward in growth, and in which manner that you decide to halt or further your evolution. So you see, "sinning" is the inability to allow growth, to disallow creative expression in a positive manner, or to stop expansion of the soul, which is damning to oneself. When one's soul does not learn the lessons or the experiences in a lifetime, and continues them with unsatisfactory results, then this is the damnation chosen for oneself (by constant replay of this illusion in torment). So indeed, you are self-damning your eternal soul - keeping yourself tortured by your own doing. In that way, sin does equal unhappiness, torment, never-ending pain, and what one may feel as an unending thirst, which seems to go forever unquenched. A soul goes from lifetime to lifetime repeating the lessons until they're learned and graduated from. This is the soul's evolution. Everyone sins, and as they sin, this allows each to experience their disconnection from God, opposite the love of light - only to seek their reconnection again when ready.

Historic scholars claim that, somewhere in the development of humanity, there was a large change in DNA, where understanding of duality occurred. Scriptures metaphorically describe the human upgrading of DNA in the story of the Garden of Eden. The example of the Forbidden Fruit and the symbolism of wisdom (the snake) were explained by the act of eating the Forbidden Fruit, causing man to separate from God and thus creating good, evil, and sin.

6.3 Where Did the Idea of Hell Come From, and Who is Satan?

Dualistic thought, as the idea of good vs. evil, may be traced back 3,500 years ago to ancient Persia, where currently Iran, Iraq, and Syria reside. At that time, there was a belief in many gods that were both good and bad. The more popular gods were favored as good, while the less favorable happenings were attributed to bad gods. There was a religious teacher, a Persian prophet named Zoroaster (or Zarathustra) who took all the gods of his time and simplified them into two gods. Ahura Mazda was the god of light, order, and good; while Ahriman was the god of lies, darkness, and chaos. Before this time, there was no notion of a single, omnipotent, malicious force that would torment a soul in hell, and the concept of Satan didn't really exist. Zoroaster taught the idea that the earth was a battlefield, and humans had to make a decision of which side to take. If you decided to take the side of the good, you would be rewarded in the afterlife, while if you chose to be bad, you would be tormented for the bad you did to others. Under Persian emperor Darius the Great, the teachings of Zoroaster became the official way of the Persian Empire, which included the land of Israel. In time, Zoroaster's teachings found their way into the Jewish writings and Old Testament. Personification of the Devil and thoughts of a divine leader of evil have existed in Scripture since this time. When Alexander the Great defeated the Persian Empire, the Greeks introduced their Gods and Goddesses, which included the god of the underworld, Hades, who judged the dead and granted wealth and abundance, but was not thought of as evil. Tales of the "Evil One" were mixed through cultures, growing more and more frightening, both in looks, and in deeds against humanity. Greek myth included a well-known story where Zeus, the ruler of the Olympus gods, defeated Typhon, a winged serpent, and then tossed him into the underworld's lowest level under the earth (Tartaros), where souls were thought to be tormented. Over time, this story turned into the story of how Satan was thrown from heaven for disobeying God.

Similarly, in Jerusalem, a city called Gahanna (the valley of Hinnom) was a landfill that disposed of surrounding waste, and was also the place where Jerusalem authorities would burn the bodies of executed convicted criminals. The fires would burn for weeks at a time, followed by the foul stench of trash and rotten flesh. The stories spread about this mysterious place, which established the idea about what it would be like to die and go to a place of foul stench and torment, a possible display of what hell would be like for a bad soul. This is also where fire was introduced into the place of torment, for Hades' underworld was a dark place of loneliness and seclusion, but believed to have no fire in it. Later, the Caesars of the Roman Empire, which persecuted the Christians, became known as the enemy of God. It even says, in the New Testament, that the beast is given the human number "666." Emperor Nero Caesar's name in Aramaic numerical value (when added up) was exactly "666." The idea of Satan also progressed when church images, portraying him as an angel, showed his wings looking like those of a dragon's, rather than one with traditional angel feathers. The feet were also drawn as a dragon's claws. The image of Satan morphed into one of great fear and pain, representing evil over a long time by the mixing of mythical legend and culture.

About four centuries later, Constantine the Great converted to Christianity and made heresy illegal. This helped the Church rise quickly into a superpower, with authority to do as they pleased. At the same time, Pagan Gods were still being worshipped, so the Church decided to eliminate any threat to their power. In particular, the harmless God of music, happiness, and sex was the Pagan Arcadian God, Pan, who looked like a happy, dancing, goat-like creature. The Church, which had all the money, power, and wealth, convinced people that these gods were evil, and even went to the extent to tell people that if they were in any way connected to material possessions, that they were worshipping the devil, and they must surrender wealth to the Church. When the Inquisition came from Pope Gregory the 9th, anyone questioning the work of the Church would be aligned as working with the devil and put to torture or death. The Church had a self-appointed license to torture and kill in God's name. However, the charge of "patronizing with the devil" was used by the Church to seize land, riches, and silence anyone who was in the way of their agenda. For centuries, the church used this weapon to gain power. Those in their way were branded as witches, sorcerers, necromancers, Satanists, or enemies of the church. This practice still goes on to this day.

If we are to look at the Bible's explanation of Satan, it states that God originally created archangels Lucifer (who became known as Satan), Michael, and Gabriel. Lucifer, along with his angels, rebelled against the government/kingdom of God, and today he leads these now fallen angels, or demons, as the God of this world. So is this demon (also known as Lucifer, Diablo, Beezelbub, Baphomet) an individual, or merely a "personification" of an idea represented by a snake, a goat, or dragon with horns, and a tail? Or is this devil the collective destructive thought consciousness? Is it anti-God - the direct opposite side of God's own creation? The idea of a fallen angel, or evil being, has indeed been personified from a long history of cultural ideas of what good and evil are.

Why would an all-loving creator, God, ever allow an enemy to contradict his will or intention? And if the one true Creator made this individual, would this Creator God also not be able to remove or delete his own creation? And did God make us humans, also his creation, inherently good or evil? Could our body, soul, or spirit be connected to evil? Certainly not the soul or flesh by itself, as neither is good or wicked, but only a vehicle to achieve a mission in the world. However, can our body be perceived as good or evil through a lifestyle chosen by our free will? The answer is found in the power of our duality.

Some theologians speculate that we may be both God and the Devil; that we are able to enact both sides of the coin since we have been made in the image and likeness of the one true God. In being gifted the free will to choose, we may pick the opposite of light, which offers contrast to what we know as good. Our free will truly offers us the choice to either exercise our connection with the Creator or choose to feel lost in darkness without Him. Hell is real to those who create it. It is a vibration held by many who co-create the frequency of being outside the light of God. We are able to live in our own daily heaven or hell, as humanity can conjure up the ideas, feelings, and experiences to realize what good or evil really means.

6.4 What Does Misunderstanding SIN Do to My Well-Being?

When we go through our path in life we construct and co-create an illusion. We have a series of events that brings us joy or pain, depending on how we handle each situation and how we want to "experience" the experience. With time, how we view our world will depend on our perceived wins and losses. Someone with a very religious background will have a much different success outcome in life than someone without. The structured rules and regulations on seeing oneself in relation to God, and their punishment or reward, lays the groundwork for how the individual will relate amongst the larger part of society when they leave the confines of the home and family. It is fine to feel that doing wrong to another will ultimately bring pain upon yourself. However, the way religious groups teach sin and the effects of sin is devastating to the soul, and its perception could scar an individual for life. Believing that a higher authority is evaluating every decision you do or make leaves one stunted, preventing you from making choices or allowing yourself the availability to grow from mistakes. Feeling that you are guilty for life, condemned to eternal fire, and not worthy of forgiveness if a sin was too large will actually trap your soul, preventing it from experiencing future freedom, or to again live in love. This jails not only those who were affected by the sin committed unto them, but also the person who committed the sin. Yet the Bible clearly states that God allows forgiveness and does not keep grudges, as the rain falls both on the wicked as well as the good. Remember, society chooses what is right and what is wrong in each era, not God. We're instructed to obey the laws of His land, and God is the Creator and observer, not the controller or punisher.

What this means, in the grand scheme of things, is that everyone co-creates with each other. This means that another person's definition of "right" or "wrong" affects the world they live in. Most people are not aware they're co-creating; however, others understand exactly how to create an environment that influences both themselves and you. You have a responsibility to others, as co-creation is not to only self-serve. The next few sections speak in depth about groups that are known to be self-serving, and influence the environment of co-creation in this illusive reality using knowledge unknown to the general public.

6.5 Planet Earth - The Grand Stage

"Political and economic power in the United States is concentrated in the hands of a 'ruling elite' that controls most of U.S. based multinational corporations, major

communication media, the most influential foundations, major private universities and most public utilities. Founded in 1921, the Council of Foreign Relations is the key link between the large corporations and the federal government. It has been called a 'school for statesmen' and comes close to being an organ of what C. Wright Mills has called the Power Elite – a group of men, similar in interest and outlook shaping events from invulnerable positions behind the scenes. The creation of the United Nations was a Council project, as well as the International Monetary Fund and the World Bank."
~ Steve Jacobson

Media is the ultimate control of a society. It molds the public view to tell society what is normal, acceptable, and "good" for us. Walter Lippmann, Pulitzer Award winner and author, spoke of Big Media and its influence of The United States. In *Public Opinion - The World Outside and the Pictures in Our Heads (1922)*, Lippmann compared the public at large to a "great beast" which was unable to make its own decisions, and needed the advice and regulation of a higher elite authority. In his words, this elite class was "a special class whose interests reach beyond the immediate vicinity." The elites were an organized group of corporation owners, bureaucrats, politicians, professionals, etc. Lipmann further defined the "bewildered herd" as "the fascinated viewers of activity," or commoners. Those who matter and make the rules for everyone else are considered "the accountable man," which is not the everyday, average laboring "Joe."

The elites (those in a high position community who have the ability, finances, resources, and power to see a particular objective through without being questioned by others), by definition, are the individuals in politics, media, legal, medical, and entertainment arenas that feel privileged in terms of brotherhood. Through unity with others in the same mentality of privilege and entitlement of elitist thinking, those with lesser means are looked at as the less desirable (or middle and lower class) workers, or as Lipmann put it, the "bewildered herd."

Mr. Lipmann believes the way he does because he is a founding father of a group called the Council of Foreign Relations (CFR), considered today to be one of the most influential "think tanks" on global events and power. To give you an idea of the power the CFR holds, some of the members who meet in secrecy include Barack Obama, David Rockefeller, Hilary Clinton, Dick Cheney, and the CEOs of significant corporations such as Citibank, BP, Bank of America, IBM, Google, ABC, ExxonMobil, Heinz, Pepsi, Walmart, and Xerox. The movers and the shakers of the world filter the information as they see fit and then post this information as fact through their own news and media outlets.

To avoid conflict of opposition to their new ideas, the elites have understood for centuries how to manipulate their agenda to become the mass agenda; using time and media to slowly interweave their needs into mass acceptance. Propaganda tactics of the elite are now down to a science, usually scripted through news corporations to impact society slowly over time through repetition without the need of brute force. Lippmann called this the "manufacture of consent," a change in popular opinion which allows the elite agenda to be the public agenda.

6.6 Regulating Human Thought – What You See is Not What You Get

There has been a huge merger of press organizations in the last fifteen years. The newspapers, magazines, television programs, movies, and songs we put our focus and attention on are controlled by five large organizations. The fewer competitors in any business, the larger the monopoly, and the larger the chance that the viewpoint presented is unfair and biased to the audience it claims to serve. By procuring more of the companies that provided freethinking and gave competition, the mega-corporations put together a control grid of influence that now provides the false idea that the individual is free and has choice. However, the choices and outcomes have been bought and paid for by these groups, as to be able to control both sides of the outcome, no matter how the actions or events unfold. As the late comedian George Carlin said, "You don't have real choices; you have limited choices – Democrat or Republican, paper or plastic, cash or charge, aisle or window, Coke or Pepsi."

The elites craft their agenda, their media makes an issue seem significant, their courts pass the laws, and their system enforces the laws that keep the people in check. Within the system, the elites can make anyone they wish rise and fall by creating their own rebels, and good or bad guys to draw the public's attention away from serious issues, as is currently the case with news stations focusing on endless coverage of insignificant events. Anything or anyone that is not aligned with the popular thought process of the elites is quickly branded as a fraud or illegitimate, and is thrown to the lions. Using the media outlets, their opposition is attacked and ridiculed until the public interest dies down after making their decision to not support the ideas and people that are in fact in their own best interest, as is seen in aspects of possibly every election to date since John F. Kennedy.

In the name of entertainment and convenience, utilizing 3D films, handheld computers, phones, and home cinemas, hidden propaganda is literally shoved into our brains every single second, with our passive acceptance. This ultimately leads us to our enslavement as we give up the right to privacy and individuality in order to be part of the latest consumer trend. The mega-corporations have infinite sources of research data that tell them how their product would integrate into our lives so that we would become addicted or dependent on them. Properly strategized subliminal audio tones, sounds, images, and colors are used in selling everything from food and water to clothing and cars. The brainwashed public spends its hard earned dollars to purchase products and services that will remove them even further from knowing more about their internal power and connection with their fellow human beings. Instead we allow the corporations to create a nation of docile zombie slaves, committed to feeding their material addictions, and being led where the elites desire society to go. This continues to feed their status and maintains them in power. If the public at large were to wake up and take their power back, this would be detrimental to the elite structure, and they would stop at nothing to return to "business as usual."

6.7 Desensitizing People - Everyone is a Salesman

It seems that, just like in the old times, kings, queens, knights and serfs still exist - just in a less visible way. Back in the day, if villagers were unhappy with the king's new laws, they would stage a huge uprising, quite a bit more fierce than the people today who go on strike or protest. When the people have power, see vast contrast in policy, and are mistreated - the people will always speak up. However, the "higher-ups" usually don't want to give away more rights, compensation, or power to their inhabitants. This is a huge inconvenience for them, as they would rather be sitting in the lap of luxury without chaos to deal with, as things go on - "business as usual." Over the years, the elites have learned how to keep intrusions to their plans at a minimum. Using a psychiatric therapy process called desensitization, over time, any idea can be implemented into a society even if it was unpopular or bad for the public interest. By including the idea in television and Hollywood film plots, sexy music videos, songs on the radio, and repeating them over and over, the suggestions - no matter how shocking or wicked - would be accepted and allowed in by society. This strategy of apathy is highly effective thanks to psychological pre-programming.

If you remember in the 1980-2000's, young men were shown certain role models to follow, and taught how to be strong man with films like *Rambo, Commando, Full Metal Jacket,* and *Platoon*. Then, years later, they are still being continually desensitized to violence and war glamorization with *Inglourious Bastards, Black Hawk Down, The Hurt Locker, Zero Dark Thirty,* among many other titles. In the summer of 2013 when the Superman movie *Man of Steel* played, there were advertisements in the newspapers, television commercials, and movie theaters connecting recruitment for the National Guard with Superman. Using mass propaganda, the individuals behind the message told young minority men and women that they, too, can be as strong and as cool as Superman by being "soldiers of steel" and serving in the military industrial complex. As teens generally idolize good things, like superheroes, a connection of something bad - like killing people and war - was attached to a good thing like Superman, in order to desensitize the idea (and associated emotions) that war and killing is a bad thing. With time, that same individual will receive further images of recruitment through high school and college, with added pressure like calls at home from local military recruitment offices when they turn 18, which eventually can lead them to enlist or give over their life "serving God and country." In reality, it's serving the elitist agenda of power and control. The mental and emotional programming starts early, folks. It is well known that elitist families do not send their children to die in wars.

Today, our televisions and movie theaters continue to numb our brains with escapism and subliminal messages concerning trans-humanism (becoming robots, cyborgs), UFO alien attack, competitive fear based survival, and zombie apocalypse, seen in the movies: *2012*, *Oblivion*, *Hunger Games*, and *World War Z* (just to name a few). The elites understand the manifestation process and the idea of mass thought. For something to be manifest in this world, it must be brought in by thought energy. Over time, a thought held in our subconscious will manifest, and it will do so much more quickly when it is in the minds of many. Negative thoughts take much more energy to manifest than positive ones, as human nature, a connection to God and what is good, are natural. With mass subconscious programming however, any message can be entered into the minds of many when they are willing, relaxed, and open in a state of allowance. So the question to ponder is this: What are we allowing into our minds every time we relax and the television or movie theater shows us successive images in rapid formation, which lodge deep into our thoughts and mind through our eyes and ears? Are we unconsciously being desensitized and programmed to accept future ideas the elites deem correct for us and society's future? How much control do we really have over our lives, and if we have lost control, can we take our power back?

The loss of personal power will show an individual the reality of tyranny. The power someone has (or is perceived to have) is an accumulation of the thoughts that the others around that individual have given over of their own power. The greatest trick a large group of influencers can play on another class is to convince its people that their minds are not powerful, and put out propaganda studies showing this perspective as fact. The elitist media is a tool of those who are in power to further amass more power and influence over those who have given up their power unknowingly. Over time even those unwilling to give up their power will feel that they must also succumb to the will of the oppressor(s).

But this idea is a total lie. The challenge of the oppressed is to regain their power once they give it over, and this can get more challenging as more time passes on. The amount of power and influence of the oppressors becomes greater with time, thus taking more public resources to bring power back to equilibrium. If a government body or dictator, for instance, shows enough force to those around them, and this force is accepted as truth, those who are of equal power will succumb to their own choice, allowing the thought of themselves as "less than equal" to be their new truth. This is a deliberate affirmation of the suppressor being validated by peers. With the growing thought energy, the dictator can further amass more power through resources, even more quickly than when the rise of power began. After it starts, it's a large domino effect. Someone's rise to power is directly related to the individual knowing their internal power, and exercising it while everyone else chooses to give them the status and energy asked of them. If the populace decides to regain their power and understands how to do so, there would be a "balancing out" of energy and power again. The people in unison have the power always, unless those people are led to willingly give up their free will over time, as occurred in Germany with Hitler in 1934.

6.8 Hidden Communication of the Occult in Plain Sight

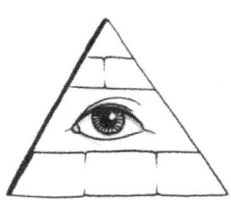

The study of occult practices includes alchemy, magick, and divination, tied in with belief structures and concepts mostly known with neopaganism, Hermeticism, Wicca, Gnosticism, Theosophy, Thelema, and Satanism. "Occult" is based on the Latin word "*occultus*," literally meaning "hidden" for only select elect individuals. Meanings of occult objects and symbolism can be challenging to decipher or be understood by non-occultists. Most in the general public doesn't give much attention or significance to occult things, and they are never mentioned in the news or daily life. Occult issues, however, are not by any means insignificant to those who secretly take part in rituals and dealings of the occult. Hand gestures, signals, secret handshakes, secret words, and symbols all exist among the ranks. A secret brother or sisterhood is accountable only to the rules within the group, and they hold them holy, even in higher relevance than the common law followed by the rest of society. Many cultures throughout history, like the Egyptians, and groups like the Knights Templar and Freemasons, have passed on many mysterious secrets and odd traditions that are still in practice behind closed doors by members of several "prestigious" institutions today.

"If this inner doctrine were always concealed from the masses, for whom a simpler code had been devised, is it not highly probable that the exponents of every aspect of modern civilization – philosophic, ethical, religious, and scientific - are ignorant of the true meaning of the very theories and tenets on which their beliefs are founded? Do the arts and sciences that the race has inherited from older nations conceal beneath their fair exterior a mystery so great that only the most illumined intellect can grasp its import? Such is undoubtedly the case."
~ Manly P. Hall

The "simpler code" that Manly Palmer Hall (1901-1990), a Canadian born author and mystic, mentions is organized dogmatic religion. The mass use of media and preaching power that it has instills aspects of separatism in beliefs, religious dogma, spiritual emptiness, materialism, and a self-centered, egotistic existence. These are the things that are contrary to the teachings and rational of all pronounced philosophical schools of thought. Christians have branded occultism as heretical, but occultists claim that Christians incorrectly labeled them as sinister by theorizing the meaning of the world occult (hidden), was a bad thing, as it was considered to be "away from the light," and labeled occultists as Satan's consorts. Occultists claim that they simply study the deeper spiritual study of the unknown and spiritual realities (outside what is known by conventional science today) with the misunderstood, rebellious angel, Lucifer, as their God.

Many of those who were outcasts or deemed "unacceptable" by society's standards have been welcomed with open arms into the family of occultism and shown their ways. Occultists are highly controversial whenever engaging in communication about their beliefs in public, as they do not feel they are doing evil, but are actually doing good in their own way. Many rock bands in the 80's like KISS, AC/DC, and Black Sabbath took on Satanism and Occult practices. They welcomed lost youths looking to belong into their fan base. Concerts, lyrics, and music played backwards all held anti-Christian messages. However, extreme Christianity served with dogma and extreme Anti-Christianity are both religious mind-control techniques, each on opposite sides of the same coin, overseen by and controlled by the elite.

6.9 Mother, Father, Teacher, and Preacher Programming

In the early 1980's, the video game systems made by Atari were all the rage as the video gaming industry started to explode, giving rise to other competitive systems, such as Nintendo and Sega-Genesis. These videogame consoles evolved to highly interactive systems like the Wii, Play Station, X-box and virtual reality consoles we have today. The gaming industry has seen enormous growth since its ping pong pixel beginnings. The systems and programs have indeed upgraded with time and advancing technological consciousness. Personal computing began as a typewriter, and evolved to programmable 386 and 486 processors that then moved up in performance through Pentium and the Dual and Quad core systems, to what we have now as laptops and mobile devices, capable of multitasking feats that make the first computers blush in shame. Even modem communication evolved quickly from the annoying dial tone 14.400kbs connections to high-speed fiber optic connections in less than 2 decades. Unfortunately, unlike the speed of which technology upgrades itself through competitive innovation, some adults choose to slow down their internal human evolution to much slower techniques, thinking, and reasoning. They choose to stay with old, outdated traditions, and stagnant dogmatic acts more indicative of the medieval ages than anything of the information age.

Chances are your parents and grandparents have not changed much. Chances are they won't. As you look back at old family videos and photo albums, you can probably agree that they look and act nearly the same then as they do now. The previous generation isn't as familiar with the current and coming ways of life; they are programmed by the 2 generations prior, like an outdated computer running old software. Although awareness is now quickly evolving, most people are still closed off to the technological and progressive nature of things these days. The speed of information is so fast, and many cannot catch up. Their fear of progression keeps their children in the same state of fear. The current generation, however, is making huge strides in thought consciousness and raising the bar on human development. They are doing away with old energy vibration.

Part III:
EMPOWERMENT - Tapping into Your Spinal Power

"If you want to understand the health of the body, you have to understand the health of the spine."
~ Greek Physician Hippocrates,
Founder of Modern Medicine

To understand how health works, we must understand that the spine is the Information Superhighway. It is your potential gateway to the unseen higher abilities that you can tap into, mostly termed as "paranormal" in today's world. Instead of being paranormal, it is actually a process of using and exercising your neural potential, connecting to the Higher Power, and activating the stream to allow flow. Jesus Christ was undoubtedly the best teacher by example on how to connect to the Father, the Source, the Universal power that created us all. However, we incorrectly implement the teachings of Jesus to suit our human egos, lust for power, and control through religion, and then wage war on others in the name of "God."

How was this man, named Jesus of Nazareth, able to bring about miracle cures just by laying his hands on people? What went on to cause such excitement in his teachings, which have endured over 2,000 years and are still spoken of to this day? Jesus surely appears to have healed people on more than just the physical plane. There was more going on behind the scenes in the spiritual, mental, and emotional dimensions of the ill-stricken, though this we do not have proof of. But what can we understand today about these healings that previously may not have been clear? In chapters 7, 8, and 9, we explore the nervous system and discuss how disease may progress from the unseen to manifest physically.

Chapter 7:
The Kousouli® Method - Healthy Living In Today's World

"To make our nervous system our ally instead of our enemy . . . we must make automatic and habitual, as early as possible, as many useful actions as we can, and guard against the growing into ways that are likely to be disadvantageous to us, as we should guard against the plague."
~ William James

It has been proven that your mind and body are like super recorders, remembering every move you make, from the numerous falls you had as a child to the sports, work, and auto injuries of today. It all adds up. Your spinal cord has been stressed by many forces both in your childhood and now, which causes communication loss between your brain and vital organs, tissues, and cells. When this occurs, there is lack of proper nerve flow from the brain, causing malfunction, premature aging, and dis-ease. Your current health condition is reminiscent of the choices you made for your body throughout all your years leading to today.

7.1 Is Your Mind Really Involved in the Dis-ease Process?

The mind is not just in the brain; it is everywhere - in every cell, tissue, and organ of our creation. Every mental state is identical to a corresponding physical state. Mental terms or "thought energies," and physical terms of "body health" are different descriptions of collaborative states, showing how our body, mind, and health conditions are all interconnected and deeply rooted in each other. The mind is a highly differentiated, functional cluster achieving high integration in a few milliseconds, thus acting as the driver for all brain activities. Scientists have noted that speaking mentally or verbally to your body results in upgraded changes within cell structure, and can vastly improve the healing of a damaged area.

Physical strain, chemical imbalances, emotional issues, environmental toxins, and the everyday stresses of life are impacting you even as you are reading this right now. The real danger lies with those who they think they are "okay," and mask a headache by taking medications, or for those who let a chest pain go on, which places them at higher risk. The most complicated health concerns hit suddenly when the container "body" can no longer hold the stress. This may end in an emergency situation, costing you countless dollars, aggravation, lost time, severe pain, and may even be fatal. So take control of your choices, and your life, while you can.

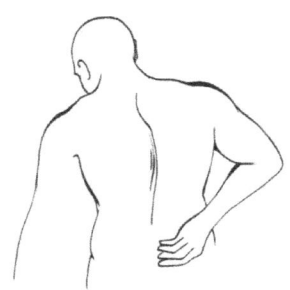

It is widely believed by laypeople that chiropractors are simply back pain doctors who cure neck and back pain by cracking or popping the back. Unfortunately, most people are ignorant about the real process that occurs once total neural connectivity is restored, and do not know the effects of spinal misalignment and nerve interference on our overall health. Many chiropractors, like myself, have experienced extraordinary success over the years in helping patients beat a multitude of health problems. Most people don't discern that, in combination with using proper exercise, lifting procedures, eating correctly and drinking plenty of fluids, upholding the spine requires a specific patient-tailored plan for periodic spinal adjustments to encourage alignment. Generally speaking, when the spine is aligned properly, innate energy flows freely throughout the entire body so that various bodily functions remain normal. In a misaligned spine, nerve interference occurs along the spinal path and normal body functions are disrupted. The sad thing is many nerve-related problems mimic severe medical conditions and patients never know it. They repeatedly get misdiagnosed by their doctors, who can't find out what is going wrong, and consume over-the-counter drugs and prescription pills to cover their symptoms. They never realize that the real cause could be spinal in nature; a misaligned spine that is not coordinating the necessary instruction from the brain to its corresponding organ(s) or tissue(s).

7.2 Retracing Your Recovery Pathway

Life is a circle of events, and lies somewhere between 2 points: the health state and the current dis-ease condition. One important way to ensure a healthy revitalization is being able to retrace the pathway of illness all the way to the starting point, where things started to go awry. Retracing essentially allows restoration of all the phases through which you progressed to the current dis-ease state. Examine these three factors when retracing to health:

1. **Time Element:** Time is of paramount importance in detailing your recovery path – if you had symptoms that were prevalent for a long time (chronic), the recovery will take

some time to retrace the path to health. When a sudden deformation happens in one of the spinal segments, impacting the neurons supplying the spinal segment, the resultant effect is acute inflammation and heat generation, which cumulatively produces a melting and flash fusion effect. The segment fuses with its conjoint bony structures, and even though this kind of a change is sudden, the resultant damage will require a much longer retrace and the recovery process that can span over a few months - even possibly years - rather than a few days or weeks. The rule of thumb is that acute diseases take less time to recover, whereas chronic conditions take longer time to heal.

2. **Extent of Involvement:** Some injuries might involve and encompass more extensive tissue damage than others; the more widespread the damage is, the longer the process of healing will be. It must be added though that no matter what dis-ease condition it is, it always has subsequent damaged tissue in the cells that are malfunctioning. A very easy way to envision the whole situation is looking at how an injury in the skin is resolved. The dermal (skin) tissue initially goes through the visible pathologic transformations within each layer of tissue, until it assumes its greatest degree of abnormality, and then gradually retraces every path of tissue re-generation until it turns normal. In some adverse cases, if the damage is too much, it leaves a scar behind.

3. **The Dis-ease Production Phase:** To remedy a disease, it is first imperative to know the dis-ease process. Otherwise, the symptoms are only alleviated and the dis-ease *per se* is never cured - only temporarily concealed. Tissue requires three things to maintain health: (i) appropriate quantities of oxygen, and (ii) quantitative and (iii) qualitative amounts of nervous-system-mediated vital energy. In fact, tissue oxygenation is also directly regulated by cognizant nerve supply to the tissue. On the flip side, oxygenation is also required for the nerve tissue to function properly. In summary, the aforementioned cues are the central cog around which the human body functions, and all malfunctions can thus be traced back to this central regulatory region. The nerve fibers are also important, in that they double as the transmitters of information from the brain to the rest of the body, so anything impacting them will impact the body's normal physiology and result in a dis-ease condition. When a vertebral misalignment happens, it causes partial closure of the entry-exit site through the spine, causing a deficiency of vital energy transfer to different parts of the body, and thus causing dis-ease over time. Depending on the

numbers of fibers affected by the misalignment, different areas of the body can be affected and will remain as such until the misalignment is treated. Any other measure will only cause temporary relief from the associated symptoms.

7.3 How Does Emotion Affect Your Health?

Our lower frequency emotions of fear, anger, and grief can all have a long-lasting, negative effect on our well-being. We occasionally feel sabotaged by negative emotions, even long after an original occurrence. When it stays with us for a long time, it gets encrypted into our subconscious system, so much so that it jumps into action when we feel a certain way, or undergo a certain stress (i.e. breakups, the death of a loved one, a boss yelling at us, etc.).

To further explain, imagine a female walking alone to her car near a dark alley at night. All of a sudden she is attacked and robbed at gunpoint by a large male. She will experience fear for her safety at first; then anger that she was robbed, possibly resentment that she could not do anything about the incident, and then finally revenge as she wishes justice could be served. Her nervous system received strong programming through that incident and responded the way it knew how - according to her previous experiences of danger to keep safe. Now armed with this new and reinforced 'programming' her nervous system files it away until it needs to react again to a similar stimulus. However, every time she goes past an alley whether alone or with others now, in bright daylight or night time, she will get a revival of the stored feelings she had from her prior alley encounter even if there is no attacker or threat present. The response sometimes serves us by keeping us alert and away from danger. However, if it is negatively affecting us, the loop . should be neutralized or 'deleted' to allow for newer more useful programming. The negativity loop is destructively harbouring the feelings in her nervous system's programming and she'll fail to realize why she is having future relationship difficulties 1) trusting unfamiliar males around her 2) feeling safe in the dark or 3) being intimate in a dark room with a lover Without intervention, the negatively programmed loop will be reinforced into the subconscious by any similar trigger with the original incident, and this is forced deeper the longer it goes unresolved. This charged negative energy affects chakra stability and leaking of vital energy occurs over the areas that were weak at the time the incident occurred. If we happen to be in a destabilized state when heightened states of emotional distress happen due to chemical stress, physical trauma, poor nourishment, or other low frequency emotions, they may lodge deep and take much longer to resolve (or never resolve).

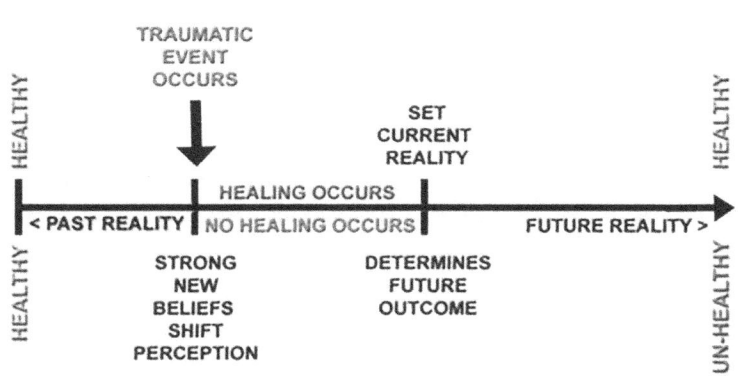

Then, years later, we encounter a comparable issue, state, or condition, and the deep-rooted previous emotive reaction kicks in and tries to save the day from any proposed danger or threat. The past event and the present-day situation is connected intimately, without your conscious knowledge. Remember that the emotional reality you hold as 'truth' can radically affect your health. Parts of our body can hold or express emotional energy too. This is the reason for sweaty palms or cold body extremities before a presentation or an exam. Many emotions plague the bodies of chronic worriers, and these people can end up with stomach ulcers!

I have developed a technique named Kousouli Neural Emotive Reconditioning or KNER® for short, which is part of a larger healing process; the Kousouli® Method 4R Intervention System. My unique technique utilizes visual imagery, hypnosis, deep diaphragmatic breathing, colour therapy, spinal adjustments, and positive verbal declarations. The therapy identifies and neutralizes negatively stimulated emotional belief or vibratory frequency running wild in the subconscious, chakras, and body organs. It closes energy leaks that are producing unpleasant results in the patient's life so that the loop can be reconditioned positively.

When applied effectively, the patient's nervous system releases the lingering stress entity through the spine and energy body. It is not unusual to sometimes find the patient go into an extreme dumping of repressed feelings during the session expressed as heavy tearing, heat, rage or laughter. Success varies per individual patient lifestyle variables; however it's completely safe, quick, and the process utilizes simple muscle testing. Patients often report strong emotional discharge that brings deep peace after the procedure. No part of the Kousouli® Method uses psychiatric evaluation and is a totally drug free therapy. KNER® is in the 4th part, Reset, of the Kousouli® Method 4R Intervention System.

7.4 The Kousouli® Method 4R Intervention System

My experience with the different aspects of chiropractic care, clinical research, energy healing, clairvoyant meditation, hypnosis, and personal experiences in and out of the clinic both as a doctor and as a patient have helped me develop the 4R Kousouli® Method of Health. **The main goal of the Kousouli® Method is to treat the patient by addressing vital energy loss in 4 main arenas (spiritual, mental, emotional, and physical) utilizing the 'antenna' called the nervous system.** The nervous system allows us to interact with our internal and external environments and is the master communicator of our health. The Kousouli® Method 4R Intervention System gives patients a daily checklist and simple structure for making sure they are on point to "Rejuvenate the Body, Empower the Mind and Free the Soul."

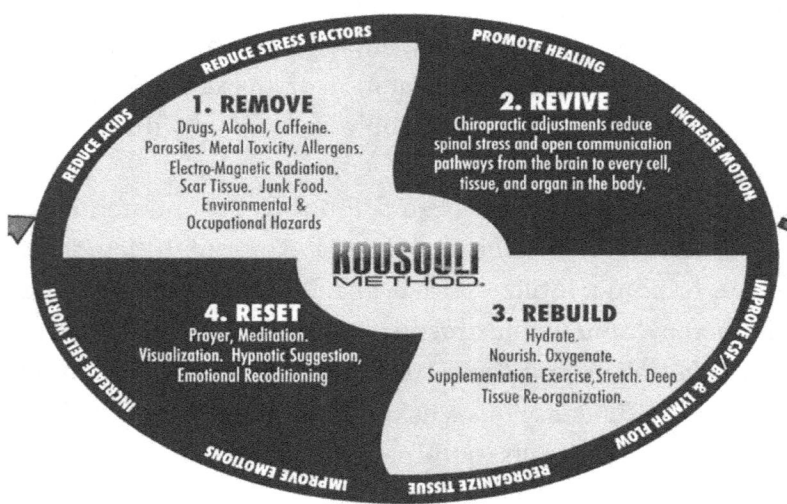

Those with healthy lives make daily healthy choices. Adding the steps of *Remove, Revive, Rebuild, and Reset* into your life *over time* will help you *regain health*.

The following diagram has three main circles; two of which are cycle states of health. The first cycle reflects where most people are when they feel something is wrong or feel ill. Because of accumulated poor lifestyle habits and neglect over time, they feel lousy and seek out a health care provider to deal with the physical body. The first cycle (left) reflects the negative aspects of health. The center middle circle represents the **Kousouli® Method 4R Intervention System**. When one becomes proactive utilizing the Kousouli® Method, they complete the 4 steps of *Remove, Revive, Rebuild, and Reset.* This is where change starts, and if maintained during a set care plan over time, favourable results will start to appear. The third circle (right) reflects the positive benefits of health after incorporating the Kousouli® Method. If maintained, the patient stays in this positive cycle until neglect over time pulls the process back to the negative cycle. **The success of the method is due to the focus of the *4R continuous processes*:**

1. ***Remove* the toxins**; Cautiously limit or remove as much as possible all drug use (prescription, over the counter, or recreational), alcohol consumption, caffeine, sodas, smoking, intestinal worms & parasites, heavy metal toxicity, allergens, electro-magnetic radiation, old scar tissue build-up, junk food and fast food, environmental and occupational ergonomic hazards.

2. ***Revive* the nervous system utilizing correct chiropractic care**; Chiropractic adjustments reduce spinal stress and open vital communication pathways from the brain to every cell, tissue and organ in the body.

3. ***Rebuild* the body through whole food nutrition and exercise**; Proper hydration, nourishment, oxygenation, supplementation, exercise, stretching, and deep tissue re-organization of spinal muscle attachments.

4. ***Reset* your thoughts and programming**; Prayer, meditation, visualization, hypnotic suggestion, Kousouli Neural Emotional Reconditioning (KNER®) and proper mind and body rest will ensure that the whole process is perpetuated within yourself and you continue to reap the benefits for the rest of your life.

Going through the Kousouli® Method 4R intervention system will ensure you get the 5th 'R' too; Recovery! My simple message is: those with beautiful posture, flexibility, strength, unlimited energy, youthful and healthy lives, make daily healthy choices. Don't lie to yourself thinking that just going to the gym, eating a few days' worth of salads instead of meat, one day of yoga, or a week of Hollywood's latest detox craze will get you healthy. To stay in the positive cycle, without losing any progress by relapse, you *must* decide your health is a priority worth maintaining over the course of your life; not just for a week or a few months. The 4R system of the Kousouli® Method 4R Intervention System now makes it much easier to keep yourself on track and move toward your health goals. With the removal of body pains and the return of your health to homeostasis, you can focus your energy and attention on exploring higher states of awareness.

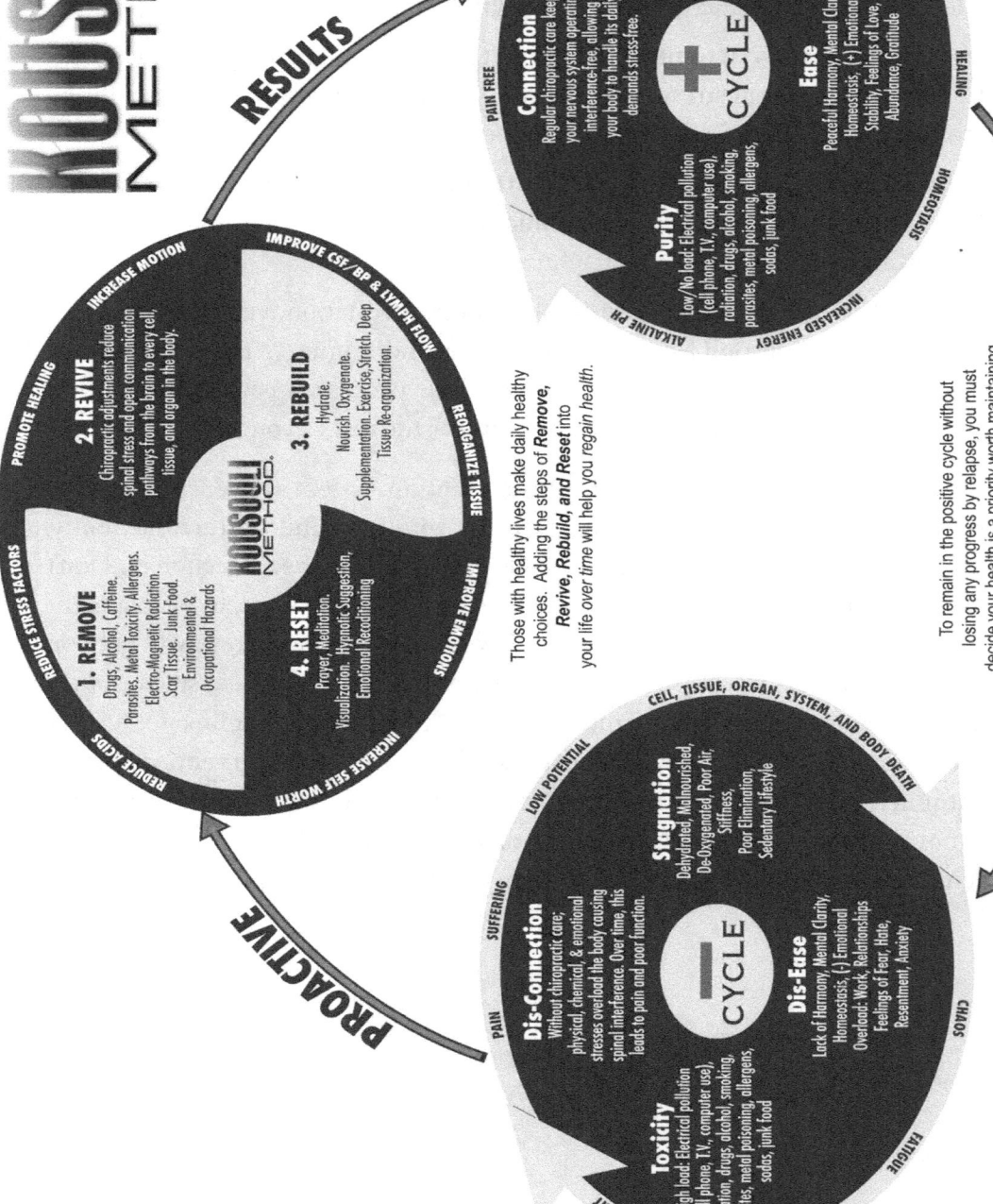

Neglecting to do the 4 steps will bring you backwards into the negative cycle. Choose to be healthy by paying the price of health. The price is dedication and commitment to a new paradigm that maintains your health priorities. Adding the steps of **Remove, Revive, Rebuild, and Reset** into your life consistently, will help you regain and maintain your healthy new perspective. I will summarize below the attributes that will help you in maintaining the positive cycle and also explain the lifestyle events that will push you towards the negative cycle.

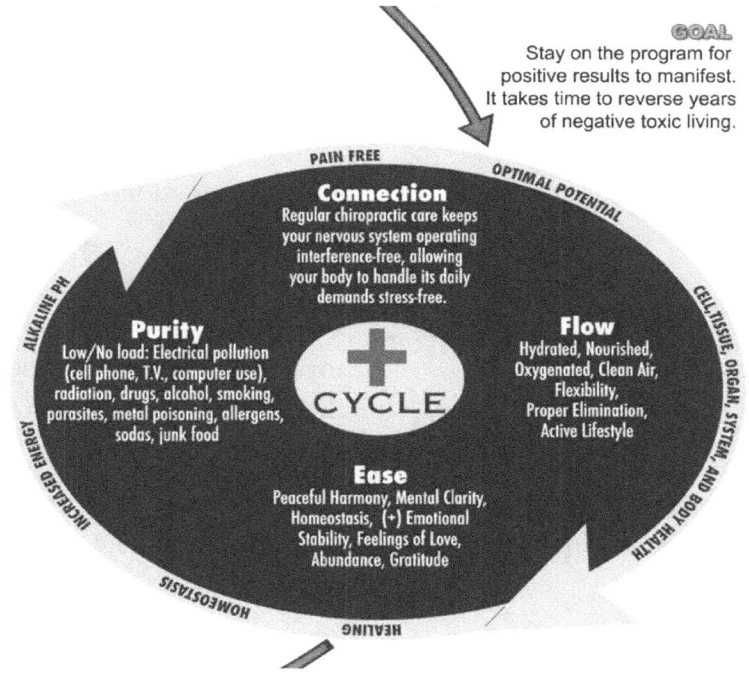

Staying in the Positive Cycle

- **Connection:** Regular chiropractic care keeps your nervous system operating in an interference-free fashion, allowing your body to handle its daily demands in a stress-free manner.

- **Flow:** Incorporating proper hydration, nourishment, oxygen, clean air, flexibility, proper elimination and an active lifestyle will ensure a smooth flow of energy within your body.

- **Ease:** Having peaceful purpose, harmony, mental clarity, homeostasis, positive emotional stability, feelings of love, abundance and gratitude for yourself and others will keep you in a positive frame of mind.

- **Purity:** Avoid or remove electrical pollution (cellular phone, televisions, and computers), radiation, drugs, alcohol, smoking, parasites, metal poisoning, allergens, sodas, caffeine overload, junk or fast food.

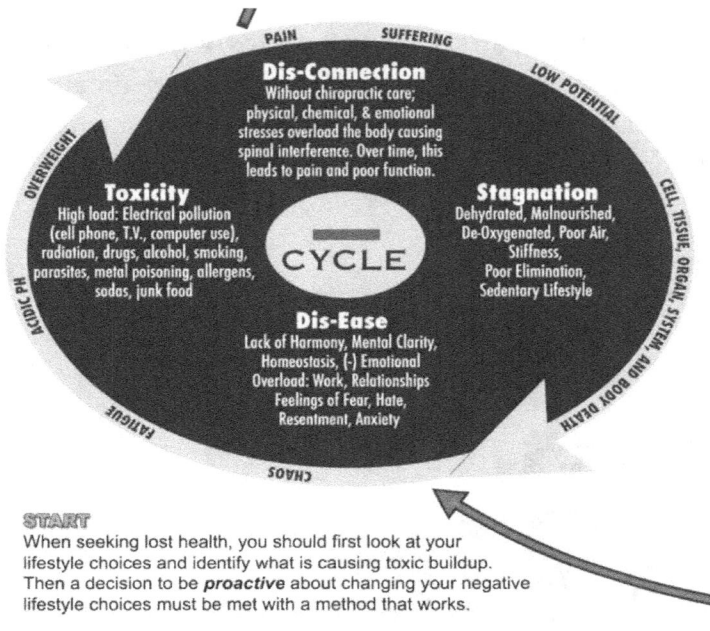

Reverting Back to the Negative Cycle through Neglect

i. Dis-connection: Irregular, discontinuous or complete lack of chiropractic care; physical, chemical, and emotional stresses all compound spinal overload. Over time, this miscommunication of brain to body leads to pain and poor function.

ii. Stagnation: Staying in a dehydrated condition, receiving improper nutrition, no or low supplementation, poor air or water quality, lymph flow backup, poor elimination, and a sedentary lifestyle are cardinal signs for bringing your health down.

iii. **Dis-Ease:** Lack of harmony, mental clarity, negative emotional stresses, work or relationship stress overload, feelings of fear, hate, resentment and anxiety all will contribute to disease conditions.

iv. **Toxicity:** High load of electro-magnetic pollution, radiation, drugs, alcohol, smoking, parasites, heavy metal poisoning, allergens, sodas, and junk food will result in an overall imbalance and a downslide of your health condition.

It becomes apparent from the above points that most of your health is a matter of lifestyle choice; being able to regulate your temptations and not resorting to the lazier lower vibration path at every whim. Sometimes taking the tougher route ultimately proves to be wiser, healthier, and perhaps easier too in the long run. The very same conditions when done properly induce and maintain the positive cycle, and a slight imbalance in any aspect can tilt the whole balance towards the negative energy cycle. Consistency is a key word in maintaining a healthy condition, and the more consistent you are with your good habits and lifestyle choices, the better you will be served by your body. This system is a great guide to allowing you the ability to keep yourself in check by referring to it often and making sure you are doing all 4 aspects adequately and are maintaining your homeostatic balance. It will help remind you if you've been skipping positive steps or neglecting yourself; like smoking, eating junk food, forgetting to get your workout in, staying dehydrated, or missing your last chiropractic appointment; all of which would start leaning you towards the negative cycle.

The Kousouli® Method 4R Intervention System is continuously being developed through clinical application and research. When correctly applied it has shown successful symptom reduction or elimination of headaches, dizziness, fatigue / low energy, carpel tunnel, whiplash pains, muscle spasms, joint pains, neck pain, back pain, allergies, depression, hormonal imbalances, fibromyalgia, numbness, limb tingling, IBS, asthma, acid reflux/GERD, arthritis, insomnia and toxicity just to name a few of the most common treatable ailments. The Kousouli® Method through KNER® also takes into account the spiritual, mental, and emotional aspects of health, which usually manifest into the physical plane as pain and dis-ease. By accessing specific energy points and balancing these points from leaking, the individual can focus their personal innate energy into their healing with quicker results. Let's now look into the intricate wiring that makes *you* up!

This system's powerful technique of replenishing health naturally goes beyond the surface scope of this book and is taught privately to interested practitioners at live seminar events. Details can be found at www.DrKousouli.com or www.KousouliMethod.com.

Chapter 8:
The Nervous System: Gateway for Turning Your Life Around

"God may forgive your sins, but your nervous system won't."
~ Alfred Korzybski

It is truly remarkable; 200 million sperm find one egg. One sperm enters the egg and that combination of energy turned into the person who is now reading this book. Congratulations - you're 1 in 200+ million! What incredible odds! That's pretty unique and special! Have you ever stopped to wonder how this energy transformed a few cells to create you? To understand the power of healing, we must understand how energy in the body moves and works. We have to understand the master system of control in the human body – the nervous system. Within just 15 days of conception, the neural tube develops from the embryo's ectoderm layer, which turns into the central and peripheral nervous systems, the brain, and organs. The nervous system then sends instructions to the rest of the body to grow what is needed. The matter that makes up our body is all energy at the core. You were created, and continue to create, through the energy superhighway called the *nervous system*. Although the actual mechanisms of healing manifestation are not synaptic or corporeal in nature, but quantum (the smallest quantity of energy), it would be wise to look at this physical system as a possible "fuse box" when things go astray in health. Let's take a look at some of its parts.

8.1 The Neuron

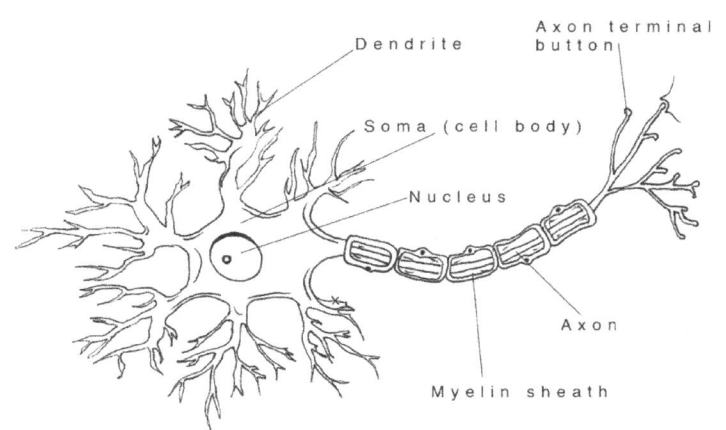

The fundamental building block of neurological structure and function in the nervous system is termed the *neuron*. Neurons receive, integrate, and relay action potentials (nerve impulses) to other communicating cells. Neurons are very specialized nerve cells that communicate electrical and chemical information, depending on the task needed in the body.

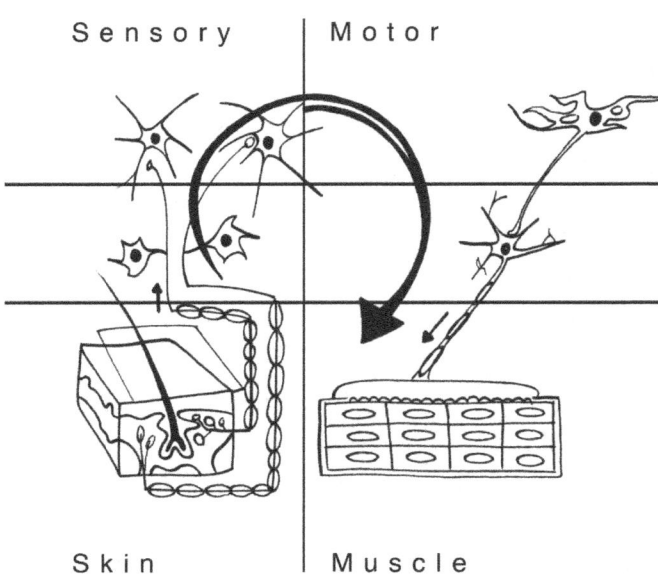

Sensory neurons take information from the body and bring it to the brain. Motor neurons transmit brain information to the muscles of our body. Interneurons transmit between neurons of the body. Here below, we can see sensory information being pulled from the skin that goes to the sensory neuron, and a motor neuron sending information to the muscle for contraction.

The metabolic needs of the cell are met by the *cell body (soma)*, which varies in position to the attached *dendrites* and *axons*. Sensory axons are like long arm projections that come off of the soma and conduct nerve impulse away from the soma. Dendrites act as threadlike extensions of a neuron's cytoplasm. They resemble treelike processes that act as most of the neuron's receptive surface. *Dendrites,* unlike axons, take information from other cells inward, toward the cell body and are usually stimulated by a neurotransmitter that is released by an axon. These structures allow energy to flow, unseen by the naked eye, which allows you to move, think, talk, and basically live your life. There are other cells, called *glia,* that support axons and form insulating coverings around axons in the peripheral and central nervous system, called *myelin sheaths*. Myelin sheaths increase the nerve impulse along the axon's path allowing the signal to essentially fast-forward its transmission speed. The flattened out cells that make up the myelin sheaths, when found around central nervous system axons, are termed *oligo-dendro-glia,* whereas when found around the peripheral ner-

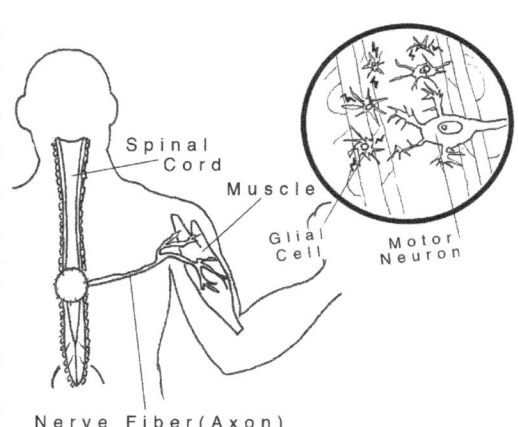

vous system, they are simply called *axon sheath cells*. The cell bodies, which have myelin, tend to have a shiny white appearance to them that has come to be known as *white matter*; cell bodies lacking myelin are known as *grey matter*.

8.2 Body Communication Via the CNS and PNS

The nervous system is very complex, so in an effort to easily explain its workings, we are going to talk in general terms. The nervous system is a vast super-network of cells that communicates between cells, you, and your environment through nerve impulses, which are transmitted along axons of nerve cells. You build brain synapses with everything you do, see, feel, touch, and experience. The nervous system communicates within itself and its external world as it uses your nose, eyes, skin, and tongue to build sensory recognition. It is sensed, processed, and your nervous system sends out a reaction to the stimulus, creating movement such as muscle contraction, like in walking or blinking. Everything learned or recalled from the system will be experienced as an image or feeling when someone is sensitive enough to receive input. This is important to understand, as it will serve you in your training on expanding your clairvoyance in later chapters.

Our nervous system is grouped into two sections called the CNS and PNS, or *Central and Peripheral nervous systems*. The CNS holds the brain and spinal cord, thus earning the name "central," and the "periphery," or "other nerves," are grouped into the peripheral nervous system (PNS). Most of the activities of the body's nervous system go on in the brain and spinal cord (located in the CNS). When signals have to go to the muscles and outside the brain, the signals travel over the PNS.

The nerves outside the head and neck that make up most of the body are located in our arms, legs, and most of our trunk. These are named "spinal nerves," and they are mixed in signal, functioning as both motor and sensory (excluding C1 and coccygeal nerves, which are considered motor). Thirty-one right and left pairs of spinal nerves (five lumbar, twelve thoracic, eight cervical, five sacral, and a single coccygeal) exit out of the vertebral canal through holes called "intervertebral foramina." The cervical spinal nerves exit above the vertebral level, except for cervical nerve eight, which exits between cervical seven and thoracic one. The rest of the nerves exit below their respective named vertebra.

8.3 The Autonomic Nervous System (ANS) and Peripheral Nervous System (PNS)

The term *visceral motor*, or *visceral efferent*, is the name given to neuron fibers that flow signal to glands, smooth muscle, and cardiac muscle, which are automatically controlled, unlike skeletal muscle which is flexed or relaxed consciously. Thus, the automatic traits of this system earned it the name "Autonomic Nervous System," or ANS for short. Striated muscle of the skeletal system, which is also referred to as the *somatic motor system* (soma; Greek for body), works through communication of a system of axons from the periphery to the CNS. The visceral efferent system further divides into the *Sympathetic* and *Parasympathetic* nervous systems. Sympathetic stimulation in the viscera (bowels/insides) causes the commonly referred to phrase, "Fight or flight," which is the reaction one has to perceived danger. Parasympathetic on the other hand, signals are relaxing in nature and recuperative, helping to recover from overproduction.

Let's take a look at the differences:

- *SYMPATHETIC* stimulation increases our heart rate and sweat gland secretion, decreases gastric motility, results in vasoconstriction, decreases secretion of salivary and digestive glands, dilates pupils, and allows ejaculation and bronchiole dilation.
- *PARASYMPATHETIC* stimulation does the opposite of *SYMPATHETIC*. It decreases heart rate, increases gastric motility, increases digestive gland and salivary secretion, and results in pupil constriction and smooth muscle contraction.

The PNS and CNS are connected by nerves that run all throughout our body. Cranial nerves of the CNS consist of 12 pairs that exit the foramina (holes) on the underside base of the skull. This is where our sense of hearing, smell, and vision come from. Cranial nerves can be all motor, all sensory, or a mix of both functions. The twelve cranial nerves are as follows:

1. ***Olfactory*** – Smell / Sensory
2. ***Optic*** – Sight / Sensory
3. ***Oculomotor*** – Moves eyeball / Motor
4. ***Trochlear*** – Eyeball depression, lateral rotation, and intorsion / Motor
5. ***Trigeminal*** – Feeling from face, moves mastication jaw muscles / Mixed
6. ***Abducens*** – Abducts the eyeball / Motor
7. ***Facial*** – Facial expression, taste from 2/3 of tongue, saliva, tearing / Mixed
8. ***Vestibulocochlear*** – Equilibrium, balance, and hearing / Sensory
9. ***Glossopharyngeal*** – Taste posterior 1/3 of tongue, swallowing, saliva / Mixed
10. ***Vagus*** – Controls voice muscles, sends signals to thoracic and abdominal viscera (The vagal nerve quiets the body systems and hinders adrenal function. It is mostly parasympathetic in nature)/ Mixed
11. ***Spinal Accessory*** – Controls sternocleidomastoid and trapezius muscles, ability to

shrug and head movement / Motor

12. Hypoglossal – Swallowing and speech articulation / Motor

The PNS sends neural information from the environment back to the CNS for processing. When information goes from the CNS back to the periphery, it is called *efferent,* or *motor,* in nature. If the information is going from the periphery back to the CNS, it is called *afferent,* or *sensory*. Signals that follow along circuits between the sensory and motor neurons are termed a monosynaptic reflex arc. Take the case of touching a hot stove: We see that the nerves in the hand send the signal back to the spinal cord and brain (CNS) for instant processing. The signal back tells the hand to get away from the stove so that it doesn't burn.

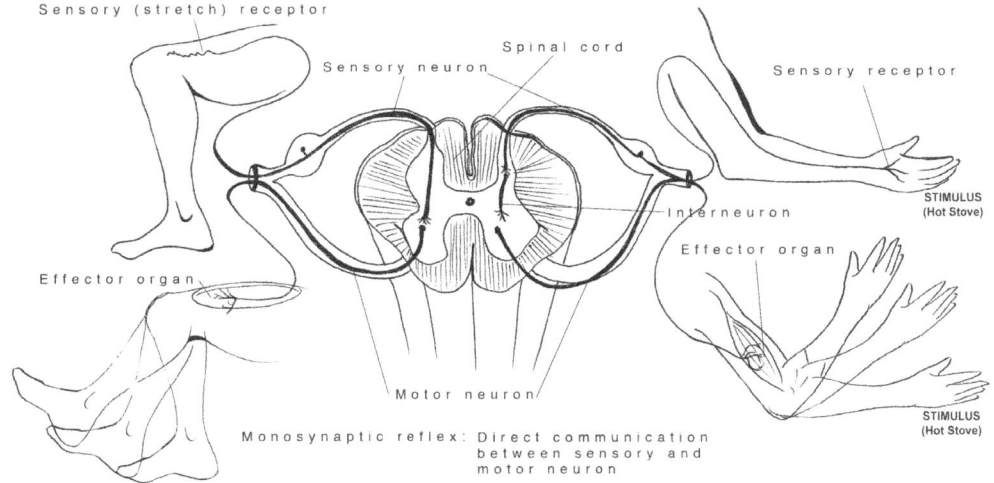

The diagram simply illustrates the path of the nerve signal when there is a stimulus. The same can be said about tapping the patellar tendon and activating the knee-jerk reflex. More complex circuitry that involves intricate movements, like dancing or feeling the texture of something, involve another connection termed an *interneuron*, or simply speaking, an 'in-between' nerve connector.

8.4 The Spinal Connection Further Explored

Our spinal nerves travel through holes called *intervertebral foramina* and emerge through to the rest of the body by splitting into two branches called *rami*. There is the *ventral ramus* that supplies the front-facing skin and trunk, extending into the limbs. The *dorsal ramus* supplies our skin over the vertebral column and the inner back musculature. Usually, each area of the body is supplied by the nerve level of the corresponding emerging adjacent intervertebral foramen, but this can also be much more complex. Skin sensations are felt by a specific area that transmits a signal to the spine, and then to the brain. These areas of skin differentiation are termed *dermatomes*. Your chiropractor uses them to check the function of sensation for overlapping sections of skin during your exam to help rule out nerve damage.

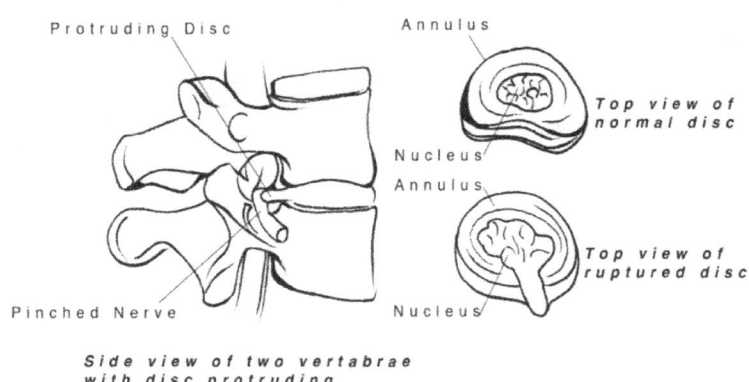

The diagram shows a spinal joint and a disc that separates each vertebral bone (except for the first bone, *atlas*). The discs also act like a shock absorber and keep you moving smoothly. The disc is made of an external annulus fibrosus, which encloses the internal nucleus pulposus. The annulus fibrosus comprises itself of several fibrocartilage layers. The nucleus pulposus encompasses loose fibers in a jelly mucoprotein gel that acts like a shockwave absorber for the spine. If the disc is injured, it may bulge out or intrude on the surrounding tissues or spinal nerves, causing symptoms like paresthesia and pain. This degrades the nervous system impulse to freely function, such as in the example of sciatic pain down the back of the leg.

Chapter 9:
Chiropractic Care and Kousouli® Spinal Stretches (KSS™) for Well-Being

"In the near future chiropractic will be as much valued for its preventative qualities as it now is for adjusting and relieving the cause of ailments."
~ D.D. Palmer

9.1 How Does Spinal Degeneration Affect You?

NORMAL SPINAL JOINT

STAGE ONE DEGENERATION

Your nervous system controls and coordinates all the functions of your body – that's how! If parts of the body are hampered, signal messages traveling over nerves will not be communicated, in turn compromising function. Hence, "*sub-lux-ations,*" or spinal misalignments that impede nerve flow and lead to spinal joint degeneration, are referred to as *SILENT KILLERS*. They start off slow and small and manifest as debilitating issues later in the life. The figures in this section clearly show the drastic effect on the spine during progressive stages of degeneration over time (a normal spinal joint up to stage 4 degeneration).

Medical practitioners usually define subluxation as a joint misalignment that is an order of magnitude less than a gross dislocation or luxation (break), though don't take it into account any more than that. Chiropractors are a step ahead in including misaligned joints, improperly moving joints, or temporal positioning and movement problems into the definition of subluxation. Therefore, the medical definition and the chiropractic definition of subluxation are very different. Chiropractic management is focused on delivering manual *adjust-*

ments to reduce the vertebral subluxation, which ultimately eliminates the root cause of the dis-ease - nerve interference.

Patients who are under chiropractic treatment are usually well aware of their precise level of functioning, and will often be capable of identifying what part of their body is malfunctioning in a particular condition, e.g. whether their spine is subluxated. However, this is entirely impossible for other patients who are not well informed of their body's level of functioning. They usually don't take any action to get better and slowly start sliding into more dis-ease over time.

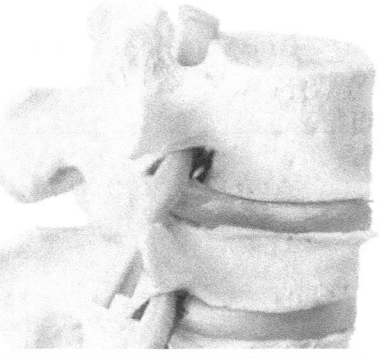
STAGE TWO DEGENERATION

Some symptoms that may be telltale signs that you are suffering from subluxation and need to visit a chiropractor are: low back pain, neck pain, headaches, migraines, shoulder problems, postural abnormalities, fatigue, breathing issues, disc injuries, nerve root irritation, sports injuries, stress related disorders, digestive complaints, hyperactivity in children, hormonal disturbances, allergies, and recurring skin complaints.

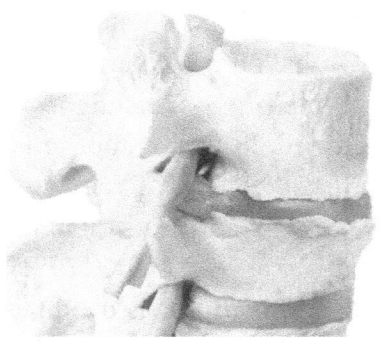
STAGE THREE DEGENERATION

The purpose of reducing a vertebral subluxation is to remove nervous system interference associated with that condition. It is believed that, all else being equal, a nervous system unimpaired by subluxation freely directs the body's innate abilities to maintain an optimum state of adaptability, including spinal integrity. This state, in turn, contributes to the overall health and well-being of the individual. When pain is eliminated and health restored, the patient can then focus their mind away from pain and turn it to higher level tasks such as extrasensory ability training.

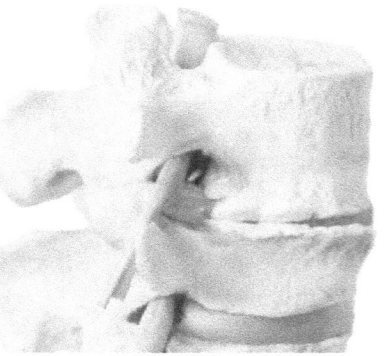
STAGE FOUR DEGENERATION

9.2 Vertebral Subluxation and Neurological Compression Syndrome

Some doctors describe the subluxation process as Neurological Compression Syndrome. The word subluxation is still used by the majority of chiropractors and is defined as less than a break; a misalignment. Subluxation occurs when one or more of the bones of your spine (the vertebrae) move out of proper position and create pressure, inflaming spinal nerves and surrounding structures. The nerves malfunction and interfere with signals traveling over those nerves. Symptoms, like headaches, cramps, etc., will then occur. These issues may be coming from your spine and may never go away if only using medications!

The perfect analogy is to imagine you were stepping on a garden hose, where the hose represents the spinal cord and the water represents the nerve flow of energy or information. Removing the pressure on the hose allows water to again flow from the source to the garden. In the case of our bodies, nerves flow and vital health instruction flows from the brain back to the deprived cells, tissues, and organs. The noxious stimulus would be the foot causing the kink on the hose. It is believed that most dis-ease conditions are a cumulative outcome of "nerve interference," which refers to an impediment in the normal physiological functions of the central and peripheral nervous system. Nerve interference disrupts motor functions by affecting effector organs, such as muscles and glands, and also the information flow from the peripheral to the central nervous system. Think of how many diseases could be a result of limited or no nerve flow!

> *"The great challenge to any chiropractor is to not merely spend one's life removing subluxations, but rather to help patients remove the cause of their subluxations."*
> ~ *V.V. Strang*

Let's now take a look at how the spine can be affected globally by subluxation. The following table highlights the different vertebrae present in your body, and the different parts of the body that the neurology directly connects to. The symptomatic presentation occurs when one or more of these connections are disrupted by subluxation.

Vertebrae	Parts of Body	Possible Symptom
C1	Intracranial Blood Vessels; Eyes	Headaches, Migraines
C2	Lacrimal Gland, Parotid Gland	Dizziness, Sinus Problems
C3	Scalp, Base of Skull, Neck	Allergies, Ear Infections
C4		Ringing in the Ears, Head Colds, Fatigue, Vision Problems
C5	Neck Muscles, Shoulders	Runny Nose, Sore Throat
C6	Elbows, Arms, Wrists, Hands	Stiff Neck, Cough, Croupe,
C7	Fingers, Esophagus, Heart, Lungs, Chest	Arm Pain, Hand and Finger Numbness or Tingling, Asthma, Heart Conditions, High Blood Pressure, Immune System Dysfunction
T1	Esophagus, Heart, Lungs	
T2	Chest, Larynx, Trachea	Wrist Pain, Hand and Finger
T3	Arms	Numbness or Pain, Middle Back Pain
T4		Congestion Bronchitis, Difficulty Breathing
T5	Gallbladder, Liver, Diaphragm	Asthma, High Blood Pressure
T6	Stomach, Pancreas, Spleen	Heart Conditions, Bronchitis
T7	Kidneys. Small Intestine	Pneumonia, Gall Bladder
T8	Appendix, Adrenals, Middle	Conditions, Jaundice, Liver
T9	Back	Conditions, Stomach Problems, Indigestion Heartburn, Gas
T10		Bloating, Ulcers, Gastritis
T11	Small Intestines, Colon	Digestive Problems, Kidney
T12	Uterus, Buttocks	Problems
L1	Large Intestine, Kidneys,	Constipation, Colitis, Diarrhea
L2	Buttocks, Groin,	Gas, Abdominal Pain
L3	Reproductive Organs, Bladder	Irritable Bowel, Bladder
L4	Colon, Thighs, Knees. Legs	Problems, Urinary Conditions
L5	Feet, Lower Back	Menstrual problems, Low Back Pain, Pain or Numbness in Legs
Sacrum	Buttocks, Reproductive Organs, Bladders, Prostate Gland	Constipation. Diarrhea, Bladder Problems. Menstrual Problems
Coccyx	Legs, Ankles, Feet, Toes	Low Back Pain, Pain or Numbness in Legs

9.3 The Importance of Scar Tissue Removal in Supporting the Spine

There are three separate phases during which a fibrous connective tissue, or *scar* tissue, is initially formed when healing occurs. During inflammation, prostaglandins act as master regulators and activate the immune system, along with trafficking the immune mediators, which helps prevent infection. We also see an eradication of scar tissue during inflammation, which is a foreword for new, healthy tissue formation by cell proliferation. This is a longer step than the previous one and may take a couple of weeks for complete regeneration. By nature, scar tissue and healthy tissue can be differentiated in terms of elasticity and lubrication. An improper processing of new tissue can cause weakened tissue formation, making it more prone to further injury. Since this can be disadvantageous for those of athletic nature, they usually follow a multistep remodeling system very carefully. Well-directed physical training helps develop stamina and endurance. Tissues are remodeled during almost all physical activity and beneficial exercises.

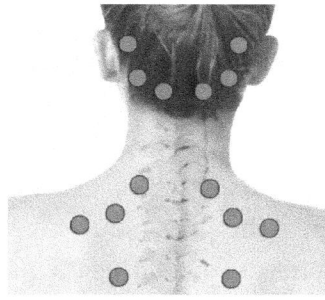

Injured tissue begins to lack elasticity and will contract over time, and damaged tissue becomes sensitive to nerve stimulation while interfering with the blood flow. As circulation is blocked, an accumulation of toxins cause various degradations, like confined movements, as injured muscles become fibrous.

Palpation during deep tissue massage can easily help identify where you have hypersensitivity due to scar tissue. Healthy tissue has more elasticity and less resistance than scar tissue, which resists movement and proper muscle toning. Removing, breaking down, or remodeling scar tissue helps oxygenate and improve blood flow to the stagnant areas that are detrimental to proper healing in the spine and associated body parts.

Subluxations also cause neurological short-circuiting in the muscular system, which is commonly experienced as spastic, tough nodules that are painful upon pressure, called 'trigger points.' These points can be found anywhere along the spine, from the neck down to the pelvis, but can occur anywhere muscle/nerve flow is interrupted. When nerve flow from subluxation is inhibited to muscles, the muscle cells cannot get the proper instruction to remove wastes efficiently, so toxins will back up and cause local pain in the area. Often, the area will

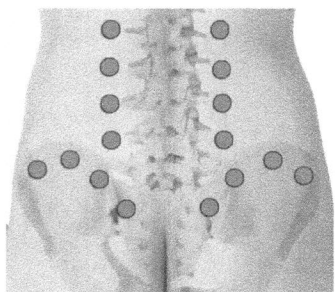

need help in the form of deep tissue cross-friction myofascial release to break down stagnation and help the toxins move along to cleanse the lymph system. Remember, no matter how much one gets massages in these areas, until the neurological component of the problem (the subluxation) is addressed first, there will always be pain from dysfunction.

9.4 Relief and Corrective Care

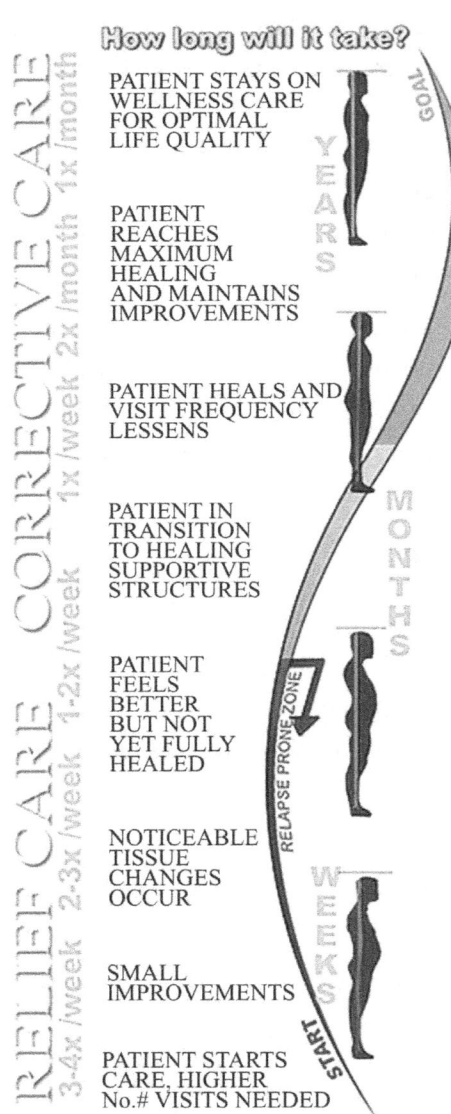

Chiropractic therapy can be done for a short-term alleviation of suffering and pain (relief care), or it can iron out and stabilize the root cause of the spinal dis-ease, thus alleviating the pain and suffering for a longer term (corrective care). Corrective care is how supporting structures (e.g. ligaments, tendons, and muscles) get a chance to repair. The chart to the left shows phases of care, along with a timetable and frequency of treatments. As one starts life healthy (optimized), but then neglects their spinal health, they drop down the chart curve. Symptoms appear at the end of a dis-ease process and are labelled at the bottom of the chart (suffering). When symptoms and pains are evident, patients are forced to address the problem and look to move up the chart again towards optimization. However, before we can correct the problem, we must first address the immediate pains and symptoms that are being felt. The tricky thing is the "relapse prone zone" that is depicted with an arrow down mid-way. If a patient does not commit to further their progress, they will fall victim to the faulty assumption that the injury or spinal issue has been completely healed since they feel no more pain, and thus may lessen or stop care, only to relapse again. Actual healing starts to happen after the immediate symptoms and issue of pain is relieved, then the body lays down a supporting foundation with more time and energy dedicated in strengthening the tissues. Time and financial constraints can sometimes force patients to choose a limited relief care program. Corrective care is always recommended over relief care, as it is more rational and provides a much more stable, long-term basis for healing. It's been proven that ligaments and muscles that support the spine require longer healing times, long after even the pain and symptoms appear insignificant. That's how important regular, non-stop care of the spine is; it's absolutely essential to ensuring the best possible outcome when the spine has completely healed. Of note, not everyone can reach complete correction or optimization. Sometimes a person's problem has reached a point where complete correction is impossible due to many limiting factors - most notably patient age and extent of damage through toxin accumulation. This is why early detection (by starting chiropractic care earlier in life) can in effect save both your life, and your lifestyle.

9.5 Corrective Care of Chronic Pain

Chronic pain is frequently resistant to conventional treatment. As recent research findings suggest, chronic pain may also result in structural alterations of the brain. Changes in function, chemical profile, or structure, also known as neuroplasticity, observed in the peripheral and central nervous systems, have been related to chronic pain. The etiology of chronic pain can be visceral, ischemic, nociceptive, neuropathic, or a combination of etiologies. Nociceptive pain (somatic/body or visceral/organ) is caused by stimulation of the nociceptors (pain receptors) located at nerve endings; arthritic pain is an example of nociceptic pain. Neuropathic pain involves pain impulses generated in the nerve, spinal cord, or brain, and is a consequence of injury to the central nervous system. Other chronic pain syndromes include chronic neck and back pain, headache, migraine, whiplash, rheumatoid arthritis, fibromyalgia, facial pain, pelvic, perineal pain, abdominal organ pain, irritable bowel syndrome, postsurgical pain syndrome, phantom limb pain, and chest pain syndromes. Some chronic pain disorders commonly found in older adults are spinal canal stenosis, osteoarthritis, degenerative joint disease, tumors and malignancy, post-stroke pain syndrome, post-herpetic neuralgia, and diabetic peripheral neuropathy.

9.6 The Kousouli® Method Spinal Stretches (KSS™)

Unknowingly, many people are adding problems to their already over-stressed spines. Some well-known malpractices are: texting on a mobile device with the neck flexed forward, carrying an oversized, heavy purse or backpack over one shoulder, long hours of slouching in a computer chair at work, holding the phone between a shoulder and tilted head, sleeping face down on an unsupported mattress or couch (causing slanting of the pelvis), creating low back issues by placing a thick wallet in the back pocket, and wearing high heels all day without taking any breaks. These bad habits remodel our spines forward into an unattractive hunched position (kyphosis), and can also eventually create large sideways back humps (scoliosis), causing us to shorten, appear disfigured, and look years older. Some even lose vital lung capacity from caved in chests, forward head postures, and tightened pectoral muscles, which lead to fatigued states of acidosis. We rarely get a chance to exercise truly correct posture, since very few chances throughout the day allow for the extension of our spinal column.

I decided to help patients improve their posture by developing nine simple and easy to remember stretches (Kousouli® Spinal Stretches or KSS™) that can be incorporated into one's daily routine effortlessly for a more erect posture.

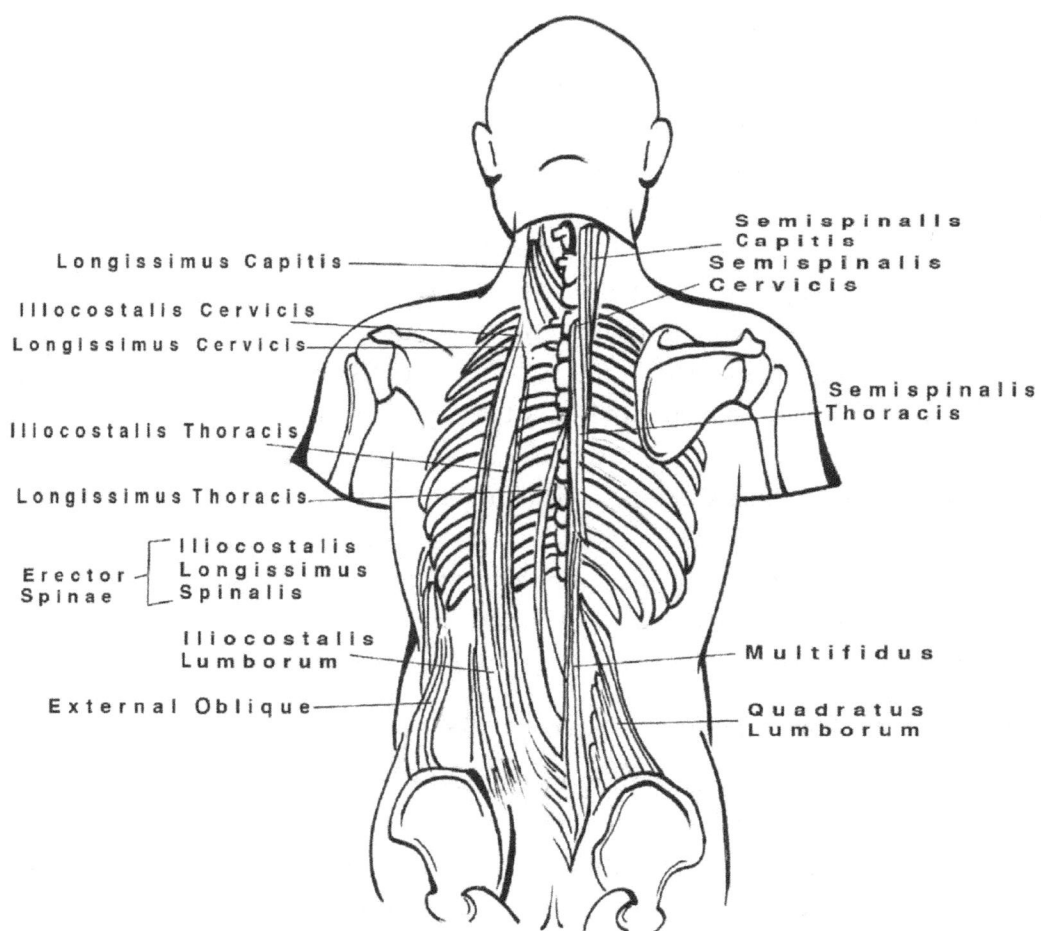

These nine stretches strengthen the very muscles that encourage proper form: the erector spinae muscle group. They consist of the spinalis, longissimus, and iliocostalis muscles of the back. In addition, focus also centers on muscles of good head, neck, and shoulder posture: Semispinalis capitis, semispinalis cervicis, splenius capitis, splenius cervicis, levator scapulae, and rhombodeus major and minor.

The coupling of my fascination with mythology and my understanding of the human body over the years has manifested into the development of KSS™, an easy to remember, practical, and fun way to keep fit, stay positive, and move with energy and stamina throughout your day.

Kousouli® Spinal Stretches (KSS™) Benefits:
- Strengthens erector spinae muscle groups; improves posture and overall physical appearance, helping you look and feel younger.
- Improves circulatory flow, cardiovascular fitness, and health.
- Releases stored tensions (physiological reduction of stress).
- May help slow down osteoporosis when done regularly.
- Burns calories and may help with weight management.
- Release endorphins and enkephelins that block pain and help you feel good.
- Positive outlet for releasing emotionally stored stress; depression, frustration, anger, and anxiety; improved connection to oneself.
- Increases oxygen to brain and breathing capacity for improved alertness, concentration, and mental ability; improved meditation ability.
- Increases muscular strength, endurance, and flexibility for improved body balance and coordination; improved ability to take care of one's body.

Precautions:
- KSS™ can be a magnificent stretch program for all ages to help bring more energy, stamina, and power into your life. Nevertheless, there are some safeguards that you should keep in mind when starting the program.
- Always consult your doctor before beginning any exercise or stretching program like KSS™.
- If you feel pain when performing any movements - stop immediately.
- Begin your KSS™ gently - do not "jump right in." Give yourself time to adapt.
- If you have had a joint replacement or are just coming out of surgery, simply limit,

restrict, or avoid major movements.
- KSS™ movements and methods may be modified and adapted to suit an individual's age, needs, and abilities. Do the modified versions labeled "M" if the original stretch is too difficult for you.
- A KSS™ program for seniors or arthritis sufferers may be applied slowly, and modified gradually over a period of time, depending on skill level. Move your joints slowly through a full range of motion several times, to help enhance overall circulation, and to decrease any stiffness. KSS™ may be resumed once tenderness has diminished and your doctor allows you back to total activity.
- Rest painful, inflamed, or hot joints with a cold ice compress at 15-30 minute intervals, and discontinue for the time being if pain occurs.
- Always breathe deeply down into your diaphragm (not chest), and allow unrestricted flow of your airway while doing KSS™ movements.
- Be sure to use a pillow or soft mat for any joints (like the knees) that make constant contact with the ground during modified stretching.
- Practice good technique; do not overextend joints beyond the normal range of motion. Maintain good form and posture.
- Hydrate often throughout the day (A full glass of water per hour awake is recommended). *See section 10.7 for recommended water requirements.*
- When learning the stretches, consult a more experienced KSS™ user for proper form and execution, rather than learning the poses incorrectly.
- Follow your stretching with a cool-down period, including sustaining the end of the stretch to avoid tenderness or stiffness. If soreness or stiffness occurs despite performing a cool-down, reduce your movements and try the modified "M" version of the stretch.

KSS™ is powerful, quick, and easy to do. Just nine key stretches total: three easy-to-do stretches in the morning, three at mid-day, and three in the evening. You may choose your favorites and make a personalized routine. Adding these stretches to your chiropractic care program, along with a clean diet, can help you gain the posture you deserve, encourage healthy circulation, and help oxygenate your entire body!

The following pages will detail the various stretches along with images for instruction. Persons with disabilities, who are not able to stand, or have weak lower extremities, can also perform each stretch. The modified versions of each stretch will be denoted by the letter "M." Let's get started!

(A.) HERMES STRETCH

Hermes was the messenger of the Gods. His symbol was a pair of winged boots. This is a recommended morning stretch you can do on your bed once you wake up. Start with one arm extended straight up over your shoulder and the knee bent towards your chest. Inhale deeply, and slightly extend your back as you hold the stretch for three seconds. Slowly switch the arms and legs as you exhale. Repeat the stretch on the opposite side. Modified Hermes is done by lying on your back. As you inhale and exhale from your diaphragm, visualize your spiritual body freely expanding past its physical container.

(B.) POSEIDON STRETCH

Poseidon was the ruler and God of the sea. His symbol was the trident. This is a recommended morning stretch that can be done once you get out of bed. Poseidon should be performed by starting in a crouched position. Inhale deeply from your diaphragm and rise up into a standing position with one leg back, as if emerging out of the ocean. Extend the spine and push the chest out. Keep your arms wide, and hold up your chin. Hold for three seconds, and then exhale as you come back down into a crouched position. Repeat the stretch with the opposite leg. Meditation to start the day: Envision yourself victorious as you explode past any current tension, body pain, or adversity you may be facing. This visualization will be powerful in your meditation practice.

(C.) APHRODITE/EROS STRETCH

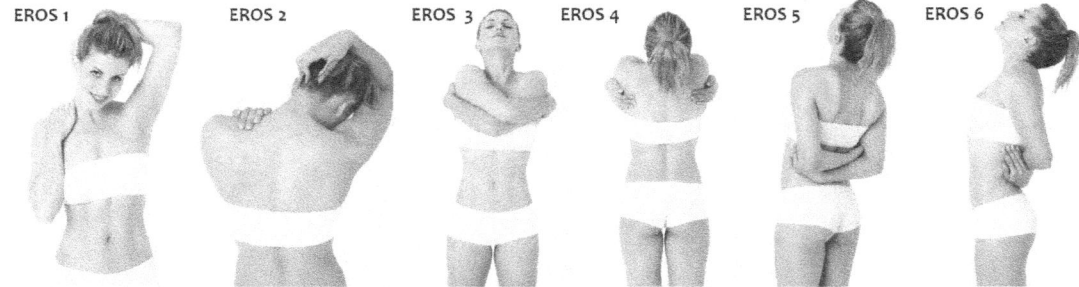

Aphrodite was the Goddess of love, beauty, and desire. Her symbols were the scepter, dove, and rose. This is a recommended morning stretch and can be performed in the shower while warm water washes over the back of the neck, shoulders, and upper back. Stand with your left hand on your trapezius and pull the shoulder muscles down and forward. Anchor your fingers from your right hand onto the left posterior inferior occipital ridge (bottom left edge of skull, see picture: Eros 2). Gently pull your head forward, down, and to the right with the chin towards your right chest. Inhale and exhale feeling the stretch. Repeat on the opposite side (Eros 1). Next, perform a loving heart hug by wrapping your arms around your chest (Eros 3, 4) as you extend your head back. With a gentle squeeze, try to move your fingers as far back to your spine as possible. Next, wrap your arms around your low back for support. Extend your upper body back gently, feeling the stretch (Eros 5, 6). The modified version of this stretch can be done seated. Appreciate yourself and feel love for the precious being that you are. As you execute the poses, meditate seeing yourself bathing under a cascading waterfall of golden light.

(D.) APOLLO STRETCH

Apollo was the God of music, healing, and archery. He was associated with the sun, light, and the archer's bow. This is a recommended mid-day stretch. Apollo should be performed in a standing position. Inhale deeply from your diaphragm, arch your spine, and push out your chest as you pull one arm and leg back. Put yourself into an archer position, and hold for a three second count. Exhale as you come back to starting position. Focus on the fluid motion of your body, as tension builds upon extension of the back and arms. Repeat on the opposite side. Modify this stretch by kneeling or sitting with legs crossed. Meditate by seeing in your mind's eye the goals of the day and aiming your intention at the target.

(E.) HEPHAESTUS STRETCH

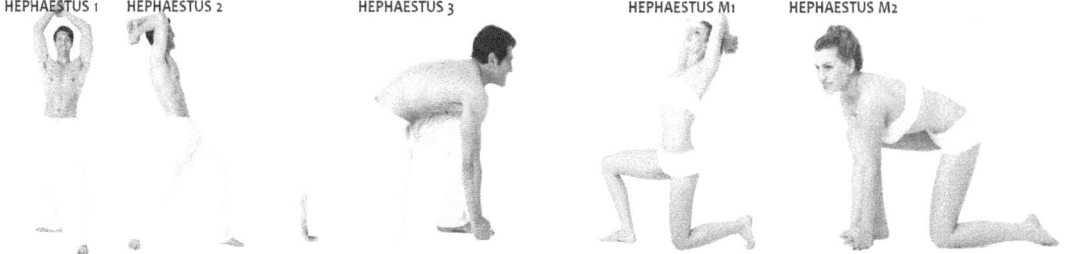

Hephaestus was the master blacksmith and craftsman of the Gods; God of fire and the forge. His symbols were fire, the anvil, axe, and hammer. This is a recommended mid-day stretch that will surely get your blood moving! Take a break from the cubicle or desk, and get your body moving with a Hephaestus stretch. It is done by going from an extended standing position to a crouched forward pose, as if you were wielding a large axe or hammer to the ground. Inhale as you slowly extend a leg and stretch back, hold for three seconds, and then come down gently forward overhead, bending the knees as you exhale. Slightly rotate your upper body through the movement to isolate the abdominals. Go slow and do not overextend your back. Repeat the stretch on the opposite side. Modified version is done by kneeling or sitting with legs crossed. Meditation: As you toil through your day, see the labor you do as being appreciated by others. With each extended movement of your arms, envision your labored efforts manifest into countless abundance. Feel the energy you manifest as you work, and sense the energy around you.

(F.) ATHENA STRETCH

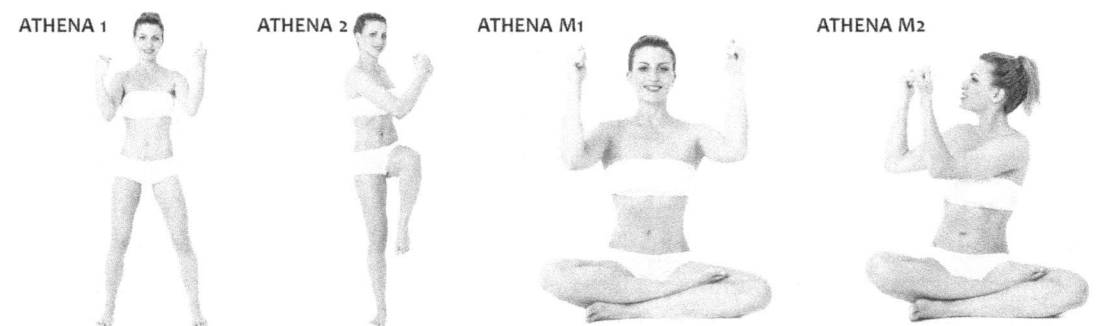

Athena was viewed as the wisest of all, and was the Goddess of warfare and reason. Her symbols were the owl and the olive tree. This is a recommended mid-day stretch. Stand with flexed biceps, as if you are holding a large shield in each arm. Extend slightly your spine and inhale deeply. Turn your arms and upper torso to one side and bring up the opposite knee. Tighten your abdominal muscles and hold for three seconds. Exhale and repeat on the other side. As you breathe deep from your diaphragm, perceive yourself as an impenetrable fortress. Any negative energy that may be coming from others is unable to affect you, and simply bounces off.

(G.) ZEUS STRETCH

Zeus was Greek mythology's king of the Gods and ruler of Mount Olympus; the God of the sky and thunder. His symbol was the thunderbolt. This is a recommended night stretch prior to ending your day. Zeus should be started with your body crouched and then slowly extend your arms up as you stand into a body X position. Inhale deeply as you slowly stretch to the sky, pushing up on your toes. Feel the stretch as you hold for three seconds. Exhale slowly as you descend back into a crouched position. As you descend and exhale, cross your arms as if throwing lightning bolts down to earth from the heavens. Repeat. Your meditation during this stretch should focus on the slow fluid motion of your body as tension builds up on the upward motion, and then releases on the downward flow. On the descending exhale, meditate by letting go of any stress you may have held on to during the day. Envision any negative energy slide off, as it is thrown to the ground. Modified Zeus stretch can be done kneeling or sitting with legs crossed.

(H.) DIONYSUS STRETCH

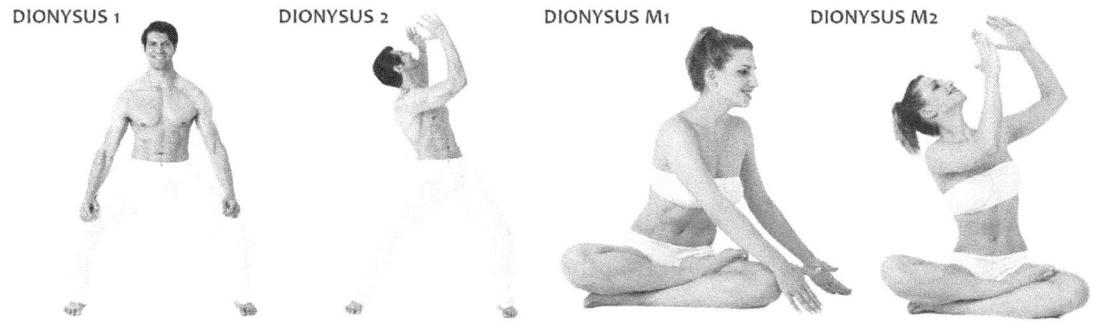

Dionysus was the God of enjoyment. He was often represented by wine, alcohol, parties, festivals, and merry occasions. This is a recommended night stretch. Dionysus should be performed while standing in a saddle stance. Slowly bring up both arms as if holding an oversized glass of wine. Inhale deeply from your diaphragm, and slowly extend your torso as you rotate to one side. Gently extend your neck and upper back as if you are drinking the wine. Hold for three seconds, and keep your core tight. Return to center as you exhale, and then repeat on the opposite side. Your meditation should focus on thoughts of a happy moment for celebration, either from the day's events, or something in the near future. You may also envision a goal you have set, and how accomplished you will feel when you complete it. Feel the energy move towards that goal, or bring that energy back to you if are celebrating your achievement.

(I.) DEMETER STRETCH

Demeter was the Goddess of fertility, agriculture, harvest, nature, creativity and the seasons. Often considered to be the deity of the farmer, she is represented by the symbols of corn, scepter, and torch. This is a recommended night stretch, easily performed just prior to sleep. Lie on your back and inhale as you squeeze your knees to your chest; this signifies fertility or pregnancy (new life). Hold for three seconds, and then exhale as you slowly extend your legs down, depicting the seasonal summer/winter cycles. At the completion, slightly arch your cervical (neck) and the lumbar area (low back). Repeat. The modified version is done with palms down, under the low back or hips for support, and makes the stretch a little easier. As everything in life is a cycle, we end our day with this stretch lying on our bed and getting ready for a good night's rest. With gratitude in your heart and mind, envision all the good that happened throughout your day. Replay any less than optimal events as more positive. As you drift off to sleep, plant in your mind higher vibrations of energy that will produce an even better tomorrow.

KSS™ can become an integral part of a healthy lifestyle.

Based on the discipline of "visual meditation and diaphragmatic breathing during spinal motion," KSS™ is a significant form of exercise, self-discipline, and empowerment. If tai chi or yoga is intimidating, difficult for you, or you're short on time, you'll love KSS™ because it feels good, is easy to remember, and it will improve your posture dramatically!

A daily KSS™ routine yields many physical benefits. KSS™ improves musculoskeletal aches and pains by stretching out stiff muscles, tendons, and ligaments that affect the spine. As your posture improves, your organs will also work more efficiently, as less pressure is put on them from slouching forward. It helps your digestive system eliminate more efficiently, and improves your sense of core stability.

KSS™ can help you achieve deeper sleep so you're more rested throughout the day. Patients report that they feel energized and focused in the morning. They feel inspired to get on with their day, and have more clarity after stimulating their circulation. While performing these spinal stretches, be sure to meditate while you move your body, and breathe deeply from the diaphragm. Encouraging movement of the spinal column's cerebrospinal fluid (CSF) pump, and getting more oxygen into the blood is vital for an alkaline internal environment and quick recuperation.

KSS™ may also help people mentally. Moving our body through space creates a sense of focus; through exercising self-will you can become more aware of your spatial alignment. Patients have claimed KSS™ to be a therapy for depression, the after-effects of quitting smoking or alcohol, panic attacks and anxiety. This is because the KSS™ system has the ability to reverse sensations that made them feel withdrawn from their body, or depressed from lack of exercise and oxygen intake. The deep, diaphragmatic breathing done in KSS™ is very detoxifying and calming. KSS™ is also a low impact form of exercise for those recovering from surgery. Osteoporosis patients, or those with disability who cannot easily get to the gym, can handle the gentle movements involved.

9.7 Sleep Well to Reenergize the Mind and Improve Body Chi

Sleep is often considered the greatest medicine available to a patient. Sleeplessness is one of the most common ways that any dis-ease takes form. Sleep affords continuous rest that is required by the body to repair itself. Normally five to eight hours of uninterrupted sleep is recommended, but it is highly person (and case) specific. Sleep duration normally decreases with age, and babies tend to sleep a lot more than eight hours as their energy goes to cell growth. How fresh are you feeling when you wake up? Do you feel like you need to go back to bed immediately? Do you hit the snooze button on your alarm often? Are you feeling more tired than you think you should be? These are cardinal signs of a disturbed sleep pattern. An uninterrupted sleep pattern has four distinct cycles, the last of which is called the Rapid Eye Movement (REM) sleep. This is also the phase where you have dreams. Therefore, a good way to know whether you are completing your sleep cycle is to keep track of whether you are dreaming often. Sometimes, in patients who have disturbed sleep or insomnia, the cycle duration is way off and a person can go to REM sleep within half an hour of falling asleep. This is the group who is known to sleep talk, and will wake up more exhausted than before going to sleep. You may want to investigate your sleep patterns by conducting your own inexpensive sleep study. Purchase and set up a video camera that has night vision or low light filming capability. Go to bed, allowing the camera to record all through the night. Review the footage in the morning in both fast-forward (6-8x speed), and normal speed. Look for how long it took you to fall asleep, how many hours you slept, how deep your breathing was, how much you tossed and turned, if you snored, if you maintained your sleeping position, if you dreamt, if you talked in your sleep, or if you sleepwalked. Do this overnight both close up and far away from your face. Compare the footage nightly. You will be amazed at the data you can attain in the course of a week. If you feel your sleep patterns are abnormal, you should discuss this with your doctor.

9.8 Sleeping Ergonomics

The most important thing that determines your sleep pattern is the relative positioning and alignment of your spine. If the spine is aligned in a stress free orientation that allows flow of your blood, oxygen, and nerve impulses, then you will have a better chance at well-defined sleep patterns and waking up refreshed.

- Try a lot of different mattresses before deciding on the best one for yourself. Choose a mattress that is firm yet can shape according to your body contours. Seek out "chemical and toxin free" memory foam mattresses without the fire-retarding chemicals. They are only available with your doctor's prescription, as companies are required by law to put these deadly chemicals in! Do your research prior to buying, so you're not stuck inhaling toxins.
- If you are sharing a bed with your partner, it is important to determine mutual compatibility as far as mattress choice is concerned. The goal is to find a mattress where one person won't be affected by the movement of the other during sleep.
- Choose your pillow properly. Neck pillows should be semi-firm. Not too hard and not too soft either - the non-toxic memory foam option works to conform to each neck uniquely. Most pillows raise your head position too high, stressing your neck and head. This is definitely not good for your overall sleep pattern and body health. The right-fitting pillows should be thinner/softer under the head and firmer/thicker under the neck. Orthopedic or cervical pillows should fit well no matter whether you sleep on your back or side.
- Do-It-Yourself Neck Pillow: Roll your own neck support if you do not have a non-toxic memory foam neck pillow, or need a quick temporary solution. Roll a small bathroom towel to the diameter equal to the circumference size of your

forearm. Place two large rubber bands on each end to hold it in place. Place it under your neck for support. That's all you need!

- The back of your head and the top of your shoulders should be making contact with the mattress. The only part supported away from the mattress should be the neck. This helps ensure proper neck curvature is maintained and allows nerves, blood, and oxygen to flow properly during sleep. Be sure to point the chin up as a checkpoint to make sure you're in proper position. Any large pillows should be placed under your knees (not your head - *see photos*) to take the pressure off of the low back. Some will need to use a large wedge pillow to bring their upper body to a 40-45 degree angle while using the above position. This will be especially true for those with acid reflux or digestive troubles, where sleeping flat would cause distress at night.

- For stomach sleepers, I recommend slowly training yourself each night to sleep either on your back or on your side. If you sleep on your stomach, you are getting less oxygen through the night because your chest is compressed. You are also sleeping with a kinked neck. When the neck is turned while sleeping on your stomach, oxygen, blood, and nerve supply gets cut off. Stomach sleepers often also complain of numb limbs due to inefficient blood and nerve circulation to their appendages. This makes them feel tired even after a long sleep session. In summary, choose a pillow that will support your natural spinal contours and slowly train yourself to sleep on your back as shown in the following photos, starting with small naps at first, and then whole night sessions.

- Limit sleeping on your side because there is less support for your spine. Sleeping on your back is the best option. Choose a firm mattress. Sleeping on the floor would be considered too firm. Sleeping on most couches is too soft. Find a happy medium that supports your spine but does not contort it. The back of your head and the top of your shoulders should be flat on the mattress. With your neck supported, your chin should point up slightly towards the ceiling. Any large pillows should be placed under your knees (not your head) to take the pressure off of the low back. If you insist on sleeping on your side, keep your knees bent at a 45-degree angle and place the rolled towel or small pillow between your knees to relax the pelvis. The pillow you choose for your head should fit the space from the ear to the mattress without kinking your neck. Your neck should be perfectly aligned with the rest of your spine.

Incorrect Neck Position Cuts Off Vital Brain-Body Chi Flow

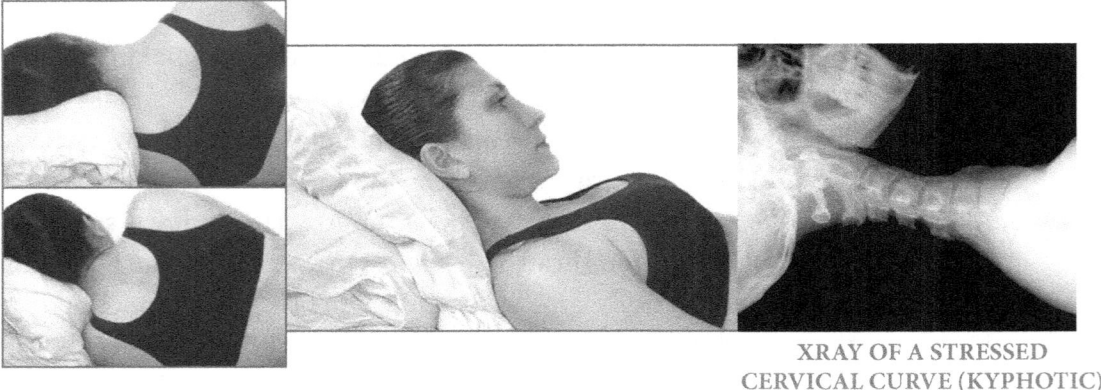

XRAY OF A STRESSED CERVICAL CURVE (KYPHOTIC)

Correct Neck Position Allows for Brain-Body Chi Flow

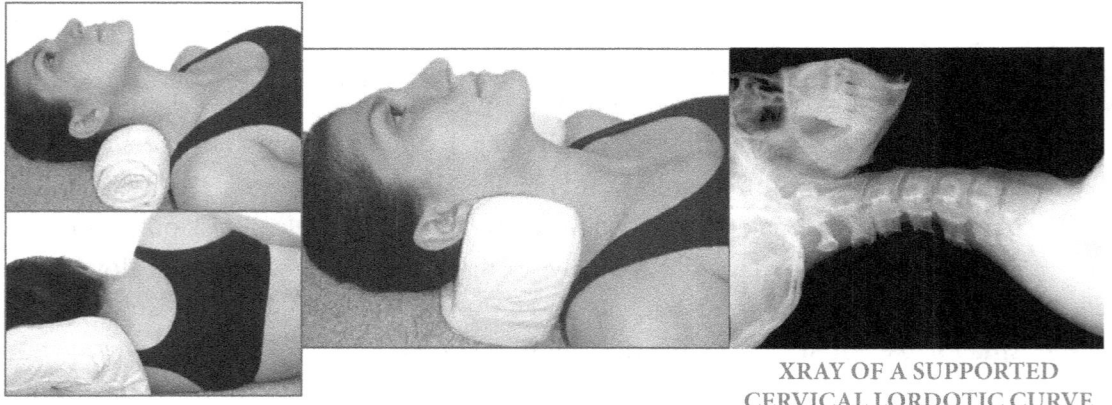

XRAY OF A SUPPORTED CERVICAL LORDOTIC CURVE

Correct Leg Position

Please keep in mind that regular bad posture while sleeping (or sitting) will nullify the efforts of your chiropractic treatments and destabalize muscles and ligaments from holding your spine in proper form. Help your chiropractor help you by adhering to correct body postures. You live in a world where the majority of your activities are done looking down (texting, reading, typing, etc.). Kyphotic (forward hunched) postures are made worse when you spend one-third of your life sleeping in improper positions.

Chapter 10:
Nutrition Guidelines for Increasing Chi Energy

"Let food be thy medicine and medicine be thy food."
~ Hippocrates, Father of Medicine, 431 B.C.

10.1 Acidosis - Starting Grounds for Dis-ease

When people feel pain, are distressed, or are grieving, they are exhibiting manifestation of the negative health cycle. A patient in less than optimum states is most likely starting - or already in - the process called the "acid state." You need to understand the basics of acidosis, as it is the root cause of all dis-ease afflicting us as humans. Our body works under a finely regulated homeostatic balance of acids and bases (a.k.a. alkalis) 24/7, 365 days a year. Our body also produces its own neutralizing buffers to keep the overall acidity under control. By encouraging a proper whole food diet and removing toxic loads through the "Remove" phase of care, the body is given a chance to come back to balance. The pH scale is measured from 0 to 14, with 7 being the neutral point. Substances that are below 7 are considered acidic and substances over 7 are considered alkaline or more basic (pH or "potential for hydrogen" is the given term to designate acidity or alkalinity). An internal environment like our body favors the alkaline side of the scale.

10.2 Does Negative Emotional Energy Contribute to Acidosis?

Any kind of negative emotion can tax body function, increase free radicals, and create acidity. An increase beyond normal amounts will lead to acidosis. Have you ever heard the saying, "I am sick to my stomach" or, "You will never amount to anything because you're stupid"? Statements like these create emotional states, which makes you highly prone to acidosis and sets the stage for dis-ease. Oftentimes, it is the fear (of rejection, rebuke, reprimand, etc., from your parents, friends, or peers) that sets you off on this negative energy phase. So choose the company of positive people who only talk of good things, and throw away the thoughts of fear and anger. Choose the path of love for both yourself and others!

10.3 Cleansing and Detoxification

"If ones bowels move, one is happy; and if they don't move, one is unhappy. That is all there is to it."
~ Lin Yutang

When performing a system of detox, it would be very wise to consider starting slowly. The body will go through withdrawal symptoms, especially if the patient is addicted to high glycemic carbohydrates, diet or caffeine drinks, nicotine, or alcohol. A successful program leads to release of toxins, harmful bacteria, parasites, and yeast overgrowth (*Candida*). This waste leaves the tissues and enters your blood stream as it travels for neutralization and elimination. Therefore, patients will usually experience issues like: fever, nausea, headaches, chills, ulcers, skin rashes, thirst, increased urination, loss of appetite, eye pain, difficulty sleeping, extreme drowsiness and fatigue, diarrhea, muscle soreness, lack of motivation, and any already known problems usually become heightened.

For example, a migraine or fatigue may become more intense than previously experienced, or a runny nose gets worse than before the detox. This detox side effect phenomenon is termed a 'healing crisis,' and generally lasts for a 1 to 2 week period after starting a detox. Although it may not seem like it at first, this is a good thing, as it means the body has begun cleaning up toxins and is removing impurities. Though after this beginning detox phase, 'healing' has not yet returned. Healing occurs after the toxins have been dealt with and the body can start to repair and rebuild in the healthier state.

We must remind ourselves of the many toxins we have come into contact with, and multiply that by the number of weeks, months, or years our body has suffered. We must further understand that getting healthy will not result from just a quick week's detox program. This is especially true in regards to cancer cleansing. The body suffers from a wide range of side effects, from radiation and chemotherapy treatments, in addition to trying to fight off cancer cells from the toxins that caused the cancer in the first place.

Therefore, as you go through your "healing crisis," expect to feel worse before you feel better as your body cleanses your "house." Follow your doctor's recommendations closely, and take the detox seriously, so that you may give your body all the time it needs to regain its health.

10.4 Home Detox Tips to Get Rid of Acidosis and Raise Chi Energy

Just because you're not sick doesn't mean you're healthy. Some are on the verge of sickness because of toxic living. Living in our first world country in the 21st century is not as clean as many may think. Our day-to-day living has toxic concerns hidden under the guise of "convenience." Imagine the small doses daily that eventually add up, and seemingly from out of nowhere, someone can get diagnosed with a seriously fatal dis-ease process. If unaware of the cause, it seems sudden - though the cause for what has manifested has been taking years, and many times decades, to compound toxicity. When the body's natural detoxing mechanisms are overpowered and drained, the body's next defense is to accumulate and store toxicity away from major organs into the surrounding tissues. Toxicity builds and the body then decays. Most, if not all health problems, are from one of two things: Not ENOUGH of a nutrient or substance the body needs, or TOO MUCH of what the body doesn't need. Let's discuss some hazards in the home that need your immediate attention.

- ✓ **Toothpaste** should contain no fluoride. Replace all future use of toothpaste with a non-fluorinated brand. Use soft toothbrushes, as they have flexible bristles that are easier on the gums and enamel.

- ✓ **Colognes and perfumes** should be made of natural botanical oils, not commercial store brands made in a lab. Chemicals unnatural to the body are absorbed by your skin and filtered by the lymph system. Overuse and accumulation of some of these chemicals will usually lead to skin, breast, and organ cancers.

- ✓ **Shampoos and conditioners** should be made from certified organic botanical ingredients, not brand commercial names with chemicals made in a lab. No parabens or laurel sulfates!

- ✓ **Shower filters** help remove chlorine and toxins contained in city water. They should be changed every six months to a year to keep hair and skin smooth and soft.

- ✓ **Reverse osmosis filtration** systems help drinking water stay healthy for human consumption by removing the fluoride and chlorine in the tap water. Tap water is just as bad as bottled water. Reverse osmosis with ozonation is the best way to purify water.

- ✓ **Throw out your microwave** and purchase a heat convection oven, as microwaving food has been linked with many types of cancers. Never microwave water (as in teas, etc.) and then drink it, as this may be linked to thyroid disorders.

- ✓ **Do not chew gum** that has aspartames or phenylketonurics, like Phenylalanine. They are proven to cause cancer in animals. Also many gums are made with rubber latex, which could trigger a latex reaction when used. Gum makers left natural gums because they wanted to say their gum did not cause cavities or tooth decay, but instead the artificial chemicals now give us much more to worry about than just bad teeth; they cause cancer. Another common poisonous artificial sweetener, saccharin, is proven to cause cancer of the uterus, bladder, skin, ovaries, and other organs in animal studies. In humans, bladder cancer occurrence is highly associated with the use of saccharin, which is disguised in gum, tabletop sweeteners, and "no-sugar-added" foods. Other chemicals linked to cancer in gum are BHT, propylgallate, acesulfame K, Red 40 Lake, Blue 1 Lake, maltitol, and the list goes on. Seek out natural gum without these ingredients; they do exist.

- ✓ **Detergents** What are you washing your clothes with? Commercial detergents have chemicals that may clean clothing but also cause cancers. Make sure you are using an earth-friendly detergent. Chemical detergents are notorious for causing all types of skin ailments, itching, color changes, and even cancers when exposure is long.
- ✓ **Garage chemicals** and **wash solvents** are highly toxic. That **new rug smell** is highly toxic. Factory chemicals on the rug gets released into the air and ends up also on the skin, causing massive allergies developed over time. **Flame retarding chemicals in mattresses and pillows** are highly toxic.
- ✓ **Avoid cooking with Teflon** anti-stick cookware, as it is highly toxic.

10.5 Overcoming the Deficiencies

The goal of this section is to help you understand why healthy eating is vitally important to both the healer and the patient. Both need the correct nourishment to manage energy for healing. Just as you cannot expect a garden to bear good yields with no water or seeds, you cannot expect healing to occur without the basic necessary ingredients in the body, our most precious garden. Unfortunately, the soil that gives our food the nutrients that we consume now has a major problem.

The soil of the United States is critically mineral deficient. In 1936, the United States Senate Document 264 highlighted the problem of depleted soil-borne micronutrient and trace minerals, concluding that the nation was coming into a crisis soon with serious mineral deficiency in its foods. America is currently in this crisis because we are growing nutrient deficient food from nutrient deficient soil, which produces nutrient deficient people and a drastic surge in mineral deficiency dis-eases! The study concluded: "Countless human ills stem from the fact that the impoverished soil of America no longer provides plant foods, with the mineral elements essential to human nourishment and health!" Between 1940 and 1991, statistics for both the UK and the US Government show degeneration in trace minerals of 76% in fruit and vegetables, according to The Journal of Complimentary Medicine.

We have indeed become a nutrient deficient country. Although we believe we are eating a healthy, nutrient rich diet, this is not the case when compared to the same food amounts and values seventy years ago. Nutrient deficient people exhibit nutrient deficiencies, and get sick much more often. It's a vicious cycle. It gets worse. It is a fact that people now are eating higher amounts of processed foods, and lower amounts of whole foods. Processed foods have been stripped of their nutrition and they are often filled with harmful ingredients such as herbicides, pesticides, fungicides, preservatives, artificial flavors and colors, unhealthy fats, high levels of sodium, and high levels of sugar. In addition, there are countless other chemical ingredients that are added to these foods to preserve shelf life "freshness" that can harm your health.

On the other hand, eating a diet full of fresh foods in their natural, unprocessed, or genetically modified form is a great way to prevent, reverse, regain, and maintain health. These foods are lower in calories and higher in nutrition; they contain vitamins and minerals that will improve health and prevent dis-ease. The Mediterranean diet has been linked to better health and dis-ease prevention, and many doctors recommend this diet. When people make the change to a more natural way of eating, they find that their overall health always improves.

When a person follows the Mediterranean diet, they eat vegetables and fruits, legumes, nuts, cereals, fish, and minimal amounts of alcohol. This diet focuses on a healthy ratio of monounsaturated and saturated fats, which has been shown to help prevent disease. In order to keep a healthy balance of these fats, it is important to focus on eating the healthy foods, as well as avoiding foods with unhealthy fats, such as heavy red meat, dairy, and certain types of vegetable oils. The following steps are recommended for an easy transition into your new and healthy diet regimen.

- Introduce a lot of variation in what you are eating. Boredom is a real issue, as it normally makes adherence to a diet regimen very difficult. You start with lots of hope, stick to the strict diet regimen for a few days, get frustrated, and then eat so much junk food that you undo all the good you achieved through your hard work. If you mix and match the healthy foods and give yourself lot of options on your menu, it will be that much easier for you to transition to your new diet, and then maintain it through your lifetime.

- Adequate amounts of protein and monounsaturated fatty acids in your diet are highly recommended, as you will get the correct nutrition and sense of satisfaction.
- Use various herbs and spices in your food, as this will add taste to your food and make them interesting and enjoyable to eat.
- Eliminate any kinds of processed food products, specifically the ones that have artificial coloring and flavoring components. It is also recommended to stay away from frozen food items, as they come with high amount of free radicals, which will compromise the alkalinity of your body. One big disadvantage of processed foods is that it makes your healthy food items tasteless and uninteresting, tempting you to cheat on your diet regimen.
- If you feel that you are not eating enough, include a lot of fruits and vegetables into your daily diet. They add roughage to your food content, which helps increase bowel movements, thus enhancing natural colon cleansing. The additional advantage of fruits and vegetables is that they are always low in calorie content, but rich in nutritional value. Fruit should also be part of all your daily diet.
- Above all, knowing why you are changing your diet and appreciating the cause wholeheartedly will tremendously help you in adhering to the new regimen. Remember, you made the choice to switch because your old dietary habits made you feel terrible. Hence, even if at the start you do not feel good about yourself, over time when you begin to feel healthy, you will enjoy your life more as your energy levels soar.

Unfortunately, practicality does not rule the society – money does – and as a result, over 80% of all food items you see in the store are processed. I call all processed convenience foods "junk foods," and highly suggest avoiding anything which has been artificially sweetened, inclusive of soft drinks, ice-creams, chocolates and candies, diet or normal pastries, and processed cereals. For them to be digested and absorbed by the body, they depend on other food items you intake. For example, if you are eating a lot of protein but not enough fat, then you do not have enough metabolic energy to utilize the entire protein intake. Hence, avoid empty calorie foods because they completely degrade your metabolism.

It is also highly recommended that you stay away from food items that your body hints you are allergic to. Typical allergic reactions your body gives you are: coughing, mucus or phlegm production, sneezing, difficulty breathing or swallowing, skin rashes, face swelling, watery eyes, and fever. These symptoms are commonly seen a few minutes after consuming processed dairy drinks or foods, like milkshakes or cheesecake. Acidic, genetically modified, and processed foods are void of good energy and deplete the body's resources, as they are toxic and must be cleansed. An excellent alkaline substance that helps neutralize and energize the body from acidity is chlorophyll.

10.6 Chlorophyll – The Green Blood

Chlorophyll is a pigment in plants, often referred to as plant blood. Chlorophyll is like the hemoglobin in our red blood cells; the protein that carries oxygen to all tissues of the body through our circulatory system. Chlorophyll's green color is what makes plants appear green, and coincidentally, green is often associated with the color of healing. Mother Nature keeps the best healing secrets! Chlorophyll is housed in little organelles called chloroplasts, which use sun energy to synthesize food for the plants; something we humans just can't do. They're considered the number one position in the food chain because of this, and they use carbon dioxide to make their food, while giving off oxygen in the process for us. We can also drink Chlorophyll to stimulate our lungs, blood, and intestines. Chlorophyll can halt foul mouth odor, slow down growth of putrefactive gut bacteria, impede bacterial growth in the body, prevent gum diseases, and even accelerate wound healing!

10.7 Nutritional and Habitual Tips *to Grow Your Natural Chi*

"He who takes medicine and neglects to diet wastes the skill of his doctors."
~ Chinese Proverb

In order to be able to efficiently send, receive, and regulate energy flow for healing, you need to have an ample supply of living energy in your body. Deciding to eat and drink a cleaner existence will keep energy levels heightened. Here are some big tips for getting the energy edge.

- ✓ **Get chiropractic adjustments regularly.** <u>This is the basis of fully expressing your life force and cannot be understated.</u> Getting adjusted regularly by a qualified chiropractor ensures that full nerve supply to different pH-regulating organs is uninhibited. Spinal adjustments will also improve your respiration and oxygen intake, thus contributing to boosting alkalinity and spinal chi.
- ✓ **Eat living enzymes found in vegetables and fruits.** It is important to cultivate more chi in your body through whole living foods. You cannot eat dead energy and expect it to be a source of life. Steam your vegetables; be sure not to overcook

them. Cooking food kills enzymes and denatures the proteins needed for vitality. No foods should be cooked to a charred black color, as this burdens the body when metabolizing the breakdown of the food.

- ✓ **Avoid eating pork or beef.** Bad animal raising and feeding conditions, cruel methods of death, and pain inflicted on animals as they suffer all are infused into the energy state of the meat. Eat quinoa, brown rice, beans, and feta or goat cheese in very small portions, once or twice a week. Seafood is an excellent source of clean protein. Stay away from squid and shrimp, shellfish, or anything that lives off the bottom of the ocean, as they tend to be more toxic. Keep in mind that wild caught, non-coastal fish can be a great source of protein, and should be eaten on a regular basis. Some healthy fish that are less likely to have high levels of toxins include: mullet, oyster, catfish, flounder, herring, anchovies, pollock, haddock, hake, pink/sockeye salmon, tilapia, whitefish, cod and calamari.

- ✓ **Drink lots of water.** Keeping hydrated allows acids to flow out easier, and also maintains normal blood pH and viscosity. Blood and water conduct the chi energy, which is how chi travels through the body. Food, water, and air all need to be as clean as possible. Saturated fats and cholesterol clog the arteries and veins so water helps push and flow impurities along for excretion. Those living in a constant state of dehydration cause unnecessary wear-and-tear on their body. Water should not be served too cold or too hot, just regular room temperature. Extreme temperature shocks the body and it has to use its own energy to bring back homeostasis. Luke warm liquids are best, as they won't shock your system. There are many formulas for what and how you should drink. Some authorities claim you should drink at least half your body weight in ounces every day. If you weigh one hundred twenty five pounds, you need to drink a minimum of 62.5 ounces of purified water a day. There are a few important benefits to drinking a lot of water, including: metabolism optimization, nutrient absorption, body temperature regulation, reduced muscle fatigue and blood pressure regulation. Under stress, the body needs much more water. If levels drop past normal range, you get classic symptoms of dehydration: headaches, brain fog, dry skin, intestinal troubles and muscle pains - just for starters.

- ✓ **Load up on antioxidants.** Antioxidants like vitamins C and E promote health and youthfulness by fighting and preventing disease. They are basically your army of good nutrients, fighting against the bad things that are happening, or could happen, in your body. One of the main functions of antioxidants is to clean up free radicals and prevent them from causing damage to your body. Antioxidants are found in fresh, natural foods such as fruits and vegetables, nuts and seeds, etc. Vitamin C sources: strawberries, tomatoes, broccoli, leafy green vegetables, and any type of citrus fruits such as mandarins, tangerines, oranges, grapefruits, etc. Vitamin E sources: Leafy green vegetables such as spinach, chard, collard greens, kale, etc. Also, wheat germ, almonds, walnuts, avocado, and many types of seeds. Beta-Carotene sources: Any type of orange colored fruit or vegetable, including squash, carrots, apricots, peppers, cantaloupe, pumpkin, sweet potatoes, etc. Additionally, leafy green vegetables provide beta-carotene, so eat lots of collard greens, romaine, spinach, kale, etc. Sources of selenium: whole grains and nuts, such as whole wheat bread, brown rice, oatmeal, brazil nuts, and walnuts.

- ✓ **Master emotional stability.** Emotions and feelings are the guiding system of a healer, and you must not be emotionally disturbed when involved in using your energy in healing yourself or others. Healers should seek out other practitioners, and each should work with one another in accepting and receiving healing. Healers understand that energy must cycle, and thus allow receiving as well as giving to occur. KNER™ in part 4, Reset, of the Kousouli® Method, helps patients stabilize emotional energy.

- ✓ **Breathe fresh air deeply for good chi.** If you move your shoulders or upper chest while breathing deeply, you are not cultivating correctly your breath. Adults who harbor lots of stress usually have shallow breathing and must re-learn to breathe like they did as a newborn - from the diaphragm. Air pollution also means a lot of our body's energy goes into detoxifying the air we're breathing in. Limit your exposure from air pollution such as: enclosed crowded office buildings, damp/musty, or moldy air in the home or basement, synthetic furniture or carpet smells, air fresheners, garages, factories, chemical colognes and perfumes, etc. All the aforementioned are known causes of acidosis and inflammation in the body. Your bedroom air should be as close to clean country air as possible. It is difficult to alkalize your body when you are breathing in toxic city air.

- ✓ **Get proper sleep every night.** Even though there are plenty of drugs on the market to help a person sleep, undesirable side effects often follow. Natural supplements are a far better alternative if you are having a hard time sleeping. The following is a list of supplements that can be taken to reduce stress and improve sleeping patterns. Check with your doctor for dosage: L-Tryptophan, L-Theanine, GABA, B Vitamins - B2, B3, B6, B12, Magnesium, Choline Bitartrate, Inositol, Vinpocetine, Melatonin, Galantamine, 5-*hydroxytryptophan* (5-HTP), DMAE and Gingko-Biloba. Also review sections 9.7 and 9.8.

- ✓ **Meditate.** Meditate throughout the day. It is best to meditate in the morning between the hours of 4 to 7am. Nighttime meditation is more difficult for two reasons: Difficulty concentrating may happen, as your mind is full of the day's stress, and because you are more apt to fall asleep rather than keeping attentive focus on creating. When you meditate at night, burn a little sage and say a prayer to clear your space and set the intention prior to beginning. Places where there are a lot of plants and vegetation are great for meditation, as the positive chi surrounds you. Masters throughout the centuries have been known to pray and meditate in gardens. The flow of good energy in a garden or forest is far higher vibration than that of a city or urban setting.

"In a disordered mind, as in a disordered body, soundness of health is impossible."
~ Cicero

- ✓ **Be aware of your energy exit points.** Chi is believed to exit the body through the hair ends, the forehead, the throat, the palms, the fingertips, blood loss, menstruation, and semen secretion through the penis.

- ✓ **Learn sexual restraint when applicable.** Cultivating your sexual energy is very important to being able to maintain balanced energy reserves for healing. Transference of sexual energy with another disciplined and knowledgeable partner is a very positive activity, which can enhance the sacral and root chakra centers. A healthy sexual appetite is important; however overindulgence or misuse of this energy can block chi flow and bring on chronic fatigue. For an in depth explanation read *BE A MASTER® OF SEX ENERGY, to learn how to focus your orgasmic chi energy, hypnotize your lover, make your relationships better, and so much more!*

- ✓ **Do not over eat.** The source of inner power integration is in the area of the solar plexus. Your personal energy is processed here and harvested. Nutrients go into your small intestines, which transfers to the blood and then the heart pumps the nutrients out to all cells. Overeating overloads the body's resources for food metabolism, and redirects blood to the gut instead of the muscles, causing you to fatigue. You want to avoid heavy oily and fried foods, as this brings acidity to the body which must defend itself from the intrusion. The body loses chi, adjusting itself back to homeostasis.

- ✓ **No canned energy or coffee drinks.** Phosphoric acid is in sodas and causes havoc in the body. Instead, load up on green drinks that contain chlorophyll. Sugar energy drinks and caffeinated drinks are horrible for your personal chi because it burns your adrenal system out and imbalances your personal chi flow. The longer it is disturbed, the longer it will take to recuperate the body.

- ✓ **Snack on seaweed.** Although an acquired taste, edible seaweed has remarkable vitamins and minerals from the ocean, and is powerful for self-healing and chi boosting. Kale and other dark green vegetables are also amazing chi boosters.

- ✓ **Eat more super foods.** Most American diets are missing the nutrients of super foods like Omega-3 fatty acids, which have a strong effect on a person's health. Omega-3s are found in sardines, mackerel, herring, and salmon (wild-caught cold water fish is healthier than farmed), walnuts, flaxseeds, and soybeans. Quinoa is very high in protein, selenium, vitamin E, and zinc. A small daily half-cup amount of chestnuts and blueberries will help improve your overall health also. Blueberries have phytoflavonoids, vitamin C, antioxidants, and potassium, plus they're a strong anti-inflammatory food, which helps reduce cancer and heart disease risks. Eating beans and green leafy vegetables are vital because they provide protein, phytonutrients, fiber and antioxidants, increase oxygen levels in the blood, and can help lower cholesterol.

- ✓ **Eat anti-inflammatory foods high in chi and supplement correctly.** Taken together, docosahexaenoic acid (known as DHA, an omega-3 fatty acid) and eicosapentaenoic acid (known as EPA, another omega-3 fatty acid) are a powerful anti-inflammatory supplement combination found in fish oil! They work together to regulate brain chemicals and repair body damage. Other healthy anti-inflammatory oils include: rice bran oil, grape seed oil, olive oil, and walnut oil. The best anti-inflammatory herbs are: ginger, basil, cloves, parsley, rosemary, cilantro, oregano, cinnamon, mint, turmeric, and boswellia. Vegetables that lower inflammation are: cauliflower, cabbage, chard, rhubarb, collards, sweet potato, green beans, broccoli, yams, Japanese pumpkin, spinach, fennel bulb, and onion. Fruits that help you heal faster are: avocado, apple, blueberries, blackberries, black currants, guava, mulberries, raspberries, kumquat, pomegranate, cherries, and pineapple. Add powerful nuts, beans, and seeds that boost antioxidants and reduce inflammation like; almonds, hazelnuts, walnuts, mung beans, split peas, flax seeds, lentils, sunflower seeds, pumpkin seeds, and soy beans. When healing or recovering from surgery, you will want to avoid foods that cause more inflammation such as: cow milk and dairy, processed and refined foods, potato, tomato, eggplant, frozen foods with trans fats, bell pepper, sugar, coffee, alcohol, and red meat. The best anti-inflammatory supplements will contain vitamins, minerals, micronutrients, and healthy fats, such as: omega-3, flaxseed oil, or fish oil supplements. These supplements can be found in a liquid or capsule form, and you should be taking at least 2-3 grams per day.

- ✓ **Chew fully and take your time eating.** Food is very often eaten in a rushed state, as we hurry to work or our next important destination. Many people eat their meals quickly while doing something else at the same time. This habit of multi-tasking while eating actually causes the mind to register stress, putting pressure on the entire body. That daily stress pattern over time can cause chronic health problems in the gut.

- ✓ **Do not drink cow's milk or dairy.** Research has clearly shown that drinking cow milk can cause anemia, bloating, gas, migraines, indigestion, asthma, prostate cancer, and serious allergies - just to name a few symptoms. Try switching to coconut, almond, hemp, or rice milk found in the non-dairy section – they are a far healthier choice.

- ✓ **Do not drink carbonated drinks.** Our bodies do not derive any valuable nutrition from carbonated sodas. Consuming sodas on a regular basis can set you up for long-term chronic dis-ease, like diabetes and osteoporosis. The pH of carbonated soda is 2.8, very acidic and opposite the flow of alkaline health.

- ✓ **Connect with the ground - go barefoot.** When we think about the amount of time our feet do not make contact with the earth because of shoes, we start to realize that we may be cutting ourselves off from important energy that our body needs for health. It's no surprise a brisk barefoot walk on the beach, or through our grassy back yard, has recharging powers. When we wear footwear that insulates the foot, we block out the conductive power of Mother Earth to our leg channels. This process is called "grounding," or "earthing," and is vital in maintaining a high level of chi and health.

- ✓ **Exercise is vital for chi flow.** The body must recycle its energy or it will stagnate.

It is important you revolve and flow the body energy in a productive manner. As long as the cycle of personal chi is used in constructive ways, it will build and stay strong. The better the flow, the better one's health. A significant factor in dis-ease risk is the nature of a person's day-to-day activities. Our modern world of technological convenience has made us move less. As a result, the muscle-wasting effects of a sedentary lifestyle are becoming more and more common. Many people start exercising simply because they want to lose weight, but there are actually many other reasons that a person should exercise on a regular basis. Aerobic exercise three times a week, for twenty minutes each day, is a good place to start.

Benefits of regular exercise include:
- Increased chi energy, blood flow, and alertness
- Lower risk of diabetes
- Control of blood lipid levels/lower high triglyceride levels
- Increased HDL levels (good cholesterol)
- Reduced risk of various forms of cancer
- Builds healthy muscles, bones, and joints
- Lowered risk of stroke
- Decreased risk of obesity
- Lowered blood pressure
- Increased muscle strength and flexibility
- Combating osteoporosis
- Increased oxygen and alkalinity throughout the body
- Psychological improvements (reduction of depression, anxiety, etc.)
- Increases mood and helps keep lifestyle active
- Improves social skills and builds community when done in groups.

PART IV:
TRANSFORMATION – 'Awe'-waken Your Power

*"If anything is possible for man, and peculiar to him,
think that this can be attained by thee."*
~ Marcus Aurelius

Just when you think it's smooth sailing, something challenging happens. You get a scary diagnosis, or start fearing one. Your aging face and thickening waist stare back at you in the mirror. Aches and pains appear out of nowhere. Perhaps it is not just the physical; you're hurting inside too. Emotions and feelings that have been long suppressed cry for release, and your tolerance for stress decreases. Your spirit no longer settles for the status quo and demands to be heard, as priorities begin to change.

In times like this, you want answers and you want help, but it is difficult to know where to turn. There is so much conflicting information out there, which only adds to your feelings of overwhelm and confusion. Try as you might to change, old habits of mind and body refuse to budge; positive, permanent change and evolution seem to elude you. Know this: You do not have to stay stuck. In this section, you will get all the information and the tools you need to create the healthy, happy life you desire with greater ease.

In the rest of the book, you will learn what other intellectuals, philosophers, and "the greats" in history knew - that their connection to God allowed them to do great things. Their wisdom reflects the original wisdom left for us by historical biblical writings. Let their truths become your newfound awareness, and use them as aids in your spiritual development. I advise all who read this book to always keep an open mind, filter the information, and use your own soul experience to arrive at your personal truth. To develop a more positive mental attitude that serves you and shifts you from negative programing, you should use the mentioned techniques regularly to allow less stress and more joy. You will be walking on the sunny side of the street after you shed the weight that keeps you from leaping forward.

Chapter 11:
Spiritual Wisdom and Laws that Allow Your Abundance

"A sad soul can kill you quicker than a germ."
~ John Steinbeck

The Bible has withstood the test of time, as it has powerful lessons in it that teach us how to succeed while incarnated in this earthly realm. Some claim that the Old and New Testaments of the Bible are the ultimate guidebooks for attaining compassionate awareness and the wisdom of the God-Self. 2,000 plus years ago, and still to this day, the teacher Christ is believed to have quite possibly been the most connected human to the source of ultimate power, or God force - The Creator - The Father. No matter what set of religious rules or doctrines you follow, you can gain benefit from Christ's teachings. The wisdom of Christ and the gospel writings have echoed over the centuries in the words of many leaders throughout time, despite their religious backgrounds or faith doctrine. In the next few sections, you will find a number of quotes that resonate with Christ's teachings, showing that the themes of his lessons span the test of time, regardless of the individual, culture, or religion.

11.1 About Confidence

"You gain strength, courage and confidence by every experience in which you really stop to look fear in the face. You are able to say to yourself, 'I have lived through this horror. I can take the next thing that comes along.' You must do the thing you think you cannot do."
~ Eleanor Roosevelt

"The LORD is my light and my salvation; whom shall I fear? The LORD is the strength of my life; of whom shall I be afraid? Though a host should encamp against me, my heart shall not fear: though war should rise against me, in this will I be confident."
~ Psalm 27:1,3

"Regardless of how you feel inside, always try to look like a winner. Even if you are behind, a sustained look of control and confidence can give you a mental edge that results in victory."
~ Diane Arbus

"For the Lord shall be thy confidence, and shall keep thy foot from being taken."
~ Proverbs 3:26

"Remember that wherever your heart is, there you will find your treasure."
~ Paulo Coelho, The Alchemist

"But they that wait upon the Lord shall renew their strength; they shall mount up with wings as eagles; they shall run, and not be weary; and they shall walk, and not faint."
~ Isaiah 40:31

"Man often becomes what he believes himself to be. If I keep on saying to myself that I cannot do a certain thing, it is possible that I may end by really becoming incapable of doing it. On the contrary, if I have the belief that I can do it, I shall surely acquire the capacity to do it even if I may not have it at the beginning."
~ Ghandi

"Nay, in all these things we are more than conquerors through Him that loved us."
~ Romans 8:37

"Skill and confidence are an unconquered army."
~ George Herbert

"Success is most often achieved by those who don't believe that failure is inevitable."
~ Coco Chanel

"Attempt easy tasks as if they were difficult, and difficult as if they were easy; in the one case that confidence may not fall asleep, in the other that it may not be dismayed."
~ Baltasar Gracian

"I can do all things through Christ which strengthens me."
~ Philippians 4:13

"Success is not final, failure is not fatal: it is the courage to continue that counts."
~ Winston Churchill

"They can do all because they think they can."
~ Virgil

"Cast not away therefore your confidence, which hath great recompense of reward. For ye have need of patience, that, after ye have done the will of God, ye might receive the promise."
~ Hebrews 10:35, 36

"Optimism is the faith that leads to achievement. Nothing can be done without hope and confidence."
~ Helen Keller

"We either make ourselves miserable, or we make ourselves strong. The amount of work is the same."
~ Carlos Castaneda

"Besides pride, it is loyalty, discipline, heart, mind, and confidence that's the key to all the locks."
~ Joe Paterno

"Believe in yourself! Have faith in your abilities! Without a humble but reasonable confidence in your own powers you cannot be successful or happy."
~ Norman Vincent Peale

"No one can make you feel inferior without your consent."
~ Eleanor Roosevelt

"The man of genius inspires us with a boundless confidence in our own powers."
~ Ralph Waldo Emerson

11.2 About Courage

"It takes courage to grow up and become who you really are."
~ E.E. Cummings

"He giveth power to the faint; and to them that have no might he increases strength."
~ Isaiah 40:29

"Life shrinks or expands in proportion to one's courage."
~ Anaïs Nin

"For I am persuaded, that neither death, nor life, nor angels, nor principalities, nor powers, nor things present, nor things to come, Nor height, nor depth, nor any other creature, shall be able to separate us from the love of God which is in Christ Jesus our Lord."
~ Romans 8:38,39

"If you develop the absolute sense of certainty that powerful beliefs provide, then you can get yourself to accomplish virtually anything, including those things that other people are certain are impossible."
~ Tony Robbins

"Be of good courage, and he shall strengthen your heart, all ye that hope in the Lord."
~ Psalm 31:24

"Seeds of discouragement will not grow in the thankful heart. Discouragement is not the absence of adequacy but the absence of courage."
~ Neal A. Maxwell

"A great deal of talent is lost to the world for want of a little courage. Every day sends to their graves obscure men whose timidity prevented them from making a first effort."
~ Sydney Smith

"Fear thou not: for I am with thee: be not dismayed; for I am thy God: I will strengthen thee; yea, I will help thee; yea, I will uphold thee with the right hand of my righteousness."
~ Isaiah 41:10

"As long as I can remember I feel I have had this great creative and spiritual force within me that is greater than faith, greater than ambition, greater than confidence, greater than determination, greater than vision. It is all these combined. My brain becomes magnetized with this dominating force which I hold in my hand."
~ Bruce Lee

"It ain't what they call you, it's what you answer to."
~ W.C. Fields

"Do not miscalculate your self-worth by multiplying your insecurities."
~ Dodinsky

> "Nothing splendid has ever been achieved except by those who dared believe that something inside of them was superior to circumstance."
> ~ Bruce Barton

11.3 Overcoming Confusion

> "Trust in the LORD with all thine heart; and lean not unto thine own understandings. In all thy ways acknowledge him, and he shall direct thy paths."
> ~ Proverbs 3:5,6

> "There is no worse screen to block out the Spirit than confidence in our own intelligence."
> ~ John Calvin

> "The man who acquires the ability to take full possession of his own mind may take possession of anything else to which he is justly entitled."
> ~ Andrew Carnegie

> "For God is not the author of confusion, but of peace."
> ~ I Corinthians 14:33

> "It is not the mountain we conquer, but ourselves."
> ~ Edmund Hillary

> "We have to learn to be our own best friends because we fall too easily into the trap of being our own worst enemies."
> ~ Roderick Thorp

> "And we know that all things work together for good to them that love God, to them who are the called according to his purpose."
> ~ Romans 8:28

> "No man has the right to dictate what other men should perceive, create or produce, but all should be encouraged to reveal themselves, their perceptions and emotions, and to build confidence in the creative spirit."
> ~ Ansel Adams

"It took me a long time not to judge myself through someone else's eyes."
~ Sally Field

"I will instruct thee and teach thee in the way which thou shalt go: I will guide thee with mine eye."
~ Psalm 32:8

"If any of you lack wisdom, let him ask of God, that giveth to all men liberally, and upbraideth not; and it shall be given him."
~ James 1:5

11.4 Overcoming Discouragement or Fear

"Because he hath set his love upon me, therefore will I deliver him: I will set him on high, because he hath known my name. He shall call upon me, and I will answer him: I will be with him in trouble; I will deliver him, and honour him."
~ Psalm 91:14,15

"What we do not see, what most of us never suspect of existing, is the silent but irresistible power which comes to the rescue of those who fight on in the face of discouragement."
~ Napoleon Hill

"Peace, I leave with you, my peace I give unto you: not as the world giveth, give I unto you. Let not your heart be troubled, neither let it be afraid."
~ John 14:27

"Nobody else can make us discouraged; it is a choice that we alone make when facing disappointments. Disappointments will come and go, but discouragement is a choice that only you make."
~ Dr. Charles Stanley

"We are troubled on every side, yet not distressed; we are perplexed, but not in despair; Persecuted, but not forsaken; cast down, but not destroyed."
~ II Corinthians 4:8, 9

"In spite of everything I shall rise again: I will take up my pencil, which I have forsaken in my great discouragement, and I will go on with my drawing."
~ Vincent Van Gogh

"For God hath not given us the spirit of fear; but of power, and of love, and of a sound mind."
~ II Timothy 1:7

"In God have I put my trust: I will not be afraid what man can do unto me."
~ Psalm 56:11

In depth: Trust in worldly security gives you absolutely no security; everything changes; the seasons change, the day becomes night, the days turn into years, your hair turns grey, your clothing wears out, money is lost, homes fall. How can we hold onto security and think nothing will change? How do you get security in an insecure world? The only way is to believe in the power inside you, the power put there by your maker.

"There is no fear in love; but perfect love casteth out fear: because fear hath torment. He that feareth is not made perfect in love."
~ I John 4:18

In depth: When you feel fear, you must claim it so that it does not bite, much like a snake. Claim it, know it is there, and know you hold it as your truth in the moment. Honor that you feel it, and then you can take actions to clear it. Do not let fear become an ever-escaping ghost in your life, as it will surely frighten you out of living a fruitful life. Bring the dark into the light – in the light you can expose the issues and remove perception of power that fear holds over you. Love is not where fear lives, and fear is not where love is. As long as you believe in fear, you cannot create or heal freely to bring the manifestation you wish for. The only real thing is your mind, beliefs, and perceptions. Truth is only within you. God is where you are, as God is in you, through you, and "of" you.

Some common fears that plague mankind are:

- Fear of death (the unknown)
- Fear of being alone, or seclusion (being unloved, deserted)
- Fear of ill health (being dependent on others)
- Fear of poverty (lacking, being without)
- Fear of exposure (humiliation, being disgraced)
- Fear of failure (being unloved, not good enough)
- Fear of success (more responsibility, lack of freedom)

Which of the above do you feel has control over you in your life? Fear can take the largest champion and beat him into defeat, or take a seemingly courageous person and turn him or her into a coward in the blink of an eye. The frequency of fear is like a silent dis-ease that sneaks into the mind and soul, planting itself as a poison so great, and so potent, that if not cleansed prior to taking root, it will wreak havoc on the man or woman it has imprisoned. The craziest thing about fear is that it only exists when it is perceived as, or believed to be, real.

However, fear may not be *all* bad. In war, fear can be a valuable resource for winning a battle when implementing it against an enemy, and it can also save lives on the battlefield. Fear can also cause you to look both ways before you cross a potentially hazardous roadway, helping you make a safe crossing. What we want to differentiate here is incorrectly placed fear (which is destructive) from that which is constructive. When fear is not constructive to your goals, it is a killer. Your beliefs and perceptions once again come into play here.

So how do you use the power of fear to change the way energy flows to you? Put it to work for you – that's how. Make it an employee rather than making it your boss. Fear now is on your payroll. <u>Fear works for you</u>, and it's a hard worker. See fear as an opportunity to bring out the unexpected good possibilities in life. Instead of fearing you won't be able to pay the rent next month, you may decide to fear having more than enough, to pay not only next month's rent but also the next month's rent, and so on. You can even be fearful that your landlord may not be able to accept your advanced check for rent for the whole year, and he will be shocked when you say, "I hope it's okay, but can I give you payment for the year now?" Your landlord may be fearful of even accepting your check because of his own insecurities - that you're pulling his leg or that maybe the check will bounce if he cashed it. Fear is now working for you. I admit that this is not an everyday reaction to a situation if you may be facing eviction because you can't pay rent next month, but this is the very turning point that either makes positive creation with favorable outcomes happen (or not happen) for you. When you "re-act" (acting the same way and getting the same outcome as before), you will declare the future and outcome. If you dare take the suggestion to change the way you think about the situation or observe the expected outcome, then you dare to create or "act out" your future in the way you want it to be. Everything you experience now is about your creation, and this example of decision-making at critical moments is no less important than any of the other examples or tactics mentioned in this book. Every moment, you are co-creating your future. You're even doing it right now – by choosing to read this book.

Eliminate the "paper tiger" called fear – it can't harm you, no matter what shape it comes in. Love eliminates it immediately. Jesus Christ said he is the Son of God, and so are you the son or daughter of God - the Father. Jesus told people that they could do and be the same as him. He told people to follow him to God, and that He is the way. He was telling the truth - not out of ego or by proclaiming himself as King, but as the *example*. Christ showed what is possible when humans exercise their highest vibration of love to govern their lives, and how to live a full potential life without suffering or pain.

11.5 About Love

"If you must love your neighbor as yourself, it is at least as fair to love yourself as your neighbor."
~ Nicholas de Chamfort

"Owe no one anything, except to love each other, for the one who loves another has fulfilled the law."
~ Romans 13:8

"The first question which the priest and the Levite asked was: 'If I stop to help this man, what will happen to me?' But...the good Samaritan reversed the question: 'If I do not stop to help this man, what will happen to him?'"
~ Martin Luther King, Jr.

"For you were called to freedom, brothers. Only do not use your freedom as an opportunity for the flesh, but through love serve one another."
~ Galatians 5:13

"If you wish to befriend someone, look for a person who loves first God then themselves. If they love God, they will be able to love their neighbor, too."
~ Peter Deunov

"Having purified your souls by your obedience to the truth for a sincere brotherly love, love one another earnestly from a pure heart."
~ 1 Peter 1:22

"The Lord commands us to do good unto all men without exception, though the majority are very undeserving when judged according to their own merits... [The Scripture] teaches us that we must not think of man's real value, but only of his creation in the image of God to which we owe all possible honor and love."
~ John Calvin

"Beloved, let us love one another, for love is from God, and whoever loves has been born of God and knows God. He that loveth not, knoweth not God; for God is love."
~ 1 John 4:7-8

"If we are to love our neighbors, before doing anything else we must see our neighbors. With our imagination as well as our eyes, that is to say like artists, we must see not just their faces but the life behind and within their faces. Here it is love that is the frame we see them in."
~ Frederick Buechner

"Let us love one another so that we may in one mind confess Father, Son, and Holy Spirit - the Trinity, ONE in essence and undivided."
~ Eastern Orthodox Liturgy

"Let us always meet each other with a smile, for the smile is the beginning of love."
~ Mother Teresa

"Love is patient and kind; love does not envy or boast; it is not arrogant or rude. It does not insist on its own way; it is not irritable or resentful; it does not rejoice at wrongdoing, but rejoices with the truth. Love bears all things, believes all things, hopes all things, endures all things. Love never ends. As for prophecies, they will pass away; as for tongues, they will cease; as for knowledge, it will pass away."
~ 1 Corinthians 13:4-8

"Love is life. And if you miss love, you miss life."
~ Leo Buscaglia

"You have heard that it was said, 'You shall love your neighbor and hate your enemy.' But I say to you, Love your enemies and pray for those who persecute you, so that you may be sons of your Father who is in heaven. For he makes his sun rise on the evil and on the good, and sends rain on the just and on the unjust. For if you love those who love you, what reward do you have? Do not even the tax collectors do the same? And if you greet only your brothers, what more are you doing than others? Do not even the Gentiles do the same? You therefore must be perfect, as your heavenly Father is perfect."
~ Matthew 5:43-48

In depth: If someone loves you because you do good things for them, or you are beautiful, then they love you based on some manifested reality that is tangible. This is conditional. The soul loves with energy before it is manifested, living in a place of pure potential. The soul sees every option. This means that the soul is powerful to create all things. Our rational conscious mind is unable to comprehend this. To unconditionally love, we must look past the physical 5 senses and practice upon what we in western society actually do very little of: daily meditation and prayer. We should be aware of our physical senses, but we have little power when we do not exercise the arena of where power actually comes from; prior to being power - in the manifested physical.

"And one of the scribes came up and heard them disputing with one another, and seeing that he answered them well, asked him, "Which commandment is the most important of all?" Jesus answered, "The most important is, 'Hear, O Israel: The Lord our God, the Lord is one. And you shall love the Lord your God with all your heart and with all your soul and with all your mind and with all your strength."
~ Mark 12:28-30

"Eventually you will come to understand that love heals everything, and love is all there is."
~ Gary Zukav

"For God so loved the world, that he gave his only Son, that whoever believes in him should not perish but have eternal life."
~ John 3:16

"God loves you just the way you are, but He refuses to leave you that way. He wants you to be just like Jesus."
~ Max Lucado

"As the Father has loved me, so have I loved you. Abide in my love. If you keep my commandments, you will abide in my love, just as I have kept my Father's commandments and abide in his love. These things I have spoken to you, that my joy may be in you, and that your joy may be full. This is my commandment, that you love one another as I have loved you. Greater love has no one than this, that someone lay down his life for his friends. You are my friends if you do what I command you. No longer do I call you servants, for the servant does not know what his master is doing; but I have called you friends, for all that I have heard from my Father I have made known to you. You did not choose me, but I chose you and appointed you that you should go and bear fruit and that your fruit should abide, so that whatever you ask the Father in my name, he may give it to you. These things I command you, so that you will love one another."
~ John 15:9-17

"God is subtle, but not malicious."
~ Albert Einstein

"No, in all these things we are more than conquerors through him who loved us. For I am sure that neither death nor life, nor angels nor rulers, nor things present nor things to come, nor powers, nor height nor depth, nor anything else in all creation, will be able to separate us from the love of God in Christ Jesus our Lord."
~ Romans 8:37-39

"Blessed is the influence of one true, loving human soul on another."
~ George Eliot

"See what kind of love the Father has given to us, that we should be called children of God; and so we are. The reason why the world does not know us is that it did not know him."
~ 1 John 3:1

"The hunger for love is much more difficult to remove than the hunger for bread."
~ Mother Teresa

"Complete my joy by being of the same mind, having the same love, being in full accord and of one mind."
~ Philippians 2:2

"I believe in the compelling power of love. I do not understand it. I believe it to be the most fragrant blossom of all this thorny existence."
~ Theodore Dreiser

"Hatred stirs up strife, but love covers all offenses."
~ Proverbs 10:12

"The way to love anything is to realize that it may be lost."
~ G.K. Chesterton

11.6 About Perseverance

"Wait on the LORD: be of good courage, and he shall strengthen thine heart: wait, I say, on the LORD."
~ Psalm 27:14

"When you come to the end of your rope, tie a knot and hang on."
~ Franklin D. Roosevelt

"He that tilleth his land shall have plenty of bread: but he that followeth after vain persons shall have poverty enough."
~ Proverbs 28:19

"If you are going through hell, keep going."
~ Winston Churchill

"He that endureth to the end shall be saved."
~ Matthew 10:22

"Paralyze resistance with persistence."
~ Woody Hayes

"Let us not be weary in well doing: for in due season we shall reap, if we faint not."
~ Galatians 6:9

> *"If we are facing in the right direction, all we have to do is keep on walking."*
> ~ Buddhist Proverb

> *"Blessed is the man that endureth temptation: for when he is tried, he shall receive the crown of life, which the Lord hath promised to them that love him."*
> ~ James 1:12

> *"I am a slow walker, but I never walk backwards."*
> ~ Abraham Lincoln

> *"Be thou faithful unto death, and I will give thee a crown of life."*
> ~ Revelation 2:10

> *"Persistence is to the character of man as carbon is to steel."*
> ~ Napoleon Hill

> *"Commit thy way unto the LORD; trust also in him; and he shall bring it to pass."*
> ~ Psalm 37:5

> *"We can always redeem the man who aspires and strives."*
> ~ Johann Wolfgang von Goethe

11.7 About Success and Prosperity

God wants you to be wealthy and prosperous so that you can do his will, and to spread wealth and prosperity to others. It is absurd to think that a loving God would want you to have anything less than all the best, or would allow you to suffer without meeting your needs. When you serve others in love, wealth (in many forms) will come to you. Enlightened souls that concentrate on gratitude and faith manifest what they need, as they need it, and have few worries in life. Unenlightened souls who worry, fear, and gripe usually focus on what they do not have or lack, and end up getting more of that lack on a consistent basis.

> *"And also that every man should eat and drink, and enjoy the good of all his labour, it is the gift of God."*
> ~ Ecclesiastes 3:13

"It's not about working for money, it's about having money work for you."
~ Stephen Richards

"But his delight is in the law of the LORD; and in his law doth he meditate day and night. And he shall be like a tree planted by the rivers of water, that bringeth forth his fruit in his season; his leaf also shall not wither; and whatsoever he doeth shall prosper."
~ Psalm 1:1-3

"The Lord is my shepherd; I shall not want."
~ Psalm 23:1

"When you are able to shift your inner awareness to how you can serve others, and when you make this the central focus of your life, you will then be in a position to know true miracles in your progress toward prosperity."
~ Wayne W. Dyer

"And they shall build houses, and inhabit them; and they shall plant vineyards, and eat the fruit of them. They shall not build, and another inhabit; they shall not plant, and another eat: for as the days of a tree are the days of my people, and mine elect shall long enjoy the work of their hands. They shall not labour in vain, nor bring forth for trouble; for they are the seed of the blessed of the LORD, and their offspring with them."
~ Isaiah 65:21-23

"Prosperity is only an instrument to be used, not a deity to be worshipped."
~ Calvin Coolidge

"Therefore take no thought, saying What shall we eat? or, What shall we drink or, Wherewithal shall we be clothed? (For after all these things do the Gentiles seek:) for your heavenly Father knoweth that ye have need of all these things. But seek ye first the kingdom of God, and his righteousness; and all these things shall be added unto you."
~ Matthew 6:31-33

"Learning is an ornament in prosperity, a refuge in adversity, and a provision in old age."
~ Aristotle

"I have been young, and now am old; yet have I not seen the righteous forsaken, nor his seed begging bread."
~ Psalm 37:25

"Prosperity is not without many fears and distastes; and adversity is not without comforts and hopes."
~ Francis Bacon, Sr.

"Honour the LORD with thy substance, and with the first fruits of all thine increase: So shall thy barns be filled with plenty, and thy presses shall burst out with new wine."
~ Proverbs 3:9,10

"Prosperity tries the fortunate: adversity the great."
~ Rose F. Kennedy

"For with what judgment ye judge, ye shall be judged: and with what measure ye mete, it shall be measured to you again."
~ Matthew 7:2

"Empty pockets never held anyone back. Only empty heads and empty hearts can do that."
~Norman Vincent Peale

"Give, and it shall be given unto you; good measure, pressed down, and shaken together, and running over, shall men give into your bosom. For with the same measure that ye mete withal it shall be measured to you again."
~ Luke 6:38

"Prosperity is a way of living and thinking, and not just money or things. Poverty is a way of living and thinking, and not just a lack of money or things."
~ Eric Butterworth

"But thou shalt remember the Lord thy God: for it is he that giveth thee power to get wealth, that he may establish his covenant which he sware unto thy fathers, as it is this day."
~ Deuteronomy 8:18

"Comfort and prosperity have never enriched the world as much as adversity has."
~ Billy Graham

"But this I say, He which soweth sparingly shall reap also sparingly; and he which soweth bountifully shall reap also bountifully. Every man according as he purposeth in his heart, so let him give; not grudgingly, or of necessity: for God loveth a cheerful giver. And God is able to make all grace abound toward you; that ye, always having all sufficiency in all things, may abound to every good work."
~ II Corinthians 9:6-8

"Prosperity is the best protector of principle."
~ Mark Twain

"But my God shall supply all your need according to his riches in glory by Christ Jesus."
~ Philippians 4:19

11.8 About Money

Let's clear up the idea many poor and/or misinformed individuals hold – the idea that "money is evil." Money, by itself, is not evil. The love of acquiring money - over health, over relationships, over living peacefully, and wanting to have money above all else - is evil. Money is only a piece of paper we give our attention to, depending on the denomination printed on the paper. We all agree to use printed paper or plastic credit money as an idea of wealth. Money is a reflection of prosperity and the flow of God's abundance. Money can build a church for good just as much as it could be used to hire a hitman for evil. Money should be used wisely to bless humanity, and to give happiness to those it flows through. Money flow is merely a symbol of your economic health; just as free-flowing nutrient-packed blood in your arteries shows status of your physical health. Restrict either money or blood flow, and stagnation produces dis-ease in both. Spiritual stagnation may show up as a lack of God's blessing to flow prosperity to and through you. Physical stagnation may show up as a dis-ease or physical ailment.

Money comes and it goes. A natural flow, as in a river, is healthy; an imbalance is not. For most, it may seem money flows out more than it flows in. Even those who win the "Super Lotto" seem to be right back to where they were barely five years down the road. Having money does not mean happiness; just ask any wealthy person on anti-depression meds! Some of the wealthiest and most famous stars on the Hollywood Walk of Fame did not die happy people. Elvis Presley, Marilyn Monroe, Kurt Cobain, and others had lots of money, fame, and adoring fans but may have lacked true inner happiness. Money is only an idea held in our consciousness. Money can serve as an idea to create your will or a means to an end; it's only a piece of paper thought to be valuable for trade. An abundance of money will usually amplify what your character already is. If you are truly kind and a good person, you will multiply the blessing of money for the good of mankind. If you are evil in thought and mind, you will squander the blessing of money for evil deeds and frivolous works.

"If you want to know what God thinks of money, just look at the people he gave it to."
~ Dorothy Parker

"For what profit is it to a man if he gains the whole world, and loses his own soul? Or what will a man give in exchange for his soul?"
~ Matthew 16:26

"So you think that money is the root of all evil. Have you ever asked what is the root of all money?"
~ Ayn Rand

In depth: Imagine if you and a friend have an idea, or brainstorm an invention together that will change humanity; you both create ideas that have the potential for many more ideas that earn money - possibly millions or billions of dollars. Don't make money your end goal, though, as you will end up short changed every time. Make serving others and being of value to your fellow human the utmost priority in your life. Follow the laws and teachings in this book, and what you desire will manifest for you, even money. After you hold the keys of manifestation, you will see what I say here, that there will be far more creative things you will desire to manifest than just paper bills with dead presidents' faces on them. It seems even they couldn't take their money with them!

We exchange our service or product for another person's money. Success is not a result of making money; making money is a by-product of being successful. If you dedicate yourself to serving prosperity, then prosperity will come back to you through the law of reciprocity. No one really gets rich unless they enrich others. Your earning is equal to your service to others. Calm, joyful, successful living comes from obeying the laws of financial success and understanding.

"Happy is the man that finds wisdom, and the man that gets understanding. For the merchandise of it is better than the merchandise of silver, and the gain thereof than fine gold. She is more precious than rubies: and all the things thou canst desire are not to be compared unto her. Length of days is in her right hand; and in her left hand riches and honour."
~ Proverbs 3:13-16

"Money can't buy friends, but you can get a better class of enemy."
~ Spike Milligan

"The fear of the LORD is clean, enduring forever: the judgments of the LORD are true and righteous altogether. More to be desired are they than gold, yea, than much fine gold: sweeter also than honey and the honeycomb."
~ Psalm 19:9,10

"Money is a strange thing. It ranks with love as our greatest source of joy, and with death as our greatest source of anxiety."
~ Joe Moore

"The LORD knoweth the days of the upright: and their inheritance shall be forever."
~ Psalm 37:18

"He who loses money, loses much; He who loses a friend, loses much more; He who loses faith, loses all."
~ Eleanor Roosevelt

"The wicked borrows, and pays not again: but the righteous shows mercy, and gives."
~ Psalm 37:21

"If money is your hope for independence you will never have it. The only real security that a man will have in this world is a reserve of knowledge, experience, and ability."
~ Henry Ford

"Labour not to be rich: cease from thine own wisdom. Wilt thou set thine eyes upon that which is not? For riches certainly make themselves wings; they fly away as an eagle toward heaven."
~ Proverbs 23:4,5

"I can live without money, but I cannot live without love."
~ Judy Garland

"For riches are not for ever: and doth the crown endure to every generation?"
~ Proverbs 27:24

"The darkest hour in any man's life is when he sits down to plan how to get money without earning it."
~ Horace Greeley

"Better is the poor that walketh in his uprightness, than he that is perverse in his ways, though he be rich."
~ Proverbs 28:6

"He that is of the opinion money will do everything may well be suspected of doing everything for money."
~ Benjamin Franklin

"He that hurries to be rich has an evil eye, and considers not that poverty shall come upon him."
~ Proverbs 28:22

"When money is seen as a solution for every problem, money itself becomes the problem."
~ Richard Needham

"A faithful man shall abound with blessings: but he that makes haste to be rich shall not be innocent."
~ Proverbs 28:20

"All is not gold that glitters."
~ Miguel de Cervantes

"I returned, and saw under the sun, that the race is not to the swift, nor the battle to the strong, neither yet bread to the wise, nor yet riches to men of understanding, nor yet favour to men of skill; but time and chance happens to them all."
~ Ecclesiastes 9:11

"The man whose only pleasure in life is making money, weighs less on the moral scale than an angleworm."
~ Josh Billings

"No one can serve two masters, for either he will hate the one and love the other, or he will be devoted to the one and despise the other. You cannot serve God and money. "Therefore I tell you, do not be anxious about your life, what you will eat or what you will drink, nor about your body, what you will put on. Is not life more than food, and the body more than clothing?"
~ Matthew 6:24-25

11.9 Gaining Financial Power

To gain monetary power, you need to ease into a vibration that is more suited for financial abundance. In fact, this is true to gain power in any aspect of life, and is particularly relevant for tapping into God's ever-abundant flow. Learn how to best align with the Law of Attraction. Simply thinking of your job as a profitable source of fun while serving humanity, rather than a place of hard work and boredom, can open the floodgates of proper connection to the vibration that leads you to more financial bliss. Your senses must all direct you towards the new desire. Your beliefs of what is possible or attainable must match up to your new desire. Your feelings about your self-worth and deserving nature must match up to the new desire. Your environment, people, places, and things must match the new frequency of your desire. The law of Intent must also be kept at the frequency of this new desire. Poverty is a mental dis-ease; a place where the mind does not create with ease. Those who have this mental disease are easy to spot by their "pity-party" demeanor, and the somber look of helplessness on their face. You must remove all those in your environment that vibrate against your new desire(s). These individuals are long-term habitual offenders who do not connect to proper thought vibrations of possibility and prosperity via their higher God power.

"Beware lest you say in your heart, 'My power and the might of my hand have gotten me this wealth. Thou shalt remember the Lord thy God: for it is he that giveth thee power to get wealth, that he may establish his covenant which he swore unto thy fathers, as it is this day."
~ Deuteronomy 8:17-18

"If they obey and serve him, they shall spend their days in prosperity, and their years in pleasures."
~ Job 36:11

"Riches and honour are with me; yea, durable riches and righteousness. My fruit is better than gold, yea, than fine gold; and my revenue than choice silver."
~ Proverbs 8:18, 19

"In the house of the righteous is much treasure."
~ Proverbs 15:6

"I go the way of all the earth: be thou strong therefore, and show thyself a man; And keep the charge of the Lord thy God, to walk in his ways, to keep his statutes, and his commandments, and his judgments, and his testimonies, as it is written in the law of Moses, that you may prosper in all that you do, and wherever you turn thyself;"
~ I Kings 2:2, 3

It all Starts as a Thought…

Look around you. Everything that you see – everything, without exception – was first someone's thought. The skyscraper or building you work in was an architect's thought, dream, or life's purpose. The restaurant chain you eat at, the toys your child plays with, and even the movies you see in the cinema. All of them - created by thoughts in someone's mind, focused on long enough to solidify into this material realm. The experiences you have as memories, from birth to now in your life, are the direct result of focused attention that became dominant vibrations, which solidified into the material illusion which is your current version of reality. In Galatians 6:7 of the New Testament we find, "Whatsoever a man soweth, that shall he also reap," or as in Matthew 9:29, "It is done unto you as you believe." The wisdom from the Bible has been repeated throughout history by others in similar ways:

"Whatever your mind can conceive and can believe, it can achieve."
~ Napoleon Hill

"Your imagination is your preview of life's coming attractions."
~ Albert Einstein

"Whether you think you can or can't either way you are right."
~ Henry Ford

"As you think, so shall you become."
~ Bruce Lee

"All that we are, is the result of what we have thought."
~ Buddha

"You create your own universe as you go along."
~ Winston Churchill

11.10 Why Isn't My Wealth Here Yet?

Just because someone may want a diamond necklace, a mansion, or a Lamborghini does not mean that they will get it immediately. One may hang up photos of these things and can visualize all he or she wants, but they never manifest it as an experienced reality. Why is this? You simply have not yet enacted the correct universal laws to make it happen for you. There is a process. The total connection to using your senses, as well as your intent, beliefs, and feelings, are what will change the circumstances for you and set the motion towards achieving that which you desire. You must create a space for abundance to bring in abundance. If your personal space is full of negativity or doubt, you can't manifest a positive outcome. Creating a space of abundance is why someone can go from having nothing to having everything quickly (or the other way around). There are countless stories of people who had nothing, and then all of a sudden abundance was brought into their life within a short period of time. Their set of beliefs, thoughts, and feelings changed their parallel universe and caused a cascade of well-being within them, which then reflected outward into the experienced reality. There are also many stories of people who have it all and then allow their thoughts of negative self-worth, insecurity, and paranoia come into their minds. This then causes their health and abundance to dwindle quickly. These stories are not mere luck, but enacted laws that bring forth the individual's new illusion as their new reality - both good and bad.

Since many people here in the earthly realm seek material abundance and their thought relationship with money is poor, I have included helpful tools to help change anyone's relationship with the thought energy of money. Let us look at some principle laws that need to be understood and practiced continually in order to cultivate abundance.

11.11 Know These Universal Laws for Creating Abundance

Those who break the teachings also go against the laws, and break the normal progression and flow of life, thus violating the flow. In historical religious teachings, this is called a "sin," which I earlier described as "Self-Inflicted Negativity," or a stunting of one's growth progression. A sin is a misunderstanding or misjudgment, falling short of the mark of perfection. As such, repentance and forgiveness are the only ways to correct the mistake, whether that mistake is physical (eating low level nutrition), or spiritual (neglecting love for self and care of spiritual matters). If one violates too many of the laws for too long, there will be repayment of the energy in a negative way, which may lead to a certain type of death or perceived pain. What is cancer or illness? A long standing violation of health laws that have been broken, and need repentance or reversal to move toward a better lifestyle. This is why in religious teachings they preach that if you break spiritual laws you will be given death. A spiritual death means disconnection from God or all your abundance. The following are the laws I have come to personally understand as paramount for living an abundantly powerful life. They all work together in creating change.

- **The Law of Attraction**

The Law of Attraction is based on the metaphysical belief that "like energy attracts like;" that when one focuses on positive or negative thinking, they can bring more of the same to them as physical results.

Invoking the Law of Attraction:
1. Decide what you <u>desire</u> in every detail, and phrase it positively.
2. Write your desire on a 2x4 card and laminate it.
3. Carry this card with you in your wallet or purse and view it whenever possible.
4. Decide to believe and know (not wish) that your desire is logically possible for you.
5. Get your emotional self to open up, and totally involve your heart in the belief that you now have what you desire in your possession.

6. Close your eyes and meditate on the vision often. Allow your imagination to have fun with your desire, and go wild with the possibilities.
7. Be ready to act now, quickly, and go without resistance when you see doors start to open in your physical reality. The doors of opportunity will appear as inspirations, and thoughts which will be shown to you. Some will be subtle, while others will be very obvious. Act upon these "nudges" ASAP.
8. Others may question or ridicule your idea or desires, but you must stay on your path. Let no one's opinion sway your focus.
9. Continue to do these steps, feeling gratitude for attaining your desire without attachment to a particular outcome. Continue to run steps 1-9 on more desires regardless of any previous outcomes manifesting.

The desires you form in your mind are impulses of organized energy we term "thoughts." When thoughts are combined with emotional feeling, your brain cells magnetize a vibration that is in line with nature's laws to attract to you the very things you wish to experience.

- **The Law of Vibration**

All things in the Universe exist at a certain vibration. Everything vibrates at its own speed. Take for example your senses. All are an aspect of a vibration that tunes into frequency. Your thoughts are in vibrational movement as well, and your feelings are also controlled by the conscious awareness of specific vibration. The law of vibration is needed to bring about the law of attraction; they work together and some say they are one in the same.

- **The Law of Imaging or Imagination – Visualization**

"Imagination is more important than knowledge. Knowledge is limited." Albert Einstein believed that, "Imagination encircles the world," and "Imagination is the preview of life's coming attractions." The famed prosperity teacher Catherine Ponder called visualization, "The Imaging Law of Prosperity." Visualization is vital in order to succeed in creating a world you love. Your visualizations can be a dream come true or a horror story realized - based on the thoughts and visions you program daily in your mind.

- **The Law of Expectation**

Working alongside the Law of Attraction, this law states that whatever we expect with confidence, belief, and focus, becomes a self-fulfilling prophecy. Mark 11:24 states, "When ye pray, believe that ye receive." If you expect something with belief and faith, you set manifestation towards that which you expect. For example, you are in a rush to quickly drop off something to a friend, but when you get to your friend's apartment there are no parking spaces (you did not create one in your mind to be there before you left) so you decide to illegally park your car. You worry in your mind that parking your car in that bad spot will get you a ticket, and due to the fact that you've received many parking tickets in the past, you feel fear, worry, anxiety, and are on a vibration that is set to attract a parking officer to your car quickly. Upon coming back to your car what do you see? A ticket! The law of expectation should be used just like when you order something from the Internet or a catalogue. You choose the item you desire, you pay, and you know it is on its way without worry or fear. You hold excitement, happiness, expectation, belief, faith, and base this on many other perfect deliveries you have experienced. And behold, before you know it, the package arrives as expected!

- **The Law of Gratefulness**

This law cannot be understated. It is what keeps you connected to your power with God, Universal Intelligence, Allah, The Source, The Father, or The Creator. When you keep your mind focused on being thankful, you immediately look for what is good in life. The more your focus and attention are directed to good, the more you invoke this law in your subconscious to manifest more good for you (more neurons build thought patterns of gratitude).

- **The Law of Increase**

The more you spend energy in a place, the more the fruits of that labor will increase. The law of increase can be used to increase anything you currently have. Increase the happiness in your life by complimenting others, lending an ear to become a better listener, investing money into good business causes to multiply your earnings, teach and spread your knowledge to youth, or simply give a senior citizen some companionship. The more of your energy you give in love, the more you will receive from the Creator. There is an infinite supply of energy in the Universe, of which you can never take more than your fair share. Your fair share is infinite, and the more you exercise it through loving and serving others, the more can come to you, just as it comes to your neighbor. Not sharing love does just the opposite. If you feel you are pinched off from life, ask yourself, "How much am I giving without strings attached?"

Take a moment to consider: A homeless man approaches… Do you give him money or buy him food? Why does the homeless person come into your experience? Is it by chance that he or she walks the same route and projected path to ask you for a dollar, or did you summon that person to you? The homeless individual and you have a co-creative experience at the moment of meeting, which allows two things to happen. 1: This happens for you to understand your overflow of abundance, and to express your generosity. 2: It's a lesson for the homeless person in finding hope, seeing abundance delivered, or possibly a chance to experience human connection. Depending on both individuals' role in their life's journey at that time, the experience will unfold as they create it together, through Divine co-creation. Lives can change if both decide to take the opportunity. It is just as uncomfortable for a homeless man to ask for help as it is for someone to engage a stranger and give them their hard earned money. However, in this discomfort comes growth. Remember that every moment you act or make a statement, you are defining to the Universe and to yourself who you are, what you believe in, and what you stand for in that moment.

Should you give money or food to the homeless? Some make the quick assumption that if they give money to the poor, the money will be used for drugs, cigarettes, or alcohol. Instead, they buy them food. Sometimes the homeless person is angry and doesn't accept the food and would rather have the toxins to numb their pain and continue their own form of reality. In both cases, it would be wise to exercise whatever choice each individual feels brings about their own greatest growth. However, if they choose to not take the experience in that manner, this is not wrong or right on either end. It is only an expression of choice and perception, which is only judged by the individuals involved in the creation of the experience, and no one else. In either situation, the law of increase will give you more of what you put forward.

- **The Law of Tithing; The Law of Circulation; a.k.a. Law of Fair Exchange - Giving and Receiving**

This law states that all things in the Universe are flowing in circulation and at an ever-expanding rate. There cannot be a giver without a receiver. Do not refuse anything good given to you by another. Doing so blocks the law of circulation and tells the Universe you do not accept good things from others, putting you at a disadvantage of receiving more good. If you are given a gift, say "Thank you," and accept it. If someone offers to pay the bill, say "Thank you," and let them. When you are not accepting by saying, "No" to good things, you block the flow of abundance to your life as well as the flow of the giver's life. In all human interactions there is a law of giving and receiving… a law of equal reciprocity. When there is no fair exchange, someone breaks the law. If there is no receiving there is no giving - and if there is no giving, there is no receiving. If you resist giving, the law will resist giving to you. Each is a function of the other. If you neither give nor receive, then you will be the kind of person who only takes. Taking creates resistance with those around you. Those who break the Law of Circulation or Fair Exchange are easy to spot because they always feel guilty deep inside, are very cheap, complain, get minimal results with what they do, ask for special attention, seldom reach out to help others, find false reasons or excuses to quit, don't try new experiences, and badmouth those who have tried to help them.

Tithing is based on giving back to God 10% of your income towards good deeds or projects that serve others or God's work. Doing so sends out the signal that you are a provider and this continues flowing God's abundance through you to many others. God puts energy in the places that flow. The law of tithing is part of The Law of Circulation; a.k.a. Law of Fair exchange - giving and receiving. You will discover a powerful manifestation correlation as taught in II Corinthians 9:6-8 of the Bible:

> *"He which soweth sparingly shall reap also sparingly; and he which soweth bountifully shall reap also bountifully. Every man according as he purposeth in his heart, so let him give; not grudgingly, or of necessity: for God loveth a cheerful giver. And God is able to make all grace abound toward you; that ye, always having all sufficiency in all things, may abound to every good work."*

- **The Law of Vital Few; a.k.a. Pareto principle a.k.a. 80-20 rule**

This 80-20 rule was developed by Joseph Juran, a 20th century management consultant that named the principle after Vilfredo Pareto, who observed in 1906 that 80% of the land in Italy was owned by 20% of the population. The principle states that 80% of the effects or consequences come from 20% of the causes. So that what we put in we get out - but there is a ripple effect. If you consistently invest in yourself, in time the 20% will overflow to affect the 80%. If you have a lot of things to do today, break down the activities to the specific twenty percent of the tasks that contribute to eighty percent of the results you seek. Give your maximum concentration to the top 20 percent of tasks which will in effect move you forward more efficiently.

- **The Law of Conservation of Energy**

Energy cannot be created or destroyed; it can only be changed from one form to another. When energy is being used, it is not being used up; only changed. God is energy. That energy can be changed into matter, and back to energy. Energy like God is eternal and is all the energy there ever was, is, and always will be. Some of the molecules you are breathing in right now were also the molecules of air possibly breathed in by Abraham Lincoln or

Elvis. Your body when it is done being used in its current state will be decomposed back into the parts needed by the Earth. Understand that this energy recycles and apply it to your understanding of life's flow.

- **The Law of Balance**

The law of balance says one should conserve personal energy to achieve the greatest proficiency. For example: consider a car with four wheels, a stool with three legs, a human with two feet, an ostrich on one leg. Balance is positive for proper living. There is a harmony that if ever upset causes chaos. Think about too much food, too much alcohol, too much sleep, too much sex, or too much work. All bring about imbalances and are unhealthy. Respect the law of balance and apply it to your life.

- **The Law of Action**

This law states that you must convert energy into action to get your desires. You cannot bring into being what you desire unless you take action towards a set end goal. When taking action, you set forth knowledge, beliefs, and feelings so that they can be created. The smartest of men are the largest of weaklings if they hold treasures of knowledge and power idle by not setting action to them. Do not stay passive. Take massive action in your life and create the magic you deserve!

- **The Law of Timing**

Life is a process of steps you must complete. You must finish sections of your youth before you enjoy your adulthood. Having the things adulthood offers as a teen rarely comes about until you do the steps that bring adulthood to you. Respect the law of timing and understand there are events that supersede other lessons down the road as you are growing with every challenge in the current experience. The law of timing allows you to feel the effects of what you are doing in the 'now' and involves the law of free will to choose the next series of events. The law of attraction then brings more manifestation to you, which in turn creates more choices and events.

- **The Law of Free Will (To Choose)**

The responsibility of free will is great as it keeps us from blaming anyone else but ourselves for our shortcomings in life. We can't blame God either. Free will is the great equalizer that allows all; the man, woman, young, old, rich and poor to feel success and triumph or agony and pain by the choices each make in their life's journey.

- **The Law of Faith**

Law of Faith says that if we have total faith in an outcome, it will come about. Unlike the Law of Expectation, the Law of Faith is specifically faith and total trust in the Divine. Faith with love dispels fear. Examples that you already have faith: Driving on the road inches away from another driver to your left which at any moment could pass the double yellow line and come head on through your windshield and into your lap. You have undeniable, unquestionable faith that you will be untouched by such incident when you drive. You have faith in your next breath. You have faith the sun will rise and keep doing what it did for centuries, yet again tomorrow. You have faith that you will have dinner, breakfast, lunch, and food to eat continuously. You have faith your heart will continue to beat without you having to think about it. You have faith the seed you planted will blossom and the rain will fall; both on the good and the bad. Understand you already have faith in the Divine plan. Build on this faith by removing your worry and allow Divinity to work through your thoughts by knowing and trusting 100%.

- **The Law of Parkinson**

Parkinson's Law, named after a British naval historian and author of 60 books, Cyril Northcote Parkinson, states that "work expands so as to fill the time available for its completion." Also explained as, "the demand upon a resource tends to expand to match the supply of the resource." So if you do not fill the time with high priority things most important to you, the time available will be filled with less productive things unimportant to you; i.e. watching television, playing computer games, gossip, or passing the time without positive results to impact your life in a forward way. Likewise, any work not extended on high priority things will be taken up by lower energy things. So if you do not spend your waking hours going towards the life you seek to experience, you will experience the lower version of that reality. Choose the high road for a life worth living.

- **The Law of Forgiveness**

The Law of Forgiveness states that when forgiveness is given, the soul is at ease. We know that disease can only form when a body is not at ease. Once you understand this law you would not want to keep from practicing it. Most people are stuck in the rut they are in without knowing that they are holding too much unforgiven anger and resentment against another person. These two emotions are two of the nastiest vibrations to hold onto in the body for they slow or stop all abundance. Growing up with guilt, anger, resentment, hatred, or rage as taught to children through religion, cultures, and tradition early in life, causes many painful experiences later in adulthood. It is no wonder that once forgiveness is given to the self or others, we say that the "weight feels as if it has been lifted" from our shoulders or chest. Our innate energy cannot flow properly when any chakra is maintaining a negative thought or emotion. Love yourself and respect yourself enough to forgive all and hold absolutely no grudges. Let go and release all negative thought and emotion. Free not only others from negative repressed feelings but most importantly, yourself.

- **The Law of Hypnotic Flow/Rhythm**

Rhythm and routine are part of our daily lives. Any conscious behavior that is repeated over and over again may become an imbedded habit, whether good or bad. When something becomes so ingrained in us that it becomes an automatic rhythm, we no longer have control over it and the cycle is nearly impossible to break. Because we know this, we also know that the brain is always acting or thinking. When we understand that the brain is never idle, only constantly moving to express action, we realize that all energy and atoms are in motion. Nothing is stale or static. Via this law, any thought (positive or negative), given time, will become permanent habits over one's lifetime and will be forced into a similar environment in which it thrives. Thinking positively manifests positive actions over time, thinking negatively over time has the equal and opposite reaction.

- **The Law of Love**

In Mark 12:30-31, Christ's primary commandment was "Thou shalt love the Lord thy God with all thy heart, and with all thy soul, and with all thy strength." No, this love is not the same as, "I love pizza, I love the internet, or I love Fridays." Nor is it a materialistic type of love, "I love designer products and flashy cars." It is a law of unconditional and universal acceptance of the highest form of divine energy connection. Christ continued, "And the second is like it: 'You shall love your neighbor as yourself.'" This is truly the greatest of all laws, for those who serve others and fully love their brothers and sisters on this planet, bring the flow of abundance into their lives. God gives blessings to those who are lovingly open and can also flow benefits to others. Those who break the grand law of love, choke off their ability to properly grow and attain sufficient abundance both for themselves and others.

Chapter 12:
Exercises for Visualizing and Manifesting Abundance

"Health is a state of complete harmony of the body, mind and spirit. When one is free from physical disabilities and mental distractions, the gates of the soul open."
~ B.K.S. Iyengar

The next 13 Kousouli® manifestation exercises I use personally, and with them have helped my patients feel and become more abundant. I suggest using a few of them together to develop a daily routine you feel comfortable with. Do them often, and do them with deep *feeling*. Although these exercises can undoubtedly bring about physical material objects, the objects themselves are not the focus; so you would be wise to focus on the process of manifestation, not just the things manifested. The appearance of the physical objects will only be proof to you that the process works, and it is the same process for all manifestation in your life here on Earth. It will further verify your connection to the abundance your Creator has for you while bringing you closer to the bliss of life, so that you are in constant manifestation of your desires. *Remember: riches manifest quickest from serving and seeing abundance for others out of love. You will be given more in a physical form (physically manifested and seen) all good things if you know, believe, and have faith that you have them already in the spiritual (unseen, non-physical) form. This bridges the gap from not having to having.*

12.1 Manifestation Method - Your Personal Valet Angel

Imagine if you could get V.I.P. treatment by the Universe and not have to walk far after you get to your destinations. Image your friends unable to figure out why you didn't have to fuss for a parking spot when they had to roam around the lot for 20 minutes in order to find a space. Imagine being at the right place at the right time - all the time. You can be if you call on your personal valet angel given to you by the Universe! You can imagine your valet angel anyway you wish him or her to be. I see mine as a mid-teen male quick to fly to my aid. He's very courteous, friendly, and willing to help at any time I call upon him. Just as the valets of 5 star hotels jump to help serve you; that is how you can picture your personal valet angel. However, unlike most hotel valets, this one really loves his/her job and doesn't do it for tips. Here's how: When you are about to leave your current destination and go to a seemingly busy place, like the mall or the food market for instance, call upon your trusty personal valet angel by thinking it or verbally saying it out loud. "I am now leaving this place and ask my parking spot be ready at my next destination". If you know the spot or area you wish to park at, visualize yourself pulling up to the destination, smiling and giving gratitude in your heart to your personal valet for making ready the space. Sometimes it may be a few seconds or a minute for a spot to open up in front of you, though if you do this correctly, it will seem as if the world has a spot for you every time. Be sure to thank your personal valet angel, as gratitude is the only payment he or she wishes from you.

Why this works: You invoke the Law of Expectation. By expecting an outcome and asking for it, you then also invoke the Law of Attraction. Holding the image of the parking spot in your mind prior to your arrival sends powerful signals to the Universe telling it to align situations around your arrival so that it is created as you like. This works also because of previous, solid, and understood beliefs. First, you understand and inherently know that there are many parking spots available and that they can be available to you. Second, you are not stuck on an outcome or particular parking space exactly; you allow the Universe to find one for you within a range of space. This opens up options to greater probability of connection. Third, you believe this is possible because of previous experience of finding a space so you have no blocks to knowing that having a parking spot is possible. If you doubt or have any hang-ups about the process, you won't be able to perform this or any manifestation. This is one of the easiest manifestations to do. Graduate from manifesting parking spaces to always getting green lights, avoiding traffic, or even having friends buy you a drink spontaneously when you're out on the town. Your imagination (and personal valet angel) is limitless.

12.2 Manifestation Method - The 'In-Vision board'

Imagine flipping through magazines, books or catalogs, pointing to what you want, and getting it. The In-vision, or envision board, is quite possibly one of the most powerful tools one can use to get what they desire. It works because it invokes several factors in the creation process. To manifest, the creator of the board uses emotional feeling, the physical senses of vision and touch, as well as the nonphysical 6th sense through thought and imagination. Many have built fortunes just from this exercise alone. You would be wise to learn and master this manifestation method.

Dr. Kousouli, How do I build a powerful In-Vision Board?

You will need a poster board, pencil, scissors, glue, favorite magazines with a lot of ads displaying goods you desire, and a quiet place with no distractions. You can find poster board at any craft store. It doesn't matter what color the poster board is, however I do suggest going with plain white for simplicity. Take your pencil and create areas of the poster board into sections marked financial, love, work or career, travel, and other. You may have many other categories and that's okay too; remove or add any kind of category you wish. The most important thing is to have fun and feel really good about what you're going to put on this board. This is your board, your rules, your life. This board is your private arena of creation and no one is to stand in judgment of it, so it is a good idea to keep your board away from anyone else's eyes. This is especially true if you are in an environment with negative parents, competing siblings, or friends that tease you. You should keep your board secret not because of shame, but because of energy. The energy you put on the board is to manifest for you, not others. When others start to look and criticize what it is you desire, their filters and their limitations will conflict with yours. When they can't see it possible for you to achieve a certain item on your board, their pessimism will counteract your optimism and sway your energy from manifestation if you allow it. So be sure to create in a place of no distraction and no negative criticism. You can be as selfish as you want on this board; for instance, you may want to put a picture of your favorite luxury car. Want a loving relationship? Put a photo of a newlywed couple on your board. Maybe your desire is to travel and you've never been to Europe. A picture of the Eiffel tower would be perfect for your travel section. Your board may contain both pictures and words. You may cut out magazine ads, photos, and even letters or word phrases for your poster board. You may put any combination of words and pictures together. You may group pictures in clumps or spread them out as you wish. There are no rules for what it is you desire and how fast you should finish the board. You do not have to finish the whole board in one sit-down session. You may work on it in sections and you may work on it over time. As you see things manifest on your board, you may want to remove and add new things to replace those manifested. Here's the key point that makes the board work: *The feeling of gratitude that the desire has been met.* In fact, the Latin word for *'desire'* means *'*of or from the Father/God/King/Sire.' When you flip through the magazines and find things that you desire to bring into your reality, claim them as yours just before you cut them out to place on your board. Feel what it's like to own that item; what it would be like to live your life with that item as yours. Feel nothing but joy and happiness in your heart, your soul, and your being as you put glue on the back of the pictures, speaking to the universe *to bring you each desire.* Continue this step until your board is filled with items, ideas, thoughts, words, and anything else you desire to bring into your life experience. Your board now is complete for you to envision the creative powers of manifestation! Put this board near your bed where it is easily visible when you first wake up in the morning and before you go to bed at night. Look at the board and your still pictures on them. Close your eyes as you envision each still image become a moving picture as you play out the scenario in your mind the way it may be when you acquire it. Give thanks to the Universe with complete gratitude as you envision your life with that item and your desires fulfilled. Be sure not to wish that you will have it, or hope for it in the future but instead think and feel the joy as if it is yours *now*. Starting and ending your day on a creative note with joy will magnetize the item(s) or situation(s) closer to you by switching your current dimension of reality.

Why this works: You may not be able to see the big picture of your magnificence prior to this exercise. Allowing yourself to put the images of your desires on the board enables you to construct a roadmap of your next possible growth cycle. This exercise allows you to invoke the feelings of fulfillment as you tangibly attach the image with the idea of 'manifestation' in this current dimension of reality, thus experiencing that version of having; not lacking. When you see results start to manifest, this will be your 'proof' that you have Divine ability to steer your life as you like.

12.3 Manifestation Method - The 'Never-Ending Gratitude List'

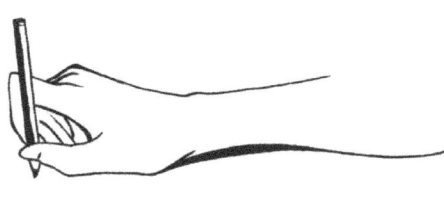

Get a piece of paper and the writing instrument of your choice. This exercise empowers you to see the positive in what you already have in your life in order to improve your attitude and allow more good to come in. If you are a pessimist, this exercise is mandatory for you. You MUST see the good to attract more good into your life. If you have been thinking bad vibration you have been attracting other bad vibrations. "Like attracts like," "Birds of a feather flock together," "The apple doesn't fall far from the tree;" these are all sayings that mean the same attracts more of the same. So if you have been unhappy with what is around you now, you won't attract anything different unless you start appreciating even the little bit you may already have.

Take out a white lined piece of paper. Fold the paper into thirds so you have three columns. At the top of the paper write in large bold writing '**I AM GRATEFUL FOR.**' In column one, line one, start by writing something you are thankful for. This can be as simple as your pet, family, friends, mentors, health or home. Keep writing everything that comes to mind without stopping. Write even if it sounds like it is silly to you like: air, wallpaper, ground, mud etc. Just keep writing. This is an excellent exercise to do when you are feeling underappreciated or less than abundant. Bringing to mind the things you are abundant with will invoke the law of attraction to bring more of what you want into your life. Move to column two, three and so on. Keep going. Keep writing. From time to time, pick up the list and read all the abundance you've listed in your life, but may have forgotten about.

Why this works: A common practice in schools was to punish troublemakers by making them stand for hours in detention and write "I will not start fights with other kids" (or any other message the teacher wanted to get across to the student) onto a blackboard. The purpose of that exercise was to alter a negative action through repetition, since an action when repeated over 21 times starts to become part of the person doing it. The same thing is true about learning how to do a special skill like learning a language or playing an instrument. The technique uses this exercise in a similar but much more positive way through gratitude repetition.

12.4 Manifestation Method - The 'Big-Money multiplier'

Some say "seeing is believing" or "fake it till you make it" and these sayings come to life with this powerful exercise. Of all the exercises listed, this one makes the top five for the simple fact that it puts to use four of your five physical senses, and utilizes your current programming to expand your allowance of abundance.

Get yourself a stack of cash; the larger the currency and higher the stack - the better.

This exercise takes a little dedication. Save your money every chance you get to pile it up as high as possible. Recommended currencies are twenty, fifty, or one hundred dollar bills (best). Try to use crisp bills; when you do the exercise it will help you hear them in motion. If you do not have larger bills you may use five dollar bills, but try to refrain from using one dollar bills. The idea is to have a cash stash somewhere you can go to easily and quickly anytime you feel any sense of lack to remind yourself of abundance.

If you are bad with saving money, or feel it is unsafe to do so over a period of time at your residence for whatever reason, then you can go to the bank and withdrawal an amount you feel comfortable with from your account. As you withdrawal it, feel a sense of empowerment that this energy is moving from the bank's hands into your hands. As the teller asks you how do you want your bills, say "large please," with a smile. One of my patients Jim, has a great sense of humor and tells the clerk each time he does this exercise,

"Large please, that's the only way I roll"; adding humor is another way to boost the transaction, as the teller may get a smile or boost their good vibe as well. You are prosperous. Spread good with both with your humor as well as your money.

To put this exercise into practice you will need to get yourself to a quiet place without distraction. Take the large stack of bills and look at it. How does that make you feel? It's important to use cash, since through our ordinary life transactions we don't see it like we used to in the 1990's and prior due to credit cards and check card popularity. This is one of the reasons people are also in debt, they simply don't respect their cash flow, mostly because they can't see it! This will help you feel better about money inflow by using your olfactory (smell), auditory (hearing), tactile (touching) and visual (seeing) senses along with your mental ability for manifestation.

Now take a deep breath, relax as you take the stack of cash in your one hand and with the other start flipping down each bill as rapidly as you can. While you do this it is important that you simultaneously:

- Hear the crackle of the bills as they stack on top of each other.
- Feel the texture of the bills as they pass through your hands/fingers.
- See the rapid succession of bills pile in front of you as you lay them down.
- Smell the scent of the money every now and again as you stack the bills.

As this is occurring (at the same time) imprint in your mind the following phrase(s) in succession as you also verbally say them out loud:

- "Money flows freely, easily, and quickly to me."
- "I am a receiver and giver of money."
- "My abundance increases minute by minute, daily, weekly, and yearly."
- "I am limitless in attracting abundance into my life."
- "The Universe showers me with its abundance."
- "I am an heir to the Kingdom of Abundance."
- "I now call forth manifestation of my material abundance."
- "I invest in myself. Others see this, and also want to invest in me."
- "Money wants ME, and it finds me every time."

Once the stack has been emptied, grab the stack of bills and repeat again and again flipping the stack over as if you are counting more money. You can repeat for five consecutive minutes or until you get too tired to continue counting all that money.

Why this works: You are not counting the money in numbers or amount. That is irrelevant here. You are imprinting to your subconscious mind the above truths while repeating the physical motions and actions of your hands. Saturating the senses imprints deep into your psyche that you are capable of attaining, multiplying, handling, and holding monetary abundance. The more you practice this exercise, the more familiar monetary abundance will become to you.

12.5 Manifestation Method - The 'Journal of (I AM) Praise'

Keep a blank notebook by your bedside. Make it a habit to write in it every chance you get when you awaken and just before you sleep. This journal is to praise yourself positively for anything and everything. You can write as much or as little as you like, just be sure to be consistent with your entries; the only rule you must follow is that everything is written in the present positive tense. Start with the words **I AM**. For example: **I AM** happy prosperous and live in bliss. **I AM** in the house that I desire. **I AM** happy with my work space. Even if it is not at this time true for you in physical reality, you FEEL blissful and ENVISION it while you desire it and write it down. This is the only rule you must follow. Be positive, be present. Start it all with I AM.

Why this works: By speaking with the terms I AM, you put everything in the present tense. The creator of ALL that IS, said to Moses, "Tell them, I AM that I AM", and since you are also co-creating your reality with God from moment to moment, you are declaring what and who you are in the Universe. You change the now to affect your future through your thoughts, feelings, and words of declaration in the present moment. The accumulation of changing of the present 'now' moment will in effect bring you the experiences you desire.

12.6 Manifestation Method – The 'This was Your Life Biography'

Why wait for some lame depressing obituary or preacher to yap over your dead carcass at a burial? Wouldn't it be great if you could fast forward in time and see what you accomplished in your life by reading your own biography? You could revel in your amazing accomplishments, images of the joyful world tours and vacations you took, and your awards for bravery and valor or humanitarian efforts abroad. Well, guess what - you can! You're going to write your own legacy! If you were to pass away and someone was to read about your life, would you have been interesting? Did you do all that was to do in your life? Did you see the world? Did you fly to every continent? What did you do in your life that was amazing? You're going to take fate in your hands and write a roadmap of your achievements and accolades the way it should be read. Start out with the obvious past factual data like when you were born and who you were born to. If you are an orphan or adopted and don't know who you were born to - I suggest you write that you came from a royal bloodline! If you're the type that is moving up in the world, you can say you were born a street beggar and are now going from rags to riches. Anything goes; you're making the rules here - it's your story, and your life!

Remember:
- Be as grand as you wish to be; there are no limits
- Any talent you want to do or learn and any goal or reward you aspire to attain; you write them down as accomplished!

Why this works: When we write our thoughts down on paper we transform thought into physical manifestation. Even this book had to be transformed from the information in my brain to the book that you hold in your hands. Likewise, what happens here is a creative process that must go through the necessary steps to bring it about. By writing down what you did in your lifetime, you leave things less to chance and more to written law. By creating your story, you put into effect situations and circumstances to fulfill your prophecy the way you desire before you leave this Earth. Make your stay here AMAZING!

12.7 Manifestation Method - 'Things to Do Before I Leave List'

Don't want to leave the earth plane just yet? Make this list really long so you can better the chances that you'll stick around much longer to accomplish all your desires and goals. Start with a hundred things, and then grow it to a thousand items. No matter what it may be, if you want to experience it, write it down and put it on your 'bucket' list.

Why this works: It is well known that those who retire don't live long after they declare their retirement. This is because the purpose or mission that the soul performs feels fulfilled, and they become restless as to its continued purpose here on Earth. Retirees start to pace around and eventually fade away when they feel their use is no longer needed. When you plan your list, you are ensuring your time here will continuously be active in purpose. Once you reach a goal scratch it off and put another in its place. Give yourself thousands of reasons to stick around longer. The longer your list, the longer you will decide that staying youthful, active, and in life's enjoyment is a full time priority for you.

12.8 Manifestation Method – '365 Days of Calendar Power'

Make an agreement with a friend to get together once a week to discuss events and goals that are on your agenda. Both of you should have a basic flip calendar for this exercise to encourage each other to stay on track. Maybe Susie needs to lose 10 pounds by next month, and John needs motivation for a project that could get him a promotion at work. The objective is to ensure neither of you become lazy in manifesting your desires, because you're accountable to each other. Both people would write down the important dates for their friend's various events and goals. Throughout the week quickly check in with your friend(s) to see how their goals are going. Meditate and pray at various parts of the day on the goal being achieved. Guess what? Susie will lose that weight and John will eventually get that promotion because of this support keeping them aligned and on point to what has been envisioned.

Why this works: When you have more than one person on an idea the power of the combined creative consciousness flows solid through the combined efforts of all minds involved. Also see Chapter 17 on Group manifestations.

12.9 Manifestation Method - The 'Universal To-Do list'

Make two columns on a piece of paper and list your daily activities in a positive way. Title the first column *My Responsibility*. On the second column, title it *The Universe's Responsibility*. Split the work between what you can give the Universe to do and what you can do to help the Universe carry out your desires. Sometimes the tasks you take upon yourself are not supposed to be your job; it's the job of the higher power. Are you taking too much responsibility on your shoulders when it's a job better suited for the powers of the Universal God? You're probably feeling the heaviness of the weight if that's the case, so jump out of the pilot's seat and into the co-pilot seat! That means: letting go of your ego's need to control every detail and allowing the Creator to take over for you when you need it the most. Don't try to control; create instead! A big secret of those who are successful in life is that they do not sweat the small OR big stuff; They outsource it to God and do not worry or get anxious about the how-to.

> "***Be anxious for nothing***, but in everything by prayer and supplication, with thanksgiving, let your requests be made known to God. And the peace of God, which surpasses all comprehension, will guard your hearts and your minds in Christ Jesus."
> ~ Philippians 4:6-7

Example: *My Responsibility*: Be more sociable by joining a softball league. *The Universe's Responsibility*: Unite me with loving people I relate to and I can be friends with.

Why this works: When you are focused on your skills available for co-creation, you do not need to know the *how*, just the <u>*what*</u>. Being clear in the <u>*what*</u>, is paramount; the *hows* are taken care of by the Universal forces that are already set in motion to work in your favor. God only requires you to start the process by asking for *what* you desire.

12.10 Manifestation Method - The '4-D Experience'

In a meditative state: envision feeling, seeing, touching, tasting etc. as vividly as possible any experience you desire to bring into your current reality. YOUR inner experience, emotions, thoughts, consciousness, and awareness are all different expressions of the higher mind. Actual development and transformation happens only when you promote growth in all the aforementioned dimensions. Take for instance the fact that you usually see yourself only in 2D. Standing in front of a mirror you only get height and width. For depth (3D), you need to see a holographic projection of you in order to get an accurate idea of your reflection; how others view the physical you. We don't have a clear concept of ourselves in 3D, and you can't view the back or side of your head. However your imagination can implement all axis of rotation, view, angles, depth, as well as timelessness, to bring upon you the feelings of actually experiencing it in all dimensions, aspects, or ways.

Why this works: Imagination is a powerful tool of manifestation, which accesses parallel universes, lifetimes, situations, or versions of you that you wish to experience. You literally *pull* closer the version of reality that you desire to actualize as your truth with intent, focus, and inspired action. With this exercise the alternate parallel universe where what you desire is located will be pulled closer to manifest in present time.

12.11 Manifestation Method - 'Chalk on Glass or Mirror'

Gather materials: liquid chalk marker, pen, paper, and mirrors.

You have been exposed to this very powerful technique many times, and may have even been influenced by it to spend your hard earned money. This is a technique used by salesmen, car lots, and store window displays to get your attention to aspects of a particular special store sale. If you have ever been car shopping and purchased a car or clothing due to initial interest, yet found yourself suckered into buying something you didn't really need, then this technique has worked on your subconscious. Now, we will open up the secret of this method so you can quickly accelerate forward in both your purpose and desires.

You will need a liquid chalk marking pen found at your local hardware or craft store. White chalk will suffice, but if you want to get other colors, and are an artistic type, then go for it! Be sure it is water based and easily removable. You don't want it to say 'permanent' on it – or your roommates or spouse will surely be upset with you.

Next, you want to get your positive thoughts and goals aligned. Make a list of 10 and prioritize them from most emotionally moving to least emotionally moving for you. Now remove the last two to five least emotionally charged ones and keep the top 5-8 powerful ones. A quote from your favorite author or philosopher will do; keep it short and sweet. The mind likes things that are powerful but easy to remember. A four word quote that delivers the message is more powerful than a paragraph that babbles on.

After you have your inspirational words and thoughts, you want to find target sites in your surroundings you can put your messages on. The targets are anything with a reflective surface you see or look at often. Ideally mirrors, because you can see yourself in its reflection are the best. The bathroom mirror would be the optimal target, since you see it right when you wake up and again prior to going to sleep. Your bedroom window or wherever you look at the sunrise or sunset daily would be second best.

Regularly change your quotes to keep you moving toward your desires and keep you on track. You can also give your quotes a break intermittently, and just write one word feeling or desires on your mirror such as "LOVE," "YOU ARE BEAUTIFUL," or "I AM ABUNDANT."

Why this works: This is a ridiculously easy method to help focus you on positive aspects of your life, and turn you towards abundance. You think it, you write it, you feel it, and you continuously repeat the thought when you see it; which brings about a changed belief system and the process of manifestation. This process of self-hypnosis helps retrain your brain automatically when you wake up and go to sleep, as the positive messages are still in your mind. Your environment maintains being positive without falling to the negative thought patterns of others. This method helps bounce you back quickly and holds you there throughout your day. After about 21 days, the pattern will become your new programming, and results can start to show up for you.

When you write a positive message and associate it with your image, it ties in together as one image subconsciously. For instance, walking up to the mirror in the morning with the message "I am Beautiful" will automatically put you in a positive state of mind to reflect that feeling. Throughout your day this energy will also be felt by others around you and this will bring you more positive reinforcement. Your day will be different than if the message was not there. When it is repeated, it makes changes to your belief system and in turn your factual reality. Just as you see a beautiful sports car with words written on the windshield claiming "A Beautiful Must Have Car" it infuses the adjective with the item to move you to a response. If every day you pass the car dealership seeing that car and message, and you have a feeling inside that makes you emotionally connected to the car, then you may stop and take a closer look. If the salesperson appeals further to your emotional need, you're more likely to buy the car, suit, or anything else that's marketed. You are your own personal positivity sales consultant now, so pitch yourself the best lines for a happier, purpose-filled, and more productive day!

12.12 Manifestation Method - The 'Previously Manifested List'

Here's an exercise that will help you realize that you are a powerful manifester who is divinely connected to the laws of the Universe. Title a page of paper with that acknowledgment; "I Am A Mighty Manifester." Now, think of everything that you've successfully completed in your life already. We've successfully manifested more things than we're usually aware of. You learned how to walk, ride a bike, drive a car, completed various levels of schooling, and many projects that you've done for yourself or someone else. Maybe it was a vacation or job you materialized, a contest you won, or you created a home. Don't attempt to perceive whether the outcomes are good or bad, just focus on what your actions and beliefs have manifested through faith over the years. Include those little miracles in your life that you have no explanation for, or that you attribute to 'luck.' What seems insignificant is highly important for this exercise.

Make a long list of previous manifested activities, and study it. Examine each entry and become aware that to get that result there was a creative process of manifestation that occurred! Weren't there thoughts, ideas, feelings, and choices that came into play that made you choose the route you took? Weren't there challenges you had to overcome? Did you envision yourself in positions or think about how to make your desires your current reality? Did you ask for a certain relationship and manifest that type of person? Were you clear or unclear about the traits of this person? How close to what you wanted were they in fulfilling your desire of being with them? Did you learn or grow from the experience together? When this exercise is done correctly, it is powerful in revealing your manifestation power as one thing becomes very evident: You are a powerful creator and the process has always been working for you. If you have been creating things and situations you are not happy with, then you can change things. If you are happy with what you have manifested so far, you are once again conscious of the process to further and multiply your abundance more consciously.

Why this works: You've just created the proof your awareness needs to gain confidence in your ability to manifest. Now you know you can do it again whenever you wish, because you have manifested miracles and desires before.

12.13 Manifestation Method - 'Big Brother Benjamin'

You often hear the phrases, "If you want to be rich, you have to think rich," and "Fake it till you make it." These little bits of wisdom are only half of the magic formula. Where the real magic lies is not in thinking and pretending till the cows come home, rather it is more important to have the *continuous feeling of abundance throughout your being*. This is what will rocket you toward becoming more abundant. A great way to feel abundant is to hang out as much as possible with your big brother Benjamin. When big brother Benjamin is around, you'll feel and act more confident and financially secure. You will need a crisp $100 bill. Simply earn yourself your next $100 dollars. Feel appreciation for your health and ability to earn this money as you cash your paycheck. Envision how this money will allow you to express your free will to purchase anything you desire. Or you may even decide not to spend it but rather keep it around to remind you of your absolute abundance.

Place the $100 bill in your wallet or purse where it is easily seen by you every time you reach for your billfold to do a purchase transaction. See big brother Benjamin pop out and say hello as he reminds you of your abundance. Don't spend big brother Benjamin, rather know he's there to help you use your money wisely. Big brother counsels you quietly as to make important purchasing decisions which could bring you more purchasing power from sound investment choices. Envision that you could spend this bill anytime you wanted to and you can afford anything it can purchase. Also know that you can earn many more Benjamins if you wanted to easily. Just as you have this one, you can have many more. One thing not to do is worry that you will lose big brother Benjamin. Worry or fear that big brother Benjamin will leave you is not the way of a positive rich abundant thinker like you. Abundance means exactly that: Abundant; as much as you would like, never ending, refills automatically. The thought virus that there is little money out there for you is a very limiting one that is just not true and based on your previous lack mentality. It's time to forever delete that thought from your being. You know very well that the Federal Reserve prints so many hundred dollar bills and that there are many of them in circulation (especially since all those crazy bank bailouts) that you shouldn't be the least bit worried about 'lack' of money available for you. Instead, know that if anyone was to actually find your lost bill, chances are they needed it much more than you did. Be thankful and happy that you were able to shine some good fortune on another human being. You're an abundant provider and God source used you to flow money through to another less fortunate! When money flows, it grows! Simply replace big brother Benjamin with another big brother Benjamin as soon as possible and don't even sweat about it.

Why this works: Your mind does not know the difference between what is real and what is imaginary. Having the vibration of a hundred dollar bill in your pocket has an effect on how you see your buying and spending prowess. The longer your vibration matches with that of a rich abundant thinker, the faster your old programming will fade and physical material manifestation can occur. Though know it is the continual *feeling* of your abundance you are achieving here. This is the key.

For example: A man who can convert his creative thought energy into money, food, and housing for a family is perceived highly by society as they declare him a provider. This individual is continuously blessed and given more by Source when the flow is used in accordance with Universal laws. On the other hand, an individual who cannot even take care of themselves and surrounded by lack mentality is looked at quite the opposite in terms of personal power and ability to flow energy unto himself and others.

12.14 Formula for Successful Manifestation

A logical common sense step to maximizing your material abundance is to maximize cash flow in while minimizing bad habits and stopping all frivolous cash out flow. You will have to be advised by those who have more experience than you in financial matters and it is good to ask for help from financial advisers as you use the methods explained herein to attract new wealth to you. You should set up a plan to get rid of bad debt and control your cash flow as you keep yourself from repeating negative habits like credit cards and frivolous spending. Need help? Simply contact organizations like the National Foundation for Credit Counseling at 1-800-388-2227; http://www.nfcc.org, or contact Debtors Anonymous at 1-781-453-2743, or through their website at http://www.debtorsanonymous.org for help.

Don't keep worrying about the past debt – let the guilt leave your mind! You won't be able to manifest wealth if you are worried and stuck in the vibration of debt and lack. Set up a manageable monthly re-payment plan and take action for slowing down all current and future expense leaks. Then focus ALL your attention on abundance and growth of your income. Focus on what you can do now in the present moment which will unfold to you a magnificent new future!

Your senses must all direct you towards the new desire of wealth. Your beliefs of what is possible or attainable must match up to your new desire of wealth. Your feelings about your self-worth and deserving nature must match up to the new desire of wealth. You must remain fearless in creating your new desired wealth. Melt any fear with unconditional love for yourself. Knowing this is easy; practicing it every time you are confronted with the opportunity to do so is the challenging part.

√ *Dr. Kousouli's Manifestation Formula: Add the Power of Intention + An Open Heart of Gratitude + Clarity of Focused Visualization + Total Emotional Allowance + Inspired Action = High Manifestation Potential*

Your intent locks onto the invisible thought vibration, or wavelength through thought. You focus on it with clarity and vibrancy, which slows the vibration down into a materialized visual object in the current parallel dimension you are physically experiencing. You feel compelled to take an inspired action, or act on a thought to quicken the signal transference. Manifestation can then occur.

12.15 The Key is FOCUS

Focus helps create your world. Set your full attention on good thoughts for you around the perception of what 'good' is for you. You will get what you focus on with intention. You are worthy of all good things, no exception. Think about the Sun and its magnificent energy. What happens when you bring those rays together and focus them through a magnifying glass and onto a piece of paper? It goes right up in flames. Your God force is like the magnifying glass. Either your rays will be spread out or focused and on point.

Resistance is always about you not matching to the vibration you are seeking. Focusing on any vibration that is not what you want is your resistance. It's not your friends, your family, your boss, etc.; it is you and only you that is in charge of what you FOCUS on. Every second of your existence is about what your focus is on, without exception. This is important as what you are experiencing in your life is a direct manifestation of your current thoughts collectively. Anything against what you desire is a non-matching vibration with your desire. When you are focused on your vibrational match, this is when you feel 'in the zone' or on point and on purpose.

Chapter 13:
The Chakra System – Healing Through the Unseen

"The doctor of the future will give no medicine, but will interest his patients in the care of the human frame, in diet, and in the cause and prevention of disease."
~ Thomas Edison

I consider the marvel called the human spine to be the framework for communication, not only between our brains and our bodies, but also between the earth realm and the spiritual realm. It is this structure's health that acts as an "Antenna" to allow you to access all information from the cosmos, as well as inner and outer well-being and homeostasis.

13.1 Remedy Through the Invisible

The placebo effect is a process that involves providing the patient with a made-up treatment, which actually contains no medication. This treatment is generally "prescribed" in order to reinforce the patient's expectation to get well when a medication is administered. Studies have found that the placebo effect can be just as powerful, or even more effective, than the medical treatment given. It is good for a person to have a strong understanding of the placebo effect so that they understand more about the power of mind-body connection and healing.

For example, when a person is given a sugar pill, (a treatment containing no medication), their perception of treatment will cause a therapeutic effect, which means that the person will experience their condition improving. The brain is expecting the change to occur, so it will start the process to produce the healing elements that are needed within the body. The placebo effect proves that the brain plays a big role in the healing process. It is interesting to see that patients can actually be healed by the suggestion of medication if they believe the medication is positive for them. The mind is so powerful that the body works through the healing process, even if their medication is simply a sugar pill. Even the doctor's verbal cues can have a placebo effect on the patients they are working with. For example, if a patient is told that they will be better soon, the patient will be more likely to get rid of their symptoms in the near future.

The human mind is very powerful, and physical symptoms, or healing, can develop based on suggestion alone; especially when it is coming from a person of authority. For example, an experiment was done where patients with specific allergies were told that they were going to have skin contact with the offending plant. Even though patients did not actually have an allergy to the plant (because a different species was used), over 80% of the subjects had a physical reaction: redness, itching, boils, etc. This example shows how effective the power of suggestion can be when the patients' bodies actually created the physical allergic reactions, even though they were not initially allergic to the plant that they came in contact with. Likewise, there are multitudes of researched instances demonstrating that the human body is able to heal itself, if the patient believes that they are receiving a treatment that will help their condition.

As a person understands that it is possible to get well without medication, it increases their faith in their own ability to find better success in alternative treatments; through a healthier mind-body connection. Patients with a good attitude will actually have a faster and improved healing response when they actively participate in the treatment. Health is deeply rooted in the belief system. A person's beliefs, thoughts, and expectations have a strong impact on brain functioning. Understanding this phenomenon will empower them to make lifestyle and belief changes towards a positive attitude about their condition and life.

The Kousouli® Method enforces clear communication to create an environment of positive energy via the *4th step - RESET,* which helps reprogram the subconscious mind for success. Remember that positive communication is more effective for healing than negative communication; whether it is from a doctor, family member, or friend. Surround yourself with loving people who will build you up with positive language. You can tell your family and friends that you are looking for positive verbal support, and ask them to help you in your communication also. A positive environment is vital to mind and body.

13.2 Hypnosis

The Kousouli® Method reflects aspects of sound biomechanical therapy, meditation, spinal neural emotive reconditioning, color therapy, biofeedback, diet modification through whole food nutrition, and hypnosis as approaches to pain management. Hypnosis is an exemplary mind-body therapy that uses the patient's power of intelligence, imagination, and concentration (deep focus), and entails accessing multiple dimensions as deep relaxation increases comfort and control over pain through dissociation, time distortion, pain displacement, sensation alteration, and pain decreasing distractions.

Dr. Elena Gabor, a Medical Hypnotherapist, and author of "Home at the Tree of Life" excellently defines hypnosis as, "A deep meditative state that helps shift the brain activity from the stress-prone areas to the calmer areas, leading to the release of happiness hormones, and, as a result, to good feelings. It also leads to an increase of immune system strength, which protects us from disease. The exploration of the subconscious mind through hypnosis helps identify, dismantle, and replace both conscious and subconscious negatively-oriented, fear-based, and disempowering patterns of thinking. It is a process that leads to overcoming major health challenges such as depression, suicidal thoughts, anxiety, insomnia, pain, and many more. Basically, hypnosis is a natural state of the mind that favors healing."

It can be logically supposed that hypnotherapy entails inclusion of physiological, behavioral, and phenomenological impact on the subject. In the clinical setting, the hypnotic protocol is tailored to the individual based on his or her response to the induction and hypnotic suggestions. Hypnotic suggestions for deep relaxation are increased comfort, decreased pain, increased control over pain, and decreased aggravation by pain. Hypo-analgesic suggestions are most often followed by post-hypnotic suggestions for decreased pain sensation.

13.3 Hypnotherapy and the Mind-Body Problem

Dualism versus monism is at the center of debate in the relationship between the mind-body phenomenon. Mentalists consider the mind a spiritual substance, and consider the body as a sensation of the mind. Physicalists may attribute mental states to a physical process within the brain. Psychological, neurological, endocrinological, and immunological communication systems have been discovered, and a shift towards holism (the whole body and mind together) is beginning to occur. The Kousouli® Method focuses on wellness of the physical, emotional, mental, and spiritual levels of development. The nature of the relationship between the mind and body gives us an option of identifying natural remedies for different diseases.

13.4 The Influence of Mind-Body Theory on Medicine

For over two millennia, Chinese and Ayurvedic medicine has embraced the integration of mind and body. The Western philosophy of medicine was holistically oriented, and treated the whole person, prior to the emergence of the monopolistic biomedical model. Charcot, a French neurologist, is credited with being one of the first scientists to use hypnotic suggestion to treat hysteria, a condition characterized by the presentation of a physical symptom of psychological origin. Many indigenous cultures continue holistic treatments. Energy therapies, herbs, massage, trance, rituals, and natural remedies are found in holistic health regimens that interconnect the mind, body, and spirit. In fact, the Kousouli® Method is also an integrative treatment regimen that incorporates each one of the above holistic principles.

13.5 States of Brain Wave Activity

When hypnosis through subliminal advertising is put into effect it is usually inserted when the person is operating in an alpha or theta level (meditation splits between these two states also), so it is important to deliver suggestions when people are more susceptible in those states. Advertisers also know sex sells so they appeal to the lower primal chakra energies through subliminal sexual advertising. You never see late night personal ads or 'impulse buy infomercials' run at 5pm time slots during the nightly news. This is why late night advertising is so effective. Most people at the midnight to 3am time zone are dozing off into an alpha or theta pattern as they watch late night television. Without knowing they are being programmed, they end up buying products and services they later regret. Let's now discuss brain wave states...

- **Delta waves**: The deep sleep state. Range from 0/.5 to around 4 cycles per second (cps) and are considered total unconscious. Individuals in a coma are in this state.
- **Theta waves**: The drowsy sleepy state. Range from 4 to about 7 cps and are considered to be where our emotional experiences are stored – a subconscious state where psychic phenomena could also reside. Results with hypnosis suggestions are best here. REM Theta with spikes up to alpha (dreams).
- **Alpha waves**: The relaxed state. Range from 7 to around 14 cps; where our normal subconscious resides. Daydreaming, hypnosis, usual sleeping take place in this range and at times dip into theta.
- **Beta waves**: The alert awakened state. Range from 14 cps and up creating our conscious awareness that includes reasoning, thinking, and does not allow too much opening to outside suggestion.

13.6 Covert Hypnosis Is All Around Us

Read this sentence to yourself internally and then externally out loud ten to fifteen times. Do not continue until you have done this at normal pace and also at a much slower pace. **"A buddy of mine who *knows you*, said that you enjoy those *scratch 'n sniff* stickers because *scratching* is *your desire*, and she *knows this to be truth*."**

After you have read this about fifteen times, think back to your recent actions. Did you scratch your nose or touch your face at all while reading the sentence? If yes, then you are currently susceptible to a form of hypnosis called covert text hypnosis. The command is to 'scratch your nose.' The subliminal command is cleverly hidden by '*italicizing*' and increasing slightly the font size of key words (*scratch*, sniff, *your*, scratching and knows) in the sentence. If you did scratch your nose, don't feel bad, it doesn't mean you suffer from a low I.Q., it only means your conscious mind was bypassed and were not aware of it. If you were tired or in an alpha or theta state, it would bypass your conscious mind easier than if you were in an awakened beta state. Try it on a friend, or make up your own hidden message and commands which are hidden in different fonts. Hopefully now, you will understand the power of hypnosis and how those with the knowledge could use this to sway the public mind into doing whatever they like; such as voting for a certain candidate or forming public opinion on any topic through newspaper articles, magazines or billboards.

13.7 Common Myths About Hypnosis Exposed!

Hypnosis as a whole is one of the most-misunderstood practices ever thanks to the propaganda and mistruths of Hollywood films. Clinical hypnosis is safe when performed by a qualified practitioner whose intent is to help a patient heal their disruptive subconscious programming. I am going to help clear up some common misconceptions for you.

1. **Dr. Kousouli, I saw a hypnotist make someone do odd things; what is going on?** The type of hypnosis used in an office session is very different in delivery style and intention, than the hypnosis done in front of a large crowd or stage. Clinical hypnotherapy promotes health and well-being, whereas stage hypnosis is done purely for entertainment value. In stage hypnosis, the carefully selected subjects are chosen on their willingness to let go of inhibitions, and gain approval as a good subject. The reptilian, primitive part of their brain is rewarded by the applause and positive reinforcement of the hypnotist's suggestions, so that the subject acts in a manner that makes for a good show. The volunteers allow themselves to act out the silly suggestions as their conscious analytical mind temporarily lets go. In clinical hypnosis, you relax and focus on the sound of the hypnotist's voice while you are guided to remove stress, heal an addiction, toss a bad habit, or gain more self-confidence.

2. **Can hypnosis be used for brain washing and does the hypnotist control my brain and mind?** The hypnotist is actually a chaperon, who helps guide you through the path to self-hypnosis. If you are unwilling to follow suggestions, unable to relax, or can't focus while the process is being conducted, there is no force

that can still hypnotize you. You still have free will, and it cannot be taken from you unless you give it over willingly.

3. **Can hypnosis be used to enslave me?** Hypnosis can be used for positive intent as well as negative, but no one is permanently taking your conscious thinking mind away from you. The intended process in your doctor's office is focused on helping you; teaching your mind to relax and let go of the negative stress or subconscious programs that no longer serve you. If you continuously watch negative television or movie programming, the television or film acts as your hypnotist. The programming will input negative thoughts (fears, violence, or other unacceptable behavior) into your mind over time because you allow it to; by giving your focused attention to it. This is why parents tend to blame television, video games or movies for the changed behavior of their children. However, the parent or individual is to blame for allowing the wrong type of guide to influence their subconscious mind. When you use hypnosis for the right reasons regularly with a relaxed open mind, you can literally change your life for the better.

4. **Do you forget everything that happened during a hypnosis session?** As I mentioned above, all that hypnosis does is teach your mind to relax and focus. If you do not remember anything from the session then your mind won't remember to utilize it when you need it. The body and mind always remember subconsciously; it is what we choose to recall consciously from the stored information that shows up for us to use in our lives. You will not remember your session consciously, if you act upon any suggestion given to you by the hypnotist that upon waking, you will not remember the session.

5. **Can I lie while under hypnosis?** You will have all thinking capabilities active. In fact you'll be more focused and more active because your mind is freer to create. It is your choice to 'create' the truth or lie, even though it is never advisable to lie. The suggestions you make or are given will be more real or true to you depending on what you feel the 'truth' is.

6. **Isn't Hypnosis against the basic principle of Christianity?** Seventh Day Adventists and Christian Scientists have religious doctrines that speak against using hypnosis; but not because it goes against Christianity, rather for possible traditional and political reasons. All Christians practice meditation through a modified form of self-hypnosis or what some religions like to refer to as prayer, which helps them relax the mind towards asking God for divine intervention.

7. **Dr. Kousouli, I've heard Hypnosis is very common in our day to day lives; how**

so? Hypnosis is a natural process and all of us have experienced a form of it at some point of our lives. Road hypnosis is common for those who drive often on highways and suddenly find themselves at their destination in little or no time at all, wondering how they got there so quickly. Prior to bed every night, the body goes through a shutting down cycle referred to as sleep hypnosis. Some spouses claim their significant other unknowingly talks in their sleep but seems very awake. Unresponsive teenagers staring at the television with solid focus while mom is telling them dinner is ready, is the effect of covert hypnosis. Covert hypnosis is a sneaky and well known practice among large corporations to manipulate people into trusting and buying their products. The mass public is subtly conditioned over time through image, text and font manipulation of print in magazine articles, billboards, or newspapers, hiding brand logos in hoax viral videos, or transmitting television and radio frequencies that affect the mind. A usual trait among hypnosis episodes is that time seems to have gone by quickly, or that time simply does not exist at all. Everyone at some point in their life has been in a self-induced hypnotic state without even knowing it. Clinical hypnosis refocuses and targets its use for positive changes in one's life.

8. **Dr. Kousouli, what is regression hypnotherapy and how does it help?**
    As defined, to regress is to go backwards. Regression hypnotherapy is a specialty within hypnotherapy that looks at possible unresolved previous lifetime emotions, events, feelings, or traumas that may be lodged far down in the patient's subconscious. Patients under regression hypnotherapy report reliving and 'seeing' the root cause of their issue that has been unknown to them in their conscious day to day life. They find their path forward seems much easier as they explain that the 'issue' that held them back has been forever understood and resolved. Regression hypnotherapy is usually sought out as a last resort to help a patient when every other modality or therapy has not produced effective results.

13.8 Dreams

Dreams are direct communication from that which we call "God," or the soul. It is the space in time where truths are revealed and passed down to us in a manner our limited vocabulary or primitive brain can understand. The life you live is a byproduct of the beliefs, thoughts, and feelings you are bringing into your consciousness. Nightmares or bad dreams can form from unresolved tensions and stress thoughts, which upon waking could give you special insight for problem solving. Dreams are very important. Pay attention to your dreams and have them decoded (there are many books and online dream interpretation sites that can help you) for they can give you information needed for the Earth realm. Tell yourself you will dream right before you go to sleep, telling yourself that you will be retaining the information that is most important to you. Right upon waking, ask yourself if you dreamt and ask yourself how it felt. You may want to keep a daily dream journal. Quickly write down what you remember; the longer you wait, the faster it will be harder to recall what you saw.

While your body rests, your soul is in the astral realm solving all types of problems for when you come back to your physical body. You even orchestrate and flow through to future potentials or other dimensions, playing out scenarios you may choose to create. You will even experience Déjà vu moments here in your linear earthly life, when you feel that you have lived the same scenario before. This is like your spirit's confirmation to your conscious mind that you've been there before and you are making the correct decisions, thus letting yourself remember that you are on track. Inventors have brought back with them life-altering inventions, artists have created epic works of art from their dream sequences, and directors have spellbound us with their visions on the big screen; all from dreams experienced in other realms. The astral and dream state is the real home base of our souls. Experiences here on Earth are formed so that we may expand ourselves as creators. The Creator has truly made us in His image and given us His most beautiful gift, the ability to create as He has, over and over again. We feel like God when we create original art, music, build homes and skyscrapers, or bring a child into this world. Isn't it wonderful to look at a beautiful work of pottery art and sigh with joy as we realize that it was created from just a glob of clay? Pay attention to your dreams, as they can empower you to work closer with your higher self for quantum level manifestation.

13.9 Astral Projection

Astral travel, or astral projection, dates back to the times of ancient China. It is a version of an 'out of body' experience that occurs while awake, in deep meditation, or while lucid dreaming. A person's awareness is shifted into a 'spiritual body double,' which is in sync with the physical body in a comparable realm recognized as the astral plane. This 'subtle body' is connected with the physical body through an energetic link, which often appears as a shiny grey or silvery cord inserted into a chakra.

Some theorize that it's impossible to truly leave the body, and that our physical world and the astral plane exist as intertwined points on a field of awareness together. Others speculate that our physical and spiritual bodies are separate and can experience various parts of creation independently from one another. During an astral projection, people say that flying like a bird, viewing future scenarios, communicating with those who have crossed over after death, visiting other planets, seeing the past, and similar phenomenon are all possible.

13.10 Understanding the Third Eye

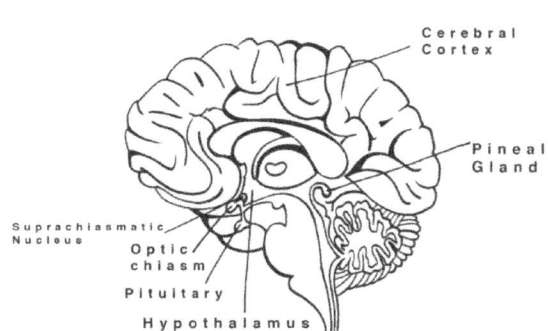

Although the term third-eye can be used for various purposes, it always relates to chakras, enlightenment, and the activation of psychic potential which is related to the clairvoyance. The third eye is associated with the pineal gland; an endocrine gland in the middle of the brain that is shaped like a pine cone and is the size of a pea. The pineal gland deals with melatonin, sleep patterns and circadian rhythms. Keeping it decalcified and soft is important for its function and your health. Garlic, parsley alfalfa and Iodine from dark greens like kelp, can help keep It healthy. The third-eye is one of many main energy portals, or chakras, in our aura. It is closely linked with the senses of awareness, and the spiritual realm. In Buddhist and Hindu religions, the third eye is understood as the symbol of insight and illumination. Spiritually, many of our psychic abilities heighten during meditative awakening of the third eye. Telepathy, remote viewing, and telekinesis, are just a few of the skills that can activate. Unravelling the third eye has been the goal of many ancient civilizations for its power can open up a new world to those previously naïve of its existence. The third-eye is associated with the sixth brow chakra and the color indigo (dark blue). See 13.25 and the Kousouli® Master chart for more information.

Activation of the Pineal Gland/Third Eye using Herbal Medicine

The medicine Ayahuasca is an entheogen, which means 'spawning the divine within.' An entheogen is plant matter with hallucinogenic effects utilized in religious, shamanic, spiritual, and medicinal practices. DMT (N, N-Dimethyltryptamine) is a psychoactive chemical in Ayahuasca, closely related to serotonin in the tryptamine family. DMT activates intense visions that are naturally produced in small quantities within the human brain, giving access to the spirit world and literally allowing you to dream while awake.

It is believed Moses was given manna in the desert, which may have had miraculous effects on him, assisting the abilities he was divinely given to create the miracles that were witnessed. For centuries, Man has wanted to communicate with God, and the Bible conveys that Man was able to do so in deeply profound ways. It certainly seems possible that our ancestors were more connected with herbs, the Earth, meditation, and the paranormal than we are today. Could the prophets, Jesus, Moses and all spiritual greats have been able to meditate to the point of activating a rush of their natural DMT reserves, and not only create miracles but live in more than one dimension at the same time? It can also be suggested that the human brain in ancient times produced more DMT than we do today. Let's examine a passage from Isaiah 6:

"Above him were seraphs, each with six wings: With two wings they covered their faces, with two they covered their feet, and with two they were flying. And they were calling to one another: 'Holy, holy, holy is the Lord Almighty; the whole earth is full of his glory.' At the sound of their voices the doorposts and thresholds shook and the temple was filled with smoke."

If someone told you they saw the above events while awake in full consciousness, you would believe they were either referring to a dream, or they were high on some sort of drug. What if this was seen in a normal state that occurred when one connected with their natural state of God? Today, we do not eat, drink, or keep ourselves as pure to connect with God the way we used to in ancient times as shown through disassociated living with technology, toxic lifestyle and busy work stress.

Those who experience Ayahuasca today, claim seeing visions of unimaginable creation and beauty. Some report witnessing the very essence and meaning of life itself. Time, and reality as we know it, cease to exist when in the presence of Divine consciousness. The world we know is broken down into pieces and the knowledge of God becomes clear; as you are one again with all energy, leaving the material world for a glimpse into all possibility. The experience can be frightening to some, while blissful to others, depending on the ego mind and state of the person's mood and beliefs when entering the experience. Fearful thoughts would bring on fearful worlds, and loving hearts would explore more loving realms. Those who go through the DMT experience describe it as spiritually awakening. Whatever the journey, Ayahuasca always leaves the observer humbled by the experience. They say they feel they know the truths of the Universe. Those who experience DMT assert that this life we know physically on Earth is not 'reality,' but merely a created illusion of our focused intention in a constant accumulation of experience.

Some benefits of chelation therapy using EDTA and/or UV therapy are associated with the decalcification of the pineal gland. It doesn't happen for everyone, as calcification of the pineal is a natural part of the aging process unfortunately. Quick calcification of the pineal gland occurs in a large percentage of people over 60 years of age due to high toxic load of fluoride and chlorine levels, bad diet and prescription drug use.

13.11 Love, Sex, Relationships and Auric Spaces

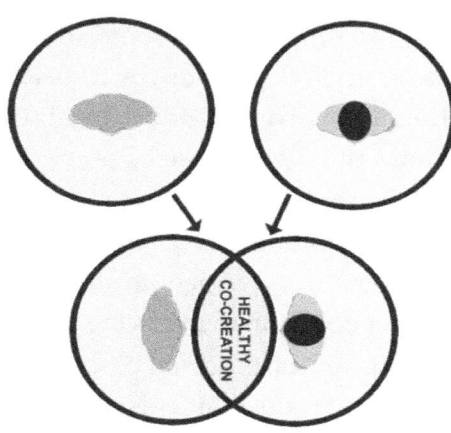

Now let's take a look at how relationships are affected by auric space. Each circle shown surrounding an individual represents one's identity and personal auric energy space. The figure shows a female and male separately and then together interacting where their circles cross. The first diagram shows a healthy, positive co-creation for both the female and the male; neither invades on the other's personal freedom or will. They each have plenty of their own identity and space to be comfortable, yet are still present within the relationship. This is positive, normal, and healthy for all parties involved. When two or more people spend time in close proximities together, their illusions/worlds/space is shared and they enter into co-creation. In any relationship, as long as both individuals hold on to their identity, personal power, and self-worth without giving over their power to another, they will continue to appreciate both themselves and the other person. This is evident when two people meet and each like the other in the infatuation stage of a relationship. Both are accepted for who they are in their own power. No one has yet to cross any personal boundaries and no one causes another to sacrifice needlessly. There has not been any 'giving up' of personal energy, free will, or identity.

However, if the personal boundary is crossed there will be an imbalance as shown in the diagram here. When a partner decides to be overbearing to another or tries to exert their will-power on another (i.e. tries to 'change them'), a conscious or subconscious agreement by one partner for loss of power and the other for gain of power may occur.

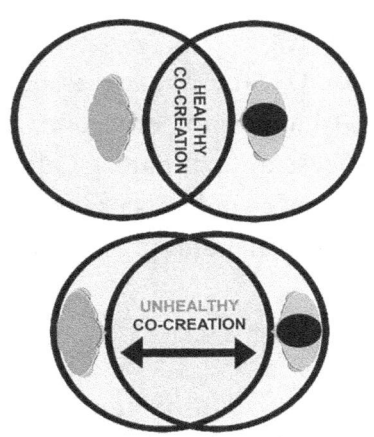

The one who is submissive will be under control of the other's energy space, which holds the images, ideas, and desires of the overpowering partner. This new energy is foreign in the aura of the oppressed, and after a while this will weaken the submissive one into depression or revolt. It takes a tremendous amount of energy to be out of balance in one's personal space. This causes explosions of emotion that end up in disagreements, fights, and violent breakups. It's a natural process because each subconsciously wants their own space and identity back. The imbalance cannot go on too long without some sort of compensation in life occurring elsewhere, such as sadness, grief, depression, or dis-ease. The truth, however, is that this all happens by choice. The submissive individual, by his or her own free will and on some subconscious level, allows the interchange of power to occur. The reason one allows giving up of their power can be many. It could be a repeat of old incarnation patterns, the soul's need to experience vulnerability in a relationship, wanting to overcome abuse and become an example for others, an agreement to strengthen areas in this life they are not strong in (i.e. attractive and poor woman marrying a man for money), or to simply gain a new experience on handling contrast. Loving co-creative relationships can occur as long as each one's personal auric space and identity is respected and allowed to be maintained by its original owner, not by anyone else; parent, sibling, lover, etc. Successful married couples that last, always allow the mate to be themselves. Although they may interchange energy by compromising day to day for small things, they always retain their original energy as to not create personal imbalance for too long. They both cherish and respect each other for who they are as individuals as well as a close unit.

We tend to find people we like by psychically feeling what it is in their illusion, world, or auric field that lights up ours and feels familiar. When two auric spaces cross for the first time, whatever matches between the two spaces gives us the feeling of familiarity in our field and we say, "I feel like we've known each other forever." When we connect to this feeling, it drives us to learn more about the other person's illusions/world, or auric space. Likewise, if there is something in their space that you wish to

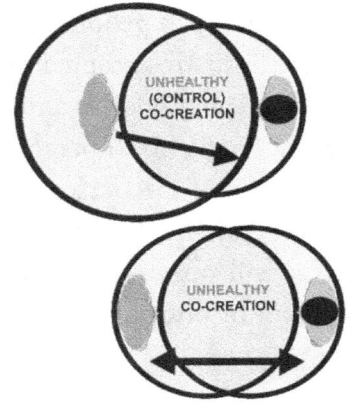

experience or learn, that too will pull you into that illusion or world, so you may experience that through your desire of it. These feelings usually start as little hunches that may be ignored at first.

Eventually, they can become so powerful it brings two people to the point of sharing their root chakra energy (sex) and co-creating /connecting energies for new creation; a new life, a baby. Thus the process of creation and bringing a once departed soul with no physical body back into this dimension for new experiences continues. The more two people share this co-creation experience, via their root chakra and through the act of sex, the more the two illusions/worlds/ auric spaces combine; to the point that both partners involved will know what the other is thinking, complete each other's sentences or share similar tendencies. They are now not only 'joined at the hip,' but in auric space and in this worldly illusion state as well. His story is her story, and vice versa. When the case does not end up in a child being born or created, the union will be strong as long as both are happy with the path of growth as a bonded unit. However, eventually the female, who is biologically created to move toward motherhood may want to complete the natural cycle of her biological identity as a female reincarnation and become a mother. If the male is not ready to perceive his world as a father and enjoys the single life to continue creating his world and experiences as such, then this will create a disharmony in the union and a separation of that co-creation will occur. Anytime there is a separation of such created worlds, the invested or misplaced energy must be relocated back to each individual. There is bound to be emotional outburst or movement of this energy in the direct proportion one invested. There will be a void or emptiness where an auric field had the other's energy until you recall your energy and move forward in your creation by yourself, or with another you signal to you who now matches your new illusion or reality based on your new perceived experience.

Identity Within the Family

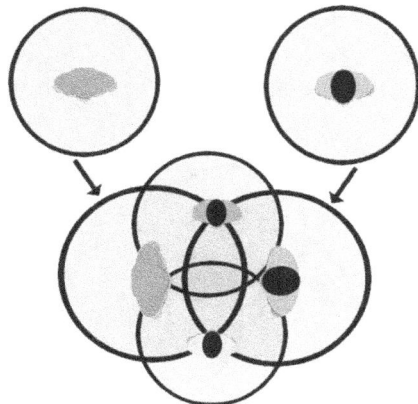

In the case of a family where energies are co-mingled in close quarters, family quarrels can be quite frequent when energies of co-creations clash. This is especially true when children growing up are trying to find themselves and maintain their personal space, aura, and identity. They have quite a task as they fight off the deceptive mind manipulation of mass marketing through billboards, television, and radio telling them how they should think and act to be happy. It is further

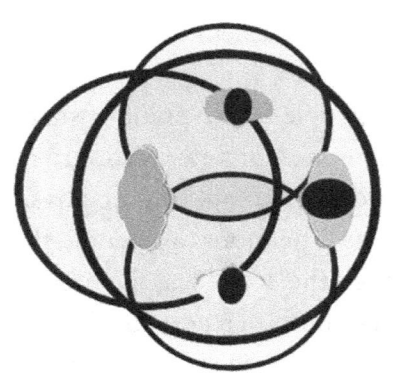

challenging to do this when the school system is flawed and home life is overly saturated with the desires and demands of an overbearing parent; one who often lives their life vicariously through their child. For example, an overpowering mother can overtake a growing boy's identity and handicap them later in life when he is an adult by not letting him complete his creation of identity, missing personal energy which his mother had taken and shaped for years. The 'mama's boy' grows up to be a young man with socially awkward tendencies and co-dependency issues. He will subconsciously be trying to find his missing energy, or identity he had as a child by attracting a woman who has similar qualities as his mother. The same is true of women in abusive relationships where an overbearing father disciplined with force or 'tough love.' These women feel in their identity that, to be complete or happy in their world, they must be with a male which is a protector through violence, and this is what love means to them. They end up attracting someone like their father or worse yet, mimic the actions of their father towards their children. The images and ideas in our auric field can multiply and copy to others quickly like a mutating virus.

The key to loving relationships is the ability to unconditionally love another to the point where you allow them to be who they are, and understand they are growing at their own pace within their space. As long as growth is happening with everyone at the same time in a positive manner, the unions will maintain their strength. If one decides to exert pressure through trying to change another, they will most surely be disappointed when the relationship explodes with emotional charge. This is always the case, as one who doesn't grow or feels stuck, repressed, or taken advantage of with pent up anger, resentment, guilt, etc. is sure to make fireworks occur in order to be heard.

Auric Spaces in Children

We can also think about how this interaction affects children as they grow. A parent-child relationship develops when the children who do not yet have their own complete understanding of the world absorb like a sponge the energies in the parental auras. The sum

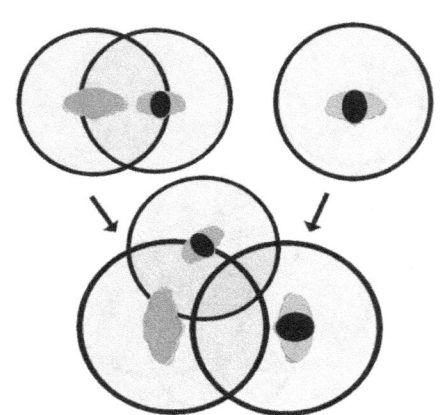

of how we act as adults can be attributed to this time where our spiritual and physical DNA intertwines to develop those characteristics, thoughts, prejudices, quirks, habits, and solutions to the challenges we experience in our worlds. Our interrelationship with family members and the strangers we allow into our auric space, gives us the illusions we choose and pick from. From there, we incorporate those illusions as we see fit, or those that are helpful to us on our individual journey.

You Are In Charge of YOU

People forget their power of free will is to choose. This is most evident in those who are in relationships where children are involved. They often feel trapped and that there's no way out, mostly due to their definition of commitment. Their happiness is sacrificed for others constantly. People stay in abusive relationships or situations and say, "I can't get divorced, I can't leave him/her, I'll have to give her/him 50%, I can't because of the kids." etc. etc. These are all excuses that keep them enslaved to their insecurities within that relationship. People choose to make their life miserable by not enacting the positive aspects of the law of free will. They choose 'not to choose,' and in return they become slaves to others who are using the law of free will. Those who live true to their free will are happy, cheerful, clear, and create colorful worlds others envy. All choices have consequences, some more and others less. All consequences also lead to more choices. It never ends. Growth always occurs; even if the seemingly wrong choice is chosen at that time, it may end up being the right choice down the road. Relationships are a way to massive growth and personal change. We help each other reflect aspects of ourselves which may need growth. We should be in appreciation of all relationships, and to all people we've shared our space intimately with. When we usually look back to where we were and how far we've come in life, we can see just how we have been transformed into a better version of ourselves.

13.12 Attracting the Right Mate For a Lasting Relationship

The word "love" is misused so much that it has created difficulty in relationships. Consider a father who tells his child that he loves him, and that's why he's beating him. This same child grows up thinking love is pain, and then gets in relationships that are painful so that he can understand the feeling of "love." Or a woman may create her current reality in such a way that all her personal relationships come to a quick end from self-sabotage, due to previous events she saw as a young teenager when her single mother would repeatedly date abusive men. Unknown to her now, she's set herself up for an emotional loop of repeatedly ruining her own intimacy. Many who get into a relationship end up looking to please others first, and end up surprised when they get their feelings hurt. Don't expect to live your illusion looking to find love in others and then think your life will be complete when you find "the one," as that will set you up for failure and will continue the lesson of self-appreciation. You cannot expect another to appreciate you unless that same frequency is being emitted by you. Everyone has their own soul and their own body, feelings, thoughts, etc. Each, when used correctly, acts accordingly. Achieving the vibration aligned to that which is our desire, without resistance, allows the desire to be fulfilled. When one decides that they are not missing their mate, the mate can appear. We cannot have high hopes for a perfect mate but not be their equivalent in energy. How can someone expect a princess to be their mate if they are still a frog? Fairy tales may have convinced us of this possibility, but only a spiritual understanding and working on oneself can enact the law of Attraction so that "like may find like." When we expect that there is no one that's perfect for us, or when we feel there are "no good women or men out there," the law of Expectation is in effect all the time, especially when one looks for relationships to go their way. If you expect someone to not respect you, you bring on more of that disrespect. The key is to maintain as much of your own vibrational frequency, and know when that vibrational frequency is overpowered or knocked off its point by surrounding energy. If so, it would be important to get it back onto the proper vibration once more by purifying more of your auric field to be in line with that which you are and removing that which you are not.

Do not try to please others without taking care of yourself first. It is not selfish, but a logical necessity. You must be satisfied where you are in your soul development, and remove the thoughts or negative loops that are giving you what you do not desire. The key is to understand you first and foremost, before you ever try to share yourself with someone else. If you do not focus on your own soul work first, the energy you attract in another will not match your expectation of the level you really wish to be with, and this almost always ends in disaster.

13.13 Relationship Misunderstandings

Lies in relationships come from misunderstanding another's illusion taken as a reality. When each partner comes to terms with who they really are, they will not have to put up a smokescreen to convince the other with falsehoods, nor feel the need to "get away with something" and not have to give truth. If both do not reach for their core love and see their partner in the light they want them to be, appreciate them for who they fell in love with, or speak and act towards them in a loving manner, then the loop of deceit will continue to evolve into a co-created reality that both will desire to get away from as it brings them pain. The more focus on the pain, the greater the separation from whom they truly are, or were to each other, and in that sense a separation will occur. Not that it is wrong, but can only be right considering the way each mate's emotional guidance system is moving each away from what they don't want and more towards what they do want. Peace. For them to find peace and happiness together, they will have to find their center and reconnect to where they want to be. They cannot keep focusing on their current negative vibration, as that will only bring more separation. Neither must blame the other nor make them feel guilty. An immediate dis-connect of attention to where they are and an immediate reconnection of thoughts, ideas, and desires in themselves and each other must be implemented to get them to where they wish to be as a team. Both must feel good immediately - right now, right away - and then find out how to stay in this feeling of harmonious vibration, both as individuals and as a couple. Clarity will come in due time, as long as the focus diverts from what is not working and is placed on what is working. As long as anyone is in a negative vibratory state they will not and cannot see the options and opportunities available to them.

13.14 You're In Charge of Your Own Life

Remember, you are in charge of your own vibration at all times no matter what is going on around you or even with a spouse or child. Patients often come and complain that their spouse is no longer looking as attractive as they once did, or that their loved one has lost hope of staying healthy. The loving spouse tends to look beat up, anxious, and beside themselves because they surely are about to give up "leading a horse to water and forcing it to drink." Yes, you should be there for your mate and helpful to them when they are having challenges, but ultimately they have their life journey and you have yours. You came into this life alone and you will leave it alone. Everything you own is 'temporarily borrowed' and everyone you meet you will see again in another energy form. This illusion is fleeting, as they say, "Life is short." However, love is forever and that is evident in how you can effectively exude it without compromising yourself. It is not easy to upkeep your own vibrations of happiness and joy when another close by is experiencing illness, pain, or discomfort. You cannot think for your loved one, and ultimately that's what is going to make the difference if they are in a low vibration. What your loved one thinks and feels is what will guide them to recovery or more illness. So you cannot and should not blame yourself for any final outcomes, but be there to support by giving love and helping them paint a picture in their mind of high vibrations and total health. The only thing that will help another is bringing them back to alignment with their highest vibration of love and joy. You cannot do this for them, nor can a doctor, but what both can do is be a reminder and picture of what perfect health is, and you can help them see that they, too, can reconnect to that frequency and get it for themselves by taking your example.

13.15 Take the Lead Role in Your Play

"The world is a stage," they say. Everyone has their role to play and we're all participating actors. Hold on to that character which you wish to become and evolve him/her through your journey. Do not sacrifice your desires for what others want you to become for them. Sacrificing yourself brings resentment for the other person, but ultimately also for yourself, as regret reminds you constantly that you did not live up to your greatest potential. You are here on Earth to develop your story. Through your spiritual struggle, you will face many who will want you to conform to their illusion and tell you that your version of illusion or reality is illegitimate or untrue. They would like you to conform to their ideals, their morals, their laws and way of experiencing life. In time you lose who you are and you deny your truth because you are not living for you, but rather for them. You remove yourself as a lead role character in your play and become a supporting actor or 'extra' in their illusion, as well as yours.

Check in with yourself from time to time by asking yourself, "What do I think of the role I am playing in my life right now? Does what I am doing, thinking, acting out work for me? Does this match my version of moving toward my life goals?" Be real with yourself. If you do not re-center your thoughts back to your purpose, you will be drained by others' illusions, or their reality, and get stuck in it.

13.16 Changing Who You Are to Who You Can Be

If we desire to be successful, we must be honest with ourselves in understanding our weaknesses. Recognition and awareness are the initial key steps to starting to change things, but then we must take action. Reevaluation of self is the key step that leads to removing the things you are afraid of. There are many things that are hidden in the Akashic record of your spiritual DNA, typically shown through behavior when triggered by something that 'triggers' you. Third dimensional ego must be submissive to your higher self. A sign that someone is working through higher consciousness, is that they hear others out and listen without judgment, anger, or damnation, and offer only solutions, not more problems. They offer calm in the midst of chaos. Higher consciousness doesn't desire to be the center of attention at the peril of others. Higher minded people are proactively cooperative for the win-win situation of all involved, and don't react defensively. There are no outbursts, or judgments against something being said against them, only love. No matter what circumstances surround them, they saw the God in all. Everyone finds their path to God in their own way. Be honest with yourself, and evaluate with direct, dedicated study what it is that makes you - you.

Are you divorced or separated from someone you once loved, and now dislike and hate the idea of meeting up with your ex-lover? Are you holding onto a grudge by taking unfair alimony from an ex, holding them hostage while you remain able bodied to work and create for yourself? Do you see the love in others, or are you keeping yourself from true forward movement in higher assertion of self? Is racial bigotry in your heart? Where is your love? If you are a Republican, do you respect a Democrat and see them as a brother or sister? Or are you judgmental, reactive, and angry when communicating your ideas if others disagree with you? Are you a fan of the 49ers and dislike or hate the Steelers? Are you a proclaimed Christian, yet judge your brother who decides to be Muslim? Are you Protestant and judge your sister who decides to be Catholic? Do not judge others who may not be spiritually where you are. Be joyous that they found their own source to bliss. Remodel yourself with conscious awareness and get rid of your fears, addictions, frustrations, anger, hate, and humble the ego. It is all changeable through proactive movement, not reactive past programming.

13.17 A Loner Maybe, But Never Alone

The feeling we place upon ourselves that we are lonely or alone is an illusion that presents as 'real.' We are all here on a deep personal purpose or personal experience, but we are all also connected together in making that illusion or reality happen. So yes, we are both alone and together, connected in a cyclical pattern as we go through life and death. In both scenarios all exist - some in one form and some in another, depending on how each plays their part. We choose to focus on the part of the whole that we want to experience. If you are feeling lonely it's only because you choose to feel the separation from togetherness as you forget the larger life cycle and the connection to both your higher self and to others. In actuality, both the energy of loved ones here and loved ones deceased both exist and are with us all the time; just in another form, wavelength, and energy pattern. They choose to exist or experience another version of themselves (non-physical reality) at a time we choose to experience that which we want to (physical reality).

Anyone who is reminded of his or her connection to *'all that is'* doesn't really feel loneliness on this earth. Feeling lonely usually means you are less connected to the power of the Source. One may choose to be a loner and go about the journey themselves, but feeling lonely is not an option for those who are on their path. Never forget that you have a legion of angels with you at all times, ready to act on your command - always. If you have been successful to cross the spirit realm through meditation or altered states of being, you will see how the other side is real and not mere fantasy or false doctrine. This physical world and its rules are malleable like clay. Thoughts and words are the tools we use to make this clay our experience within this realm we call 'reality.' I tell you the Truth, my brothers and sisters: This all is an illusion we co-create together; this is the dream.... so let us all make it a dream worth dreaming.

13.18 Victim Mentality

Relationships are all energetic attractions. When the vibrational field changes, the relationship changes or ends. The vibrational connection is what brings it in. When you think you are a victim, the vibration going out will bring you victim circumstances to validate your thoughts and feelings of being victimized. It will keep you enslaved to your current lower frequency attraction. Even the jobs you hold are the vibrational match to the relationship of what you believe about your skills, and your ability to serve others. Your worth is what you feel and believe it to be, so when you get into a great new loving relationship, you feel amazing because you sent a vibration that matched yours and now feel higher than before. The law of intention sends out the signal to help bring about a 'victor' vibration of attraction. The intent to be victorious must be strong enough for it to manifest. It must overpower the previous lower frequency to see the movement towards the new experience or new reality to validate your thoughts and feelings of visualization.

13.19 Sex and the Creative Forces of the Lower Chakras

When we focus on sexual thoughts we work mainly from the first and second chakras. The second chakra is of emotional connection and sexuality. The first controls the feelings of primitive creation. When all our focus is upon the act of sex, we are creating or enacting upon our being the awesome force of creating another human being. The energies brought forth are tremendous and they can feel energized and then depleting as in the case of male ejaculation. The male ejaculate is life force energy leaving the male and entering the female which is able to cultivate that energy and present an environment for the entering soul needing a physical body.

When sex is used as a creative or expressive energy combined with the thought and connection of love, it is indeed a beautiful thing. However, if used with the thought of lust or intent to do harm or hurt another, those negative thoughts will cause harm to an individual such as in the case of rape or sexual addiction.

Energy is neither created nor destroyed - it is however transformed, harvested, projected and absorbed. When energy is projected upon another person with negative intent the energy has to go somewhere. If the person being projected upon is strong willed and has a working understanding of their aura, body, and thoughts then they can ward off and deflect this energy. However, those who have no conscious abilities of their internal power may be more susceptible to outside influence of this energy.

"We should not lust after evil things."
~ 1 Corinthians 10:6

"Watch and pray, that ye enter not into temptation: the spirit indeed is willing, but the flesh is weak."
~ Matthew 26:41

"Ye have heard that it was said by them of old time, 'Thou shalt not commit adultery:' But I say unto you, That whosoever looketh on a woman to lust after her hath committed adultery with her already in his heart."
~ Matthew 5:27-28

Women of all ages run their energy through males to control men usually through the root, sacral and heart chakras. Mothers do it to control their sons' lives (i.e. momma's boys), and many women try to control their husbands or boyfriends by throwing sexual energy in order to persuade or manipulate.

13.20 Sexual Consciousness

It has been said by some scientists there is an actual gay gene that makes people become homosexual. Some priests say it is demonic and they can "pray the gay away." Others say that the spirit which comes into the body has brought too much energy from a former life or their experience from another life was so eventful or unfinished that their transition into this life mimics a lot of the last one which could have been the opposite sex compared to this life choice. Others say souls purposely choose to come in as a homosexual or transgender person to offer contrast and uplift the consciousness of the population to open their minds to other possibilities and in turn sacrifice themselves to the harsh comments and derogatory statements people make to cause them to feel bad about themselves when in reality they are full of love and take on the world's hate as their own burden. And others say that there is an uneven level of male or female energy in the auric field either from the mother or the father which is overbearing to the new soul coming in. Mixed with environmental factors it could explain why some men or women grow up to be homosexual while others are just born that way and know that they are. Whatever the case, it is time humanity set aside differences of race, color, creed, sex, and went forward with the knowingness of love in their heart, for God is not about separation but of unification and loves all his creation regardless of choices and classification. It is Man who is quick to cry out, "You're going to hell", and points fingers full of hypocrisy; not a loving forgiving and understanding God that created everyone in his image and everything for our conscious expansion. For more on sexual consciousness and developing your power of persuasion in love and relationships, read my book, *BE A MASTER® OF SEX ENERGY*.

13.21 Clear the Mind and Heart of Burdened Thoughts

You must believe before you see the manifestation. Think new thoughts that change your belief system. God will give you that which is in your predominant thought. He always says YES to you, even if you want bad things that are not good for you. God knows if you go through rough times, it will only give you more growth, so this is why you can have anything you like without exception. Beliefs are only a collection of thoughts held onto for a period of time. Beliefs coupled with time leads to experiences, the experiences further solidify your beliefs and it keeps going. Truth is when enough thought was given to a belief that the belief became concrete in its earthly manifestation. The more people connecting to a thought, the more powerful it becomes. Pure thought over time without resistance becomes unstoppable.

"At that time the disciples came to Jesus, saying, "Who is the greatest in the kingdom of heaven?" And calling to him a child, he put him in the midst of them and said, "Truly, I say to you, unless you turn and become like children, you will never enter the kingdom of heaven. Whoever humbles himself like this child is the greatest in the kingdom of heaven." ~ Matthew 18:1-4

"Be like children," said Christ, "Do not hinder the children to come unto me" (Matthew 19:14). What do these

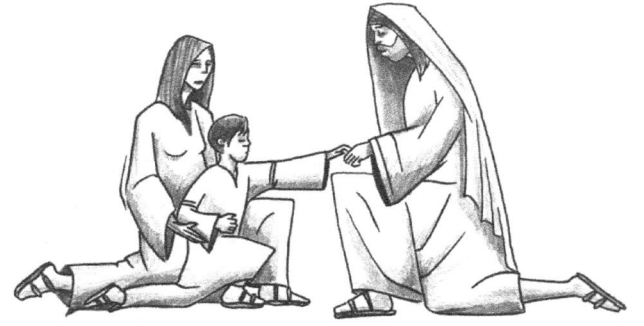

words mean: "Be like children"? We're not speaking here about faking simplification, to deny growing up, or to be in somehow less activated in the mental, emotional, or physical maturation of oneself. "Be like children" does not mean infantilism; or suggest that we need to be airy fairy about being serious in what we do or say. This would be opposite the meaning of what Christ is saying, dismissing the notion of being child-like as unimportant. What is meant here is in terms of innocence, faith and love. The words tell us to be un-programmed of this world. Little children are pure and still remember their not so long ago connection to God since being born; unlike adults who get caught up in the worries and continued pain cycles they trap themselves into. Look at little children play. When they get mad at another child they don't stay mad long. Before the day is over the incident that caused them vibrational discourse is over and they all play together again as if nothing had happened. Children have no sly thoughts or negativity towards others and feel no shame about their bodies running around diaper-less, laughing and crawling around as they explore the awesome possibilities of being in a new world. They come into a physical reality focused only on the present – the here and now - ready to explore and create new experiences. They are not stressing about the past or focused on the future. As new, pure and shiny beings we can feel and see how connected they still are to the other side just by being near their energy. This 'innocence' begins to quickly fade after age six, as the environment of this world reprograms them. As adults we love looking at babies because something amazing happens. Our heart chakra connects with the baby, filling us with love and wonder again. There is an undeniable movement in our soul that reminds us of the 'home,' where we also came from not too long ago. It's a very familiar moment in time when we instantly know we are all right here, no matter what difficulty we may be going through. We smile, we look back, and our soul says, "Thank you," as we get a little reassuring encouragement that our journey here is blessed. We know we are eternal the moment we see a mother experience a newborn in her arms. The next time you look at a new soul traveler here from the other side, look into their eyes and feel that connection to our maker, the universal source of all abundance, and all that is. I bet the sight of the newborn will follow your mouth with a smile. What a big contrast from our now rugged and overly emotional adulthood.

    As adults we tend to hold grudges, make lists of who has wronged us, gossip about our latest misfortunes, downgrade those we find to be different than us, plot against our enemies and in the end the only one we hurt is our self. Do we think and act as children, or do we appear as hardened programmed robots? Be like a child, laugh, be innocent, and quickly forgive. Connect to the source of love, just as you did when you were a child.

13.22 Angels in the Auric Field

Some metaphysical experts claim that we give ourselves a reason to believe in angels. In reality, the larger, intangible part of ourselves, the unseen 'higher-self' part, (which is always available to us), transforms into a physical persona that allows us to experience miracles. According to Genesis 1:1 of the Bible, God created angels while creating heaven to help humanity through its evolution. Even though the Bible does not say how many angels exist, we see in Hebrews 12:22 and Matthew 26:53, that the number is described as 'vast.' Angels vary in their appearance during sightings, but generally are believed to resemble peaceful, loving, handsome young men. Angels, however, are considered sexless, androgynous, neither male nor female in origin, and rarely reported as a chubby-cheeked, winged baby cupid. Those who claim to have seen an angel usually are in shock and awe, claiming radiant light as is described in Daniel 10:5-6 when the angel rolled out the stone from Christ's tomb. Angels reside in the non-physical realm, so they do not have actual bodies, but when here to perform their duties, they express a fearless form that would be understood and accepted by us. The size of angels in my research has varied from regular adult height to filling the size of the entire room with massive wingspans that cover and protect.

The Greek word *aggelos* gave rise to the word "angel," which means "middle man or messenger." In Hebrew, the word *mal'ak* has the same meaning. Angels have significant value in the Biblical texts, and are mentioned 108 times in the Old Testament, and 165 times in the New Testament. There are angelic classes like the Cherubim (Ezekiel 1; guards of God's domain), the Seraphim (Isaiah 6; sing praises to God), regular angels who rescue the distressed and deliver messages to humanity. Archangels such as Gabriel and Michael are considered protectors and enforcers of God's word. There are also the angels whom God created who have fallen from grace and led by Lucifer. These 'fallen angels' are also referred to as lower entities, bad energies, frequencies or demons. Satanic energies are the energies that cause grief, resentment, anger, rage, pain, panic, and destruction which are all fear-based. These low darker energies work opposite the light of higher consciousness and cannot express themselves as anything else higher than their negative state.

Through our free will, we choose to connect to the light, or disassociate from it, just as the fallen angels have. The great unseen battle of duality that occurs in the Cosmos may *seem* equal, but it is not. Everyone comes from the one source, the Light. The Father Creator is everyone's starting point of existence. This God is always in charge of all things; allowing duality to exist for the ability to offer contrast and change of experience to the human free will. In essence, no harm can come from the dark if one holds true to the light.

Some historians offer an interesting viewpoint that history has incorrectly deciphered the concept of angels, and misinterpreted them; pointing to their real identity as possibly originating from supernatural extraterrestrial entities from other worlds that intermingle with our planet, consciousness, and lives since even before the time of Jesus on Earth. Further, claims of interbreeding with human DNA is where the offspring became super-human, as described in Genesis:

"There were giants in the earth in those days; and also after that, when the sons of God came in to the daughters of men, and they bore children to them, the same became mighty men which were of old, men of renown." (Genesis 6:4)

Many ancient civilizations including the Mayans, Incas, and Sumerians believed in giants and even worshiped them. Many of their teachings and ways of life may have come from these demi-gods. In mythology, Greek mythology in particular, each God had their powers or purpose in what they did best and people would pray to each per their 'specialty.' Fishermen would ask for help from Poseidon, god of the Sea and farmers would ask for good graces of Demeter for the gift of the harvest and good cultivation of the soil.

Whatever the source of the angels or their history, one thing is for sure. They were created by a supreme force, God, and this force helps humanity when it is called upon. The angels carry out a range of duties all throughout Scripture. The chief action of Angels is praising and singing to God (Isaiah 6:1-3; Revelation 4-5). Angels also disclose and communicate God's will to humans on Earth. Angels protect and remove physical danger, like in the example of Daniel and his friends needing help out of the blazing oven (Daniel 3 and 6). Its further biblically substantiated that angels provide physical items, such as food and water for Elijah (1 Kings 19:6), and angels tended to Christ post temptation, (Matthew 4:11). Finally, angels are sent to some when prayers are answered (Daniel 9:20-24; 10:10-12; Acts 12:1-17). There are so many modern day unexplainable cases we see shared in the news today that show angels are still serving amongst us.

Angels transcend all religions and are believed to exist among all the peoples, regardless of nation, creed or color. Angels are a reflection of your higher mind and do not interfere with the karmic lessons, free-will, or trials you'll go through to better your soul. Be aware that negative energies can also transform themselves into angels, saints, and even

God during a dream or waking state to mislead, misdirect, or confuse those who are not firm in their 'God' power. People then are tricked into becoming self-righteous, proud, and ignorant as they try to persuade people to their cause. Contrarily, God works in humility, charity, and love. Be careful as it is said many will come in his name and bear false witness; there will be many false prophets. If you are experiencing a vision or are experiencing something extraordinary, immediately say the Creed, Lord's Prayer and/or claim that "Any energy not of the highest vibration of Christ's love and light be gone from me this instant!" and if the vision continues, it will be confirmed truth, and it can be trusted.

13.23 Common Angels

Angels are not to be worshipped, only understood as helpful forces under God. Some believe angels to be merely manifestations of our higher selves, or the highest part of our own God link into the other, unseen dimensions. Either perspective connects us to what we want to achieve, and allows us to gain the help we need at the moment we most need it. Whatever the explanation or mechanism, you may be familiar with these ten 'popular' angels.

Archangel Michael, meaning "He who is like God," is the leader of the Archangels, and the Angel of protection, courage, and strength. Call upon him for help during weak times. The patron angel of healers, **Archangel Raphael**, whose name means "God heals," is called upon when someone is sick or injured. **Archangel Uriel**, whose name means "God is light," sheds light on situations and also has insight into what is to come. **Archangel Gabriel,** whose name means "God is my strength," helps anyone whose life purpose involves art or communication. **Archangel Raziel**, meaning "Secret of God," can help you increase your ability to see, hear, know, and feel Divine guidance. **Archangel Sandalphon**, Greek for "like a brother," brings human prayers to God so they may be answered. **Archangel Metatron** led the children of Israel through the wilderness and onto safety. He continues to lead children today, both on earth and in heaven towards unity, truth, and owning their power. **Archangel Chamuel,** or "He who sees God," provides comfort, protection, and intervention in world events. Love, tolerance, and gratitude are his gifts to strengthen your hearts and relationships. **Archangel Haniel**, meaning "Glory of God," helps us find beauty, harmony, and the company of wonderful friends in life, and helps us recover lost secrets of natural healing remedies and clairvoyance. **Archangel Jophiel**, the "Beauty of God," helps us to think beautiful thoughts to create, manifest, and attract more beauty, wisdom, love, and illumination into our lives. This is the patron angel of artists. And finally there is…

Archangel 'You'

You could be the angel that God chooses to help others. Be someone's angel, mend a heart, listen to someone in pain, visit someone in a hospital. People need you, we all need each other, and there are so many opportunities to serve. You can change lives. Allow the divine plan to flow through you, and work for you.

13.24 Angel Numbers and Their Sequence Meanings

Astrology and numerology are not religions - they are tools given to humanity to be used for good, not worshipped. Numerology, or the study of numbers, has been around since man could count his fingers and toes. Numerology comes up a lot in the Bible as well, and it is not evil to use numerology as a way to strengthen your intuition, or enhance personal interactions with God. Don't listen to those who claim astrology and numerology are 'evil,' for they are fear mongering. Numerology, as well as astrology, was used often in Biblical times You may recall, according to the story of Jesus's birth, he was found by three wise men seeking him under the bright North Star. They did not use their cell phone, nor did they travel by way of camel GPS; instead they travelled using the stars.

Numbers have been correlating with both positive and negative meanings throughout the centuries. Here are some basic meanings of the numbers zero to nine our angels and guides use to communicate with us (i.e. seeing patterns of numbers randomly and repeatedly on a clock, license plate or receipt).

ZERO (0, 00, 000) – When you see zeros, this usually means completion. Whatever situation you were thinking about, or had in mind has gone full circle in its path. It may also signify death and void.

ONE (1, 11, 1:11, 11:11) – The number 1 by itself points to the self, the beginning, the God head, the Creator, the oneness of singularity, confidence, leadership, esteem, strong will, positivity, the ego, or possibly the doubting of self, manipulation, or fear of the 'I can'. The master number 11 means revelation and represents Christ's faithful apostles (minus Judas).

TWO (2, 22, 2:22) – When you see two's it usually represents our duality. This means that whatever creative ideas and thoughts you have been planting, are seeds that are now about to grow. The number 2 also represents harmony, balance, compassion, cooperation, union, passiveness, submission, or peaceful surrender.

THREE (3, 33, 3:33) – Three's are a powerful sign that an ascended master is also guiding your path. The number 3 represents communication, gossip, impulsive attitudes, children, and expressing joy. Three also refers to the Trinity or God force.

FOUR (4, 44, 4:44) – When you see fours, this is usually a sign that angels currently surround you. The number 4 relates to work, building sound foundations, discipline, creating things, taking action, and doing whatever you said you would do. It is also the number of Mother Earth, Gaea, having to deal with nature and animals.

FIVE (5, 555, 5:55) – When you see fives, this is usually a sign that you are about to go through, or are going through, a major life event. The number 5 in the Scriptures sometimes refers to death or a rebirth, and it represents change, freedom, life experiences, excitement, variety, addictions, adventures, physicality, distractions, and energy. Focus on the positive and know you will be helped through the challenges ahead.

SIX (6, 666) – The number 6 is the number of physical man. The triple six (666) is usually associated with Lucifer or the 'Dark Side'. Do not fear when this comes up, but understand that it's a sign of contrast that may be suggesting that you balance your thoughts on a more positive and healthier 'service to others' attitude rather than serving yourself or your ego selfishly. The number 6 alone in a positive sense could mean motherhood, marriage, home and family life, or could negatively reflect feelings of smothering, guilt, dread, or a martyr mentality.

SEVEN (7, 777) – When you see sevens it is an extremely positive sign that you are in your flow, and in the zone to co-create miracles. The number 7 also represents divine timing (what most consider 'luck') as well as the analyst, thinker, student, or genius.

EIGHT (8, 888) – When you see eights, it is usually an alert to get you ready to end the current phase of whatever task, project, or cycle you are in. It also means material and financial abundance is now on its way to you as you have put in the work needed to manifest it. The 8 is all about the power struggle, money, business, fame, organization, willpower, bossiness, and high stress levels to perform.

NINE (9, 999) – 9 is the number of humanitarianism and dedication to others, which tells workers of the light to keep illuminating their peers. The 9 is the number of the philosopher, humanitarian, teacher, and may be directed to correct feelings of self-centeredness, selflessness, the hiding inside oneself, or detachment of the emotional self. Also means finishing, or final step towards completion.

13.25 The Chakras

Chakra is a word that is derived from the Sanskrit word for "wheel-like turning vortices" and is a concept of traditional Indian medicine. The anatomy and sustenance of our qi (chi), as it refers to our body and spine, i.e. how the energy is circulated and expressed between our organs and physical self, is very much dependant on the balance of our spiritual, mental, emotional, and physical health. The colors and chakras themselves are always changing, and are in constant motion; they can also interweave in color. The chakras reside over major points of the spine as energy portals that interchange unseen spiritual information between our body, other's bodies, and our environment. The Kousouli® Method master chart (end of Chapter 15) shows the chakras, their positioning over the spine, and the relationship between the spiritual, mental, emotional, and physical aspects of health. When helping a patient find their way back to better health, it is these focal points that Kousouli® Method practitioners must fully investigate, in addition to lab results, and imaging procedures prior to administering treatment.

1st Root Chakra (RED color) EARTH element "Muladhara" Located at the base of our spine; the coccyx, tailbone. Relates to the grand human potential, primitive life force energy, natural survival needs, grounding, assertiveness, aggression, power, ambition, adventure, impulsiveness, lustful passion, raw attraction, competition, determination, sense of danger, hurriedness, the need for feeling secure, our connection to physical fitness, energy, vitality, material harmony, and physical strength. There is also a connection to the color red and primitive feelings, such as anger. Red in this chakra also is related to the power hormone testosterone, temperature increase, heat, hemoglobin production, and cell growth. It's for this reason also that envisioning red is used in energy healing to help stimulate blood in anemic conditions, but never used as a healing color towards cancer patients (since visualizing or wearing red is believed to stimulate tumor growth). Red is used where heat or warmth is overpowered, or is missing in the auric space. Red should also not be used to overpower those A type personalities already strong with red in their auras (i.e. sleeping under red bed sheets or wearing a red shirt) as they will feel agitated, irritated, burned out, anxious, overly hyper, or out of control.

2nd Sacral Chakra - Spleen or Splenic (ORANGE color) WATER element "Svadhisthana" Located at the level of the genitals and reproductive systems. It relates to primitive life, reproduction energy, raw emotions, clairsentience, primary interpersonal relationships, and emotional stability. Energy disharmony here can show up as a disturbance in the digestive and reproductive systems. Feelings of sexual or emotional repression may be linked to physical manifestations of diverticulitis, urinary trouble, fibroids, infertility, or cramping.

3rd Navel Chakra - Umbilical Solar Plexus (YELLOW color) FIRE element "Manipura." Located at the navel under the breastbone, this chakra relates to power integration and life force management. Digestive system, pancreas, liver, stomach, adrenals, and the spleen connect here. The 3rd chakra is the psychic energy battery, and storehouse for positive energy. This chakra links to the mind for processing negative feelings and is the area of your life force distribution. It's why you say, "I had a feeling in my gut that she wasn't being honest." Lost or misplaced energy here, leads to feeling 'out of place' within the body.

4th Heart Chakra - Cardiac (GREEN color) AIR element "Anahata" Located at the center of the chest, over the heart. By location, it separates the higher three chakras (5th, 6th, 7th) from the lower primitive three chakras (1st, 2nd, 3rd). Affects heart, lungs, upper chest, back, bronchial tubes, thymus, and immunity. Green is the associated healing color that is used for any health issue to give support, warmth, comfort and rejuvenation. The 4th chakra is the seat of higher emotions of true love, tenderness, compassion, honesty, feelings of affection and human connection. Many spiritual teachers claim that all of humanity is "plugged in" to each other through this chakra. A lengthy loss of healthy energy in this chakra level can lead to depression, seclusion, hardness, and coldness described as a difficulty in loving others, or allowing to be loved.

5th Throat Chakra - Laryngeal (BLUE color) ETHER element "Vishuddha" Front and back of the throat; relates to the power of thought through communication, speech, self-expression, and self-identification. Some health connections with this chakra are metabolic rate, thyroid gland, vocal cords, eyes, ears, nose, mouth, and neck. An important chakra in relation to the spine, as this is the area where the 6th and 7th upper chakras and cosmic channels gateway energy to the rest of the body. Repression in this chakra level is commonly seen in those who tend to be shy or scared to 'speak up' in public to represent themselves. Repressing the 5th chakra can lead to upper respiratory weakness, sore throats, migraines, and head colds.

6th Brow Chakra - Frontal Chakra 3rd eye (DEEP INDIGO color) "Ajna." Located between the eyebrows; relates to powers of mind and heightened self-awareness, psychic abilities, precognition, connection to physical and psychic eyes/vision, surrounding head and auditory nerves, head, brain; Linked to the pineal and pituitary glands. This energy is usually activated through a deeply focused and relaxed meditative state.

7th Crown Chakra - Coronal (VIOLET color) "Sahasrara." Located on top of the head, for self-realization and enlightenment, knowingness, seat of the soul, perfection of mind, body, and spirit; connection to God Source. The 7th chakra is usually depicted in religious iconography as a gold disc or circle around the head. This energy is also usually activated through a deeply focused and relaxed meditative state.

13.26 Color and Possible Frequency Interpretations in the Auric Field and Energy Healing

We use colors in our lives more than we realize (i.e., clothing we wear, home and office décor we choose, etc.). Colors are used to describe certain personality characteristics, emotional moods, or states of awareness. Color, like sound or temperature, is made of a vibration. Every color vibrates at its own specific signal. There are no 'bad or good' colors, only more favorable ones (bright solid colors) or less favorable ones (darker murky colors). I have found color therapy to be a very useful tool in helping patients heal quickly.

RED	Love, passion, sexual desire and activity, fast / quick speed or hurried, heart, blood, circulation, menstruation, masculinity, independence, strength, stimulation, courage, active action, determination, freedom, ambition. **Light Red or Pink:** Softness, tenderness, youthfulness, romance, caring, femininity, emotional love, child-like essence. **Dark Red:** Anger, rage, lust, war, internal conflict, stifled aggravation, competition, revolt, survival, impulsive, needy.
ORANGE	Warmth, cheery, openness, freedom, creativity, enthusiasm, relieving of repression, new ideas, abundance, fortune, prosperity, success, encouragement, kindness, celebration, achievement of personal and business goals, sensual enjoyment, zest for life. **Dark Orange:** Materialism, over sensitivity, over indulgence.
VIOLET INDIGO	Spiritual, divine, prophetic, royalty, compassion, transformation, renewal, stress reduction, pain reduction, dreamy, meditative, astral projection, psychic ability in healing and power, electric, calming, purifying. **Dark Violet/ Indigo:** Slow movement, trickery, lowered potential.

WHITE	All colors, purity implied, spiritual energy, balance, perfection, cosmic consciousness, protection, positivity, enlightenment, prayer, meditative, breaking of spells or curses, divine inspiration, innocence, simplicity, oneness, absolution. **Foggy, Off –White, or Grey**: Deceitful, depressive, apathetic; Unconscious energy usually related to religious control, church dogma, lower entities can hide and disguise themselves in this color.
BLACK	Mystery, stealth, hidden, secretive, lifeless, staleness, death, deep grief, negativity, dealing with the underworld or occult. The void of life or light; if feeling over sensitive, black can help shield you temporarily. Not usually favored; as the goal is to express color in an aura. Usually avoided, only used if one wants to hide or mask something from self or others. Overuse of this color can unbalance the chakras. Extreme hate, rage, seclusion, depression, stagnation, or fatigue may indicate a malfunction or dis-eased state.
GREEN	Inner peace, harmony, healing energy, monetary wealth, stimulation of emotional and mental harmony, honesty, soothing, rest, hope, nurturing, recovery, family, safety connection. **Earthy Green:** denotes grounding, nature, and connecting to Mother Earth; see Brown also.
YELLOW	Joy, exuberance, excitement, cheerful, happiness, hunger for nourishment / food, digestive tract, logical mind, decisions, optimism. **Golden Yellow:** Authority, abundance, social power and status, absolute self-confidence, sun energy, luxurious, feeling like a winner.
BROWN	Practicality, stability, grounding, clay, earth, elemental, solidity in relationship, connection to one's roots and having a "down to earth" quality, primal, material wealth, home, family, woodsy or tribal. **Dark Brown:** Similar to Black.
BLUE TUR-QUOISE	Healing, miracle energy, cleansing, angelic in nature, awe, flow. Increased intuition and sensitivity, stress relieving, intellectual, insights of higher mind, original, inventive nature, freedom of emotion, vast and limitless like the seas, cleanliness, water purity, **Dark Blue/Turquoise:** Depression, heaviness, sadness, longing, feeling stuck.

13.27 The Chakras and Auric Field

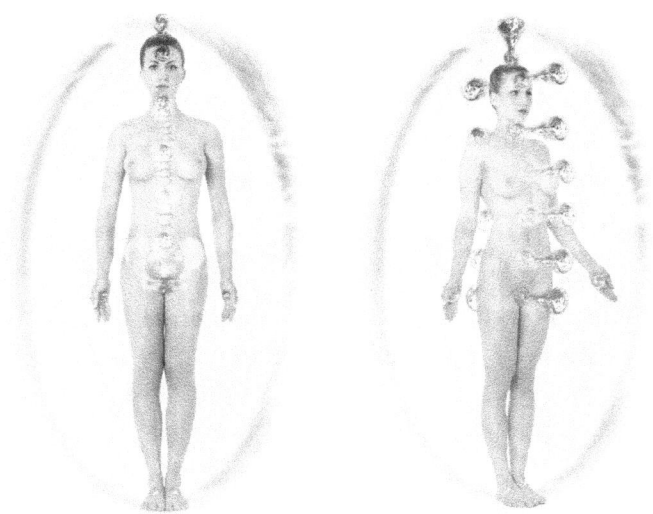

Familiarize yourself with the positions and locations of the chakras. These seven chakras are funnel like vortices that are on both sides of the body and act as energy centers for each part of the body. The chakras spin in either a clockwise or counter-clockwise rotation depending on what energies are present at any given moment. These chakras can be open or closed, smaller or larger than normal. They can be sickly or healthy as pictured in section 15.3 case studies. The energy collectively spilling from the chakras is referred to as the aura or the sum energies that make up and are around living things and can be seen by clairvoyants very sensitive to energy or seen by everyone through Kirlian photography. The chakras work between the physical body and the unseen energy body and are important to access during the use of the Kousouli® Method 4R intervention healing system.

13.28 Energy Channels

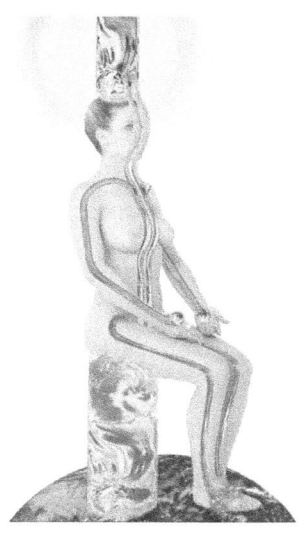

There are unseen channels which flow vital Source energy through the human body. Highly sensitive people can feel and some can even see them. Injuries can heal faster or slower depending on the 'life force' flow ability of that limb through these channels. Traditional Chinese medicine usually refers to these types of channels as energy meridians. Here we will refer to them as simply energy channels. It is important to know these for our discussion later into the more advanced concepts of clairvoyance and tapping into universal information.

Cosmic Energy is energy that comes in from God, the heavens, the air, universe, the sky or however you perceive it and can be pictured as radiant electric blue energy entering through the top of the head at the crown chakra level. This energy can be felt when one leaves chaotic areas, peacefully meditates, and feels the elation of energy bathing the body like a warm waterfall. After the experience they feel invigorated, peaceful and full of natural energy. This is because they activated a much needed intake of cosmic energy, and cleansed their upper body channels. The cosmic energy flows down into the body through the spinal channels and mixes with the Earth energy.

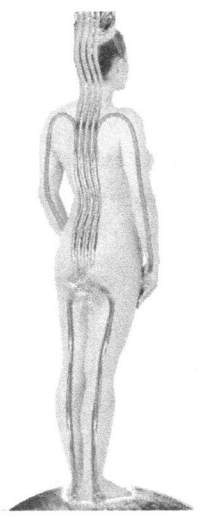

Earth, Gaea (or Gaia) Energy comes in from Mother Nature through the leg channels represented by a clay, reddish green color. This energy can be felt when one leaves the city life and walks barefoot on the beach or hikes on a trail. After the experience they are elated, peaceful and full of natural energy feeling refreshed. This is because they activated a much needed intake of Earth energy and cleansed their leg channel flow. Earth energy comes into the root chakra by way of the leg channels, mixes with cosmic energy at the root chakra and flows upward bathing all the chakras on their way up before splitting out the arm channels and up out the crown chakra.

Palm Chakra Energy located at the middle of each palm and noted for channeling the transmission of energy into creative endeavors, i.e. sculptors painters, musicians, writers, etc.

Foot Chakra Energy located at the middle arch of each foot and responsible for energy uptake from the earth through the leg channels towards the root chakra.

Arm Channels extend from the spine channel down through the shoulders to the hand chakras.

Leg Channels pass up through the ankles, knees, and into the pelvis. A lot of unexplainable aches and pains in the knees and pelvis can be attributed to poor energy flow in these channels.

Spinal Channels flow down the back of the head through the spine towards the root chakra where it mixes with the Earth energy. It then comes forward bathing all the chakras on their way up splitting out the arm channels and up out the crown chakra.

Grounding Cord extends from the end of the spine (root chakra) and connects into the Earth's core. Envision this energy line like a large hollow tube that removes any negative or stagnant energy away from your body and aura. Any such energy is dumped from the body down this hollow slide and into Mother Earth's care for recycling or redistribution of that energy. More on this in the next two chapters.

13.29 Trifecta Palm Chakra Energy Exercise

Sit still in your chair with your feet on the floor, and back up against the chair. Take a deep breath all the way down to your core through diaphragmatic breathing.

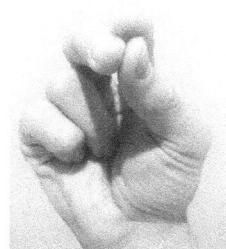

You may have heard that the sign of the cross has power behind it. It does because of the belief in what the symbol stands for. In general Orthodox Christian practice, the right hand is used to bless the body. The thumb, index, and middle fingers are brought to a point as to signify one unity. This signifies the Father, The Son, and the Holy Spirit together as one unit (see photo variations). Together they are then placed on the forehead first (brow or third eye chakra), then moved down to the solar plexus or sacral chakra – around the navel. Lastly, the hand is moved to the right shoulder and ends horizontally across the heart chakra to the left shoulder. The crossing of the fingers and sign of the trifecta however, means nothing without the understanding of that meaning and belief of faith in the God power. It is a declaration of your mind and body connection sealed as one energy with God.

To physically feel the energy of the trifecta meditate to clear the mind and then pray that you are given the ability to feel the energy. Gently rub your palms together in a circular motion for ten seconds to activate the palm chakras, stimulate blood flow and focus your attention to the feeling of your hands. Form either sign of the trifecta with your right hand and extend your left palm out exposing the palm where the left hand chakra is located. Without touching the skin of the left hand  and with the right hand in the trifecta position make a gentle slow clockwise circular motion a few inches away from your left hand's palm (left hand chakra). Focus intently as you send love energy from your right hand to your left palm. Experiment with closing your eyes and also performing it by pulling your fingers further away from the palm as well. Then perform the same on a friend and see that they will also feel the same energy. Perform it with eyes open as well as closed. Note your results during different parts of the day, when in different moods, and different environments (indoors, outdoors) and note the power of each attempt, according to your focus.

Chapter 14:
Prayer, Meditation and Aura Healing Basics

"Courses in spirituality and healing are now in place in eleven major medical schools in this country. These are historic developments, and they will continue. The research documenting these effects is so abundant that it will not go away. We're going to have to deal with it, and it will find an honored place in medicine of the future."
~ Larry Dossey, MD.

Everyone has the innate ability to heal both themselves and others. This is evident when a cut on our body takes care of itself or we console a friend through hard times. Ability to heal is inborn, and as described in this book, the energy flows through the body when unrestricted through both the spinal cord and the chakra system. To understand healing from a healer's perspective is to understand love and service to thy neighbor. We heal each other all the time, we just don't know we do as it's so automatic we don't consider it unnatural or a 'big deal.' However, healing for some is faster and more powerful than others. Also, some can bring it on in a more pronounced way when they do it consistently. In case of healing or psychic connection, it's a matter of tuning into the frequency, focusing, and connecting so many times that it becomes second nature.

When a client comes for your services, it's like a confession of their self-inflicted negativity. They tell you 'what's wrong' and confess all their aches and pains to you on the intake form; they want freedom from their invisible shackles. They tell you everything when they are on your table as they put trust in your guidance to lead them to a better place.

14.1 Just Get Out of Your Way

As a healer you understand one cardinal principle. You stay neutral; humble yourself. You must understand you serve others and you are not curing or healing anyone. You are a vessel channeling the energy from Source's total connection to the one who needs the connection - a bridge. Healing has no room for ego. To have ego is to be in direct conflict with love for the patient by putting yourself above the connection which should be the primary objective - not you. This does not mean you don't take proper care of yourself while serving the patient. It means that you keep focus on the goal of healing and do not deviate. Be honored you are chosen to serve and be the one to help deliver energy and change a life. Stay neutral and sensitive to the messages, energies, and cues that come from the healing sessions so you can distinguish a clear transmission and deliver without doubt.

I want you to think of a television. When you watch it, it moves its pictures and sends to your ears sounds which you pick up and understand. But what is making it do that? Something is operating it. If we look at the television cord we can examine a plastic coating on a wire but that's not what's making the television work – its only what insulates the wire from what's really doing the work. The electricity can not be seen but it sure can be felt if you're hit with it! Likewise in healing you can feel energy but sometimes its not easy to see unless you are very sensitive and develop the ability to sense auras. The Greek word 'energia' or energy means operating of activity or motion. The animation our body has is because this energia is there just like in the television example. Compare a living body to a dead corpse and you know there's a big difference in energy. This energia is what chiropractors, reiki healers, acupunturists and other holistic practitioners understand and work with daily. Even though it is difficult to measure or see, it is very present and very real in this realm. Energy can also be transfered in a handshake, a hug, or a passionate kiss. In healing it is transferred through thought and love by the way of the chakras, particularly via the hand chakras. Energia can even be transcended through realms to be used by a non physical entity to throw objects across a room. Energy is everywhere and everything in our universe consists of it.

14.2 We Are All Healers

"I've experienced several different healing methodologies over the years - counseling, self-help seminars, and I've read a lot - but none of them will work unless
you really want to heal."
~ Lindsay Wagner

Having the ability to choose, some choose not to heal. Believe it or not, the choice of not healing is chosen by many who seem stuck in a back and forth endless search for an answer to their health difficulties. The guide (doctor) helps the patient find their way by bringing clarity to their situation. The awareness and choice of choosing to heal must be switched 'ON' to allow the healing to flow.

When you get a cut, you heal naturally without resistance. This innate power is in all of us. Some have dealt with the healing arts through many incarnations and their ability to guide healing is higher than others. Although we can say that everyone can heal, some are great at also healing others as well as themselves. If as a healer you have been validated time and time again that you are well along in your efforts, your faith in your ability and skill will grow. Some know they are here again as healers, and others are here to be healed.

As a healer you know there is something different about you than most others around you. You are sensitive, and you ponder deep soul yearning questions that others may never ask. You have certain qualities that hint to your ability to heal, and you understand that the outer world you see is a direct manifestation of the internal world you feel and think. You feel you have a responsibility to yourself and others to do good, and progress love on this planet. You have a strong sense of caring for others and desire to share information with them. You have difficulty seeing people suffer and act to ease their pain, or empathize and comfort them. You know you are a vessel that universal energy flows through for creation and healing. You are happy to just 'be' and live in the moment. You bring people together, and connect them to awareness and knowledge they've forgotten or don't remember, and they find their happiness once more. You attract people who ask you for your help, even for the smallest things, as they feel you are more knowledgeable and can confide in you. When you are hurt or sick, you find it easy to get back into health quickly. You are interested in healing matters, and researching the things that could bring about health faster. You have an internal knowing that the power which made the body also heals the body. You somehow always receive what you ask for, and usually exactly when you need it. You let go of negative emotions like anger, jealousy or resentment, and do not let them harbor long within you. You acknowledge other's frustrations and challenges but do not let them become your own. You feel energy and being around large crowds affect you, so you choose your surroundings wisely. You enjoy spending time in nature's peace. You do not fight, or resist challenge, but instead flow with it towards increasing goodness. You often know the mood or energy predisposition of people without them telling you. You feel extrasensory perception and psychic phenomenon like déjà vu, clairvoyance, and clairsentience often. You remain diligently centered in seeking your truth, but also remain understanding that you are moldable and in constant expansion of your truth. Your ability to be sensitive is an important skill. You know in your heart and soul you are eternal.

The real challenge for a healer (especially in their beginning years), is to assimilate the information they are getting through their sensitivity and put it into a useful and understandable system that they can use or explain to others. It is also imperative you know how to discern the good habits from the bad habits as you mature in healing ability. As you conduct your practice you love everyone without judgment and allow them to grow into themselves. You do not blame, condemn or vilify anyone who may stumble. You offer solutions to people's problems, but do not solve their problems for them. You guide, direct, and cheer on someone seeking your help but remain humble and do not act as their martyr, savior, saint or God. You do not use your ability to force, seduce, manipulate, or control them but instead look to see them as free from their pains and sorrows. You do not allow anyone to dump their negative energy onto you but redirect the energy towards positive resolution. You see each person as unlimited love potential and do not eliminate or control their free will, or stifle their journey with negative criticism.

Believe it or not you have healed many people to this day. You did the moment you were born in the hospital as nurses and doctors handled you upon arrival while witnessing your magnificence. They smiled and felt amazing joy and peace inside when they came in contact with you. You did something very important for them. You reminded them of who they are too. You reminded them of where they also came from. Parents, uncles, family, and strangers alike were healed when they saw and touched your pure, brand new, supple little body. If their life troubles made them forget where they came from, you reminded them by healing the sadness which came from their forgetting. You reminded them to connect more often to their 'higher self' or 'God.' The more they smiled and felt your presence, the more they felt alive and child-like again. People would come visit you just to get this reminder often, especially your proud grandparents who were soon to return to where you just came from. They eagerly wanted to have you remind them of what it feels like to be a child again; so full of imagination, wonder, and a carefree spirit in a brand new body. Even the toughest ice cold hearts would pop open when they saw cute baby you. You healed many and had this effect until about age 6 or 7 where you tried to continue doing so, but it did not have as much strength as it did when you were fresh from the non-physical side. As you continued to learn the ways of adults here on Earth, you also lost your ability to remember where you came from. You stopped practicing the innocent ways of the child, and the magic began to fade. You doubted what you saw, or felt you inherently knew to be true, and instead you adopted the illusions of adults who were less than open to stories of angels, invisible friends, and subtle colors around people. Some have held onto this child-like essence however, and have worked on fulfilling their path as sensitive intuitives openly without care of judgment.

14.3 The Path of a Healer

Healers are often tempted by senses and splendors of the earthly realm. They will be shown contrast by distractions, and often their willpower is tested more often. They will be held to higher standards, and often unpure thoughts will challenge them as they assume more responsibility than others are willing to accept. They are usually born leaders at managing their energy and helping others do the same. In the past it has been a rocky road for healers. Sometimes shunned to the corner of the village, misunderstood, not appreciated by their community, and even humiliated publically; which was the case of our most famously Divine healer, Jesus Christ of Nazareth.

Understand that once you open up to the idea that you want to lead a more spiritual life, temptations will swarm you. The law of opposites will be in full swing, and everything opposite from what you wish for will come into your awareness to test you and change your reality. The one who wishes to cut back on sweets will be tempted by cake. The one who wants to give up alcohol or cigarettes will be tempted by friends who ask him or her to join for a drink or smoke at the party. Be ready for the temptations, which are a natural phenomenon that beckon for you to make a 'new' choice. You must leave the current vibration to break the cycle of the old pattern and move forward to a better version of you.

14.4 The Healer's Tool Belt

Prayer and meditation is not a daily thing for healers; it becomes a moment to moment thing that you taste smell, feel, see, eat, hear and ARE. Healers are energy balancers. They do not cure anyone; they help the patient open their portals for healing through prayer and meditation, to balance the chaotic and misdirected energy that blocks healing. Healers channel God's Divine healing to the patient by holding a sacred space for them to reconnect to their highest self, and most helpful path, or truth within the Eternal Source. They must shine the light in ways that show they do the work, and they must be lighthouses to lost souls amongst the rocky shores of life. Earth is a never ending examination of one's 'self' to challenge abilities and soul growth within the dualities and laws governing this realm.

14.5 The Healer's Wardrobe

I usually get this question from practitioners new to energy healing: "Dr. Kousouli, what should I wear when I want to do a healing session? Should I wear a certain color or specific gem necklace? Should I eat or drink specific things prior to beginning?" My answer is always: "Keep it light." Wear light color clothing in light fabric that allows you to feel comfortable and move effortlessly. Be sure to adequately hydrate yourself with pure alkaline water, and do not eat heavy meals, or wear constrictive items that would inhibit blood flow or your ability to discern feeling cues that you need to be sensitive to. If you have gemstones, lotions, potions, herbs, or artifacts that you've developed a positive association with, feel free to use them; if you believe they will be helpful to you being able to relax and bring forth your highest vibration of love. You don't really need anything but YOU, aligned with clear intent and thought; nothing material is needed. Materials are NOT the source of the healing or the vessel. You DO NOT need to put on special candles, talismans, jewels, burn sage, rub magic lamps, listen to chants or drink pig's blood to become worthy of healing work. Various tools may help some people get into a state of letting go easier so that they can experience healing, though all that is just ritual to make one feel good about what they are about to do. God expresses though you all healing, and your whole being and essence is the channeling vessel He uses to deliver healing. The healer needs no attachments to see and feel their God power, which is our continued lesson of mastery; to get to that place where we know we know. Look at the master healer, Christ. He traveled light and did not pass out prescriptions, potions, lotions or carry herbal remedies. He only touched the ill gently as he gave a reassuring or validating word to those seeking healing.

14.6 Creating and Respecting the Healing Container (Healing Space)

Most doctors are unaware that when they are pointing out only what is wrong, they raise the patient's fear level. Healers have a grand duty to convey a place of calm and peace that allows the patient to activate their vibration of hope for healing. When doctors and patients focus only on the symptoms and pain, they keep the patient hostage to an illness or diagnosis; removing positive outcome possibilities will diminish hope, which changes the atmosphere of healing to one of chaos and panic. Cells in our bodies are consistently responding to vibration at every moment, so a dis-service is done to the patient when they come for hope and healing, but leave with the misunderstanding that the disease is greater than their body's ability to maintain their homeostasis of health. As a healer you should always give your patient options for holistic natural avenues and positive reinforcement for connecting back to their healthiest possible state.

14.7 Know There's Healing Happening

Ask for trust, and know that Spirit will give you validation. For me, validation comes in threes; it repeats to me three times, and then I know it's the right message. Even if I fight it, if the message is true it will appear in three ways, either the same way or slightly different ways representing the same thing. And if I am still being dense, Spirit will nudge me right in the gut. I have to let go of the ego's resistance and allow messages to be delivered to the client, even if it doesn't make sense logically to me, and may make me feel foolish for saying what I am feeling or seeing. The message, however, is exactly what the person being given the message needs to hear, regardless of the healer's filters. As a healer you must stay neutral to incoming information. We are either visual, auditory, or kinesthetic (feeling) types, and process information differently; everyone has their own way of getting the spiritual data through intuition.

14.8 How to View Aura Energy

This dense realm we live in is linear and hides higher vibrational understanding. However, virtually everyone can view the difference in energetic state between a person, animal, plant and their surroundings if they tap back into their ability. In order to see it you must believe you can see it. Doubters will have difficulty experiencing this phenomenon and other extrasensory abilities. When you were a child this was much easier to do than it is now as an adult. Why is that? Because there was no doubting in your mind, and as a fresh energy being from the other side of a non-material realm, you knew inherently of this energy being 'real.' The aura is transparent; it follows the outline of the body and can expand out to over 8 meters off of the skin in all directions. As you start to re-experience it, you may not see the color at first, but as you progress in time, you will be able to see colors, the more you connect to this energy frequency. When I see auras on patients I see them as hazy mists as if you look on a hot summer asphalt road beaming heat a few feet above ground.

Depending on the person I am viewing, it can be just off their skin surface a few inches to even a few feet away from their body. In some parts of their body it can be clearly seen, while in others it is missing or very hazy. When really focused and the conditions are just right, color can be seen even with the naked eye. However, the colorless transparent blurry mist is much more easily seen. Since it is easier to see the color patterns when in a meditative state, pair up with your meditation partner and try the following exercise.

Aura Viewing Exercise

Start off by saying in your mind the phrase, "I can see auras and see them now clearly." Believe it as you say it, and relax your mind. The best way to see an aura is by relaxing your eyes and using your peripheral (not direct) vision. Focus on the space above the shoulders, sides of the neck or top of the head. What you are looking for is a white, grey, or colorful mist emanating half an inch to a few inches away from the body. It is similar to a hazy summer night when the asphalt of the road is giving off a hazy smoky halo when looking down into the distance or the energy around a candle in the dark. If you are doing this exercise for the first time you may be likely to miss seeing this, however with patience and practice, you will learn to trust your eyes and see that what you are looking at is in fact true. Similarly you can do this with viewing someone's hand or palm against a black background. Again, in a slightly dimmed room (pupils will dilate for maximum light intake from the environment), place your hand up with fingers separated in front of a black wall, sheet, or background. When looking at the palms look between the spread out fingers as well as around the hand or palm. Keep the palm steady or slowly move it to check for changes in outline. Using your peripheral view, look lazily (don't stare) at the areas around your hands and between your fingers. I have noticed that the more connected to being relaxed and allowing the student is, the more they were able to see not just the haze, but also the colors of the aura. This has to do with the level of belief you hold without denying your ability. I have also seen that when the exercise is done in groups and after a deep meditation and prayer, the phenomenon is much easier to witness and comes to students quickly. Another amazing thing is that if someone does not see the aura, they can simply get into the aura of someone who does see it, and the one who was unable to see it will be able to see it quicker; meaning that in a group effort, the ability to 'see' is intensified.

How to View Energy in the Ether and Air Around You

Using the tactics above, turn down the lights in your room. Close your eyes and visualize bright white light filling the room and surrounding you. Inhale deeply as you pull in the air in the room and become part of the room as the air mixes with you into one. Breathe in and out deeply and slowly into your diaphragm several times. Relax and now breathe normally as you open your eyes. Use your vision to view the darkness in your periphery. You will notice a white haze that looks like static floating in the air. This looks similar to the pixels on a computer screen or television. You may want to turn down the lights completely if you are having trouble noticing the energy. Observe for a few minutes looking lazily from your periphery at the blackness around you. Tune in to the energy and you will eventually notice that some of the energy has a red tint while other pixels have a blue hue. With time you may even be able to see forms take shape or become aware of other entities in the room with you.

14.9 Your Spiritual DNA and Aura

Although I stress practicing the above exercises until you are proficient enough to see colorful auras on your own, the use of technology today can help anyone see and believe in the aura phenomenon. The next set of aura photos were taken on different days over several months' time using aura imaging that is highly sensitive to the aura frequency. It is notable that the color changes in combination, depth, range, and intensity. Depending on what is going on in your life and how you are handling, will depend on the energies vibrating and picked up by the aura camera equipment. Over time you notice your most prominent colors. Mine are blue, green and violet, as are usually the colors of those in healing professions.

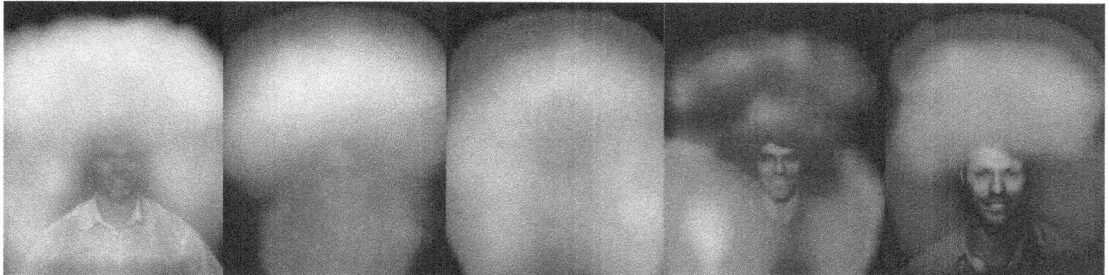

We all have a certain personality and with this set of characteristics we also tag upon each person a set of emotions or traits that equal them. Johnny is usually sad, and down on his mood. Sally is always chipper and has a sense of happiness about her at work. James loves to play jokes and pranks his classmates but is sometimes very annoying. Individuals, when examined closely, will present a certain combination of energies that make up the totality of who they are or what they are portraying to the world. This energy can be felt when you are near them or around their presence. You feel "good" energy or "bad" energy as perceived by your own energy field when in proximity to theirs. When an individual is sick, their aura is murky and less vibrant than one who is emanating joy and total health. Telling a lie, kissing a mate, or saying a joke will all change one's aura and color vibrations. Your colors reflect what you think and feel. Everything – animals, people, plants, insects, etc. has an atmosphere around it and energy emanating outward. Emotions and personalities are as different as auric spaces which change color and are unique to each individual.

When I saw what was possible with aura Kirlian photography, I was eager to apply it to my practice and correlate it to what I felt and witnessed in my healing at the office. I postulated that I would be able to see what I and the patient felt during an adjustment using aura imaging to show there was a change in aura energy. What I postulated was correct as I further researched the effects of adjustments under this technology. In the next examples we use an aura imaging camera and software developed by inventor Guy Coggins of Progen Co. that picks up the subtle energy vibrations of the human aura and translates that into an image the computer displays as color, depending on the vibration of the bio field's energy sensed during analysis. In both examples below we can see the energy changes in the aura during and after the delivery of a chiropractic adjustment.

14.10 Pelvic Adjustment Pre & Post Treatment

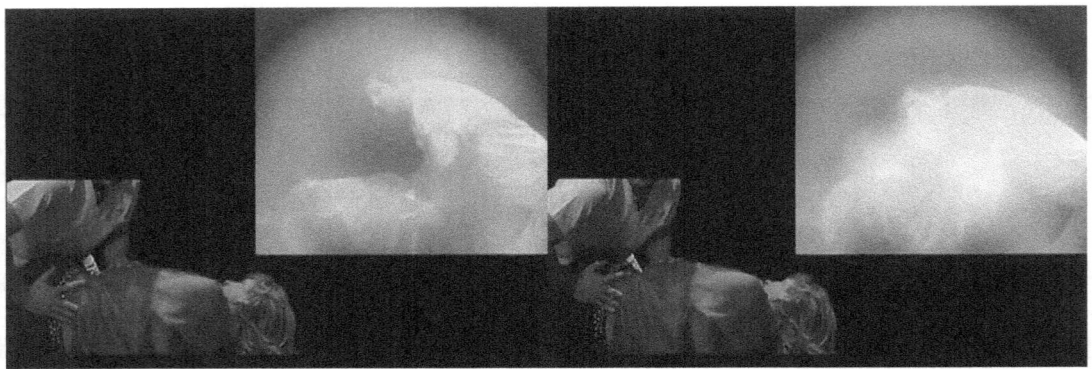

In the above example I am setting up on the patient to deliver a hip adjustment. Our auras here are very close and comingled. There is a murky or less vibrant energy seen at the side of the patient's hip. We see a burst of energy released in the second post photo just as I finish delivering the adjustment, showing an energy exchange occurring.

14.11 Cervical Adjustment Pre & Post Treatment

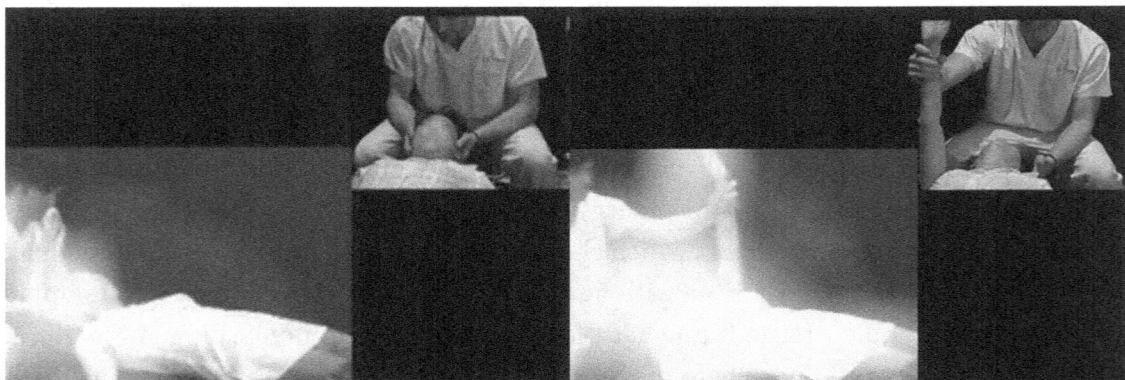

My aura here is comingled with the patient in the left pre photo. We see a burst of energy released in the post photo immediately after the adjustment is delivered, which also spreads into the patient's arm and palm chakra. The energy is also read as more vibrant in the upper torso, neck, and head in the post photo. This correlated with the patient expressing greater freedom in neck movement, relaxation of neck tension, and a rush of well-being following the session.

Through countless such interactions with patients and my understanding of the way the human body works I have developed the Kousouli® Method master chart (See Chapter 15.4) to aid me in my work. Notice that there is more to the body here than the physical aspects Western medicine usually involves itself with and the Kousouli® Method incorporates the whole system of a person paying special attention to the non-physical aspects as well as the physical.

I often see examples of spiritual or emotional trauma manifesting into physical disease in patients' later years. A male patient who is now an alcoholic admits he has never let go of the anger for his father leaving his mother during his teens which then developed into a liver and gallbladder issue. Or how an overweight woman in her mid-forties with a hormone and thyroid problem remembers when she was harshly disciplined and abused by a church elder that choked her in her youth for acting out. The combination of the traumatizing incident, lack of neutralizing that incident's negative energy, and harboring of that energy into the physical body is like a parasite staying dormant and hidden until its presence shows considerable distress to its host.

14.12 How to Meditate

While on the path to enlightenment, one must maintain patience, while constantly questioning their thoughts and emotions for answers to a deeper meaning of existence. Miraculous healing ability, insights to telepathy, telekinesis, or astral travel are all in harmony with God's laws. One of the key aspects of the practice of meditation is the attainment of inner peace while working with those laws.

When we are sitting in silence (or with meditative music) usually with our eyes closed, clearing the mind in order to get more focus on ourselves, our purpose and our understanding of self, we are meditating. Meditation sessions have no time limit and can be as short or long as you like. The main goals in meditation are to:

- Clear out mind clutter to attain a more peaceful state.
- Distinguish your energy from foreign energy.
- Remove any stressful thoughts or worries.
- Cut and remove negative cords to others.

Refer to the diagrams in 13.27 and 13.28 for help while using this section. In a quiet and private room away from any form of distraction (cell phones, other people, etc.), and with your eyes closed, sit on a comfortable chair in the position as shown in figure 13.28. In your mind's eye, allow the Cosmic and Earth Gaea energies to flow through you. Envision powerful energy flowing from the universe down into your crown chakra, and then flowing through the front and back of your spinal channels, down through the shoulders and arms and out through the palms as you also envision beautiful loving Earth Gaea energy flowing up through your feet, knees, legs, and then up into your hips. Feel these two energies mix and flow throughout your body, spin through your chakras, and flow up through your crown and then spill into your aura. As you envision these movements, allow your body to relax and sink into the chair deeper with every breath you take. Next, envision a little 'mini' version of yourself in your head (behind your eyes) as shown in the figure of the head in 16.4, step 8. This mini version of you plays 'bouncer' or 'guard' to any thoughts entering your mind. Any vibration or thought energy that enters or forms in your mind will be evaluated by this mini you. If it does not belong in your head, your mini bouncer kicks the thought vibration down your grounding cord. The grounding cord is envisioned as an energetic, holographic, one-way, slippery slide tube, or exit point away from you, leading into the middle of the Earth (the abyss). Any negativity (thought, vibratory image, entity, or vibration) that ever resides in you must be neutralized by being escorted away and buried into Gaea, as Mother Earth is the ultimate recycler of all energy on the planet. Simply envision any energy that you do not need, being sent to Mother Earth's middle core for processing. Anything sent to her through your grounding cord, is no longer your concern; Mother Earth will take care of it. Did you have a negative conversation on the phone earlier? Throw that down the grounding cord. Does someone owe you money and they just popped into your head? Throw them down the grounding cord. Did a list of chores or bills you have to pay just sneak into your mind? Throw it all down the grounding cord. Did a friend stand you up and you're mad at them? Throw them down the grounding cord. Did an ex-boyfriend cheat on you and is now trying to re-unite? Throw him and his energy down the grounding cord and let Mother Earth sort it out.

It is perfectly fine to see people, items, or whole events being sent down the grounding cord for recycling. Once you've sent something down the grounding cord, it is no longer a factor in having an effect on your energy being. See figure in section 13.28 to see what the grounding cord looks like. It is a large cylindrical channel connected to the end of your spine just like sitting on a hollow tree trunk buried deep into the ground. Some like to envision their grounding cord as a large toilet that flushes energy down into the middle of the Earth. Whatever you wish it to be and function as is fine as long as it is one way out; down the grounding cord by your mini bouncer.

Once you have run the scenario a few times and nothing else comes into your mind, you will eventually find a place of peace where no other thoughts bother you. This takes practice. At first there will be many items you will need to clear and it may take a while to do so. This however, is a basic process for clearing the mind or getting into 'the zone' so that you may then move onto other aspects of mind mastery.

14.13 How to Pray

Praying allows us to seek the higher self, or the part of us that connects directly to God, or the Creator. I suggest that people meditate to clear the mind and bring themselves to a place of peace before they actively pray. Sometimes meditation and prayer are intermingled or considered one of the same by some. However, by definition they are different.

When we actively ask for assistance from the Universe, God, Source, Higher Self, the Father, Jesus, Holy Spirit, "all that is," or another definition of what we feel God is, we are *praying*. Prayer is a state of gratefulness for our existence, what we have and all we are. When you give thanks for that which you already have, you are blessed in its vibratory frequency multiplied to you. Prayer is not making a list of wants or repeating states of illness or need, nor is it a wish list of material wants as if you are sitting on Santa's lap. It is a chance for grateful appreciation for your already manifested creation and blessing for more of it.

> *"I lift up my eyes to the hills - where does my help come from?*
> *My help comes from the LORD, the Maker of heaven and earth."*
> *~ David, slayer of the giant Goliath (Psalm 121:1-2)*

- Ask and create new manifestation with pure intention.
- Give gratitude for already manifested creations.
- Make time to pray every day, especially prior to bed and waking.
- Pray anywhere. There is no limit on prayer locations.
- Be thankful to God of what is good and ask for more blessings.
- Ask for strength to move forward from difficulties.
- Do not dwell on negativity - always state thoughts positively.
- Prayer has no time limit, it can be as short or long as you like.

Kneeling on your knees doing multiple 'Hail Marys' until rug burn sets in is perfectly fine, if you feel that gets you to your place of peace and tranquility. However, there is a far more productive way to feel and be in the presence of God. It would be wise to come to God in gratitude and thanks rather than guilt and pain, as God wants you to be in love and health, not dwell on negativity. When you are in the zone of peace and you bring upon thanks for your blessings, more good flows to you. People who continuously sob and wail about their misfortunes and life's difficulties when coming to God, only find themselves still stuck years later in the same place in life. They do not realize that God always says, "Yes." And within the context of your asking, you will receive when you have faith and belief. If you use precious prayer time to think in a negative vibration, God will say, "Yes, you may have more of the same pain, until you come to understand how to thank me for your abundance!"

Use the time in prayer to connect and be thankful for all you currently have, even if it seems to be very little (someone out there has less than you). After giving thanks and feeling gratitude, ask for your desires in any way you wish to ask. Envision yourself putting all the things you ask and desire for into a large bubble. Pack the large bubble as full as possible and let your mind go wild with imagination. Don't allow fear or negativity to sway your decision on what to pack. It's your bubble and your prayer - no one else's. Attach a grounding cord to the bubble, just as we did before in section 13.28, and see all negativity ooze out of your bubble. Ground out any thoughts or feelings that may make you feel unworthy about owning or attaining your desires. If you put in the bubble a raise, and feel that your boss will not allow you to have it, envision your boss going down the grounding cord allowing your bubble to remain clean of any negative vibrations. Once the bubble is full of your desires, see it as sealed. Imagine signing your name on the outside of the bubble so the Universe knows to deliver the items to you. Multiply the bubble into thousands or millions of bubbles and allow them to float up past the sky and into the Universe, all the way to God. Then detach yourself from those thoughts and finish your prayer with gratitude in your heart and envision yourself as if you were already living with those desires.

14.14 How to Scan and Prepare the Aura for Healing

Before starting body aura scanning and healing work, make sure the room you are going to be working in is neutralized from any air currents, such as drafts from open windows or air conditioning. These will skew your analysis and point you to false findings. The least amount of air current is preferred, as the energy signals coming to you will be subtle and your sensitivity to them must be laser focused in order to obtain accurate data. Ideally, you would want your patient in a lying down position on a table so that you can access the arm and leg channels. However, we will need to also evaluate the main seven chakras, and for this it is better to have the client in a standing or sitting position with their arms down by their side. This will mean that you will have to do a little more moving around to scan the client's body.

Both you and the client should wear relaxed fitting clothes. Remove any electronic devices, jewelry, shoes, watches, belts, etc. Have the client close their eyes and concentrate on their bodily sensations. They may keep their eyes open if they wish, though they will be less conscious of the energy flow than if they closed them. You, the healer, will also close your eyes and feel, but you must open them from time to time to make sure you maneuver around the body correctly. You may choose to sage or incense the room prior to starting with a healing prayer of your choice. Ask that the highest love and light of the Creator be with you, while being guided by the client's guides and guardian angels to achieve deep energy healing. Using your palm chakras as tools, you will be 'scanning' the leg and arm channels first, the main body chakras second, and the general aura last. Mentally, envision yourself dropping a canal from your spinal base to the middle core of the Earth, as well as one for your client from his/her spinal base. These are your grounding cords, which will empty out any used, stagnant, low energy which needs to leave the body after being worked on.

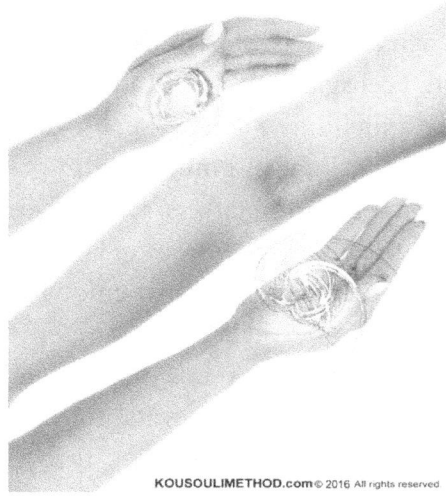

Place your palm chakras facing each other with the body part or area being scanned between your hands, as if you are sandwiching the body part being scanned. There is no need to touch the body part or person at all. You must maintain your palm chakras away at a three to five inch distance from the channels or chakra you are scanning. We will be scanning each arm channel, leg channel, and chakra vortices, which will be giving off detectable feedback through your palms which will act as the sensors (refer to image). 'Sandwich' your hands around the area or body part being scanned, and start with the client's left hand, slowly moving up the forearm to the elbow. Notice any energy shifts, such as drops in pressure, changes in heat, cold, static feeling, or pinching or scratching on your palms as you move your hands in unison. When you feel any changes, stop moving and concentrate on that area until the changes 'normalize.' Be sure to never touch the client and maintain a three to five inch distance from the area being scanned. Once you get to the left shoulder, move across to the right shoulder and scan slowly down to the right elbow, forearm, and hand, feeling for energy shifts, changes in heat, cold, pressure, static feeling, pinching or scratching on your palms. Pause for a few moments in any area you may be feeling an energy disturbance. This area may need energetic healing to help balance out the energy in that area (i.e. you can usually feel these energy shifts in sick people with sore throats or those about to come down with a cold).

We are all made up of unseen energy fields, and when these fields are out of alignment, they need healing and rejuvenation. Scanning and healing an aura helps to identify broken auric fields and patch them up for quicker healing. What you are feeling is a break or hole in the person's channel, chakra or auric field. If this is the case, hold your palm chakras in the area in question and focus your loving intention there. Say the word "healed" internally in your mind. Let it vibrate, as if it is echoing through the Universe. Then, while keeping in your mind the word 'love' and sending 'light' to this area, connect the troubled area to the Light and Creator Source, God. Allow the negative energy to release away from the client, down through the client's grounding cord and into Mother Earth who will recycle that stagnant, low energy into something positive like a tree, animal, or forest. If you heal an area on the client, be sure to also step away and heal it also in yourself before you resume healing them, so that the low energy does not copy itself to you. Repeat the healing intention several times and banish any low energy down your grounding cord. Proceed to clear the leg channels after you are finished with the arm channels. Start at the left foot, moving slowly up the calf to the knee and then the thigh. Feel again for energy shifts such as drops in pressure, changes in heat, cold, feeling static, pinching or scratching on your palms as you move your hands in unison. Those who are sensitive and more trusting of their psychic self will feel the subtle changes and energy interaction between themselves and the healer. Many times colors, angels, or guides come through while the aura is being cleansed. The client may verbalize these things to you but may choose to just enjoy the cleansing and wait to share everything at the end of their session.

Next, move onto the right foot and up to the right knee. Once you move up the right thigh to the pelvic base, you will now be working on the main chakra points, starting with the root chakra and moving slowly up through the sacral, solar plexus, heart, throat, third eye, and crown. One of your palm chakras will be behind the client's back, three to five inches off of the spine and the other palm chakra will be in front of the client slowly moving up towards the head. Again, you will be feeling for drops in pressure, changes in heat, cold, feeling static, pinching or scratching on your palms as you move your hands in unison over the chakra points.

Once you have completed the arm, leg channels, and chakra cleansing, step back two feet from the client, bring your palm chakras out about three feet away from the client's body and feel the general auric space around the client; feeling for any missed spots that need your healing attention. If you find any sticky or low vibrational energy, clean it off like you did prior with the other areas mentioned above, and send it down their grounding cord. The aura and energy of the patient should feel much lighter, and freer than prior. Lastly, close out the session by scanning and cleaning off yourself in the same way. Close up both the client's grounding cord, as well as your own. Say a closing gratitude prayer and sage the room again if you wish.

Chapter 15:
Energetic Healing of the Patient using the Kousouli® Method

"I believe that every human being endowed with intelligence, memory, and strength of character bears within him a little of the supernatural as well. The highest purpose of the conductor is to release this superhuman potential in every one of his musicians."
~ Charles Munch

Healing People with Energy

There is no way to teach you through a book everything you need to know in order to practice energy healing. Healing is a personal art, science, and technical skill that can take a lifetime to learn, develop and perfect. As everyone's rate of attaining information and assimilating it varies greatly, my goal here is to explain to you in general how I have come to practice conventional therapy with energy healing through my personal experience and how my experiences and system can introduce a new wave of systematic healing for you, your clients, and your loved ones. If you wish to learn more in depth on how to further your healing abilities you may come learn first hand through seminars and private courses. For more information please visit www.KousouliMethod.com.

15.1 The Crux of Energy Healing

When a patient desires the benefit a healer provides them, and they are in a relaxed state of expectation, the healer acts as a lighting beacon for the signal that is always available to the patient. The healer's presence reminds the patient of the signal and makes them expect the healing more. The healer does not refine, produce, or direct the energy him or herself, but only facilitates the energy stream. The patient is working with the alignment of his or her own energy vibration in terms of re-connecting to the 'God Source.' The alignment of the healer, the readiness of the patient, and the intensity of the patient's desire are key for a strong healing session. What you as a healer or patient experience when the energy flows through will be in direct relationship to the expectation and allowed connection to the Source. The healer's 'actual work' is to consistently work on their 'self.' The healer must align daily with the unobstructed energy of the Source and be a clear resistance free channel for their patients. When this is done, the healer sets him or herself as the example so that the patient feels comfortable in raising their vibration of connection as well.

Before You Begin: Understanding Energy Transference

As a reader of potentials, healer, or one interested in releasing their abundance and spiritual growth, you may be having some frustrations when things are not going as smoothly as possible. Do you feel out of the flow when you need to be doing something, or even when you have downtime? Can you stay neutral when work deadlines are pressuring you, or there are emotional expectations, responsibilities, or an urging to perform for the ego? Is there low nutritional energy within your body? Get well rested, let go of the outcome, and speak into the Universe exactly what you seek. Grounding brings more spirit into the body. Know that the spiritual aspect is the reality, and the physical reality is the moldable illusion. Frustration can overload the body with stress and cause fatigue, making the body desire a physical hibernation of its resources and a spiritual recharging of innate energy. Meditation, martial arts, Qi Gong, sleep, and prayer all help rebalance the energy body with the physical body. Yawning may not necessarily be a sign of fatigue; it could be a sign of energy transference, especially when you are already well rested. Energy is moving constantly, so learning how it moves while healing is important.

Some terms you should know in order to allow for healing of yourself or others:

Transmission – Sending or receiving visions, thoughts, or ideas. Healers or readers may show physical signs of energy transfer, i.e. yawning, twitching, burping, coughing, tearing, etc. while performing energy work.

Receiving – Being in an allowing, non-thinking, neutral, meditative or relaxed state without doubt, fear, or resistance for accepting visions, images, or messages.

Sending – Actively visualizing, making requests, or asking questions of the Universe (praying).

These are the dynamics of a healing session, where energy is transferred from the Source, through the healer vessel, and into the patient. In order to receive healing you must understand all three of the terms above as we move forward.

15.2 Understanding Yin and Yang for Healing

The duality of energy in Ancient China was defined as the synergistic yin and yang energies - a method of explaining the interdependent nature of all phenomena. In medicine, yin and yang is used to describe physiological functions and body parts. Yin is considered anchored around the lower part of the body (like the perineum) and the interior, while yang is found more in the upper body (around the naval chakra) and the exterior. The back trunk and bowels are yang, while yin in the viscera and abdomen. Yin is considered the negative, dark, feminine, rough, moist, rich, slow, and cold energy, while yang is considered the warm, hot, bright, positive, male, fiery, rapid, slippery energy. It is believed that possessing knowledge about these energies and their effects within the body can unlock massive abilities for humanity to do extraordinary things. It is incorporated in many martial arts and yoga breathing techniques.

Breathing in draws energy in, while breathing out projects energy out. Pulling or pushing the mixture of Yin and Yang energy through the naval chakra accounts for the effects experienced when projected. Yin and yang counterbalance each other and exist affecting one another. When one is high the other is low, or imbalanced, the immunity lowers and can lead to dis-ease. High blood pressure for instance, is considered a high yang activity and a loss of yin. When yang is low and yin is high, the body becomes cold with symptoms of diarrhea and swelling. Healing modalities like chiropractic and acupuncture correct the innate balance of qi (pronounced 'chi') forces, thus rebalancing the system. Having a basic understanding of balance between these two forces allows us to appreciate that when something is out of flow in the body, there may be reason to harbor energy that manifests as pain or illness. Becoming sensitive to feeling these energy changes around you allows you to be able to better facilitate yourself as a healer.

15.3 Kousouli® Method Energy Healing Case Studies

"The intuitive mind is a sacred gift, the rational mind a faithful servant; we have created a society that honors the servant and has forgotten the gift."
~ *Albert Einstein*

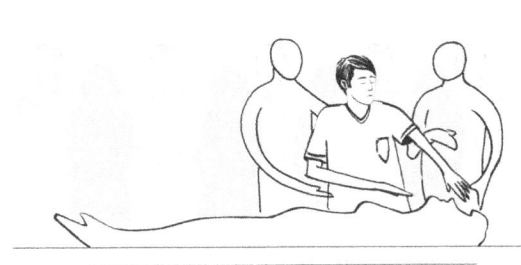

The following case scenarios will demonstrate how the Kousouli® Method helps patients heal by balancing the chakra zones. The first case scenario is one I see often, and find with patients who are entertainers such as dancers, artists, actors, models, etc. in Los Angeles.

Case Study Example #1

This next scenario pertains to healing a singer so she can perform at her highest potential. Chiropractic examination and x-ray findings showed the patient had cervical, thoracic and lumbar subluxations throughout the spine which caused her physical pain, restricted range of motion in neck and arm movement, shoulder and low back tenderness, loss of right leg extension, a rotated pelvic girdle with sacrum tilt and edema in the associated spinal areas. The patient reported difficulty sleeping, fatigue, and increased irritability. When questioning the patient further she said she has performance anxiety about an upcoming performance and she has not quite been able to get back into her 'zone' with an inability to hit her proper range during studio time. A recent breakup with her boyfriend left her less than confident in recent weeks. Checking the patient for energy leaks and lower potential spinal areas, she tested positive for energy leaking in two chakra zones - her throat chakra (self-expression, being heard) as well as her solar plexus (free will, empowerment, internal power integration).

Interestingly enough both these areas are connected anatomically to important spinal structures for singers; the vocal cords and diaphragm. Further body scan analysis showed the breakup with her boyfriend also affected the heart (love affinity) and sacral chakra (gut feelings) with broken energy cords which left her in her current state of heartache and loss. This energy void affected her by blocking her physical ability for allowing her to perform fully in an effort to get her attention. Traditional chiropractic application as well as Kousouli® Method energy healing of the associated leaking chakras immediately brought back all function to the physical body as well as a renewed sense of self-empowerment to perform at top levels. By reconnecting the energy lines through the spinal column and energy body, the patient quickly made a full recovery post treatment. The photos further explain the general process of energy healing using aspects of the Kousouli® Method after initial analysis.

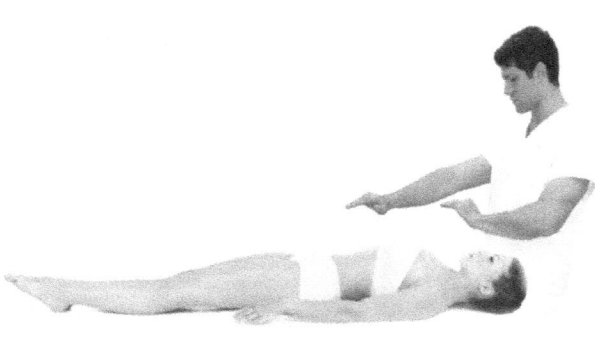

Healer and patient prepare for healing. Photo depicts how our physical eyes see things. Patient lies down on table for healing. Healer holds intention to heal. Patient holds intention to be healed and allows for the process to occur. Both hold the belief that healing is possible. Permission to heal is established. Grounding cords are set for both the patient and the healer (review grounding cord content in sections 13.28 and 14.14). Healer states prayer or personal healing mantra to set healing intention, bring in Divine help, and provide a positive healing space. Both healer and patient may now request Divine intervention to be present and assist. Healer keeps a general distance of his or her hand chakras 6-12 inches from the patient's body chakras. Healing of the 3rd (solar plexus) and 5th (throat) chakras is shown here.

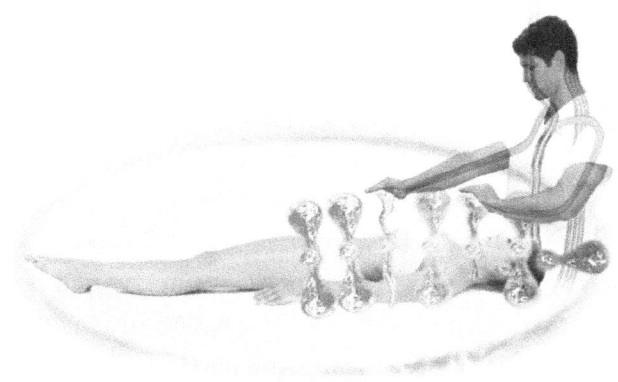

Healer feels the patient's chakras from a 6th sense perspective. Healer performs a general aura scan (review section 14.14), walking around the entire body checking the auric space and then each leg and arm channel separately for sensation changes. Healer then places hands over chakras starting from 1st root, to 7th crown, scanning for changes in pressure, temperature, vibration, pulling or pushing, pulsing, heat, cold, or tingling, twitching, tickling or a static feeling representing a change or alteration of the natural calm state of energy patterns. Notice that the 3rd and 5th chakras do not flow or feel like the others pictured.

Healer connects to Mother Earth and allows cosmic energy in. Utilizing the connection to the infinite and grounding him or herself from the bottom of the spine to the ground, the flow of energy can pass through the healer into the patient and then back out the healer's grounding cord. Likewise, the energy or sensations the patient feels can be directed to pass down their grounding cord. It is not unusual,

when energy clearing starts to occur, to have the patient claim they feel energy sensations throughout their body, go into a dreamlike state, or see visions.

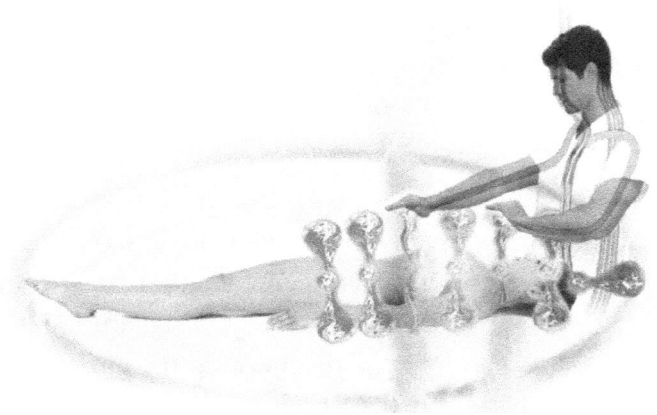

Healer identifies negative, misplaced, or stagnant energy in non-operating chakras. Unclean, stagnant, hard energy will usually be felt as muddy, dim, slow, sludgy, cold, or damp on the palm chakras when attempting to move the energy out. This low vibratory energy has no option but to move when directed by you via cosmic consciousness. The healer must guide the energy and give it an outlet for release. This release process is intertwined both with the physical body as well as the mind through the 6th sense. The healer directs these energies out of the patient and into the abyss through the grounding cord

Healer activates his body channels and works on balancing chakras via Divine cosmic inflow and grounding outflow. The healer must not use his or her own personal energy or take on the patient's energy. This would drain their life force, upset their own chakra balance, make them sick and cause what is commonly known as 'healer burnout.' The

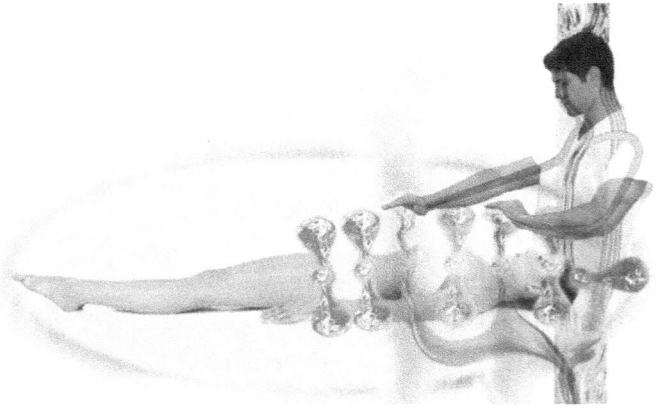

healer holds hand chakras in place as energy flows in through cosmic consciousness and out towards the grounding cord. The patient can help their healing process by also opening their energy channels and envisioning release of the blocks with instruction from the healer.

Healer drains energies and balances deficient chakras to bring patient back to proper flow. The cleansing time per case will vary but there will be a identifiable point that the healer feels a return of all sensations to a healthy medium, or return to what feels 'normal.' At this point the healer checks all chakras once more as well on the posterior side (patient asked to turn over) to be sure all work is completed and the chakras are balanced. The healer also checks the arm and leg channels as well as the auric space for tranquility and even disposition of energy. The session ends with the healer performing a post session muscle test on the patient and self cleansing on themselves (review section 14.14).

Case Study Example #2

The next scenario is one of a mid-thirties female patient who had been in multiple car accidents, two of which she was rear ended and one was a front end collision where she was ejected from the seat and cracked the windshield with her forehead. Patient was never referred for chiropractic treatment after being released from the hospital. Patient complains of constant migraine headaches, difficulty concentrating, thinking, sleeping, irritability, tingling sensations around her body, extreme fatigue, and constant body pains despite the accidents all being over six years ago. Prescription pills and diet modifications failed to alleviate her migraines. Patient reported all imaging and testing from other specialists seen was 'normal.' Specialist seen could not find anything wrong with her despite her list of symptoms.

Chiropractic examination and x-ray findings showed the patient had extensive cervical, thoracic and lumbo-pelvic subluxations throughout her entire spine which caused physical pain, restricted range of motion, tenderness, chronic trigger points throughout her upper torso and edema in the associated spinal areas. Of particular note, the patient had unresolved upper cervical subluxation of the atlas and axis vertebrae. The associated sub-occipital triangle tissue was also chronically scarred and improperly set. Upon further questioning, the patient admitted that since the accidents, she was having nightmares and odd dreams of separation, which upon waking up gave her feelings of anxiety and loneliness.

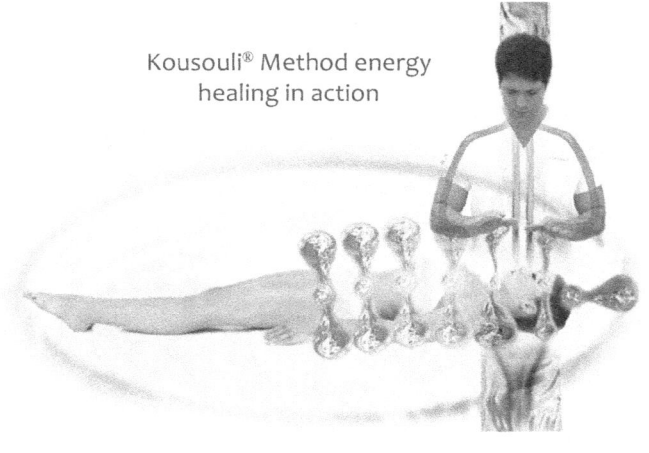

Kousouli® Method energy healing in action

Traditional chiropractic application as well as Kousouli® Method energy healing of the associated leaking chakras immediately brought back all function to the physical body as well as a renewed sense of self-empowerment in the spiritual body. By reconnecting the energy lines through the spinal column and addressing the energy body the patient quickly made a full recovery. In head trauma cases, the energy body and the physical body can separate causing a disharmony of the two, improperly flowing energies throughout the nervous system. Let us examine the healing process.

Energetic Healing of the Patient using the Kousouli® Method

Clearing of the 5th (throat) and 6th (3rd eye) chakras. Following chiropractic application (to clear patient's neural stress, and allow their mind to focus on healing instead of pain), I redirect focus to the throat chakra for healing; I pause, set my grounding cord run my energy channels, hold my intention, connect to the greatest physician - God, and then begin my work. I allow myself to be neutral after I set my intention. As a healer, I understand I mold aether, and influence matter through my mental and emotional capabilities when I'm open to receiving Divine energies. As an energy sensitive, I 'feel' and am 'led' to the different parts of the body that need assistance. I remove my ego from the equation, become the vessel, and let the energy flow do the healing. Sometimes my chest will ache or I will get a twinge in my leg which is Spirit telling me to either ask the patient about that area or to go to that area for focused energy healing. As a practitioner of energy healing, you should regularly pray for the people you work on while holding unconditional love for them in your heart. Bathe the patient in light. They don't have to believe or be faithful. As long as permission for you to help them is given, prayers will work on the non-believer as well as the believer. The non-believer's physical conscious mind may offer considerable resistance, so instead communicate healing to their 'higher self' and give them the healing they desire. If the patient is a believer and agrees to the healing process, they will allow their healing much quicker when they offer no resistance and are in like mind with you.

When healing, the intellectual mind is not the driving force. Instead, it is the quantum intelligence (i.e. the same energy that beats your heart, gives you the breath, and flows your blood) that does the magic. The focused thought of intention to heal, mixed with loving belief that the patient is healed, while surrounded by Divine love and joy without re-

sistance to their healing, is what heals the patient on a quantum level. This energy is brought forth through a loving intention without judgment, ego, doubt, fear, or pride. It happens in the heart, not the brain. You must get out of the brain and into the heart; this takes much discipline, patience and practice. Taking into account that healing is multi-dimensional; the success of the Kousouli® Method is because of its ability to address energy leaks in more than just the physical plane.

When systems of healing address only the physical component, success comes only if the issue's trauma resides purely in the physical realm. We see an example of a failed healing application relayed in Matthew 17:19, when Jesus' disciples were unsuccessful in removing a negative entity from a diseased person. Then the disciples came to Jesus privately and said, "Why could we not cast it out?" Jesus said to them, "Because of your unbelief; for assuredly, I say to you, if you have faith as a mustard seed, you will say to this mountain, 'Move from here to there,' and it will move; and nothing will be impossible for you. However, this kind does not go out except by prayer and fasting." Jesus meant that certain diseases are rooted into the body, so much so that the body must be starved and restarted (both spiritually through prayer and meditation, as well as physically through fasting and diet) to receive the full healing. So we can reason that it is far better to address illness with a 'toolbox of tools,' rather than improperly using a hammer to turn a screw. When looking to heal on a quantum level, you can't think linearly like most doctors today are trained to do. This can be difficult, especially in America's medical schools where doctors are trained to diagnose by only using previous tangible knowledge passed down by peer review journals, books, and instructors. The scholarly information is, of course, valuable and useful, though it will always come short if not applied in quantum ways. Doctors must know and understand that their duty and priority is to serve mankind by being teachers and guides to the ill stricken. They do this by providing hope and showing an alternative, positive perspective while transferring well-being to the patient. We can serve humanity by being examples in our own 'God power' to help usher others into their 'God power' as well. Jesus claimed that we all hold God's force; able to connect to and command this force, as we are extensions of the most High.

"I have said, Ye are gods; and all of you are children of the most High."
~ Psalm 82:6

"Jesus answered them, Is it not written in your law, I said, Ye are gods?"
~ John 10:34

The key to health and higher human potential increasing from 35% to 75% and higher is dimensional alignment and activation of the spiritual DNA in living matter. Human DNA has multidimensional properties which, when activated, can cause miraculous healing or reversal of disease - a concept not expressed or explored deeply by old science. Again, it is *quantum intuitive thought,* not the brain synapses, which is the working force in quantum healing. Intention held with total belief, without fear or doubt, affects all quantum levels. Healer and patient hold the healed version in mind while healing, and they will witness the final result of the healing.

15.4 Kousouli® Method Master Chart

See next page, 244.

Spiritual	Mental	Emotional	Chakra	Physical		Function	Malfunction
				Spinal	Organs		
Trance mediumship Knowingness Higher self Cosmic energy intake	Clarity Pure awareness Optimism/Pessimism Imagination	Peace, Tranquility Chaos, Blame, Arrogance, Dissatisfaction	Cranial Crown 7	Skull Bones Cranial nerves	Brain Pineal gland CSF ventricles	Cognition Critical thinking	Mental disorders Head pain Dizziness
Clairvoyance Abstract intuition Precognition Inner voice	Trusting Memory Intellect Reasoning Ignorance	Fear, Pride Inflexibility, Self conscious Confusion, Envy Humiliation	Cranio- Cervical 3rd Eye 6	Occiput C1 Atlas C2 Axis C3-C7 Cervical & Brachial plexus	Brain Cerebellum Hypothalamus Pituitary Eyes, Ears, Nose Throat	Brain-body communication Hearing, Seeing, Smelling, Tasting, Chewing	Head & Neck pain Dizziness Eye, Ear, Nose, Throat issues Migraines, Jaw pains Sleep disorders
Clairaudience Telepathy Pragmatic intuition	Authority Creative identity Inner drive	Expressionless Feeling Stuck Sadness Vulnerability Disgust	Cervical Throat 5	C1-T1 Cervical & Brachial plexus	Thyroid Vocal cords Heart Lungs Neck & shoulders Brachial plexus	Brain-body communication Verbal communication Hormone regulation	Neck pain Sore throat Arm & Shoulder pain Stiffness Hormonal disorders Sleep disorders
Love Affinity	Self acceptance Harmony Equilibrium	Compassion, Love, Tenderness Joy, Abundance Heartache, Betrayal Grief, Rejection, Hatred	Upper Thorax Heart 4	T1-T6 Sympathetic ganglion	Heart Lungs Thymus Liver Gallbladder	Circulation Breathing	Chest pain Breathing issues Asthma Heart circulation Heartburn
Out of body experience Life force energy distribution Inner integration	Will Power Egotism Restlessness	Paranoia Anger, Low self esteem Resentment, Nervousness, Worry, Guilt, Anxiety Jealousy, Regret	Lower Thorax Solar Plexus 3	T7-T12 Ileocecal valve Celiac plexus Pyloric valve	Kidneys, Diaphragm Liver, Gallbladder Spleen, Pancreas Stomach, Adrenals Large & Small intestine	Breathing Detoxification Elimination Digestion Assimilation	Kidney Stones Liver, Pancreatic failure Gall Stones, Gastric disorders, Sleep disorders Allergies
Clairsentience	Sexuality Emotional need Relationships Social ambition Addiction	Enthusiasm, Inner conflict Peeved off, Frozen will, Fear, Lust, Manipulative	Lumbo-Sacral Naval 2	L1-S1 Lumbar plexus Celiac plexus Sciatic nerve	Bladder, Sex organs Prostate, Uterus Large intestine Appendix	Reproduction Elimination	Low back pain IBS Allergies Sciatica Kidney & Urinary issues Constipation
Survival Material harmony	Safety Security Emotional Physicality Sense of Lack	Vulnerability Neediness Insecurity Control Issues Obsession Materialism Distrust	Sacro-Pelvic Spinal Base 1	S1-S5 Sacral plexus Sciatic nerve	Rectum Anus Colon Bladder Sex organs	Reproduction Elimination	Menstrual pains, Cramping, Sterility, SI pain, Leg circulation Knee pains, Numbness, Digestive disorders Allergies
Psychometry Healing Telekinesis	—	—	Hands Palm center	Radial Medial Ulnar nerves	—	Creative manifestation Energy transfer	Arthritis Swelling Gout Inflammation Cramping Carpel tunnel
Grounding Earth energy intake	—	—	Feet Foot arch	Tibial Sural Peroneal Cutaneous Plantar Saphenous Nerves	—	Transportation Physical manifestation	Arthritis Swelling Gout Inflammation Cramping Tarsal tunnel

Note: Points will cross and may affect multiple chakra sites. This chart displays the most basic relationship between the spiritual, mental, emotional, and physical human planes.

KOUSOULI METHOD

Copyright 2004-2016. All Rights Reserved.

Chapter 16:
Performing a Clairvoyant Reading

"I believe that art and healing are one. They cannot be separated. I think that everyone is an artist and everyone is a healer. Through art, people can get to a place of luminosity, of pure spirit within them-selves, where they can expand - change in time and space. This allows them to merge the two sides of their spirit. As the two sides of the spirit merge, people become open to their deepest truths; and by seeing and accepting those truths, inner healing can begin."
~ Michael Samuels, MD.

Clairvoyance is the ability to receive visual information through extra sensory means without using your physical eyes. When accessing extrasensory information it comes into your mind and displays just like a continuously moving movie in a dream, however you are fully awake and able to interact with the moving images.

16.1 Energy Potentials, Not Prophecy or 'Future Telling'

Anyone who tells you they can tell you your future is actually misleading you. No one really knows the future. There is only what is known as the reading of potentials, or possible futures. The God-self knows all the possibilities of what you will choose, and each choice's outcome. However, the big unknown is *what* you will pick. The future cannot be foretold by anyone other than each individual who enacts their free will. Although there is a changeable plan, the future is not written in stone. Together, we all co-create the possibilities of what we see happen on our Earth and how we experience it together. There are those who are sensitive to being able to read the energy potentials and possibilities of others. It is also true that everyone has this seemingly unique ability. However some individuals, who are called psychic, have exercised their sixth sense and allow their abilities to be executed, until they become second nature, like breathing. Those who are sensitive to subtle energies in auras or their environment can feel or see the energies, and can interpret them into people, pictures, places, and events that can be read as energy potential. So in essence, energy sensitive people (psychics) are interpreting the energy potential in your aura at the time you are receiving the reading. There are many avenues the energy in your aura can take, and the psychic will give you possibly one or two versions of what they feel could occur in your future reality. However, no psychic can be 100% accurate all the time, as energy potentials change every second and depend on the free will of the individual's life - not the psychic's prediction. Some can argue, that their psychic is always right: "She hits the nail on the head every time." This can of course be true because just as a doctor skilled in routine heart operations can have a high success rate, so can a psychic who is in tune with her ability to decipher energy potentials. It can also be true that the person receiving the reading decides to focus all their energy on the predicted energy potential, and actually steers their whole life towards the prediction using the Law of Expectation. Then, they attract the circumstances to them just as they were foretold by the psychic, completing the expected 'prophecy.' Readers who intuitively decipher the energy potentials of your life and give you psychic readings should be taken seriously only after you have understood that the only one you really should listen to for final say is yourself and your intuition. Readings are a manifestation of your current energetic reality; you are only using psychic readers because you yourself have not come into your own power to understand your ability and your own gifts for deciphering energy potentials in your life. Utilizing the information in this book, and then seeking training with a reader you trust and can train under, would be the best course of action if you decide to take reading energy potentials as a career. Just as you would apprentice under a plumber, electrician, or surgeon, you can do the same to learn the skills of psychic potential.

Exercises to increase intuitive awareness

Card deck exercise:

Pick 10 cards from a deck and use these to start off with. Look through the ten cards to familiarize yourself with the numbers and colors. Put the ten cards in a small pile after you mix them up. Place them face down so you can't see the face. Using your intuition, say the number and color that comes to mind after you focus on the top card before flipping it. Do not think, do not guess, do not feel anxious, and do not feel uncertainty. Do not feel doubt - feel certainty. Believe you can accurately predict the number, color, or both. Ask: "What is the number or color?" Let it come to you without thinking. It usually shows up in your mind in a quick flash. If you are not correct, do not blame or guilt yourself. Forgive yourself and go on to the next card and then the next. As you see your accuracy increase, add ten more cards, repeat, and so on.

Dice exercise:

Start with one die, and do what you did with the card deck prediction. Roll the die and just before it stops call the number. When your accuracy increases, add the other die and roll both.

Whisper exercise:
With a partner, take turns closing your eyes and standing still. One stands still as the partner starts at 5 feet away in any direction, whispering a phrase that the one being tested must repeat to check accuracy. Using your hearing, allow your partner to move slowly around you, and stop in a position as they change the phrase you must repeat. Keeping your head straight no matter where your partner is standing. When you master this, then have the partner move to 10 feet and repeat the whisper, changing the phrase each time. Then go 10 feet, and so on. The more you perform this, the better your sense of sensitive hearing will become which will help raise your general awareness.

Sensation exercise:
Sit in a chair 8 to 10 feet opposite your partner and take turns, with eyes closed, to send energy to one another. Hold your palms open side by side together, facing toward your partner while aiming at their heart chakra. Try sending the vibration in thought of love, compassion, joy, and take turns identifying what and where the other was sending out. Keep in mind that if you send negative energy as in vibration of war, hate, jealousy, disease, the other will indeed feel the difference. Only do this for a few seconds just to see the major difference in how higher energies feel compared to lower energies. Always end with sending love to the chakras; be sure not to leave your partner in a lower energy state.

Swivel chair exercise:
Sit in an office chair that swivels 360 degrees. Sit in the chair comfortably and with your eyes open, view your environment. Take note of what is in front of you, behind you, to your left and right. The goal in this exercise is to see if you can, with your eyes closed, know where you are facing when you open your eyes. With your eyes closed, give yourself a good spin and let yourself come to a slow stop. Now using your intuition and not forcing yourself to "think," let the image of what you will see in front of you come to you just prior to opening your eyes. When you feel you know where you are facing, open your eyes and compare what you intuitively saw with what you see in front of you.

Blindfold exercise:
With a partner take turns wearing a blindfold and standing still. The blindfolded one stands still as the partner moves slowly around and stops in a position. Keeping your hands down and body straight. "Feel" in your aura where your partner is standing and point or verbalize their position. When you master this, add earplugs to completely block the sense of hearing and perform the exercise without sight or hearing.

With continued practice you can get into even more advanced methods of psychokinetic power and telekinesis. Lighting small fluorescent light bulbs simply by holding the negative and positive leads or bending metal with the mind, or speed reading a book by fanning the pages like a special select children newly born are doing in Japan (research 'quantum kids of Japan' or 'psi kids' online).

Perhaps the most exciting and important practice a human being can do to connect to a more fulfilling life is activate their sixth sense also referred to activating the pineal gland or 'third eye – 'clairvoyance.' This unfamiliar sense was at one time very active, particularly in youth prior to being shut off by the limiting factors and negative influences on this earthly realm. We can reactivate and empower our abilities by bringing focus and continuously exercising their use. Over time, like an unused muscle that has atrophied, it starts to bulk up and get stronger. If you do start on this journey, understand you will be in the minority of the population who is even awake enough to want to do this. Most people unfortunately, are happy in being complacent with mediocrity and allowing others to tell them what to do and how to feel about their life. Thinking, but more importantly, *FEELing* for yourself will be the biggest gift you can give yourself if you choose to continue forward.

16.2 Clairvoyant Terminology

In order to jump into this work you should be familiar with some basic associated terminology and understand the illustrations provided for you. If you become overwhelmed (which may happen) take a breath, relax, and start over the material at a slower pace. Excitement for performing the material and getting your first experience should be subdued, as understanding and clarity are vital to know what you will be experiencing soon. Not understanding the procedure and what is being presented can falsely lead you to fear and fear will shut off all progress made. Let's look over some terminology used in higher mind circles. Many of the words will be used again in the exercises later in the book.

- *Akashic records:* The Akashic records are commonly described as a massive unseen library, non-physical supercomputer, or which contains all knowledge of human experience. The Akashic records also house each human's activities, spiritual DNA, names, occupations, just about everything. It is the knowledge storefront where genius ideas instantly come from. When performing the end of a psychic reading we ask to tap into this massive informational storehouse to add to or get information for our use here on Earth.

- ***Ascended masters:*** Those who we know of historically who have set the example here on Earth for us to emulate and follow the path to enlightenment. Every religion has their list, but some of the most popular are: Jesus Christ, Mother Mary, Buddha, Krishna, St. Germain, Elijah, Enoch, and Confucius to name a few.

- ***Channeling***: Channeling is a process where a human being allows another spirit from the non-physical world to use the human body to communicate a message or carry on a task. Channeling can be a very positive experience when aligned with the highest vibration of love and the channel is coming from a loving space. All religious writings by saints where channeled messages from the great beyond and those words were passed off as God's law since the channels were 'in the light' and felt surrounded by this unworldly love. Likewise, the human that is channeling can also allow foreign energies to work through them. This can be dangerous because it can invite unwanted entities that may decide to stay in the body. Lower energy spirits seek to exist on multiple planes. When channeled, the spiritual entity will use the body without harboring any of the negative energy (negative karma) associated with its consequence of actions. An example of opening communication with the non-physical side would be tools, such as Ouija boards or spirit mirrors. These may be used inappropriately at a seemingly harmless party or gathering and turn into a possession. You must always be in charge of your own body at all times while performing the work without giving over control. Channeling correctly does not mean you must give over power to another entity; rather you maintain your position in command as you empower your own ability and see the images and visions sent to you from your higher self. Channeling through your own ability is a purer and higher vibration than allowing it through a foreign mischievous energy.

- **Clairaudience:** The extrasensory ability to clearly hear messages from other realms, not with the physical ears, but with one's intuitive sixth sense. (i.e.) Suzy heard her deceased Uncle Bobby's voice in her head, warning her to watch out in the rain as she buckled her seat belt. A little bit down the road, she just missed being in a five car pile-up only by a few seconds.

- **Claircognizance:** The extrasensory ability to clearly know, not with the physical brain but with one's intuitive sixth sense. (i.e.) Tommy wasn't sure why, but he knew, without a doubt, that the poker tournament was rigged from the start.

- **Clairgustance:** The extrasensory ability to clearly taste, not with the physical mouth and tongue, but with one's intuitive sixth sense. (i.e.) As Tara was communicating with the medium, she knew her mother was present in the room because she could taste chocolate brownies, which were Tara's favorite when mom used to make them for her.

- **Clairalience or Clairscent:** The extrasensory ability to clearly smell odors from other realms, not with the physical senses but with one's intuitive sixth sense. (i.e.) As soon as the reading started, the smell of cigar smoke filled the room. Tom knew his deceased father, who was an avid cigar smoker, was there with him in spirit.

- **Clairsentience:** The extrasensory ability to clearly feel, not with the physical senses but with one's intuitive sixth sense. (i.e.) Theresa wasn't sure why, but when Brad told her he was just at the store, Theresa had a strong feeling deep in her gut that Brad was lying.

- **Clairtangency or Psychometry:** The extrasensory ability to clearly feel and pick up information from an object; not with the physical senses but with one's intuitive sixth sense. (i.e.) Larry touched the lost keys and immediately knew the person who lost them was a tall brunette female who has a dog.

- **Clairvoyance:** The extrasensory ability to clearly see, not with the physical senses, but with one's intuitive sixth sense. (i.e.) A day before it happened, Harry had a vision that he was going to win the game by making the final touchdown.

- *Contractual agreements or Soul contracts*: A deal, arrangement, or contractual agreement you made with another spirit, person, entity or yourself prior to coming into this incarnation. Soul contracts are not written in stone due to God's gift of personal free will and with conscious intent can be broken and changed as long as one knows how to do so psychically. Thus, you do not have a 'fate' to live up to, only the progress or path you are creating and learning from. If in contract with a lower entity, the lower entity may want some control of your physical body or mind in exchange for their help. Higher angelic beings however, do not wish to take over or control you, and are happy to assist without infringement of your free-will or harming you.

- *Cosmic awareness:* The power to be aware of anything that affects the user on a universal scale.

- *Crystalline grid:* Interlinking of the crystal energy of Earth. Where this grid pattern crosses: dimensional portals and entranceways connect other dimensional realms and star systems with Earth. Ancient civilizations used strong crystalline points to their advantage by building their temples and pyramids on top of these special vortices.

- *Divided mind:* The ability to split the mind into separate personality identities; can be due to traumatic events such as rape, abuse, torture, or shock.

- *Dream manipulation or Oneirokinesis:* The ability to go into and manipulate one's own dream or the dream of another for benevolent actions such as healing, or maliciously creating nightmares.

- *Empathy:* The ability to feel and copy the mood or emotions of others. Common basic ability amongst most clairvoyants and healers.

- *Foreign devices or Alien mechanisms:* Devices seen in readings by clairvoyants that look to be connected into human chakras or around spiritual bodies which drain energy, copy entities, or are parasitic in some way. These mechanical devices do not look like devices found on Earth and can be quite menacing or difficult to dissolve or erase. They tend to multiply and replace themselves if not dealt with swiftly.

- *Ghosts:* Unlike poltergeists, ghosts are usually harmless. It is important that you don't fear when it makes its presence known. It usually looks like a shadow or hazy mist that may pass by you or exist for a few seconds. They usually make themselves visible if they want to communicate something to the living by vibrating temperature as a cold or warm feeling, static vibration, or pulsing. They often manipulate electronic devices like radios, televisions and lightbulbs to communicate with us. A process called EVP, or Electronic Voice Phenomenon uses audio signals to get messages from the other side. We can indeed communicate with relatives who have passed over using electricity and audio frequency as a bridge. Using any audio recorder, ask questions while allowing static or white noise to record in the background. Give the energies one minute per question to answer back, and then review the tape after you've asked all your questions. You will be amazed to find that they are still very much there with you; just not in physical form. Let them know you know they are there without fear, say the Lord's Prayer in section 4.11, and if the spirit is godly, it will continue to give you its message or interact with you. If it is not, it won't be able to stay in your presence if you command it in God's name to leave immediately. Again, do not fear and they can't harm you.

- *Healing guides:* Previously incarnated souls who were doctors or healers and are looking after those who do healing work in the physical realm. Healing guides help healers here accentuate their abilities and guide them to answers during healings. They choose to work with healers because they have had or still have similar purposes and goals for bettering humanity. They can appear to you as silhouetted colors and some report hearing them as high pitch tones or ringing sounds when they are present.

- *Hive mind:* When a collective thought, idea, or vision is shared between multiple people at the same time. Happens often in places like seminars, board rooms, and stadiums.

- *Lost souls:* Usually referred to as the bodiless souls stuck on a bad vibration repeatedly tormenting themselves by feeling guilty, resentful or wandering on the other side hopelessly disconnected in what seems like an eternal loop away from their God power. These souls must be guided 'to the light' and many times don't know they have crossed over.

- *Magnetic grid* or **Planetary energetic grid theory:** Referred to as the magnetic grid matrix of the Earth, sometimes known as 'ley lines' that link the planet. It is constantly reconstructing in view of the changing spirituality and new evolutionary tasks of Humanity. Similar to the crystalline grid, they are high energy portal points in various Earth vortices (i.e. Sedona, Arizona USA).

- *Memory manipulation:* The ability to alter and regulate the mindsets, thoughts, and upper brain function of another.

- *Mental manipulation*: The ability to manipulate modify and regulate the mindsets, thoughts, and upper brain function of another.

- *MerKaBa:* In Hebrew, MerKaBa means Chariot. It is the vehicle of ascension, believed to be turned on via deep strategic meditation involving deep breathing and changes in the heart, mind and body feeling limitless and boundless in reality. Everyone has a MerKaba, but it must be activated. When activated, it appears as a spinning structure of inter-dimensional high vibrational light, or gateway, which enables you to travel from one dimensional world to another. In the Bible, Elijah and Elisha cross the Jordan when a Merkaba of fire appeared (explained as a chariot flying into the sky), and Elijah disappeared in a whirlwind of light and fire.

- **Neurocognitive deficiency:** The ability to shut down the brain function of another, usually making them go unconscious or 'blank' for a period of time.
- **Poltergeists:** Poltergeists are malicious emotionally disturbed versions of ghosts. They tend to spontaneously manifest as troublesome, loud, or vicious entities. Usually inanimate objects get thrown through the air as if by an invisible person. Noises such as knocking, or banging as well as human voices and grumbling can be heard by those afflicted. Accounts of physical attacks on human beings that feel like biting, scratching, pinching, slapping, and hitting are not uncommon. Immediately say the Lord's Prayer in section 4.11 and give no fuel 'fear and attention' to the energy as it could feed and grow from any negative emotions.
- **Precognition:** The power to recognize events before they actually manifest in physical form.
- **Psionic armor or Shielding:** Immunity against another's psychic attacks.
- **Psychic navigation:** The ability to track or map items, animals, or people with the mind; to know where they are within the terrain. Used often by remote viewers (explained in later in depth).
- **Psychic surgeons:** Similar to healing guides, psychic surgeons are passed on souls that are working on the other side of the veil. They were individuals you knew or knew of anywhere in your spiritual lineage, loved ones who now protect you, or individuals who are master healers. They often are the ones who send miraculous energy for instant healing.
- **Pushing:** The ability to insert thoughts, memories, or emotions into the people's minds. Seen often with covert hypnosis and marketing techniques.
- **Soul Flame or Twin flame:** Another soul who you feel unexplainable strong emotional love or sexual desire towards, and may have been married or involved with in another lifetime. May or may not be from the same soul group.
- **Soul group:** This is a group of infinite beings of consciousness, vowed to help each other in times of distress or share in times of happiness. These souls began incarnation on this world together at the same time with a similar purpose. Each soul learns its lesson separately but may find another soul in another part of the world by what seems as chance, only to come to the awareness that they both are soul

siblings (or soul mates, incarnated as either male or female in this lifetime) from the same group. Soul groups can be a small handful of numbers or several stadium sizes large; entering the lifetime for a specific purpose or goal (i.e. research the indigo and crystal children online). People you find in school or group meditation classes who may be sitting near you, or those you find on the same path of life learning as you, may be incarnated with you in the same soul group. A chance meeting with a person from another side of the world, that shares the same exact date of birth and life lessons as you, is likely to be a spiritual brother or sister in your incarnated soul group.

- *Telepathy:* The power to mentally accept or give information by mind readers or telepaths.
- *Telekinesis:* The ability to use 'mind' for object manipulation.
- *Upper chakra transference*: Yawning, belching, sneezing, couching, twitching, and even tearing are common when activating your clairvoyance and top-level chakras of the throat, 3rd eye and crown. When clearing through visions, pictures, or negative energies in readings, energy centers can become over-stimulated in some individuals. It would not be uncommon for these energies to make the reader feel choked up, dizzy, produce phlegm or overwhelm the head, ears, nose and throat areas as these are the areas of higher chakra activity.

Planes of Existence

Physics claims a "many worlds" theory that many believe explains that our world is split 'quantum-ly' into a world of unlimited versions of this real world. The worlds are unknown to each other and to us. However it is believed we can move to other versions or realities if we so desire through thought. It makes sense if we see that getting up in the morning we have any number of choices to eat a certain breakfast; ham and eggs or a short stack of pancakes? Pick the ham and eggs and your day will go onward on one world reality and the choosing of the short stack will take you to another. Wear a shirt and tie to work or go relaxed with a golf shirt and khakis and other realities will unfold. We truly do choose our world experiences through free will and in so doing co-create any number of world realities. There are also many planes or world realities, more than we can go into in this book, but some of the more well knowns are:

- **Astral plane:** Where we go every night when we're dreaming. There we can converse with our spirit guides, or deceased relatives and friends. This is where we can also meet with others currently living during dream sleep or meditation to give a message or take part on a journey together. There is no such thing as a past, present or future in astral realm. Traveling out of body lands you in the astral plane.

- **Elemental plane:** The plane of the elements that make up air, fire, water and earth.
- **Material (Physical) plane:** The current dense realm we exist in where we experience the belief system that we are separate from one another, from animals, from rocks, from plants, even from the 'All that is' itself. We can remove the mind from this structured reality using meditation or herbal medicines which nature provided humanity for the ascension of consciousness into higher realms. This is what is meant by getting 'high.'
- **Mental plane**: Direct connection through the mind can be achieved with the Infinite Creator at this level. Within this plane you learn about the Universe and all its secrets.
- **Messianic plane:** The Christ consciousness teaches from this plane with complete love 'agape' for all creation. Here you comprehend the interconnected web of how we are all one with each other, knowing the infinite from a deep emotional level.

16.3 Psychic Visualization and Meditation Tools to Move and Clear Energy

Whether you are aware of it consciously or not, you probably have some level of psychic ability. All those 'lucky' moments and coincidences in your life are not chance miracles. Nothing is by coincidence in a co-creative universe. Someone (you) created it in some way to get more soul experience. Whenever you had Déjà vu, an out of body experience (OBE) or premonition come to pass you exhibited parts of your higher self. Everyone has had that weird feeling that it wasn't something 'usual' or normal for them. These things are not by accident. They are you, reminding you – that you're more than just a heap of flesh here.

- **Analytical stabilization tool:** The grounding of the analytical mind is important, especially for individuals who want to get to sleep quickly or slow down their analytic brain because of over stimulation or over use. Imagine a long grounding cord with the diameter the size of a teacup saucer mounted into the back of the bottom half of the skull. See this grounding cord (in addition to the root chakra grounding cord - but separate) running down to the middle of the earth removing negative energy or overuse energy and bringing you to a relaxed calm state.

- **Browning tool:** For individuals who want to relax, sleep quickly, or slow down 'static' interfering with concentration. Close your eyes and imagine stepping into a warm chocolate syrup bath completely nude. Start with one foot entering the warm heavy chocolate sludge and proceed to see yourself as a hollow body, until your nostrils and mouth are only left open, and drink the syrup, letting the chocolate enter you as you envision it filling in the inside of your body cavity until you are submerged both internally and externally. This is a beautiful meditation to do during a work break where things seem to be too much to handle around you. You may also see someone in your environment that may be overrun with high energy. Brown them by envisioning them slowly covered with thick chocolate sludge until it hardens around them. You may be pleasantly surprised to see them start relaxing a bit more.

- **Bubble manifestation tool:** Helps bring desired objects to you faster. Imagine a large soap bubble in front of you. In this large bubble you will include all the things you wish to manifest using your imagination. Once the bubble is filled with items, it is sealed, multiplied, signed and sent out to God.

- **Dissolving/Erasure tool:** Deletes or removes undesired issues. See images fade over time or pretend you have a personal copy machine with you that you copy and recopy images until they fade. A large eraser may also be seen erasing or disassembling the image or entity.

- **Draining cords:** A connection from another source to one's energy body that takes life energy. Draining cords are exactly that; they drain you and leave you feeling empty while manipulating you in a negative way. Male sexual predators (pimps, human traffickers), cord into females' second chakra clairsentience (ability to feel) and know how to manipulate them through their primal feelings and emotional needs. Depending on the hold they have on them there can be cords found also in the neck (self-expression and the ability to voice their opinion) as well as blinding their third eye clairvoyance to foresee the process being put upon them. Total obedience without objection can also come about when more chakras are corded; and worsens the longer they are left corded by the predator. Female predators are experts at cording a man's root chakra (need for survival, material harmony) and clairsentience (ability to feel) which can be seen manifested as draining to a man financially as well as emotionally. The man gradually becomes desensitized to his upper chakra power and exercises the primal lower energy which keeps him from progressing in greater self-awareness and instead stays focused on survival and not losing the mate (faux love). The illusion the predator creates is making the victim feel fulfilled when in their presence and lost when without them. The victim starts to feel that without them around; they are powerless, lonely and empty. Victims feel like they cannot live without the predator, forget their own power and fully submit to their will. Spiritual work through the Kousouli® Method, clairvoyant readings, meditation, prayer and conventional therapy methods are needed to break these strongly connected cordings.

- **Earth and Cosmic energy tool:** Vital energy lines that run through the body – Foot chakras and Leg channels to Root Chakra (represents Earth energy flow from Mother Earth into the body) and Crown chakra through the Spine to Root chakra (represents cosmic influx from Universal flow, See figures in 13.28).

- **Grounding cord:** Most basic of tools for negative energy neutralization or removal set at the base of the first root chakra (coccyx tail bone) and connecting straight down into the middle of the Earth. Usually a little wider in size than the hips and expandable as needed for bulk negative energy removal. Examples could include hollow tree trunk, large chasm or hole, heavy industrial electric cord, hollow metal tube, large waterfall, or a slide. Any person, place, thing, feeling, or idea that causes a feeling less than joy should be envisioned as being thrown down the grounding cord and flowing to the middle of the earth's molten core for energy recycling. You can ground anyone and anything during stressful or negative situations.

- **Rose petal or flower protection tool:** A non-threatening visualization that helps relax chaos and remove negativity. Since the beginning of time, the rose has been a symbol of love. It is for this reason many who use visualization techniques use roses and rose petals as neutralizers to negative 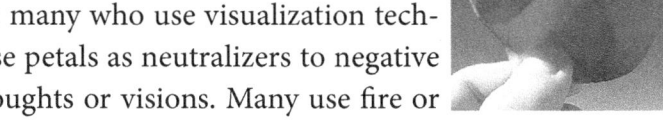 thoughts or visions. Many use fire or walls, or shields as visual protection. This is not as beneficial as a rose for the very energy associated with the mental thought of fire, walls, or shields is one of defense and war. Immediately this would put one at an energy disadvantage. It would be better to envision a semi-permeable membrane such as a rose petal or full rose bud. Or you could envision the rose petal wrapped around any entity or unwanted image and neutralize the energy. Roses also come with built in grounding cords – their stems! Using the rose tool helps delete negative energy by, "killing them with kindness."

- **Sun tool:** Replenishes vital energy by calling back your energy and uplifting or refilling the aura & chakras. While awake in physical reality or asleep in the astral plane, energy from oneself may be left with others or other places. You can call back your energy anytime you feel depleted. Envision a large sun over your head with the item or description intended to bring back. Examples include: power, forgiveness, love, patience, joy, health, etc. Various colors such as reds, pinks, etc. will be seen as they come back to you. See the warm sun burst over head as it pours its forgiveness, love, vitality etc. over you and bathes you in its calmness.

16.4 Performing a Clairvoyant Reading Session

In this section, you will learn my straightforward step-by-step techniques for performing a reading session on a client. There are many ways to attain this type of information, but I find this way most effective for my students. It will take practice and dedicated application to master the contents, so don't get discouraged if you are having difficulty receiving the energy and images. The images are all around you, just as radio waves and Wi-Fi constantly are. If you cultivate the proper sensitivity like the right station on a radio receiver, you can pick up on them easier. If you're really having a challenging time with it, you may have to be in the energy of others who are already sensitive enough to pick up on these signals. While they perform the readings you may absorb the ability to see and understand the process up close, firsthand. This is why the seminars are so powerful, as they help skyrocket people's natural psychic abilities. Some new readers will ease into their natural psychic ability once they feel it is "safe" to participate and do this type of work again. Remember, as an eternal spiritual being you are able to do all things, and this is a natural ability for you. Past incarnations (where you may have been persecuted for your abilities or burned at the stake for what was considered witchcraft) could have made your spirit reluctant to opening up your higher ability in this life's incarnation.

1. Prepare for the reading. Before starting a reading it is important you are fed well about an hour prior to starting. This work takes a lot of mental power and chances are you will

Performing a Clairvoyant Reading

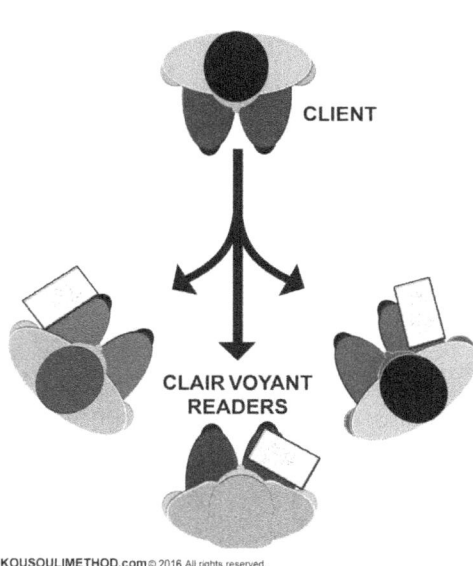

deplete your glucose reserves, making you very hungry. You do not want to go into a session hungry, as that will make it much harder for you to concentrate on the session. Keep some light crackers nearby just in case you need to get your blood glucose up. If you wish to light incense or sage the room, you may. Sit on a chair in a quiet comfortable room directly across the client. If there is more than one reader, position yourselves in a semicircle in front of the client as shown. You will each have a clipboard with paper and a pen. It's not important to be neat with what will be written; this just serves as a notepad for any information coming in. You can write anywhere on the paper whenever needed. Some readers will jot letters, numbers, doodles, or messages that come in which must be relayed to the client. These things may not make sense to the reader, but it may to the client that needs to receive them. It is not a requirement you use a clipboard, pen and paper but it is greatly advised you do so. Close your eyes (client keeps their eyes open so that all their energy remains present in the room. If they close them, they may fall sleep which will make their energy leave the room) and relax your whole body starting with the top of your head all the way down to your toes. Notice your breathing cycle. Bring fresh breath in. Exhale used breath out. Let your breathing be effortless (recall the sun tool in section 16.3). Call back any of your life force energy from anywhere in the Universe that you may have lost it: to others in your daily interaction (I.e. yelled at someone in traffic, boss was hard on you in a meeting, you lent an ear to a distressed friend on the phone who was crying, etc.) Pay attention to your heart beat while it pumps and feel its tempo. The idea here is to slow down the speed of daily life and allow your mind and body to rev up psychically while slowing down the physical body. Breathe deeply into your upper chest and let that flow down to expand the diaphragm. Let the exhalation leave and relax your abdominal muscles. Let the wave of relaxation flow down to your toes and back up out the top of your head. See yourself showering under a tropical rainforest's waterfall. Feel the fresh rush of the water running through you as you get ready to receive insight from your Creator.

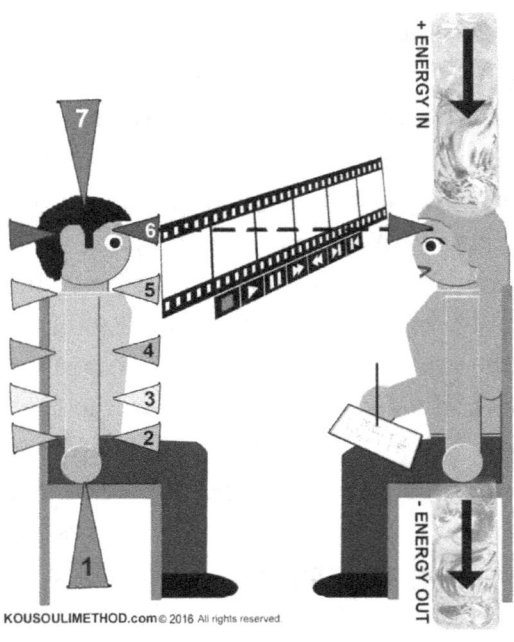

2. Set your grounding cord. Envision from the bottom of your spine through your root chakra down into the middle core of the Earth a hollow tube which is a one way, no questions asked, permanent exit for negative energy. When anything is commanded down this hollow slippery tube, it is no longer of your concern and is recycled by Mother Earth into something positive. Husband or girlfriend got you stressed and gave you some negative vibes today? Envision yourself sending him or her packing down the grounding cord. Bad dream or vision got you anxious? No problem, send it down the grounding cord as you watch it go far away from you and becoming smaller with every second it slides away. Are you fearful of your stingy overbearing boss? Simply envision him sent out of your brain and down the grounding cord as he slides into the middle of the Earth. You are not hurting anyone with this neutral exercise, but energetically you are doing something big - removing their energy vibration from affecting yours. Since energy is neither created nor destroyed - only transformed - we use this tool as a recycling center, sending any negativity to the Abyss, or core of the earth and then letting Mother Earth handle it. You can ground anything or anyone at any time when you want a direct exit point to send negative energy for neutralization. You can also decorate your grounding cord as you like, and if it gets a bit used up or raggedy looking, you may renew it. Add diamonds, make it shiny, or whatever you like. You're in charge. Use your imaginative mind and let it run wild.

3. Center your head's bouncer and silence the random thoughts. This means get all the junk out of your mind so you can get ready for the reading. No one should be in the center of your mind except YOU. Anything or anyone that is not YOU needs to go down the grounding cord. Set your "Bouncer", which is a little mini version of you sitting in the middle of your headspace. Give the mini bouncer his/her own grounding cord so they can also clean out any trash going on in the mind. Start monitoring your thoughts and if anything pops in, like "oh I wonder if I left the stove on", or "I really have to do laundry when I get home", it must be sent down the grounding cord quickly. These thoughts are NOT YOU; they are wandering thoughts that disrupt the connection to your psychic abilities! These thoughts may be other people's thoughts or things programmed into your head by the radio, television, society, friends, a parent or priest. Bounce out anything that is not a neutral silence. Once you spent some time in neutral silence, and there are no more intrusions to your mind (this may take a while for some people - keep bouncing out the negative energies and random thoughts down into the grounding cord), proceed then to pulling in your aura.

4. Pull in your aura. Our auras span out approximately 8 meters in all directions and in doing so they can be involved with things and people we do not want to associate with when we're trying to do readings. By consciously bringing in your aura, you keep your energy focused in the room and the reading happening at the present moment. Envision your auric space about four to six feet out from you, well within the room, not any further out than the walls around you.

5. Connect to cosmic and earth energies. Once your mind is centered, cleared, and you're present in the current moment in time, you will want to enact the Cosmic and Earth energies to support you. Envision a beautiful electric blue energy coming in from the Cosmos into your crown chakra as it washes through down your neck, shoulders, arms, and through your chakras into the root base. See the crown chakra burst into a beautiful golden glow that encircles your head, just like you see on holy figures depicted in icons. At the same time envision your leg channels being fed by the Earth as beautiful reddish green clay colored energy entering through your feet and into your legs and groin. Here the Earth energy mixes in the root chakra with the incoming cosmic energy that is bathing you in radiant light.

6. Run your body's energy lines. Take a few minutes and envision your arm and leg channel energy glowing and flowing throughout your body as a healthy vibrant liquid light. See every cell tissue and organ in harmony as you are fed by the Cosmic and Earth energies.

7. Dump negative energy out of your grounding cord. As these powerful energies are pulsating throughout your body, envision all negativity and any lowered vibrations from any person, place, thing, or idea being forced out down your grounding cord and straight to Mother Earth for neutralization.

8. Open your viewing screen and ground it. Once you're cleared all destructive energy, envision a screen in front of you in your mind's eye. It's just like a television or movie screen. This is where you will be receiving images, pictures, visions, etc. clairvoyantly (see image for reference) from your guides and your client's guides. This is their projection screen and your viewing screen. Just like with your grounding cord, you may decorate it any way you wish and make it look any way you like, just be sure to have it in front of you and keep it blank until you start reading. Just as you have a grounding cord at the base of your spine, and your bouncer has one in the middle of your head, ground also your viewing screen so that it can easily send energy down to Mother Earth. You may clean off your screen by throwing rose energy at it.

9. Dissolve energy roses at negative energy and clear space. Rose energy has always symbolized love. There is a never-ending supply of rose energy on this planet. Envision it in your mind's eye. You are this love energy at your very core. By that energy anything stagnant, negative, or low vibration is cleansed, forgiven and removed. You will use rose energy anytime you are looking to convert negativity to positivity. Envision yourself throwing roses to all four corners of the room blessing it in love and truth prior to saying the intention and a protection prayer.

10. Say intention and a protection prayer prior to starting session. Once you complete all the previous steps and have prepared your space and viewing screen, you're ready to start the reading after you state your intention and say a protection prayer. Failure to bring in the benevolent forces of good to aid you in your reading session will allow any energy currently present to participate. You do not want tricksters and low energy beings on the other side meddling with your mind or the messages you will receive. If you don't bless the space, they will interrupt the session or cause you to enter into fear. In order to maintain the space in high vibration, call in God's archangels (see Angels section in this book), Christ consciousness, master teacher, healer or guide you know is watching over you to be there with you while you read the incoming energy.

The Reading

1. Ask the client to keep their eyes open and stay in the chair relaxed with feet firm on the ground shoulder length's apart, feet pointed forward and palms facing up resting on their thighs. Close your eyes. Ground the client by envisioning their bottom in the seat corded to the middle of the Earth.

2. Start with a general question and intent of the client. Ask the client, "What would you like to know?" or "What is the general reason you are here today?"

3. Ask the client to say out loud their FULL birth name, first, middle, and last as it appears on their birth certificate in this incarnation, three times slowly. Have them repeat if needed. Once they end saying their name, the flow of energy will start to show on your viewing screen as still images or moving pictures. It is usually described as a hologram type of image, sometimes infused with a feeling.

4. Proceed with eyes closed to receive images and information for the general aura and question the client asked first. After this question you will move on to reading each chakra starting with the root chakra. You will all focus on the first chakra together once the client ends saying their name again. Allow 3 minutes of silence and meditation to absorb the visions, energies, and colors coming to you. With eyes closed do your best to write down what comes to you.

5. One at a time, open your eyes and share what you saw and wrote down with the client and the other readers pertaining to the general aura, or question the client asked. Do not be surprised if you and another reader saw the same thing or similar versions of the same thing. This is common and will confirm that aspect of the reading. Keep in mind that different readers will see different things as they are seeing the client from their own life filter. Everyone will be able to give the client valuable information which they could use for their life's journey. Sometimes the information you see as a reader will not make any sense until the client confirms or tells you what it means to them. Do not concern yourself with its meaning; simply deliver the message as you see it. Some tact will be needed if the content is of delicate nature, so be cautious when giving sensitive information to the client. You are a vessel for the client to get extrasensory information; this is a major service to them. Close your eyes and resume the reading.

6. Keep clearing your viewing screen after energy is viewed. Throw flower energy (any bright color you wish; see color meanings chart) at the screen and dissolve energy so that the next vision comes up clearly. You must continue to clear the screen after each vision.

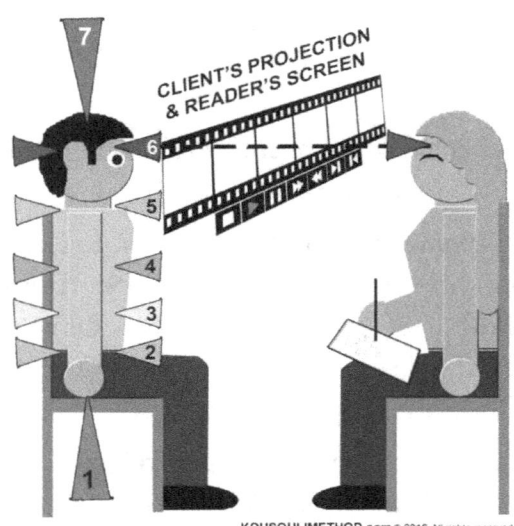

Send all cleared energy down the grounding cord. Do these two actions in your mind's eye repeatedly throughout the reading. When all readers are finished communicating the visions and information obtained on the client's general question, proceed to focus all your intent and energy at the first root chakra.

7. Have the client verbalize their FULL birth name as it is written on their birth certificate again three times slowly. The client will say this prior to the reading of each chakra's energy. Repeat the process and read the energies coming to your viewing screen still with your eyes closed. Take about three minutes to view, feel, analyze, decipher and write the information you receive as best you can on the paper. One by one, readers can open their eyes and share the information collected, with their client and all other readers.

8. Repeat #7 for the remaining six chakras. Chakra number two (sacral), three (solar plexus), four (heart), five (throat), six (third eye) and seven (crown). Refer to chakra list and Kousouli® Master Chart in Chapter 15 for chakra locations and explanations.

Be Ready for the Flow

Just as in dream interpretation, various images you see will mean different things. I.e. spiders may mean fear and snakes equate to pain. Dragons can also point to negativity or the darker side of things. While some other images will not have a meaning unless a feeling is felt along with the vision the reader is having. The reader will be experiencing and feeling the messages come through them and this is sometimes difficult as their body is being energetically "plugged into." This can feel very draining by the time the reading is completed. It is important that clients understand the reader is performing a great service for them and they must respect the process. Readers should go into sessions only when fully healthy, hydrated and well-nourished so that they can expend the energy needed to perform such a heavy task. Not respecting the reading process by not fully preparing for it, is like going into a boxing match against a heavyweight champion without any boxing training. As a reader and interpreter of energy you will be using a lot of your clairvoyant sixth sense and it may take a lot of your physical energy at times. The longer the reader is able to learn how to use their psychic ability, the better they will know their limit(s) and when they need to recharge the physical self. Although the mind may be willing, the body's stamina is the limiting factor in the reading process.

Inflow of Massive Energy

Images will start to flow to the reader as fast as the reader can handle processing them. Newbies will be sluggish and sloppy at processing these mental images, causing them to burn out and tire quickly. It's common for new readers to hit a wall of 'white fog,' where their viewing screen becomes dull, thick and hard with nothing clear showing up on it at all. They usually feel stuck, get dizzy, experience a major headache or fall into a deep sleep. Throwing flower energy and being diligent at reading without quitting will eventually pay off and the reader will break through the 'funk.' Usually, the longer one's gift of clairvoyance has been shut off, the longer their belief system needs to be re-trained in order to activate their ability again. More senior readers or those who are least analytical will get the connection faster than newcomers who have more resistance. Spirit shows the messages that the client will need to know, and it will show images or messages in terms of the reader's ability and vocabulary. For example if the reader is Italian, a point will be made in a way the Italian will be able to decipher the meaning as opposed to sending the same message through someone who may be American or Russian. All will get the same message, though it will come in different images or scenarios according to what the reader's life experience or understanding is.

Why are the readers making odd faces and noises?

When the higher chakras are activated, it will become apparent in the reader that they are releasing the energy they are receiving with physical activity manifesting in the 5th, 6th, and 7th chakras. When this energy is moving through the reader's upper senses it will appear as yawning, sneezing, coughing, choking, burping, tearing of the eyes, clogged ears, headaches, neck or head pain, dizziness, fainting, passing out, fatigue, finger tapping or twitching, short yells or noise making. Everyone receives and releases energy differently. Just as everyone walks and talks in their own unique way, so do they process this energy. The process is harmless and changes with the experience level of the reader, becoming more controllable as the energy syncs with their body.

During processing as a reader, you will see many different things, some of which are:

- **Alien beings and foreign machines:** Images of parasitic extraterrestrial or foreign entities that have been set or implanted into one's chakra(s) or auric field for energy manipulation. These can be erased, removed, healed, and sent down the client's grounding cord (with the client's permission first). Always ask for permission prior to removing what could be a spiritual contract between the client and the external force.
- **Colors:** You will see a lot of color patterns as a reader which will have various meanings. Spirit uses colors often to set meaning and feeling. (Refer to color chart in section 13.26) If you see a blue blouse in a reading, it will have a different meaning and feeling than a brown or black blouse.
- **Death image:** An image of death usually pertaining to an ending of a lifetime or how the lifetime or subject in question was ended. For example, if the client is asking about a prior lifetime, the reader may see a noose around the client's neck on his viewing screen, indicating that possible death in that lifetime was death by hanging. If this was vividly seen, it is likely that the reader also has this death image in his or her own past life and it's a matching image between them.
- **Martyr image:** An image of past life persecution for one's beliefs or service to particular sects or groups. For example, seeing a vision of the client flagellating themselves (a form of penance by self-whipping in the Catholic Church around the 11th century), or dying by being burned at the stake for a cause they believed in, which would be a death and martyr image.
- **Matching image:** An image the reader sees that matches similar events the reader has in their Akashic record as well, which allows the reader to empathize or feel for the client. If the reader has lived similar events or images in their own life that parallel the client's, this would make the images or visions seen in the client much more vivid for the reader. Always clear the screen right after viewing any matching or death images.

Finishing Your Session

1. Akashic record read. After you read and process all the seven chakras (in order from first root chakra and finish with the crown chakra's reading), you will read the client's Akashic records. This is the client's spiritual library which holds all their spiritual DNA and energy from all their lifetimes. It is the data of who they are and how they relate to themselves and to others here on the Earth using the information they obtain from all their lifetimes. The information just obtained for them from this reading and cleaned out will be added to their Akashic records for future soul growth and use. Focus about a foot above their crown chakra and intend to be shown the status of their Akashic records. After the client verbalizes their name three times slowly, proceed to see what is projected by the client onto your viewing screen for the Akashic records. Sometimes the records look ransacked and pillaged, and other times their records will look in order with just a little bit of organizing still needed. Envision yourself calling forth a spiritual record keeper (can be a guide or angel that you call out for; see who steps forth to help) who you will hire and put to work for the client. Their job is to help the client organize and process all the old and new information obtained from the reading, which will now be put into use. Set angels outside the Akashic record library to stand guard for the library and protect it from spiritual attack.

2. Envision a large open book with the client's name on it. Put the book in front of all the readers as everyone reviews the session's images and information seen for the client. Command the images and thoughts discussed into this large book. Go through all the chakras remembering what was handled and send it into this book. You must all dismiss all energies from the client and the reading into the book and close it shut.

3. Dismiss & clean out. Once you have shut the book, all readers will send the book via upload in your mind's eye to the client's Akashic record keeper so they may add the experience of the reading session to the client's spiritual library. Remove the client's grounding cord, thank them for their participation, and send them on their way. Reflect on yourself, sensing any foreign energy, negative thoughts, or low vibratory feelings that may be lingering in your own aura and dismiss everything down your grounding cord.

4. End Reading with gratitude prayer. All readers must finish with a gratitude prayer before departing the room. Thank all the high vibrational beings, healers, and guides who helped with the reading and maintained the space in love with their protection and guidance. Rehydrate your body, get rest, and proper nourishment prior to doing another reading.

Chapter 17:
Performing a Group Manifestation Meditation

*"For where two or three are gathered together in my name,
there am I in the midst of them."*
~ Matthew 18:20

17.1 Power in numbers

It is good to bring people together for a just cause. To meet with a friend and speak of good things is therapeutic stress-release from a long tough day at work. It's a practice done in cafés, parks, and lounges all across the world as people congregate and enjoy the healing energy of each other's advice, or lending of one's sympathetic ear. When positive like-minded individuals gather for a purpose, the energy magnetized is unstoppable. This is what Jesus meant by saying "where two or three are gathered together in my name, there am I in the midst of them." This is most celebrated when many gather together in the asking of healing prayer. This is the reason for having a church – to gather and pray as one large body. Church was first established as a gathering of like-minded individuals who prayed or gave thanks to God for the good in their lives. Since the first church's humble beginnings this has drastically been altered to be more about political power and the passing of trays for monetary funding of the sect or religious views of that particular church, and not so much for the unification of like minds or the progression of mankind in unity and love. It is now more about: Our church raised this much compared to last year, or this much more than that church, or we're below our goal this year so we need more stewardship - so send out more mailers and convert more people, or make more sermons to tell church patrons how giving to the church is good and not giving is bad because you won't have favor with God. Jesus never said to go to a building for worship. His church is the people. The church is each and every one of us. The house of God is your heart, your mind, and his temple - your body. When you learn the true essence of your Divine makeup and apply it, you will be again one with your Creator. The more who join in the same intention, their power magnifies exponentially. That means two people praying together is not times two, but times four. And so on. The following exercise will help you magnetize and leverage the abilities of not only more people, but the guides and angels of each person as well.

What you will need:

- Gather the most positive like-minded individuals who are unbiased, pure loving, without judgment and open to patiently working with you through this exercise. Find the closest to this description as possible. Not all of your friends and family members fit this description, but just involve the most supportive ones. Even if you just have one person who fits the description, that's much better than three that don't. Quality people will produce quality results.
- A quiet location.
- A timer able to be set for ten or fifteen minute increments
- Turn off or remove of all other electronic devices (cell phones, televisions, computers, etc.)
- The desire to powerfully manifest

17.2 How to Perform a Group Manifestation Meditation

Sit in a comfortable chair and form a circle; or across from each other if you have only two people. Your feet should not be crossed but touching the floor and your hands palms up on your lap. Your eyes open. Pick a leader to start the process.

Start the session with a prayer said by the group leader:

Creator of the highest good, giver of life and light, maker of all things visible and invisible and of the highest vibration of love known in all Universes, we _____ (list each person's name) _____ ask you hear and grant our hearts desires for we know limitless abundance in our life is your wish for us as your eternal son(s) and daughter(s). Gift our guides and angels full ability to guide us in attaining with ease these ideas we ask to manifest in physical form. We give gratitude in this and ask for our blessings to multiply in accordance with our highest good. Amen.

This brings the group's frequency together and unifies for purpose.

Next, each person in the group shares what they desire (not 'need' because 'need' usually denotes 'lack') to bring to manifestation with the rest of the group. At this point nothing is off limits, and other members should stay unbiased and non-judgmental no matter what the desire mentioned may be. This can be difficult sometimes as people could ask for lavish material things (money, mansions, cars etc.) that may seem selfish to another member or much too grand for someone to imagine (go to space, climb Mount Everest, etc.) and all must know that this is perfectly all-right. No one should judge what another's wish would be to manifest in their life and if anyone has a problem with such, they must excuse themselves from the group. There can be no one in the group that has any personal limits, jealousy, envy, or prejudice towards another person attaining the desire they ask for. All members participating should desire each other to attain what they seek. If anyone fears or doubts towards another, it will hinder the power of the group's intention and purpose. For example: Johnny desires to manifest winning the lottery but Samantha feels Johnny is being unrealistic, selfish, or 'too superficial.' This may be because Samantha has personal hang ups about money and her beliefs are limiting. Samantha must excuse herself from the group as her thoughts will not be beneficial, but counterproductive to the group and specifically towards Johnny. Same goes with those who may think small. Brad may want to travel the world but Greg is jealous of Brad because he has been to more countries already than him. Greg needs to excuse himself and take care of the inner turmoil he has against Brad in order to participate and be effective in the group. Each member must understand the Universal law of giving and receiving. When you see the other person being fulfilled without any negative hang ups; you yourself are fulfilled. You must relish in the joy and happiness of others first. This is the KEY! When you are happy for the other person, you see no competition. You certify abundance. You exude gratitude. The Universe rewards all!

Your group should be made of people who want to see each other's' best and have unlimited imagination potential. Be honest with each other about your desires and hang-ups to others' happiness as moving forward without pure love and intention will yield less than satisfactory results.

Start the process with one claiming member. The claiming member states his/her name, birth date, and desire out loud to the group. The claiming member then states the positive reason(s) why he/she feels this would bring them more joy in their life.

Each supporting member going in a clockwise direction affirms that the claiming member deserves to have the happiness and deserves the desire manifested. The claiming member will give as much detail as he or she can about their desire.

Let's say Greg really wants a potential real estate deal to close for a certain house on the Hollywood Hills that he's been dreaming of living in.

GREG: "I, Greg Smith, born in this lifetime on June 8th 1979 desire and deserve to own and live in my Hollywood Hills home."

There is a large circular driveway. The landscaping is beautiful. There is a crystal clear underground pool in the backyard. The lot is 1 full acre in size. The kitchen is huge, is made of marble, and there is beautiful hardwood throughout the house. There are five bedrooms and four full baths. The guesthouse fits three comfortably. The garage fits all four luxury cars securely. There is a beautiful cascading stairway to the upper part of the home. The chandelier hangs from the large vaulted ceiling. There is a grand piano in the room to the left of the grand hall. Etc.

The desire should be given with as much color, vision, detail and feeling as possible. It is recommended that the claiming member close their eyes while they do this part as they may be able to envision it better than with their eyes open due to current visual distractions.

Each supporting member then says this line in a clockwise direction:

JOHN: "I John believe and affirm that you, Greg, deserve to have a house on the Hollywood Hills."

SUSAN: "I Susan believe and affirm that you, Greg, deserve to have a house on the Hollywood Hills."

And so on.

Next, the leader, or claiming member, sets the timer for 10 minutes.

Everyone (including claiming member) closes their eyes while seated in the chair with both feet firmly on the floor (uncrossed) and palms face up on their lap.

Envisioning a new grounding cord (pick a bright earthy color, like grassy green or autumn reddish-yellow) the diameter of double your size from the base of the bottom of the spine rooted to the middle of the Earth (like a large hollow tube) and a large energy line directly from the heavens entering the top crown of the head (as a beautiful sky blue or gold color) as the energy enters your head from the crown, envision this energy mixing through all of your body and chakras, and then into the root chakra and swirling around up into the higher chakras to the shoulders, arms, and out the palm chakras as you will direct this light energy for manifesting. See all blocks or sludge that you previously may have felt in the body – especially in the neck, arms, and hands melt away as you see yourself ready and able to mold and shape this light. Any negative energy is flushed down your grounding cord and into Mother Earth's core where she can take the energy and transform it into something positive. With the timer going, each member of the group envisions and creates the claiming member's desire as they see it. Using the descriptions given by the claiming member, the supporting members all start with that but in their mind's eye allow much more to be created. For instance: Susan could see herself invited over to the house when it's all completed and moved into for dinner or a BBQ. John may see Greg having fun in the backyard with his family or in the study reading a magazine or his favorite book. Each member of the group "runs the movie" with themselves visualizing and co-creating POSITIVE experiences. Focus only on positive events. If anything negative happens or creeps in, immediately surround the idea or thing in a rose petal and send that as a package down your grounding cord as 'trash.' Let Mother Earth take care of it by neutralizing the negativity. Restart the thought with a positive vibe and keep creating.

When the time is up slowly end the movie by seeing you hit the "save" button. Put everything you saw in a big bubble, multiply it thousands of times with all the desires the claiming member asked for and you saw in your vision. On the outside of the bubble put the claiming member's name (and birth date if you remembered it) and send it out to the Universe away from the Earth. Open your eyes. It's time to share your creations. One by one take turns sharing what you saw while you created. Again only share the POSITIVE. Negative thoughts or distraction energy that may have creeped in need not be mentioned and should be thrown down the grounding cord. What is shared between members may amazingly correlate with another's mind creation (called Akashic entanglement; two share the same reality), and you may find yourself saying "Me too, I saw that exact thing too." This is very common and you should know that you were on the same frequency together. It is further confirmation that the power of the mind is uniting in the creation process.

When all supporting members are done, the claiming member shares last if they wish, but does not have to. The claiming member thanks the supporting members and gets ready to become a supporting member for another person who becomes the claiming member in the group.

Repeat this process with all group members (in a clockwise direction) until everyone has had a chance to claim their desire(s) and be supported. When completed with all members, end the session with a gratitude prayer:

Creator of the highest good, giver of life and light, maker of all things visible and invisible and of the highest vibration of love known in all Universes, we _____ (list each person's name) _____ , thank you for hearing our desires. We trust in the process of allowing. We now detach ourselves from the desire(s) as we have asked and put our trust in the process of attraction which you have built the whole Universe on. We open our hearts to receive as in accordance with your Laws of attraction and abundance. Amen.

Collapse your grounding cords, and let go of any neediness or expectations. Trust in Universal abundance and know that what you asked for is coming to you in the appropriate way it is supposed to come to you – Divine timing. You have asked and now you must allow in order to receive. See yourself as living your life with the desire and being grateful for receiving it. "Let go and let God," as they say.

Chapter 18:
Remotely Viewing Universal Information

"We know from the experimental data of psi research that viewer in the laboratory can focus his or her attention anywhere on the planet and, about two-thirds of the time, describe what is there."
~ Russell Targ

18.1 Communicating with God

Connecting to Collective Consciousness - Higher Power - Holy Spirit

The son of the Father, Jesus, was undoubtedly - psychic - a word the Church does not like to use as it is too taboo; and could mean anything less than God-like and more strange, weird or even satanic. Though he was indeed psychic compared to any average man. He was indeed strange against the norm and his works were indeed out of this world. However, Jesus taught how to think, how to feel, how to have everlasting life, and showed others how to be like him. He spoke in parables so that he could communicate higher level knowledge to common folk. Jesus performed miracles by laying of the hands which today could be considered as the practice of *Reiki*. He was also clairaudient which means he could hear God the Father, and spoke directly with him. He was so advanced that it seemed he could also manipulate physical properties and the molecular structure of matter through his thought. Could it be that through Jesus Christ's teachings and examples, he was trying to show us that we too could perform miracles as well? Why would it be difficult to think we couldn't reproduce his examples since we too are made in the image and likeness of our maker?

> *"And God said, Let us make man in our image, after our likeness: and let them have dominion over the fish of the sea, and over the fowl of the air, and over the cattle, and over all the earth, and over every creeping thing that creepeth upon the earth."*
> *~ Genesis 1:26*

18.2 Can I Talk to God?

God does not favor any certain elect or religion. God talks to everyone, all the time. The problem is that not many listen to him or are confused about how to raise their sensitivity to match the divine vibration. God talks to us through our environment, images or visions, our bodies, and uses 'feelings' the language of the soul - to communicate with us. Spoken words are far less effective means of communication. Think of a movie that churns internal emotions and brings you to tears or a picture you see that "is worth a thousand words." When one has a personal experience with God – they usually say to those they are trying to describe it to – "there are no words to do the experience justice." The real question is: Do you keep the communication going from the time you are born here from the other side, or do you turn it off when things in life get too tough or scary due to the word's many distractions?

God speaks to with us constantly through his written word as well as his unspoken one. As humans we try to humanize God so that we bring him down to our level so we can understand him. Why do we not want to raise our vibration to match his level? Why are so many people spiritually lazy and do not seek more than just the surface (asking for help only when in trouble or ill)? How small our thinking as a human species remains. God clearly responds to us all the time. However, when we get the answer we doubt it immediately. We second-guess it, and we feel so 'unworthy' by listening to our preachers (the ones we appoint as worthy) that we abandon any notion that God would want to talk to us or that we are actually able to speak directly to the almighty without a middleman. God does not limit communication to his creations. We do. We attach strings to our relationships and our communication with ex's or people we are less fond of. We give the silent treatment to those we anger towards, and we block people that hurt us off of our social network profiles. Why would God not love that which is of his own? The Father does not hate the Son as such the Son does not hate the Holy Spirit. It all is one of the same – eternal love. Just as you are one with your Creator, there is a part of you in Him and a part of Him in you. God speaks to you as He has always spoken to you from day one. Open not just your ears, but open your heart and your mind as well. Listen to your feelings more than trusting your ears. There is much more information coming in from your heart and gut than from your ears and eyes. The communication can also come in more than just feelings. It can appear as pictures in photos or billboards, signs, number sequences, color patterns, words in a book, music in your car radio, day dreams, or dreams when you sleep, being around spiritually aware individuals, meditation, sudden thoughts (flashbacks), prayer, or a whisper from a chance crossing with a stranger. But do you have faith and believe? Do you believe that what you are getting is really God's word?

You cannot talk linearly to God. You must think inter-dimensionally. This process will be different for everyone; no one connects to God in the exact same way. Case in point: different religions. Healers push the envelope and question linear thinking, the world, and the curing of physical ailments. Sometimes patients are merely looking for their reconnection back to God, and it's the experience of physical disease that provides a chance for this to occur.

The physical mind is separate from the spiritual mind, like the left-brain is separate from the right. However, they are connected to each other by a single part – the corpus callosum. Similarly, so is the spiritual mind to the physical.

God can also speak to us through very direct ways, like taking control or influencing the brain with images and ideas unknown to the person, so they can be divinely inspired to write messages, letters, and even books (like the Bible). There have been many instances of this throughout history, and many great writers and artists know that they are channeling the God source when they create epic masterpieces.

Animals communicate via intuitive speech, via multidimensional translation through the pineal gland. This can be thought of as a non-linear whispering of information to and from connected beings. It is a "whisper" because you have to be super-sensitive to pick up the subtle vibration. Psychics, or intuitives, can feel and hear the energies left behind in buildings, forests, battlefields, or places where acts of murder or emotional difficulty have been invested. The same way these phenomenon are communicated between humans and animals, or humans and nature, is the way humans talk to God; through soul communication. It is not through synapse, but intuitive thought without doubt or disbelief. This same intuitive thought is the higher self, angel of God, core innate being, or any other one of many definitions given by man over the centuries.

When people claim that they spoke to God, no one usually believes them. Though all legit accounts are said to have one thing in common about their communication with God. They didn't hear Him by ear as much as they heard him through thought and felt Him in heart. God thoughts are energy vibrations that can permeate the body - setting off energy waves of emotions and feelings inside us. Talking to God is something that is easy - not difficult, if you understand how to connect. A form of receiving information from Spirit by 'tuning' your mind to know the unknown, is a process known as remote viewing.

18.3 Remote Viewing: Using the God Eye to View Faraway Places

The amazing ability of tapping into the 'God Eye' was introduced to the world by psychic Ingo Swann, and used by intelligence and military agencies such as the DOD, CIA, and NSA for over 25 years. Remote Viewing is the skilled talent to attain precise straight-on data unavailable to the usual physical senses, of events, targets, or things distant in time or space, including the present, past, or future. Remote viewers are psychics (though different from usual psychics). The remote viewer tries to keep the focused info obtained clear while not allowing other outside information to influence the data coming in. Remote viewing activates intuitive flow, which usually takes the form of images and symbols. Those who use it to tap into the God Eye gain phenomenal insight to any question they seek.

18.4 What Do You Want to Know?

Becoming an expert in this field takes much dedication and training. However, I have been able to teach students how to attain quick results in record time, even without any preparation whatsoever. In this chapter, I provide my method for connecting to the 'universal super-mind' by remotely viewing information and quickly gaining the insight you need. When you become proficient in remote viewing, you will be able to ask the Universe anything you like and get correct answers. The process of remote viewing mimics 'automatic writing,' where information is transcribed from the ever present open channel, the Higher Self, Holy Ghost, Holly Spirit or cosmic consciousness onto a piece of paper. The program takes about 30 minutes to 45 minutes of dedicated honest meditative application to get trustworthy data. If you seek to get better understanding you may attend a seminar where you will be in the company of like minds developing the skill.

18.5 The Elusive Aspect of Time

The problem encountered when tapping into the Universe's information super-mind, is that time does not exist there. Time is a construct of our reality here on Earth, not of the God mind. So, when we ask about a 'when,' we don't get any solid answers that seem to be relevant to the target or phrase identifier. Thus, asking when you will win the lottery or when you will find that new boyfriend or girlfriend, will not yield precise information and gets frustrating. What you could do to find out the answer in our linear current reality is to find the key event(s) that would precede the main event in question. So if you wanted to know when you would be getting married, a great question to ask would be, "What is the prior significant event to my marriage?" When you receive that answer, you will then know that your marriage is soon to come after that now 'reveiled' event.

Receiving Messages From Your Higher Self

Let's take a look at the three circle image on the next page which we will call 'Program A.' Program A includes the smaller Initial Sketch Impression (ISI) and Imagination display area (IDA) circles alongside a larger central circle where you will be describing the information attained from the higher mind. The larger circle has icons which describe color, smell, taste, hearing, temperature, texture, dimensions, and emotions of the self and non-self. There is also a code or phrase identification section, where the targeted information will be displayed. The clockwise order that Program A is executed is shown with the numbered steps 1 – 12.

18.6 The Program A Template

Beginning Steps

You will need:

1. A quiet place without distractions where you can focus as you execute the programs. Be sure you are at a quiet location without interruption, background noise, or computers or telephones. Total focus and diligence to this exercise is important.

2. Sit at a table with a comfortable chair, take a few deep breaths and relax.

3. Pray that only the highest frequency of love and light be with you as you proceed, and dismiss any low vibratory frequencies down your grounding cord as previously described in aura scanning section 14.14. You may recite the protection or Lord's Prayer, mentioned earlier in section 4.11.

4. A pen and blank template charts of Program A, B and C.

Procedure:

- You will be using three programs. You will run Program A three times and compile that data into Program B. Then, you will combine all the information of Program B into one final composite, Program C. **Programs A+B = C.**
- First you will execute Program A, step #s 1-12 clockwise for the first round and then #s 3-12, moving clockwise again in the next two consecutive rounds, for a total of three rounds, harnessing as much information (descriptive adjectives of

what you sense) as possible.

- Second, you will compile all the information (word descriptors) you gained from Program A into a Program B, drawn as a simple line drawing.
- Third, you will execute as many Program As on various aspects of the topic or question, in order to gain more information to compile into another Project B.
- In your Project B diagram, label the data you received in level of importance from I to IV+… formulating new targets or phrase identifiers for each object in question.
- Finally you will gather and analyze all your information and compile it into a final diagram, Program C. This will be the answer you were seeking, pertaining to your question (code or phrase identifier).

Remotely Viewing Universal Information

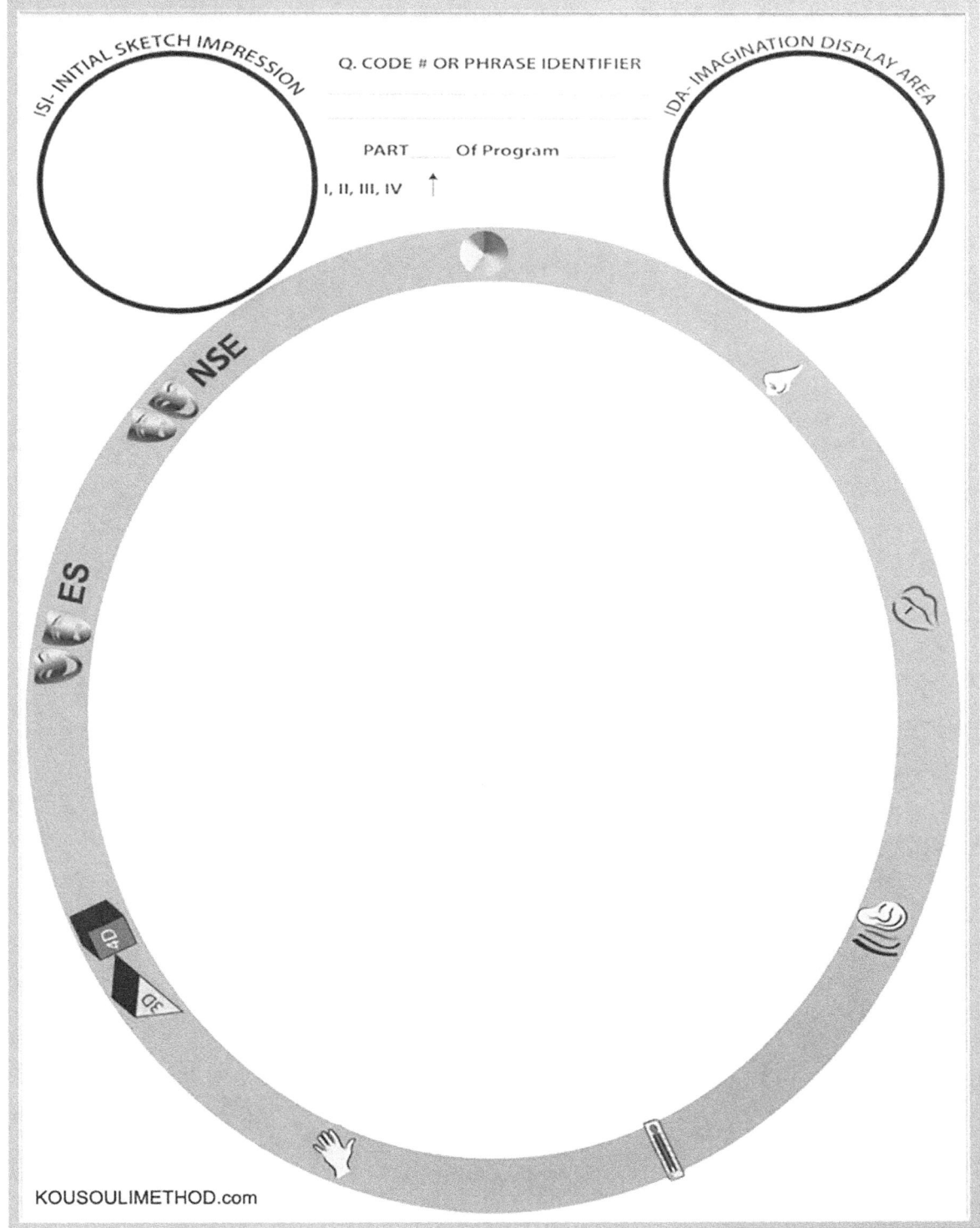

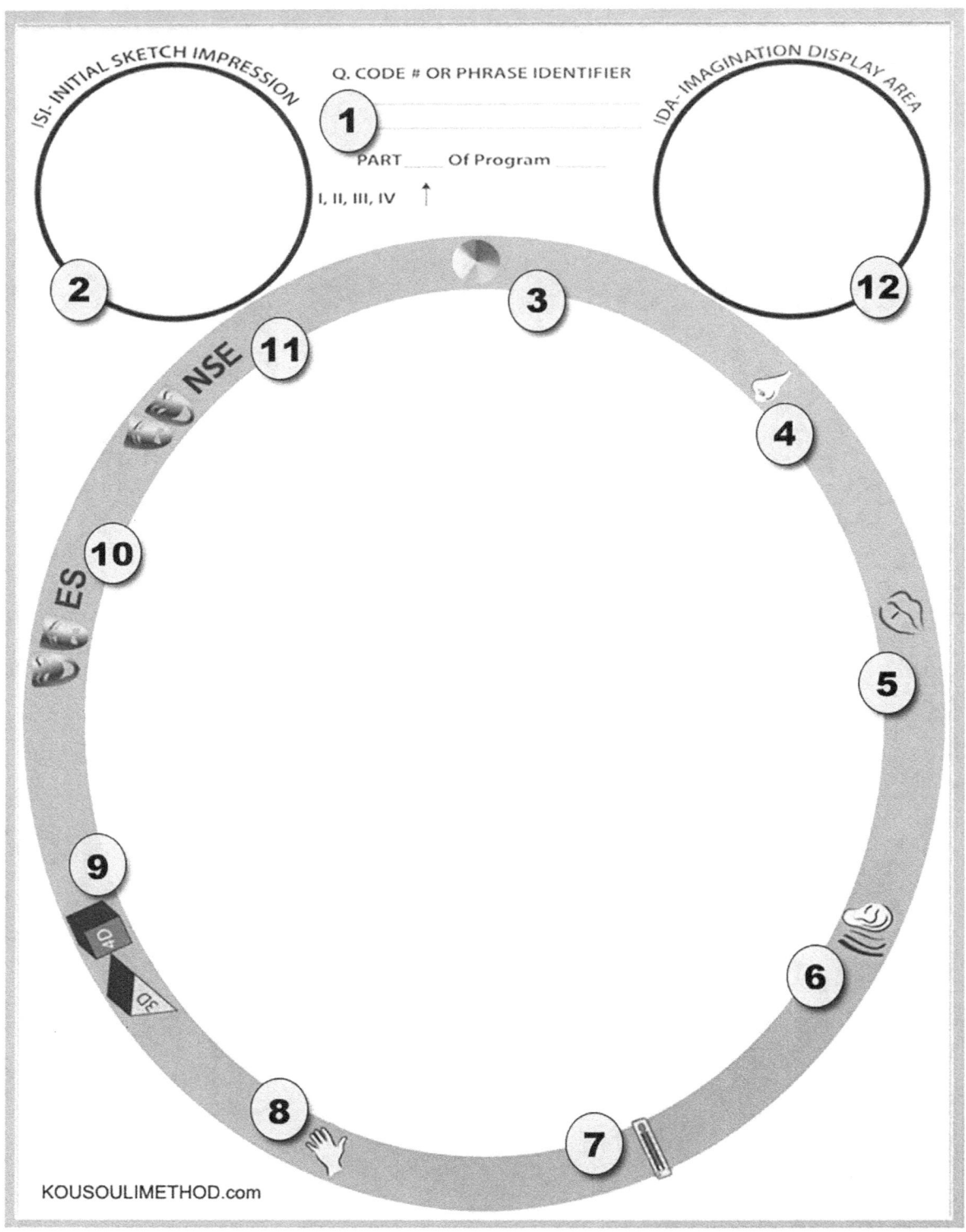

Preparing to Access the Information Super Highway

Glance over the adjectives in each of the following paragraphs and look at the adjectives that describe our world through our senses. You should not memorize or rely on them side by side as you do the exercise, rather just glance it over to bring the adjectives into your consciousness as a refresher. Your higher mind will automatically relate what is needed to you as you go through Program A. Sit at a desk firmly in a chair alert and ready to begin. It is best to feel contently relaxed and not stressed. Do not take any drugs or stimulants such as caffeine or alcohol prior to starting and give yourself time after a meal (1 hour) to digest as your blood is needed in your brain and should have left your stomach.

Picking your Phrase Identifier and Target

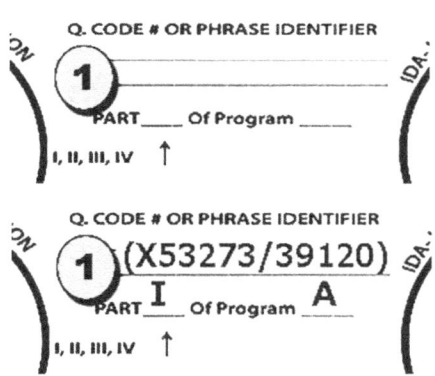

To successfully target information you need to narrow down the scope of what information it is you are looking for. There is an immeasurable amount of information out there. In order to bring you the most accurate information you desire, you must be specific. For example, if we are looking to find out where Johnny's current location is, we would not simply ask that because there are countless Johnnies in the world and many locations where these Johnnies could be. Instead we would group facts about the particular Johnny we are looking for in parentheses separated by slashes like this:

(Info here / Info here / Info here) or

(Person place or thing / Personalized information identifying only that person place or thing / Information you desire to know about that person, place, or thing)

This really narrows down the who and what you are searching for. Note: Narrow down what you are looking for; the more specific, the better. An example of a target or phrase identifier would look like this:

(First Middle Last Name / Birth Date, Birth Time, Social Security Number / Current location)

Guidelines for Setting up the Right Target and Phrase Identifier

- First write the question or target info in general terms.
- (I.e.) I lost my keys and can't find them, where are they? **Too General** Which keys?

Home or Auto? There is still unspecified information here, so we must narrow it down with the least amount of words to describe best what we're searching for.

- Restructure and narrow down into more specific phrase or code. (I.e.) (My keys / automobile /current location) **Very Specific**

- I lost my dog Ruffles and want to know where he is. **INCORRECT** (Ruffles / white poodle / current location) **CORRECT**

- Who is my friend Billy asking out to the prom? **INCORRECT** (Billy Smith / 6.9.79 /this year's prom date) **CORRECT**

- If you are seeking to target information such as guessing what is on a random page in a magazine you have never seen or trying to connect to a lost item, code the item with a random number you can connect to it that is original for that item. Let's just say we tag the completely random sequence 34673DAF467, and use this as our code. We must put this on the image we are looking to target. This way our mind has a way of finding the content anywhere in the Universe. The likelihood of 34673DAF467 being somewhere else on the planet is not as likely as coding something as simply 123, because that is more likely to identify countless many other objects and things in the world. Use a unique set of characters, symbols, numbers, or letters to identify your specific target.

The Initial Sketch Image (ISI)

Once you write down in parentheses the Identifying characteristics of what you are searching for, you will need to translate what is given to you by making a line drawing in the ISI area. This area is designated to take the first impulsive 'data' which is the information package prior to being 'opened.' Think of this information as a gift in a wrapped box. You get a nicely wrapped package from the Universe which you must then unravel by taking out its contents to inspect. This is the same idea here, only the contents we are unpacking is the informational 'bits' we will be analyzing for our Program A. Simply draw an initial sketch in the ISI circle IMMEDIATELY after you finish writing your target/identifier phrase. As you write it, do not pick up your pen. It should be one continuous line without any breaks. It can be a squiggle, zigzag line, it can loop and then curl around, anything as long as it's within the circle and quickly drawn. Draw anything that comes naturally to you in that moment without thinking about it. Once you have written the ISI you can move your focus onto reading color vibration, #3. **Examples of ISI's:**

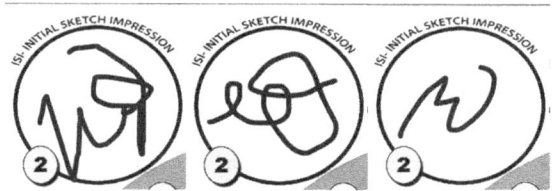

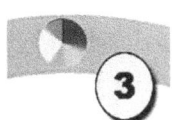

Color wheel Icon Adjectives (CLAIRVOYANCE)

Blue, Black, Brown, Beige, Green, Gray, Silver, Gold/Golden, Bronze, Red, Purple/Turquoise, Pink/Rosy, Orange, White, Yellow/Amber, Luminescent/Lit, Faded/Dim, Light/Dark, Fluorescent, Pale, Bright, Dull, Pattern, Reflective, Shadowy, Shiny/Metallic, Speckled/Dotted, Tan, Transparent/Solid

Reading Color Vibration

After you have written your ISI (Initial Sketch Impression), immediately put your attention onto the color wheel icon. This area deals with information you will access that is of color vibration. As colors pour into your consciousness write them down in #3 section. You are using your Clair-cognizance (inborn ability to 'just know' something without any physical data using only your sixth sense). Don't think; let whatever 'pops' into your mind come without effort. If you start to guess colors or draw blanks then drop your pen for 2-3 seconds and then pick it up again. If you are still feeling that colors are not coming easily, quickly move on to the next icon: smell.

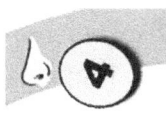

Nose Icon Adjectives (CLAIRSCENT)

Fishy, Colorful, Fresh, Damp, Earthy, Ozone, Flowery/Sweet, Fragrant/Aromatic, Toxic/Chemical, Mothball, Moldy, Dusty/Stale, Clean, Woodsy, Burning/Smokey, Ashy, Crisp, Rancid, Misty

Stay still and notice if you smell anything that would trigger your thought process and write it down. You do not smell your current environment; this is a different type of smelling - intuitive psychic smelling. Allow the information to come to you and write what comes to your mind effortlessly. If you start to guess odors write them in the Imagination Display Area or (IDA). If you draw blanks then drop your pen for 2-3 seconds and then pick it up again and retry to see if new information comes. If nothing comes to mind, quickly go to the next icon, taste.

Mouth Icon Adjectives (CLAIRGUSTANCE)

Salty, Sour, Sweet, Bitter, Bland, Metallic, Rancid, Chalky, Chemical, Fresh, Earthy, Stony, Tart, Woodsy, Spicy

Stay still and notice if you taste anything that would trigger your thought process and write it down. Open and close your mouth a little bit and see if you taste anything. Allow the information to come to you and write what comes to your mind effortlessly. If you start to guess odors write them in the Imagination Display Area or (IDA). If you draw blanks then drop your pen for 2-3 seconds and then pick it up again and retry to see if new information comes. If nothing comes to mind, quickly go to the next icon, sound.

Sounds/Ear Icon Adjectives (CLAIRAUDIENCE)

Distant/Nearby Voices, Thunder, Whooshing, Clanging, Thumping, Tapping, In/Out of Rhythm, Cracking, Clicking, Buzzing, Banging, Humming, Hissing, Scraping, Singing, Squealing, Splashing, Squeaking, Squawking, Booming, Chirping, Clanking, Dripping, Echoes, Grinding, Gurgling, Moaning, Jingling, Mechanical Sounds, Metallic Sounds, Muffled/Noisy, Rattling, Ringing, Roaring, Rumbling, Rushing, Rustling, Tinkling, Whirring, Crashing, Distant/Close, High/Low Pitched, Quiet/Loud

Stay still and notice if you hear anything that would trigger your thought process and write it down. Try to discern between your immediate environment and what is actually coming through psychically. Allow the information to come to you and write what comes in effortlessly. If you start to guess sounds write them in the Imagination Display Area or (IDA). If you draw blanks then drop your pen for 2-3 seconds and then pick it up again and retry to see if new information comes. If nothing comes to mind, quickly go to the next icon, temperature.

Temperature Icon Adjectives (CLAIRSENTIENCE)

Breezy, Cool/Warm, Frigid, Cold/Hot, Ambient, Arid/Dry, Body Temp, Room temp, Stable/Unstable, Humid/Damp

Stay still and notice if you are suddenly becoming hot or cold and write it down. Got sudden goose bumps? Did you feel a sudden breeze or drop in pressure? Allow the information to come to you and write what comes effortlessly. If you start to guess write it in the Imagination Display Area or (IDA). If you draw blanks then drop your pen for 2-3 seconds and then pick it up again and retry to see if new information comes. If nothing comes to mind, quickly go to the next icon, textures.

Textures/Hand Icon Adjectives (CLAIRSENTIENCE)

Soft/Hard, Moist, Wet/Dry, Slippery/Rough, Smooth/Bumpy, Grainy, Coarse, Semi-Soft/Semi-Hard, Fuzzy, Fluffy, Hairy, Ropey, Rubbery, Greasy, Prickly, Gritty, Slick/Slippery, Oily, Powdery, Glassy, Edgy, Feathery, Leathery, Lumpy, Matte/Glossy, Metallic, Mushy/Firm, Spongy, Velvety, Wooden, Woven, Sandy, Sharp/Dull

Stay still and notice what feeling comes to mind if you put your hand out to touch, using your mind's eye. What feeling comes to you; write it down. Allow the information to come to your mind effortlessly. Don't push yourself to think. If you start to guess feelings or textures instead of allowing them to come to you effortlessly, write them in the Imagination Display Area or (IDA). If you draw blanks then drop your pen for 2-3 seconds and then pick it up again and retry to see if new information comes. If nothing comes to mind, quickly go to the next icon, 3rd and 4th dimensions.

3d/4d Icon Dimension Adjectives (CLAIRSENTIENCE)

Above/Below, Across/Diagonal, Back/Front, Big/Small, Huge, Tiny/Massive, Tall/Short, Vertical/Horizontal, Angled, Around, Circling, Circular, Close, Near/Far, Vast, Curved, Curving, Cylindrical/Rectangular, Square, Down/Up, Empty/Full, Enclosed, Open/Closed, Fast/Slow, Flat/Round, Heavy, High/Low, Hollow/Dense, Horizontal/Vertical, In/Out, Inside/Outside, Light/Dark, Long/Short, Looping, Medium, Moving, Narrow/Broad, Thick/Thin, Oblong, On/Off, Oval, Peaked, Pointed, Scattered, Shallow/Deep, Fast/Slow, Spinning/Spiraling, Straight/Crooked, Tubular, Over/Under, Vast, Wavy, Wide

Stay still and notice if you see in your mind's eye any indication of dimensional perception. Are you suddenly up on a cliff looking down a gorge, or perhaps you see out into a vast prairie or feel as if you're suddenly in outer space? Write it down. Allow the information to come to your mind effortlessly. If you start to guess, write your guesses in the Imagination Display Area or (IDA). If you draw blanks then drop your pen for 2-3 seconds and then pick it up again and retry to see if new information comes. If nothing comes to mind, quickly go to the next icon Emotions of the self and non-self.

ES & NS Icons (Emotions of the Self & Non-Self) Adjectives (CLAIREMPATHY)

Dizzy, Dreamy, Excited/Bored, Nervous, Anxious/Calm, Afraid, Fearful/Fearless, Peaceful/Vengeful, Pleasant, On Alert/Relaxed, Amazed, Awed, Bored, Cheerful, Confused/Clarity, Content, Curious, Depressed/Joyful, Pleased/Disappointed, Friendly/Hostile, Frightened, Frustrated, Happy/Sad, Impressed, Interested, Intimidated/Secure, Intrigued, Aloof, Observant, Overwhelmed, Tense, Thoughtful, Tired, Unfamiliar, Reflective, Relaxed/Stressed, Respectful, Shocked, Surprised, Familiar, Lonely, Lost, Lustful, Loving/Hateful, Needy, Hopeful, Expecting

Stay still and notice how you feel. Are you suddenly feeling happy, content, sad, depressed? Feel a headache? #10 Emotional Self is the area for writing how you feel looking at, or participating in the scenario in question. #11, Emotions of the Non-Self is the area you write about what others in the scenario may be feeling. Are they running for their lives screaming? Are they relaxed on a beach or wet in a pool? Allow the information to come to you. Write what comes to your mind effortlessly; close your eyes and 'feel.' If the information you are getting isn't effortless and you feel like you're guessing, put this in the Imagination Display Area or (IDA). If you draw blanks, then drop your pen for 2-3 seconds, pick it up again and retry to see if new information comes. If nothing comes to mind, go back to #3 color and give the circle another clockwise round for two cycles. If nothing else comes effortlessly, and it feels too 'forced' you are done with Program A and ready to go on to merge your information for Program B.

Imagination Display Area (IDA) #12 While you run Program A, some images or thoughts will trigger in your mind which your imagination (not your higher mind) created, and they will need an outlet to get out of your mind. We 'store' these images and ideas in the imagination display area. These may not be precisely correct answers, but may just be what our ego and linear left brain want to direct us to. If we get information such as long yellow and cylindrical, our mind may automatically think the answer is banana, but it would not be correct. However the mind must remove banana and it needs to be written down to get rid of it, thus this is the area for helping the mind gather any random thoughts that the imaginative ego steps in to provide. Once the thought is dumped into the IDA space, go right back to the number you were working on prior. Trust that even though the information or words coming in does not make sense, write it all down! You will not care much about analysis of data until Program B and C.

Ready, Set, Go! Tapping into the Super Information Highway

Get a friend or a few volunteers to try your first attempt at asking the Universe a question. Keeping an open mind, know that you are new at this so be sure to allow yourself to make mistakes. However, after a few of these attempts you will start to see how quickly the information comes to you and your excitement will build as you find out that there is nothing you cannot know. The only difference between those with information and those without is their ability to access it. With this technique you will be able to find lost items, current locations of people, characteristics of future mates, next major catastrophic event(s), winners of sports game or even lotteries (the 'time element' however causes challenges in determining number sequence and date of drawing); the list is endless. Remember that the information you attain is based on probabilities of energy potentials, not prophesy - and anyone can do this.

Exercise:

Take a magazine and find a one page photo of something interesting. Make sure you pick a photo that is engaging and there are people places and things happening in it. Let's for instance take an ad of a romantic getaway vacation. In this photo there is a couple having a romantic meal on a beach in some exotic location somewhere. The lady is wearing a red hat, burgundy top and there is a green scarf around her waist. The man is in a greenish black shirt and brown khakis. The scene is pleasant and outdoors on a sandy beach with an ocean view in the background. The feeling is happy, fun, and joyful. The woman looks like she is hopeful and expecting an engagement ring.

Let's now take a pen and circle the woman and tag her on the magazine page with the completely random and 'made up' code of (X53273/39120). You can take a line and arrow and point the code at the woman or put the code directly on the woman. The code is the phrase identifier and the woman in the picture is the target. Now keep the image hidden, and let your friend run the Program A-C to find out what is going on in the picture. As we run Program A, we have our intent set to pull information about the woman onto the paper using the various images spirit sends to our minds as cues to us for specific information. So when we look at the color wheel, the colors of the woman, couple, or scene will come pouring into our mind if we offer no resistance. This is not imagination because imagination requires some effort on your part to make the imagery in your mind. This should be a totally effortless process where you allow the information to flow in by being open like a blank slate. The canvas of your mind will be filled with the information needed to paint you the picture of what is happening in the scene even if you haven't ever seen the photo! Once you hit the sweet spot and are in the 'zone,' you want to keep going as the flow picks up momentum. The more you freely allow receiving of the energy, the faster you can receive data. Once you doubt the data or try to 'think,' you will lose the flow. If you delay with more than 3 seconds where no information comes in, drop the pen and then pick it up and wait another few seconds for more flow write it down, and then drop the pen again. Pick it up and if no new information comes, move on to the next image cue and so on.

If you happen to get imagination coming into play and a whole picture is painted in your mind about what you think it all means you must toss this information into the (IDA) Imagination Display Area #12, as the information must go somewhere so that you may continue. Do not get caught up on the word or the idea of the imaginative information. You should put anything that comes up while running Program A which was not automatic and felt 'imagined' into the IDA area, then continue running the program onto the next visual iconic cue.

When you are finished one full round of the program go through it again in a clockwise fashion at least 2 more times. Do not read what you previously wrote in each area; allow more information to come into your mind through the visual icon cues. Once you are done and feel there is no more information coming through you then put down your pen and move on to combining all the Program A information into Program B.

As you go through the circle in clockwise fashion you will be getting immediate information about the target. In Program B you look at what you have on your Program A and put everything into a temporary primitive line drawing. You then pick out the top three to five characteristics in the line drawing by labeling them I, II, and III, IV, V etc. on Program B.

18.7 The Program B and C Templates

Program B is where you will be gathering all the data collected from all your Program A input and organizing it into usable data. Once you finish program A, go directly to Program B.

- Form a very basic line sketch of all Program A data, quickly taking 12-18 seconds to do so. Don't overthink it.

- Label the most prominent objects in Project B of most to least importance. I, II, III, IV,V, etc.

- At this time you may run Program A again on any object(s) labelled I-V in Project B to gain more information on that particular object. I.e. If you gathered data through Program A that suggested there is a house (using the house as the target) involved in the full picture, you may want to run a whole Program A just on the house to get more information on the house specifics so you could add information to your Program B and C. You can run Program A on anything to gain more information, with no limits. You may end up with multiple pages of Program As, which you will compile together into your Program B and then into a final Program C, which will be your final answer.

- Program C is a final diagram or image of the amassed data from all Program As and Bs into a more precise drawing. You can take a few minutes to put this together and this will be the answer or image you were seeking to your initial question.

Program B
(12-18 sec to draw)

1. Form a very basic line sketch of Program A

2. Label the most prominent objects of most to least importance.
I, II, III, IV, V, etc.

3. Run Program A on each object to obtain many Program B's.

Program C
(up to a few mins)

Detailed collection of all Program B's with descriptions on or near all objects.

KOUSOULIMETHOD.com
©2016 All rights reserved.

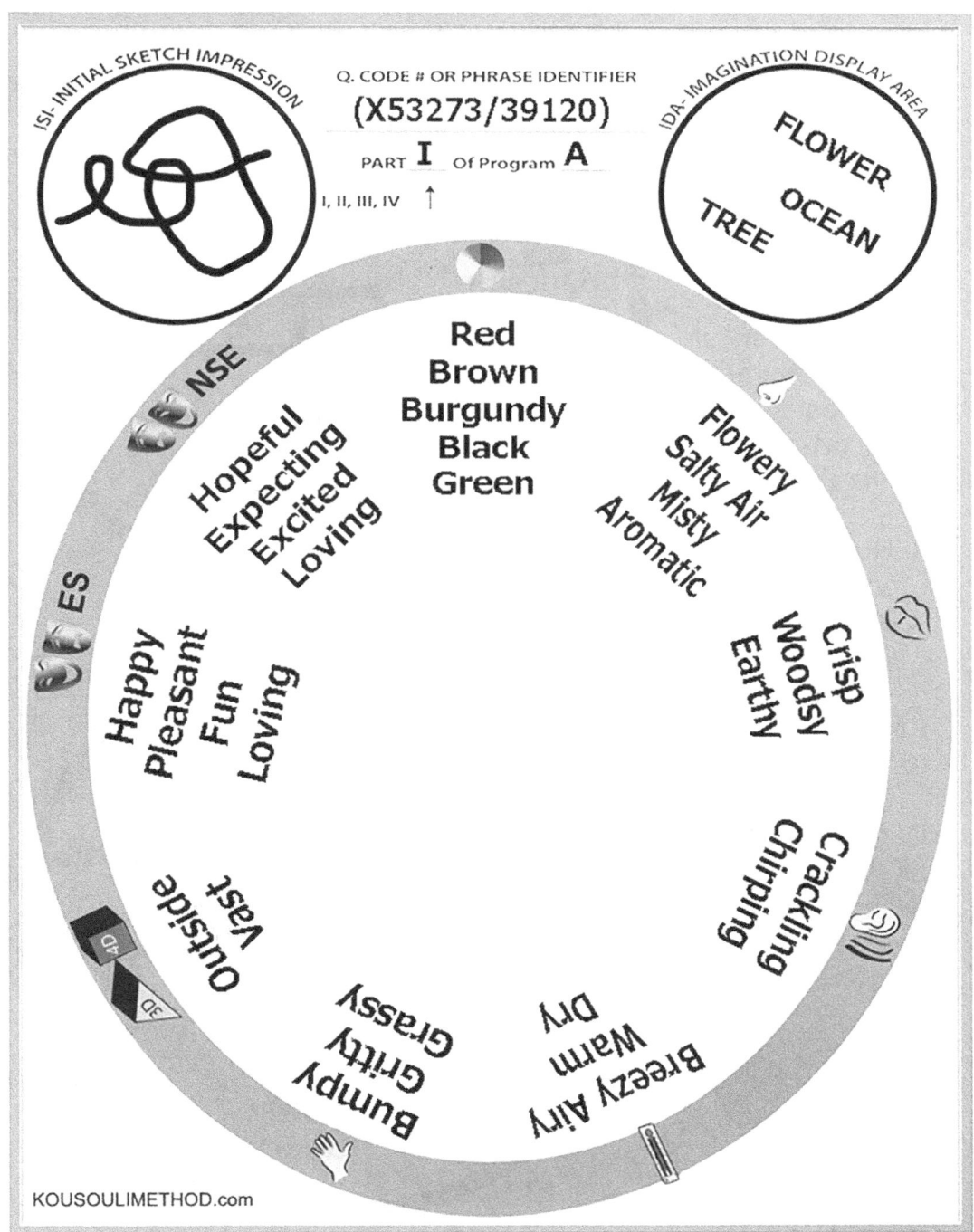

Be A Master® Of Psychic Energy

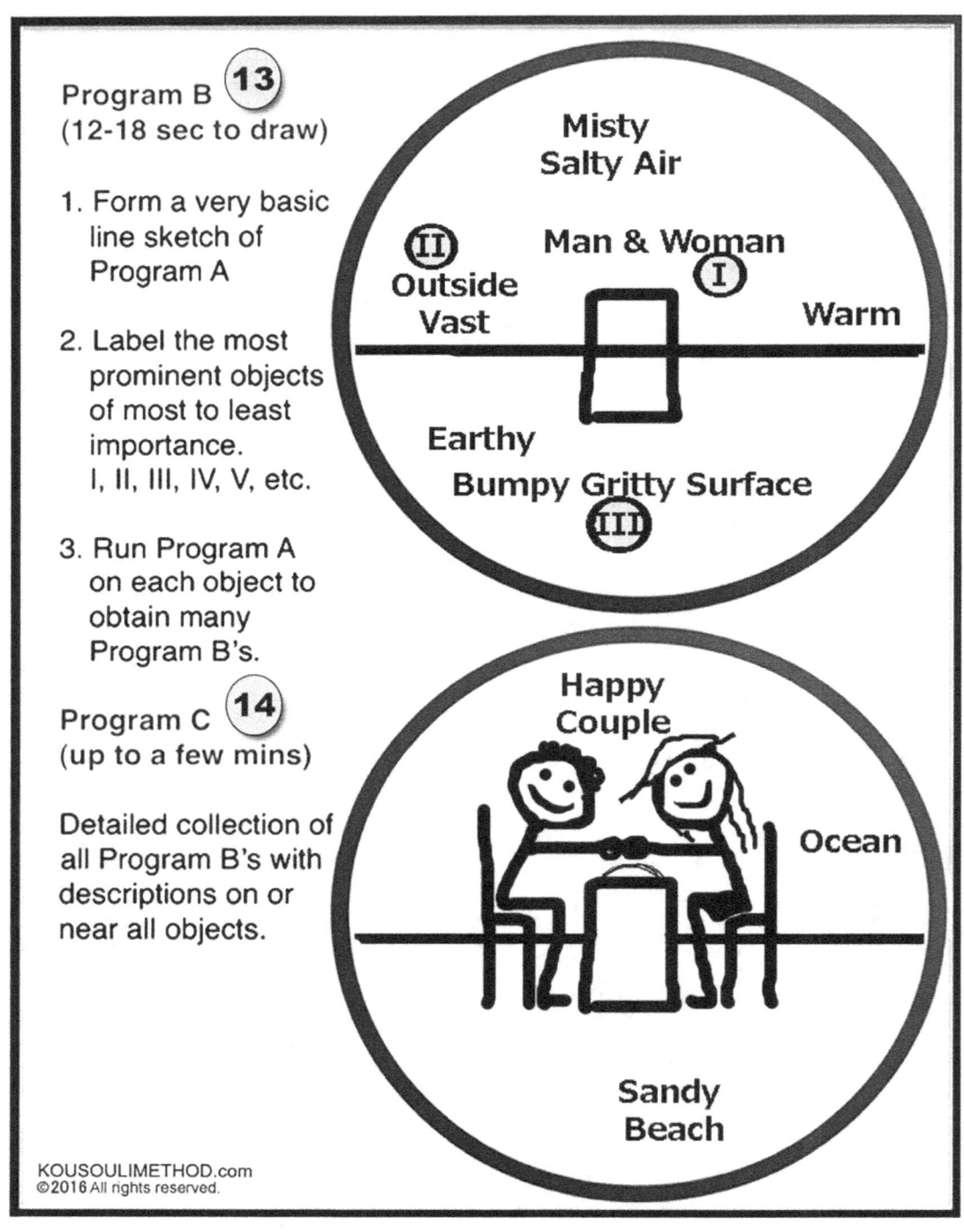

Program B (13) (12-18 sec to draw)

1. Form a very basic line sketch of Program A

2. Label the most prominent objects of most to least importance. I, II, III, IV, V, etc.

3. Run Program A on each object to obtain many Program B's.

Program C (14) (up to a few mins)

Detailed collection of all Program B's with descriptions on or near all objects.

KOUSOULIMETHOD.com
©2016 All rights reserved.

The uses for this technique are limitless and can bring you answers to virtually any question or target you are asking of Source. Again, the only limited item in this procedure is the idea of time. Since we live in a three dimensional plane of existence, length width and height, time is an illusion which does not exist in Source's thoughts of eternal, so to find out how things appear to us in an earthly timeline, we have to think of things in a linear fashion. In this case if we wish to find some information concerning a 'when' then we would run several rounds of programs A to C to find events which would happen around that 'main event.'

18.8 Troubleshooting the Program

Don't get frustrated. This exercise takes time and proper discipline to master. Read over the steps of this chapter several times before attempting to run your first Program A, as it could take a few tries to get it right. Please keep in mind that this section is a very basic explanation of a fifth dimensional activity explained down to a third dimensional instruction which presents limitations. If you are still having trouble, *you may want to attend one of our seminars where we learn together this and other valuable skills of self-awareness, clairvoyance, and spiritual awakening.* You may need to work in a group to get confirmation as you trust your abilities and grow your intuition.

- ✓ When in doubt or trying too hard to find or imagine the answer- stop. In order to be successful with this aspect of information retrieval, you must be in the 'zone.'

- ✓ You should meditate prior to attempting the exercise so you can be in a relaxed neutral, loving, peaceful and 'open to allowing' the Universe to speak to you and give you what you seek. Any pressure or resistance will immediately break your connection and the data you receive will be skewed with your ego brain bringing forth wrong information. Perform this exercise at times when you can be calm and relaxed without any interruptions. If you are not receiving adequate information, try rephrasing your question or further simplifying your code or phrase identifier - you may be doing too broad of a search.

Chapter 19:
Spiritual Warfare - Neutralizing Negative Energies

"For we wrestle not against flesh and blood, but against principalities, against powers, against the rulers of the darkness of this world, against spiritual wickedness in high places."
~ Ephesians 6:12

19.1 The Thoughts in our Heads

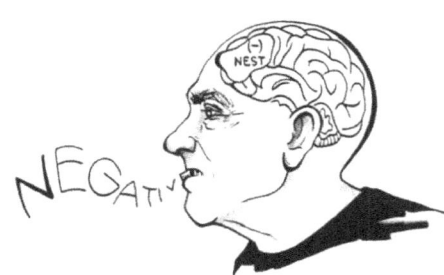

We are not the thoughts in our head, although it may feel that way if we've let them run wild long enough. It can sometimes feel as if we can't get any peace of mind, or our minds are running a mile a minute. Where do these foreign thoughts come from? They can originate from many places and over much time. Most of them come from childhood as the thoughts and words of an elder, the council of a naive friend, the limiting ideas and rules of a teacher, parent, or preacher. They could come from a doctor in a white coat giving you a scary diagnosis, or any social official, like a judge or policeman, making you feel guilty or 'bad.' Were you always sitting in front of a television while growing up? Then much of the things in your head are from subconscious programming and subliminal advertising. Have you bought into the politics of party sides between Democrats and Republicans? Possibly all you think about is a sports team's colors or emblems ruling your world. The importance of being aware is crucial to the enlightened individual seeking to quiet the chattering mind and bring in divine peace. What is the remedy? It is awareness, repentance, meditation, and deep prayer. Meditation clears the mind and helps us differentiate what we are thinking from what others may be thinking, or can clear negative, obsolete programming that does not belong in our mind anymore. The way you thought about society and your role as a teenager does not work as an adult, and needs upgrading. Awareness comes after the clearing of the thoughts and leads to repentance. Repentance does not mean wearing a black robe, selling everything you own and moving into a cave, feeling guilty about your soul or worrying that if you don't do *this*, you'll be going to Hell like many religious fear doctrines tell people. Repentance simply means you understand what went wrong and now you decide to change that program and follow a new path. Once you repent, then you give thanks to God for all the good in your life and with gratitude you ask to be blessed with more blessings, with clear focused intention on positive thoughts.

19.2 The Vibrations of Darkness

If you are a healer yourself, or interview one who deals with deep soul healing and the rooted source of patients' problems, you may find a unanimous agreement by all that there are seemingly 'out of this world' energies working in our realm. We must remember that evil forces of darkness are always powerless by default. It is us humans who make them grow strong when we distance ourselves from our creator, the ever-loving power and source of all life. When humans do this, they surrender the rights and responsibilities of their power to whatever vibration surrounds them – which is usually the 'less than' love energies. This always brings pain and ill health.

When one aligns with their Creator, they align with the one true force that made all things visible and invisible. When one pledges allegiance to anything other than the original Source of All Creation (fallen angels, other people, idols, or attachments), they pledge allegiance to a lower energy, less than the total whole. It is not that this lower energy does not have power, it does; but it will never be as strong as the Source or prevailing power of the Creator. Those who practice the Dark Arts are invoking powers lesser than the Source of 'All.' These are still powerful energies that can do extradimensional things, like conjure spirits, move objects, or levitate people. However, each and every time this power pulls fear energy from those it comes from or is sent towards; it draws from fear energy and multiplies itself. The lower energies can summon great power and bring great distress, but only because a human being gives up their power to the lesser energy by merging into that lower, negative thought pattern and accepting it as greater than their original God Source within. Thus, with great deception and trickery, evil is what it is because people allow it to exist in many forms within them. God allows humanity free-will to experience and learn from both their loving and fearful choices.

Grow Up

Spiritually evolved persons live by the rule: Do me first. You may need to grow up, whether spiritually or inwardly. You cannot expect another to make you feel secure or happy. You need to figure out what you want to create in your life and leave behind as your legacy.

Be joyful, successful; achieve all your goals and attain whatever you desire. Don't be distracted by your surroundings during your journey, or other people's creations. Separate yourself from others' demands, jealousy, envy, and do not make their problems your own. You came into this world by yourself and one day you will leave it by yourself. Become friends with you, love you, and love your 'alone' time. Do not fear being strong when you're alone. When alone, you can be in your own energy field and receive clarity. It is when you are alone that you have true tranquility and can fully investigate the depths of 'you.' Also, remember that you are not ever truly alone. You are always with Divine guidance of the higher self. Spiritually evolved persons realize this. Any lonely feelings experienced, are merely temporary illusions and a strong indicator that your thoughts are currently misaligned from feeling the connection and abundance of your Source.

Translate this into your relationship with others. When you become committed to a relationship, you will be giving up your identity to create a new identity with your mate. You must be 100% completed in your own journey in order to create a new journey with another. Ask the Universe for the right people to come into your life, not just any one - the right ones. Ask yourself with conviction, "What do I want to do in my life?" and let nothing take your focus and energies from that until you complete it.

It is not your responsibility to make people feel good, better, or worthy. They are responsible for their own happiness and worth, just as you are yours. You can't forget about your well-being and needs while trying to fix the world or others. You will only end up being worthless to everyone if you are not there for yourself first. You are not here for your mother, father, sister, brother, in-laws, etc. You are here for YOU. Let go - let it all go - start to not care so much about others' stories, issues, and negative energies. Let go and watch how their energy will then try to find you without letting up. You need not chase others, for they will in effect chase you, especially if you are of good, clean, and pure energy. The dark always wants to find the light; it desires the contrast, it wants to be cleansed once more. Keep yourself in meditation and prayer to see your life unfold in miracles.

Know that overemotional girl/boyfriends will continue to come and go, and negative family members may always be a pain in your side. Everyone will have their opinion and they will force their insecurities and poor personas onto you. It is up to you to be aware of when this is happening, and to not allow it to affect you. Knowing when the energy coming at you is not yours and of foreign origin is a major step in becoming aware of your inner being and inner power. Once you become aware of who you truly are and grow as a spiritual being, you can connect to your higher self and be unaffected by others' low vibes.

How do you connect for further levels of awareness? Heal through Levels 1, 2, and 3.

1. The human consciousness – safety and survival level of 3rd and 4th density

2. The innate body intelligence – healing occurs in DNA through pure loving trust & intent. (I.e.) practicing Kousouli® Method

3. The higher self – experiencing divine nature through pineal gland activation

When you are in survival level, you cannot ascend into the higher levels as doing so takes energies that are being put into finding safety. This is why it is so important to remove the pains and aches of the body, to allow for higher thinking and movement to a higher self. This is why deep meditation, learning from others who can read energy, and intentional prayer are key, so that if you are attacked or criticized, you can stop and deal with it in a neutral way where that energy does not affect you any further or inflict more harm on you. Your internal abilities and gifts flourish faster when you are around the energies of others who can already lovingly deflect negative energy and practice high spiritual awareness. Intent is how a healer sends multidimensional energy to change the aspects of a distorted perception or reality (dis-ease) a patient holds as their truth. The human DNA is changing rapidly, not in a way we can see in a textbook, but in the ways we can see in action in our world (i.e. extremely gifted children with super-power abilities being born). As healers improve their connection from Levels 1 to 3 (above) with quicker connections and teach this to others, they will change each individual, and that will eventually enable society to change in massive ways.

19.3 How Do I Break Away from Self Inflicted Negative (SIN) Energy, Sorcery, or Possession?

The first step is to be aware that you want a change from the negative path (**SIN** 'missing the mark' also known as hamartia from Greek ἁμαρτία) you are currently on, and decide to change your focus towards a better, more positive way of being without returning to that old way. This step is called **Repentance**. Once you are aware that you desire change from the current state of affairs, you must verbally and mentally acknowledge the mistakes made. Then, forgive yourself and others involved in the wrongdoing, or the negative ways that you wish to move away from. This is called **Confession**. Men and women perform acts of confession all the time, usually talking amongst themselves in groups by getting things 'off of their chests' in order to feel better about themselves or the troubling thoughts on their minds. In the old days, people would do public confessions where the whole town would gather weekly to 'get out all the drama' so that harmony would continue to rule in the town or village. Confession today, however, is kept confidential between one's spiritual mentor, as information could be used as gossip. Sometimes, it would be better to keep some information to oneself to avoid unnecessary public shame or scrutiny. You would also need to **identify the source of the negativity,** which started the process to begin with, as this is important so that the new course can be mapped. Then you must **forgo all temptations**, including people, places, or things that bring you back to that source of negativity. This also includes disposing of any items, jewelry, clothing, or music given to you by any negative, black magic, or sorcery individual. **Have no fear** in your heart or mind. Say the **Creed or Christ prayer** continuously, see your **Spiritual father** and hold yourself accountable to him. Just as a family doctor is close in need of a health emergency, a Spiritual Father is nearby in case of a spiritual emergency. A spiritual father is a knowledgeable, non-judgmental, loving mentor who is much older in years here on Earth, and has the spiritual wisdom and humility to help guide you correctly in God's Love. Spiritual Fathers are different than nuns and priests, as they have a huge responsibility to the individual they mentor. They will not only pray for you and with you when things get rough, but will also take on this responsibility even through their own difficulties.

19.4 How Do You Know if the Negativity Means You Need a Psychiatrist, or If It Is Possession?

A clear sign of possession is that the negativity is so deep and compounded over a long period of time that the individual seems to have lost all control of themselves, and appears to be a totally different individual (or many individuals). However, the main determining factor is taking this individual and introducing them to holy relics or holy places where many believers reside. That is, getting into a church, finding a person of faith, or a holy object. Seeing whether or not the person can drink holy water and sing hymns of praise to God will also be a telltale sign. Those with a medical condition will be able to do all the above without a problem; the ones who are influenced via external negative influences on their spirit will not be able to be amongst the faithful or partake in holy positive acts, and will remove themselves, panic, react violently, or look shaken up.

19.5 How Does One Fall Prey to Being Possessed By Negativity?

Lower frequency energies are cunning and can take time to do their 'dirty' work. Simply saying that negative energy doesn't exist or that Satan isn't real are some of the major tricks in dark energy's arsenal to enter into a physical body. Understand that giving focus or paying any attention to Dark Arts allows one to 'give the Devil rights,' which means they demote their own God-given power over to darkness and take second place to the negative energy by going into a soul contract with the negativity. Humans can become desperate at various points in their life where they let go of their connection to God and think God is not caring or loving anymore. They claim, "God's not listening," but this is all due to their own lack of faith and connection, nothing more. At this time they make the big mistake by considering help from elsewhere - looking to other people, groups, sects, clans, cults, gangs, and even make personal pacts by saying with desperation through thought and words, "I would do or give anything to… (Fill in the blank with: be famous, be rich, get a certain someone to love me, etc.)." Miraculously, the demons that do have power (given to them by the thoughts and actions of man) manifest the desire, and the human allows this negativity to harbor in his or her mind and body. The human and the negative energy unite. For a short while the ride is great, as the manifestations appear one after the other, but the human knows that they are playing a dangerous game. Slowly the human being's true self and spirit is concealed as their agreement with their dark side emerges. After a while the human feels strong in his or her power and starts to exhibit lower level actions and behaviors that are not usually them, including anger, hate, and rage. The demonic lower energies eventually end up in revolt against the possessed human and take over the body, throwing it into dis-ease, drug use, alcoholism, or worse. The drug use is even a larger connection to more enslavement of the mind, which becomes a reinforced behavior that is harder to remove. Eventually, the poor human's mind and soul feels nothing but torment and fear in their life, with what looks like no way out. These energies grow out of control with time and can multiply into an infestation called a legion (thousands in numbers), where the individual becomes very lost. The negative energies ravage the human, even to the point of suicide where then the soul loses the body, and the soul is in a negative state of torment on the non-physical side of The Veil (Catholicism calls it purgatory). This is often termed as a person's own hell, which is actually an illusion within itself, as the soul can still be freed by remembering to connect to its power and disown its disconnection just by calling out to God. Gentle prayers from loved ones to the deceased soul may help, but ultimately it is the journey of the soul itself that must make the disconnection and turn back to God through repentance. Sometimes, souls choose to reincarnate into a similar situation to relearn the lessons they missed the last time around.

19.6 Sleep Paralysis

"The worst hell to be in is the one you don't know you're in."
~ Father Paisios of Mount Athos Holy Monastery

Each night you simulate dying. When you close your eyes, your body goes into a paralytic state that mimics death in many ways. Your breathing slows down, your mind shuts off. Have you ever thought of where 'you' go? Your body is here on Earth, but where is your mind and soul? I am honored to have been able to shed light on this subject for patients suffering from sleep paralysis, which is a very frightening thing for those unfortunates afflicted. Spiritual attack may occur at any moment, especially at night, if you allow negative thoughts to accumulate and run wild from a hard day. This is why it is important to meditate and pray to clear the mind, both before sleeping and when awaking.

Demonic or lower energy forces want to separate and dismantle unity in love at every chance they can, because they don't work in that frequency and therefore don't understand it. They are opposite of light. Ever hear the phrase, "Misery loves company?" That's exactly the job of lower forces and energies. They will look for any opportunity humans give to them to entertain themselves through games, rituals, or other rites of passage. They seek out those ready to give their free will over and harbor that individual's body. These lifeless vibrations want to feel the one thing they can't feel without a physical body; to experience what it feels to be alive again.

Prior to sleep or during an attack, state boldly with confidence, "In the name of Jesus Christ and the Father of all Creation, I rebuke all, demons, principalities and low energies that are not of the highest vibration of God's love and light. I cast you now to the abyss so that you never return." This immediately clears the room of any demonic low-level energy. Don't take my word for it, search online for the countless people who have had near death experiences or are stuck in sleep paralysis and have used this armor of God for protection. The verse in the Bible states:

> "Behold, I give you the authority to trample on serpents and scorpions, and over all the power of the enemy, and nothing shall by any means hurt you. Nevertheless do not rejoice in this, that the spirits are subject to you, but rather rejoice because your names are written in heaven."
> ~ Luke 10:19-20

Demonic 'low' level energies are always looking for the opportunity to spread like a virus because that's their only reason for existence. However, they cannot harm or activate any of their power unless they get an invitation in. Unless someone invites the energy into their life through free will, they cannot be harmed. The power of love and light *always* supersedes as the authority. Demonic forces know this and will tempt those who are of weak willpower with promises of fortune or thoughts of jealousy and coveting. They will promise false happiness and grant illusions of power. They do have power, but they are much weaker in power when compared to the light of the Creator, God.

Low vibration will always try to use your fears against you to convince you that they are not affected by the above statement. This is an illusion, and will be their last trick before they flee from your presence. Demons want to know you are weak in your mind and thoughts in order to keep their hold on the current domain (your life) they inhabit.

19.7 Do Not Trust Plural or Negative Voices

"You are not good enough, not worthy enough, not pretty enough, not successful enough,"…etc. It's all lies. The voices in your head may be many and they should not be trusted. The mind expression should be one voice and clear. The voice should be loving, positive, and compassionate. The one true voice will never lead you astray, curse you or anyone else (especially God) or give you false hope. This loving positive internal voice of your soul is the only voice to listen to. Any voice or vibration lesser than the utmost highest love, is false and a deception from surrounding energies being transmitted by foreign sources (earthly or otherwise). It could be your own deception, your neighbor's, your parent's or preacher's false teachings. It can be the faulty programming of your grandparents, boss, or trusted friend. One must first become aware of the faulty thought and then observe themselves scrutinizing their thoughts, words, and actions. Question every thought and see if you can figure out its root. Was it a thought of yours or a sibling's? Perhaps it was your father talking through you? Was it a negative vibration or was it positive? Taking the time to meditate and pray to discern between the vast waves of thought is constant work a healer must go through as they go towards mastery of self. Singing from the heart and mind praises of love and gratitude towards your maker is a good way to keep flowing positive vibrations and hinder empty lower vibrations from entering your mind. Develop a cascade of constant good pure thoughts for yourself and others in your mind and you will claim victory over negativity in your illusion/reality.

19.8 A Simple Prayer For Protection

I pray to you Father, Creator, King, Lord of all creation, and the highest vibration of love. I ask with humility that you oversee me through this time of distress that I may come through it unscathed and victorious by claiming your name and glory. I ask that any foe or entity of lower vibration that seeks to harm me, your son/daughter _____ (your name here), succumb to your light and be cast away to the Abyss, powerless from my path. Amen.

19.9 Commanding Negative Energy Away From Another

As an heir to the Kingdom, you have been given 'dominion over all' as written in the Bible. However, many forget or neglect to rise to their position of power.

> *"Then He called His twelve disciples together and gave them power and authority over all demons."*
> *~ Luke 9:1*

> *"For this purpose the Son of God was manifested, that He might destroy the work of the devil."*
> *~ 1 John 3:8*

> *"Behold, I give unto you power to tread on serpents and scorpions, and over all the power of the enemy: and nothing shall by any means hurt you."*
> *~ Luke 10:19*

Calling Out Dark Energies

Dark spirit, I command you in the name and authority of the Father, the Creator, King, and God of all things, both visible and invisible, to at once leave _____ (name of individual, place, or home). I ask the loving light of Christ consciousness render you powerless and send you now back to the Abyss. You are commanded in the name of the Living Loving God to never return to _____ (person/place) or interfere in the lives of _____ (persons) ever again.

19.10 Seeing the Good in All

It is spiritually good to be able to see even the unpure as pure. There is God in everything and everyone, even those afflicted with the worst of negativity. Just as you know a basket of crops gained from farming is a good thing, you can also see the value in the manure that provided the material for the crops to grow. So spiritual thoughts are like good crops, however even the manure, what most see as bad or low energy can be converted into the good. Find the good (God) in all and call out the negativity to allow the good to shine in them. Remember that even if you see someone's human form acting out the negative low vibrational energy, they are still a son or daughter of the most high; they have only forgotten temporarily their connection and power to their Father.

19.11 Unpure Thoughts Are Wild

Unpure thoughts (thoughts not of a higher vibration) if not brought into the light by Christ consciousness will multiply through fear insecurities running wild in the mind. One may perceive two people in the distance talking and they may automatically think, "Those individuals are talking negatively about me!" or they live in fear thinking the world is out to attack him/her, thus the world is evil and they can trust no one. The spiritual state of a person is dictated as the sum quality of thoughts that can be measured by the actions of the person. Taken backwards, the actions were words. If we trace back the actions even further the words were first thoughts. Unpure thoughts are wild and can leave someone's mouth before the person has a chance to tame them. These words can cause harm to another who takes this in as their truth. How many times have people said nasty things to someone and wished they could take them back? Making matters worse, unpure thoughts are a beacon to others of like thought and mind to mingle and co-create at that level. After all, birds of a feather do flock together.

19.12 Dr. Kousouli: What Do I Do When a Client is so Overwhelmed With a Negative Situation?

There are times patients come in and feel no one is hearing them out in their private life. They may unknowingly dump all that negative energy on you knowing that you will listen with an empathetic ear. As a good healer you have the ability to soften their perspective, divert their attention to positive matters, remove their pain, and make them feel much better physically as well as spiritually. However, if you do not empower them to consistently monitor their programming; you would be giving the man a fish to eat one time instead of teaching them how to fish for themselves and eat for a lifetime. A great healer must also be a great teacher.

When things are so overwhelming that you feel so much like erupting and negative emotions overtake you like a runaway train, you must immediately stop that train. When a patient is emotionally listing off all their problems and essentially dumping them on me, I softly say to them "Stop." They may keep going and I again gently but more firmly say, "Stop" with a smile. If they still are emotional and have not stopped spewing the negativity I gently place my hands on their shoulders, look them straight in the left eye and again firmly say "Stop." They usually stop and give me the deer in headlights look and then realize what they were doing. They were 'running their program' as I like to say. They run the same program so often that it becomes engrained in them as their truth. It's not that they really want to run this negativity over and over; they just are so used to it that's the only tool they have to work with. It is good to neutralize the negativity and bring about a new proactive way of dealing with the triggers of life instead of being reactive to them.

19.13 Change the Programming and End Suffering

1. STOP. Immediately stop the verbal or physical action of negative energy dumping or looping.

2. Realize you have become *AWARE* of the programming and desire to delete or erase it. Once you *know*, you cannot UN-*know*. If you repeat the issue it becomes a 'choice' you make and no longer an automatic unknown loop.

3. Immediately close your eyes and **run the meditation program** earlier in this book (14.12) to release all random and destructive thoughts in your mind on the issue.

4. Pray (14.13) and envision what you desire to acquire it as your new future outcome.

5. Acknowledge with gratitude your creation, knowing you are now consciously taking the necessary steps in changing your past programming.

6. Thank the negative programming for showing you its lesson, where growth was possible, and **command it to release you; let it go.**

Do not give focus to negative energies, believe in them, or entertain them. If you do, they draw strength from your fear associated with your lack of connection to Source. Instead see them as solved, unimportant, completed, and removed. Re-create using clear thought to bring about the illusion you wish to experience as your new reality.

19.14 Negative Subliminal Messages and Covert Commands in Music

They say that music is the language of the soul. Many listen to music and are blind to some of the messages being pumped into their minds day in and day out. Have you ever wondered why there seems to be the same 12 songs on the radio for a period of time from the same 12 artists, day in and day out, for months at a time with little variety - if any? Do you wonder why the songs seem to promote the same sexual, money worshiping, and derogatory lyrics day in and day out? Have you ever caught yourself wondering with frustration why you can't get high vibration music on public radio? Have you ever heard of subliminal messages being put into music, or music, when played backwards, has hidden meanings? There's a good reason this is all happening, and until you're spiritually awake, you would never know to question it.

If you do a little research into subliminal occult music symbolism and study the lyrics, words, music videos, and purposes of the individuals making this music, you will find something very dark behind their 'works.' The ones you see on stage and in public are only the front men and women, who act like the faces of the industry they are slaves to. It doesn't take much intelligence to ask the right questions and do the necessary research on this topic. Once you do, you'll think twice about your favorite popular rock or pop artist, and may decide they are spreading poison - not just to your ears, but also to your soul. Beware (Be Aware) of the lyrics and audio-visual input you give permission to influence your mind. Search online the topic of 'evil in the entertainment or music industry.'

19.15 Is Your Self-Esteem Low From Negative Self-Talk?

Examining the real you exercise

Find a private room where you can perform this important exercise. You may choose to do this exercise prior to undressing to take a shower. Stand in front of a mirror (full-length mirror if possible). Turn off all distractions, phones, radios, etc. Turn down the light in the background of the room to bring focus to you in the foreground. Do not turn off all the lights, as this would defeat the purpose.

As you stand in front of the mirror, start to remove the things that are not 'you.' As you remove each item, declare, "This is not me." If you are wearing a hat, take it off - it's not you. If you are wearing any jewelry, earrings, necklaces with or without religious markings, piercings, etc. remove them - they are not you. If you are wearing a shirt, especially with any branding on it - take it off - it is not you. Repeat with every article of clothing until you are standing completely nude in front of the mirror. Look at YOU. What do you see? Do you like who and what you see? Be honest with yourself.

Truly ask yourself: "Am I happy with what I am feeling and reflecting back to myself visually? Was this exercise difficult to do? Was there any resistance to you removing or declaring any part of your wardrobe? How do you feel looking at your face, your body, your eyes, your chest, your backside? Did you notice any feelings of shame? Inadequacy? Or do you feel good about yourself no matter what? Are you in judgment of yourself saying mentally, "I should be taller, thinner, this or that…"

If you are feeling anything other than 100% pure deep and undeniable love for the being both in physical form and internal soul, then you have been programmed by society. You would be wise to drop any and all feelings, thoughts, concepts, or actions from this point forward that are not serving 'You.'

I want you to think back to your birth. That little baby loved itself and others without judgment, without shame or prejudice. That vibrant little soul vibrated so high that everyone in the room felt the love emanating from that tiny being; a soul that took a body and just crossed over from non-physical into the physical reality we call our Earth. What is the one major difference between you the baby born then and accepted with love and 100% awareness of spirit, and the you now that is looking at you in the mirror, possibly doubting your power and abilities?

The answer, my friend, is negative programming.

19.16 Recognize Your Negative Thought Patterns

Some of our negative thinking patterns are so automatic we don't even realize we're being negative! Ask yourself how a thought feels to you immediately after you have it. Is the thought positive or does it feel heavy? Does the thought give life or take energy out of you? The more you stop and discern your thoughts, the easier it will become.

Here are some common negative patterns. You may find that you project these onto yourself or others.

- **Not taking into consideration all possible data.** I.e. everything always goes wrong for you and nothing is good. Discounting your blessings, you tend to focus only on what you don't have and negative outcomes.
- **Projecting negative thinking.** Chronic conspiracy theorists and worriers are guilty of this one. Project positive thought and take positive action instead of bringing others down to your level of suspicion and worry. I.e. "Did you hear about the secret underground civilization that wants to burn the world?" Decide that you want to leave the future open to positive possibility, and don't project negative thoughts to the future.
- **Blaming others for your problems.** I.e. instead of taking responsibility for your own well-being, you put blame on others when something 'inconvenient' happens to you. Focus on reversing the downhill spiral without getting even more negative.
- **Victim mentality.** You take all responsibility for how someone else is feeling or for things that go wrong that really have nothing to do with you. I.e. blaming yourself for the whole loss when it was a team effort.
- **Internalizing trivial things as emotional truth.** I.e. July was teased since grade school for her nose, and now as a model she still feels unattractive because her nose doesn't look 'flawless.'

- **Negative thinking while jumping to conclusions.** You find yourself worrying about the possible negatives to a situation no matter how positive something about it may be. You may also dump the negativity on everyone around you. I.e. telling someone what 'bad' things happened today.

19.17 Get Out of Negative Vibrations ASAP

You know you're in a bad mood. Now what? Great! The first step and the most important one is that you have acknowledged a vibratory state you do not like. Without this crucial first step in awareness, it would be impossible to change anything you could not identify. However, even when identified some choose to not progress to the next step and prefer to stay in a 'pity party' or 'problem dumper' phase looking for others to bring down to their negative level seeking comfort or manipulating others into feeling sorry for them. This is counterproductive. It does not raise vibrations of people around you and brings them down, zaps their energy, and pushes your low vibration reality onto them. In time you will look around and see you've lost some friends. Once you identify a negative vibration, stop immediately any activity that you were doing prior to your acknowledgement. It's okay to have a dear and headlights moment for a few seconds, but then become proactive and think about something humorous, fun, and happy that puts you in an incredible mood. With abundant focus, concentrate on that very thought. If you can, act on that thought immediately.

Have a favorite song? Play it. Dance around your room like a maniac, it's okay to laugh! Do you like to draw and be creative? Have a pencil and pad ready to go. Want to exercise and get some frustration out? Time for some step aerobics, a short trail hike or track run, some spinal stretching (see section 9.6), or get the weights and pump a good curl in on those biceps. Have a family pet? Do not abuse it, rather pet it and hold it close to your heart while feeling its unconditional love for you. These are some of the more basic activities, but you can find what you like and have it ready to go when you feel your frequency is going down the tubes; especially in life's highly charged moments like when family arguments hit hard, a lover leaves you, a death in the family occurs, the boss is having a bad day and takes it out on you, finances get rough, etc. Negative vibrations do not serve you, so drop them fast. It is not easy, however the more you practice getting back to your joy and happiness the easier it becomes. There is no other way; you must do it in order to move forward in creating the life you wish to live. If you must have your pity party or 'boo-hoo' moment do it fast and get it over with quickly so you can move on to the better you. We can learn from babies and pets. Both are 'live in the moment' experts; they may fuss and anger for a split second, but they move on and get happy again fast!

They hold no negative vibes or grudges against anything or anyone. They let no one take them out of alignment from the pure care-free energy that they are. If someone with negative energy is in their auric field they can feel it and they get away from them! They are unconditional love and exude it. Be likewise.

Unconditional love means you are connected to all that is love and who you are in connection to that love regardless of conditions or challenges that may arise to contraindicate this connection.

Immediately raise your vibration:

- Listen to your favorite motivational songs
- Sing out loud no matter who's around
- Spend time with good friends
- Play your favorite game(s)
- Smile at yourself in the mirror
- Dance like a child in your room
- Hold a pet close to your heart
- Take turns exchanging full body massage with your lover
- Send another love from your heart holding them in your mind.
- Read an inspirational book
- Play the guitar or exercise your particular talent
- Watch a funny movie or videos online
- Kiss and hold a baby

How do you know if you have changed?

You react differently than you once did to a trigger. You are proactive rather than reactive and keep calm and cool about your choice of action. Low level emotion does not overtake you and you feel clarity in making choices out of love, not fear. You no longer feel needy or act out of lack mentality. Those who have not seen you in months say, "You look different, lighter; your energy is different - something about you has changed." This will be the clear sign that you are doing well for yourself and confirmation others also feel a shift in you.

19.18 Keeping Your Attitude Positive

Do you have a positive mental attitude, or do you focus more on negative thinking? Do you notice the sunshine or just the clouds? Do you entertain possibilities, or believe all is doom and gloom?

Studies show that thinking positively and having a positive mental attitude make people happier, more optimistic, and healthier than their pessimistic counterparts. Positive people aren't blind to the problems and challenges in life. They may have as many, if not more than others. But people who practice thinking positively tend to approach life with acceptance and faith. They have a can-do attitude. They believe they can have joy in the face of trouble and can heal even if they can't be cured. They extend their positive view to others and life in general.

The good news is that even if you have persistent negative emotions and thinking patterns, you can benefit from emotional and mental healing techniques to develop a positive mental attitude. You just need to be patient and take one step at a time.

If you are in resistance, you will never be well. If you FIGHT cancer you give cancer power over you, just as you try to FIGHT drugs, you will not win the War on Drugs. Anything that you resist will persist. The key is to not give it focus and turn your focus to your true desires. If you wish to win the War on Poverty, focus on the goodness of abundance for all. If you want to stop the drug problem, focus energy on programs that give people reasons not to use drugs.

Negative thinking patterns are common and easy to identify. Shifting them to a more positive mental attitude can be a bit more challenging. Fortunately, releasing negative thoughts is very much doable with commitment and help from loving, open-minded, and experienced healers.

19.19 Dumping Negativity

Think thoughts that are true to the positive loving you. Focus on an aspect of something good that is true to you without resistance to that thought. Think about only this thing, nothing else. Let your mind wrap all its power through that one thought. Increase its color. Heighten its emotion. Raise its sounds.

Say this mantra internally, and let it echo in your mind for healing: "I am thankful, I am forgiven, and it is all well within me. I love myself and acknowledge my connection to my higher self. I release all resistance of health now to God. I now am and feel gratitude, humility, forgiveness, hope, and love." Then ask, "Where is my resistance? Where does it feel tight, stiff, dull, achy, cramped, heavy, sharp etc. on my body? What color is this feeling (See section 13:26)?" I.e. dark red, brown, slime green, black, etc.? "Does this feeling and color have a sound?" You will be shown the color and you will feel the sound. Let out that sound. Start by asking the questions, "What chakra level? Which is least optimal?

Does this energy reside in the spiritual, mental, emotional, or physical realm?" See a Kousouli® Method practitioner for assistance.

Grand leaps are doable, though they are very uncomfortable. Well-being is an energy flow that continues to move, with or without you- it's not dependent on whether it is moving or not, it is dependent on your understanding that it is or is not, your belief that it is or it's not. You choose to perceive its function. As we age we attain experiences and with these we have emotions and feelings with each event and experience.

19.20 Self-Appreciation, Not Selfishness

There is nothing more important than appreciation for yourself because as you appreciate yourself internally, you vibrate powerful energy outward. All of the YOU-niverse creates for you when you appreciate the ALL being that you are. Self-confidence is actually self-appreciation. You need not look to others for this appreciation as it is not something that can give self-appreciation to you. You must come to the realization that you matter. You are also made of 'matter' and thus, you matter. Just as everyone else matters too. You matter so much that you exist and the 'Universe, Source, Creator, Higher self, or God' has put you here for a reason for your (and their) existence. You play a part of the whole. Without you, there is no 'us' or 'we.' In this way everyone is special and special in a personal way. This is why you cannot look to others for your own appreciation because they cannot give you matter. You can only give yourself matter. Insecurity, loneliness, fear, or other emotional pain is all illusive vibratory matter made real by your mind. You do not come here to prove in some way that you need to become worthy, but know intuitively that you were already made worthy. You have no lack or disconnection unless you believe you do from previous programming; by believing other's perspectives or your own faulty negative disconnected thinking. You also do not have to fight with another person for them to give you appreciation, as this is a losing battle. You do not have to compete for a medal to feel as number one either; you already exist, thus you are number one in your world.

Competition, or seeing someone else's accomplishments compared to yours, could make you feel that you are 'less than,' thanks to the false illusion that you have not manifested in the physical that which you see another has. The only difference here is that they have put in the desire, focus, and actions that brought forward their physical manifestation. When you know the process is available also to you, you need not lower your worth to feel this lack. Anytime you feel that the opinion of others matters more to you than what you feel, your appreciation becomes unhealthy. Move all of your focus to thoughts of self-appreciation and act upon doing all the things needed to maintain self-appreciation at the highest levels; let nothing take this value from you, as anything less than full self-appreciation does not serve you. Acknowledge your worth without thoughts of lack. If you do not appreciate yourself, you vibrate a very strong energy that others can feel. Lack of self-appreciation verbalizes thoughts of "I'm not good enough," or "I'm not pretty enough," "I'm not smart enough," "I'm not rich enough," etc. These thoughts became your appearance and others can subconsciously read and feel these thoughts as you wear them. People treat you based on the way you energetically 'feel' about yourself.

You cannot do well for others unless you do greatness for you first. Is there anyone in this world who has ever done great things for others if they themselves were not strong internally through self-appreciation? Most people look at others or the world and claim emotionally powerful thoughts of lack, i.e.: "It is the economy, that's why I can't get a job," "It is the government holding me down," "It is the weather's fault I'm late to work." In truth, you are projecting your lack of worth to others. You must stop this programming at once, or risk continuing losing your power and falling into more desperation. The natural forces of the universe will separate you from all the things that are worthy and good if you do not maintain the same good vibrations you had when you came forth in this physical realm. When you were born you knew how appreciative of yourself you were and you did so much that your energy vibrated to others, and they smiled when they looked at you. They wanted to be around you; even strangers wanted to experience you when you came through the veil to this realm. If you're no longer feeling self-appreciation like you did upon arrival as a newborn, you have allowed the thoughts and vibrations of negativity through your journey here to disharmonize your connection to who you really are. Nothing is more important than you adoring yourself from a healthy, non-conceded perspective. You cannot and must not worry about other's thoughts of their own lack of appreciation for themselves. Always focus on your own ability to keep your self-appreciation at the highest levels - this is your work, no one else's and no one else can do your soul's work. You can start to change any negative feelings of yourself, just do the exercises of gratitude daily as instructed in this book.

Chapter 20:
Becoming a Spiritual Super-Human

*"When your desires are strong enough, you will appear
to possess superhuman powers to achieve."
~ Napoleon Hill*

When we advance our spiritual life and continuously examine ourselves within our new ascending structure, we may find ourselves becoming less complacent with previous acts that seemed 'okay' about our personality or character. We may start to feel like a hypocrite when we do the least opposite act from what we live or preach. Expect this to be a phase of transformation you will go through until you do walk the walk and talk the talk.

We cannot be perfect, but we all will strive daily to become as close to perfect as possible through events and challenges that allow us to put ourselves to the test. What do we need to progress beyond our merely human abilities and become *superhuman*? Mental, ethical, spiritual, and physical upgrade modifications need to happen. A superhuman doesn't settle for the current state of mediocrity – he or she does what needs to be done to become a better, higher version of him or herself. The powerless man or woman is satisfied with the blissful ignorance of their current world, handed to them by the established puppeteers of their society. In contrast, the superhuman is eager to discover the depths of his or life through thought, mind, meditation, and prayer to live an unbound existence.

Let's take for example an entertaining yet useful example: Batman, who is a regular guy doing extraordinary things for his community. He wasn't bitten by a radioactive spider, and wasn't born with cool powers of flight and invisibility. He simply used his mind (and monetary energy) to modify Bruce Wayne into Batman; his higher self. While you'll probably never want to wear leather and a facemask while combating evil at night, you can do really amazing things and become more than 'just another human.' While it sounds nice and worthwhile, you're probably wondering, "How do I tap into my own real superpower(s)?" In essence, it boils down to stepping out of your comfort zone right now, and learning to build spiritual awareness. Bringing to light your bad habits and also harnessing your inner strengths can help you embrace your good and truly become superhuman.

20.1 Building Awareness

If you are tired of feeling bad about yourself, and making choices that aren't in your best interest, take a look at your thoughts. Thoughts, feelings, and actions flow from one to the other in a continuous cycle. So the first step to building super thinking is mentally healing negative thought patterns for new awareness. When are you already thinking positively? Celebrate that success. You can use it as a model for other areas. What inner dialogue do you engage in? Is it limiting or negative? Observe yourself and listen as you think and speak to see when, how, and why you resort to negative self-talk. Keep in mind that action takes many forms. They include the words you speak, what you do, and what you don't do. Inaction is also a form of action. Becoming superhuman means that you've accepted yourself as a superhuman in your own mind first - this is half the battle before taking massive action.

20.2 Don't Lie to Yourself

Once your awareness is heightened, it is easier to stop the cycle in its tracks and change it towards positive thoughts. Stop exaggerating, generalizing, or putting a negative spin on things so you can move forward with your life.

It's a matter of telling yourself the truth and holding yourself accountable. The truth is that you are a magnificent being of light holding within you incredible unleashed potentials. To reach these locked potentials you must move out all limiting beliefs and negative programming that has become part of your system from the day you were born until now.

- ✓ **When you hear yourself thinking a negative thought, stop yourself immediately.** Make this a habit. Shift it to a slightly more positive thought that you can accept as truth.

    Example: "I'm not going to try because I always fail." Shift to: "What if I just check into it?" Shift to: "I can easily do x. I'll start today." And so on.

- ✓ **The past is over, let it go.** To hold on to hard feelings against another, no matter how much you feel they deserve it, will only rob you of joy and the emotional and mental healing you desire. Your spirit can only rest when you forgive those who wronged you.

- ✓ **Express gratitude.** Catch your negative self-talk and turn those thoughts into thoughts of gratitude. An attitude of gratitude is a healthy mental habit to develop.

20.3 Balancing Your Life

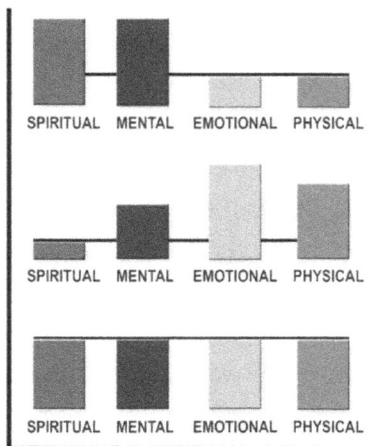

Take a good honest look at your life right now. Where are you? What could you be doing better? What plan will you set forth to accomplish it? Where do you need more help? A balanced life is a blessed life. Anytime we spend too much effort in one aspect in life (chasing after more money or getting caught up in the thoughts and feelings of others while neglecting our own) our life gets off track. We can only function at the level of the lowest common denominator. Our limiting factors are where we need to spend more time to help level out our life and bring balance. Keep everything in moderation.

You Are Not Powerless Unless You Choose to Be

You have a direct connection to the highest power, always. There is no suffering in your pure spirit. Suffering has no place in Divine peace and love. You have always been, and always will be worthy of the highest good, the highest love, and the highest power to vibrate at your top potential. All good is already there in your spiritual DNA - it is 'of' you and 'in' you. Your very essence is God power, and when you connect to that essence, you feel fully alive. Corporations, governments, religious institutions, etc. will do their best to deceive you into believing you need a product or something outside of yourself for happiness, fulfillment and self-worth, but this is the illusion they need you to 'buy' into for their power to grow. The moment someone can convince your subconscious (and conscious mind) through repeated covert hypnosis that you need or should have something you don't currently have in order to feel worthy or complete, you have given up your truth to them and allowed them to shape and create your reality. You've voluntarily stepped out of the driver's seat and become a co-pilot in your own life. You do this willingly always, and you always can take back the steering wheel. It's always your choice.

Suffering is always, in some form, put unto oneself. God does not cause you to suffer. In the case of losing a loved one, feeling constant loss and pain in the heart, the one who suffers essentially decides to feel that way about a natural life and death cycle that has existed for eternity. They create the experience of comfort and energy release through their act of grieving. However, even though they miss that person, they are very much still in communication - only the type of communication has changed from physical 'verbal' to spiritual 'feeling.' When this process is understood, instead of feeling loss and blaming the

Creator for taking a loved one from us, it can help create gratitude for the journey experienced together, rather than the perceived feeling of loss. We tend to be our own enemies and manipulate our pains and fears into what we want to experience, while growing from them or growing through them.

The waterslide: Growing up in southern NJ, each summer, I remember that all the kids loved a large waterslide. Children without pools would ask their neighbor or friend who had one: "Does it have a waterslide?" and we couldn't wait to use it if it did. Some kids would happily fly down the slide as it was meant to be used, but every now and again you'd see someone try to go against that water coming down the slide. It never ended well either; without fail, they would fly off the side scraping their body against the concrete or stumble and slip and hit their head on the railing and plop into the water, screaming in pain. I always wondered how many times I've been that kid now as a grown up, going the reverse way on the waterslide of life, only to fall back down into the water beat up, bruised, bleeding, and battered with some sense knocked into me. All I had to do was simply go down the slide – 'go with the flow.' I've applied this analogy in my life and constantly ask myself, "Am I going down the slide? Am I flowing into fun by sliding down the right way, or am I struggling up against the slide's water stream, holding on to negative thoughts, trying to prove something to myself or someone else, making life for myself difficult? Am I enjoying the ride of life…or am I about to hurt myself unnecessarily?" How often do we act as the kid that wants to prove something or act cool, only to learn the lesson that it is easier to go with the flow of life rather than to push against the laws we are created by? Our society has many who climb up the wrong side of the slide in all matters of love, health, and career.

Three-headed octopus: Everyone has their own truth and they can't stretch their self-manifested reality too fast; it's just too uncomfortable to break the comfort zone. You have to introduce small pieces to them, especially if they are very much in the dark. For example, let's give an analogy: Tim and John are friends in high school. Tim and John grow up learning about the octopus and its many tentacles through old textbooks. They both notice that the photos in the book and everything they have ever been told about the octopus is that it has one head and many tentacles. Then one summer Tim goes on a deep sea diving adventure where he sees a creature that has three heads and many tentacles! Once he gets out of the water he asks his dad, "What was that?" "That was an octopus with 3 heads," says his father. Tim was so shocked - his reality just shifted from what his previously programmed thoughts made him believe. Now Tim knows there are three-headed octopuses swimming around out there! Tim can't wait to tell his friend John what he saw.

However, when he tells John that he saw a three-headed octopus, John slams him and proclaims, "No way! You're crazy - there are no three-headed octopuses alive, everyone knows that! What did you drink or smoke? What fairytale or movie somewhere gave you this dumb idea? You are sounding like a crazy person!" Tim pleads with John to listen to the new reality and that he is telling John the truth, but John just won't budge on his position. To John it's just too odd or weird to believe the new reality that three headed octopuses exist. Tim had an experience with new information which was believed as real, but John didn't have the same information or experience to conclude a new reality. Tim's reality includes three-headed octopuses and John's doesn't. A funny thing happens when John goes on his own deep-sea expedition a few months later, and discovers a five-headed octopus. He comes back to Tim and says, "You'll never believe it! I saw a five-headed octopus!" And Tim says, "No way… everyone knows there are only one and three-headed octopuses. Five is just fantasy." This is what we do to each other, every time we challenge each other's realities with plenty of perceptions of religious views. Everyone wants their reality as truth because that's all they know and have experienced as real. However, it all exists and it is all real, co-created, co-existing. It is quite a marvelous process. Respect all creation and be open to new data from a multidimensional perspective.

20.4 Be Malleable but Decisive

When you earn such new data, as we all do in life, you should be willing to adapt accordingly. Sometimes, though, we must 'stick to our guns.' Ask from life a little and it will give you a little. Ask life to give you much and it will do so. Life will test you. It throws all the challenges it can to you in order to see if you feel deserving of what you asked for. Real successful people 'choose' their path and do not give in to indecisiveness. The Cosmos does not like indecisiveness. You are a creative being and thus your soul wants to constantly be in the creative flow; just as God is. Indecisiveness cuts the flow of creation and causes the soul to feel tormented. You have so much free will that you may even choose not to choose - putting you in limbo. However, this is self-defeating and causes internal soul turmoil. Making a decision, even if it's the wrong one at that time will bring forth growth by learning from the journey. Those who make decisions and stick to them are respected, trusted, successful, happier, and live abundant lives. You cannot be indecisive and expect definite results in your favor. Indecisiveness is a trait of people who are not risk-takers, play it safe and live average and less impressive lives. Think of people in your life that are indecisive. They are usually unhappy, fearful, anxious, negative and not moving forward in their life's expression.

20.5 Fanaticism Weakens Your GOD Power

Are you wearing someone's logo or jersey; perhaps a team or corporate company paraphernalia? If you have no vested financial or personal interest in that team, then you may have allowed the idea of belonging to a group or team supersede your ability to hold onto your own personal innate power and identity as God Force. Every person walking around with a team jersey or the latest fad gadget has given up a piece of their power to that company or team. Is that company or team worthy to hold those people's energies? How do they give back to those people for the investment of their energies? Or is it a one way deal, parasitic? In the example of sports fanaticism it seems this is the case: Consider a middle aged sports fanatic male who spends his income on team paraphernalia, season tickets, and most of his weekend time watching a game on television that contributes nothing other than short-term entertainment value to his life. He is neither a player in the game, nor a coach, not even the team's water boy. However, he has invested so much of his mental, emotional, and financial energy in the sports team that he says to his friends, "We won Sunday," pertaining to the team winning as if he is somehow affiliated with the team roster. On the contrary, his vested mental interest takes away productive time from spending it with his family, or investing the money for a family vacation or his child's future school fund. The fanatic always loses power by voluntarily giving it away not understanding that they already belong and are already whole. They try to belong and thus give away some of their identity for the sense of belonging to a group or team. This is the same with other fanaticism such as religion, shopping, gangs, overeating, alcohol and drug use, etc. Anything that is overindulged in has your energy, mind, and thus some of your power. Remember, balance is key.

20.6 Going Hunting for Lost Energy in the Home

Speaking of balance, you should find it in your home as well. If you are unfamiliar with the concept of Fung shui, you'd be wise to start educating yourself with it. I am often hired to improve the chi for prosperous home and office flow. Patients feel benefit, not only when they improve their personal energy, but also find value in improving their home and work space energies to be consistent with their forward life momentum. Fung shui (pronounced 'fung-shway' means creating harmony of chi energy between man and nature), is a proven 6,000 year Chinese practice that uses placement and arrangement of your environment to improve your life and ultimately your destiny. It is not a religion or a philosophy, but merely a principal of how you interact with your environment. Is there harmony or disharmony in your home and workspace?

Proper Energy Distribution: The Bagua

WEALTH, SELF-WORTH, PROSPERITY WOOD ELEMENT PURPLE, GREEN, GOLD	FAME, SOCIAL LIFE, REPUTATION FIRE ELEMENT RED	RELATIONSHIPS, PARTNERSHIPS, MARRIAGE EARTH ELEMENT FLESH TONE, PINK EARTH TONES
FAMILY, HOME, COMMUNITY WOOD ELEMENT GREEN	HARMONY, HEALTH, RECOVERY EARTH ELEMENT ORANGE, YELLOW, BROWN	CHILDREN, CREATIVITY, METAL ELEMENT WHITE, METALIC
WISDOM, SELF-IMPROVEMENT, INNER KNOWLEDGE EARTH ELEMENT BLUE, GREEN	CAREER, PURPOSE, MISSION WATER ELEMENT DARK BLUE, BLACK	HELPFUL PEOPLE, TRAVEL METAL ELEMENT GRAY, METALIC
MAIN DOOR ENTRANCE ALIGNED ALONG THIS WALL		

When a company or business asks me to consult with them about their workspace's energy field, I allow my intuition to guide me through the bagua. The bagua is a simple way to check if the proper placement of your room is in order for the best cultivation of qi energy. If your home and office qi is in good order, your use of that room flows much smoother day-to-day. Take a look at the blocked diagram and notice that there is a certain color, element, and theme per block, all placed in their own positions relative to the main wall that has the door opening. Many patients have claimed that upon sharing with them the information of the bagua, their life rapidly progressed, and they no longer felt 'stuck.' The new flow gave them a better sense of awareness in their space, and better reflected how they managed their personal chi (qi) we worked on together in my office. Essentially, I lay the bagua floor plan over a rough blueprint of the client's home/office/abode. I increase on the specific energy the bagua recommends, paying special attention to the heart of the home (Earth element) in the middle of the space. The middle Bagua box helps tie in all the other boxes, and brings a balanced energy and sense of peace to client's living and working areas.

Energy Flow

Are you flowing or feeling zapped of energy? Your place of dwelling is a sacred space. Everything has its proper place, color, and meaning. The elements around you are either supporting your life or draining it. This is why it is important to live and be around only the things you love. Anything that does not define who you are or what you want to create must be removed. If you are feeling stagnant in your life, this could be one of the major reasons for being so. Anything out of place will cause not only an eye sore of clutter, but also a feeling of stagnation. Your home is where you sleep, where you eat, where you were raised, where you raise your children, or both. No place means more to you or says who you are more than the place you occupy two thirds of your time; your home. Take a walk through your home, condo, or apartment. Any item(s) you are not using is considered lost energy.

20.7 Things and Spaces: Taking Energy Back

Consider your home an energy storage house. You go out to the world and bring back energy contained in articles which maintains itself in your home. Some of these things you bring back are beneficial items, others, neutral, and others not so helpful or perhaps even harmful. Harmful energies are usually identified quickly and removed from the home before they cause harm. For example trash, or waste from things no longer needed or useful, is easily identifiable. The problem here is with the items that were once perceived as beneficial though no longer serve you or your space, i.e. a BBQ grill sitting in the garage which you barely used that now collects dust and takes up space.

Or a dress you may have purchased, wore once, and put in the closet with the other three hundred dresses you purchased on sale at the mall. They both looked great in the store, though now just don't have that brand new feeling.

If we were to view these two pieces as energy, one is cloth and the other metal. Both serve no longer the desires of its master and are occupying mass and space. Energetically they are now draining, not adding, energy to the home and thus your life. "But why is it draining energy?" you may ask. It is no longer contributing to your enjoyment or further purpose in this life, thus it is like a weight on your auric space and should be viewed as such. Let's take the BBQ for example. When you purchased it in the spring, it looked great in the hardware store with the price sticker on it. It was on sale and there were photos of happy families on the ad showing them having a great time cooking together in the backyard. You envisioned yourself as the chef, making everyone a delicious burger and feeding the little ones or your buddies as everyone laughed it up and had a good time. The price was right, the feeling was right, the logic was right. You purchased the item with money, trading the money (the idea of worth), for the idea of family and friend fulfillment, which could feed your soul as well as your stomach. You used fuel energy from your car to transport the grill. The fuel cost you money (mental energy) to run the car. You opened the box in your garage and proceeded to read the instructions, trading further physical energy to put the new grill together. You have invested quite a bit of both physical labor energy, as well as monetary thought energy, into the grill thus far. You hook up the can of gas to the grill and rejoice in a manly moment of pride; the plan is complete. You make plans for the weekend and call over the family and friends to put the grill to good use on the weekend. Thursday night you watch the weather report in horror, as you see rain is eminent through Monday. Your precious weekend of hamburger heaven is sadly over. In a sad moment of defeat, you push the grill to the corner of the garage, put the grill cover on, and mumble words of disappointment as you turn off the lights to the garage and go eat a frozen microwave hamburger.

Ladies, you decide to get out of the house and go to the local mall for some fresh air. As you power walk through the mall, doing some fun window shopping, a dress catches your eye. Unlike the other three dozen cute and colorful dresses in your closet, "This one's more cute and colorful!" you reason to yourself once more. And how convenient! It is on sale, a whopping 25% off! "I must have this one," "I deserve it", "I haven't bought anything new in a while," you say to yourself as you speed off to the dressing room to try it on. You know you can't afford it even if it is on a so-called mall "sale." In the dressing room you smile as it fits perfectly. You reason how great it would be to show off the dress to your friends as they sing praises about how great you look in it. Or how great it will feel to model it for your husband, who may again notice you as attractive and hopefully give you some much-neglected affection. You charge the credit card (thought energy) beyond your better judgment (once more), and look to wear it when you go out with your friends or husband during a special event. Life then gets 'busy' and the special event is delayed or never happens.

It's two years later and both that dress and grill are not as popular to you as they looked on the selling room floor. There's no luster, there's no special feeling anymore. You look at the items and feel bad about the money you spent and the lack of joy they supplied you. They're still the same as the day you bought them. They have not changed one bit chemically or structurally. The only thing that has changed is your perception of the item's worth and what joy it would bring you. What once was perceived as an item of happiness is now an item of painful loss. Both the items are now ready for the garage sale, where they will be auctioned off at pennies on the dollar as you hope to recoup something from the transaction. You hope to transform the item back to monetary energy. The real winner is the person who buys the item now from you, as they leveraged both their thought energy (monetary energy) as well as their emotional perception finding such a great deal at such a low price. The cycle always completes. The only variable here is who will you be in it, the first or second buyer? Who leveraged their power better? Who progressed themselves faster and easier?

This puts into perspective buying a car doesn't it? We've all heard the saying: Once you buy a new car, it's used once it hits the road. Its value starts to depreciate very quickly. If you decide to sell the car the next day, it must be sold as used since there was an owner to the car's title already. The first owner of the car has the largest financial commitment to the car's perceived value. The loan, the insurance, the sales taxes, etc., etc. The person who buys the car next may have a much better deal, especially if the first buyer lowers his or her perception that the car has lost emotional or material value now, compared to when first purchased. If the next buyer leverages their power correctly (using the laws in section 11.11, i.e. law of attraction, expectation, etc.), they can get not only a great vehicle in like-new condition, but also pay much less for it. We acquire thought energy (i.e. monetary energy) from: Working a job or career, being gifted it from a loved one, bartering or trading items or services for it, or simply finding it. We use it by: Purchasing items, losing it, or giving it away.

When you put forward your money for items (trading thought/mental and monetary energy for emotional impulse purchases), energy transference occurs. If in the prior examples you had stopped and thought differently about the purchase of each item as 'creative energy expenditure' before spending the monetary energy, then you would have evaluated the value of the transaction and whether the energy transference would add or subtract from your ultimate purpose or happiness. This moment of 'choice' is where one's true power is held. If a store, car dealership, etc. can manipulate your emotions onto an item, then they can take your money and transfer monetary energy (and power) to them.

20.8 Bringing Old Thoughts to Physical Form and Deleting Them

On the subject of choice and what you give power, it's not just your physical space you can control; it's your mental space as well. If you were lost on your way to your destination, you would consult a roadmap, or GPS system to get back on track. Likewise, we will now re-chart our life course for a more positive future by forgiving and forgetting our past. Let's proceed with the next exciting exercise.

Take a piece of paper and title it "Things I feel I did wrong." Write down all the *perceived wrong decisions* you have taken in life. Take your time and don't rush this. Take several hours or days to fill up the pages if necessary. Write each decision that you believe has directly led you to your present 'difficult or bad' situation. Next, make a list of the *perceived bad influences* which you know have brought you to this present position. This includes friends and acquaintances, or bad habits. Write down each one and how you believe it has directly led you to the present point. Take as much time as you need; this is a very important assignment. Now make a list of your actual *perceived failures* (relationship, work, etc.). Did your marriage fail because of you? Did you lose a precious job because of your bad attitude? List them all - both the ones that you could have prevented and the opportunities that were beyond your fault or another's.

Take full priority and seclude yourself from all cell phone calls, Internet browsing, or other distractions and sit quietly with your thoughts. Make your lists and take breaks from time to time. Come back to them later if needed to fill in missing sections or add something you remembered at a later time. Be sure your lists are full and there are no more things you can add. Read over the lists to yourself and see if you still agree with all the things you wrote down. If yes, proceed.

Now for the most important task: Go outside to the backyard or a <u>safe</u> remote area where you can dig a small hole in the ground. Dig the hole and then crush the lists into a ball, throw the paper ball into the hole, and BURN IT. Watch the flames transform the words which were negative thoughts into something beautiful the Earth will recycle. This point of release feels incredibly magnificent. Stuff the burnt ashes into the hole, and patch up the hole. Good-bye negative energy - forever!

Why is this exercise significant? By engaging in the symbolic act of burning the written words, you have sent them back to the non-material thought realm. Spiritually speaking, you are reversing thought that had become material. You have also forgiven yourself and allowed your soul some much needed spiritual rest. Now, it's time to write your manifestation lists because the old story for you no longer applies; how exciting! Similarly, you can write all your thoughts for this year's desired manifestations on paper and plant your special list near a big tree's roots for nourishment of your intention, supported by Mother Nature herself!

20.9 Get Off the Pain Train Immediately

Many people want to change in their life and are having a difficult time seeing any movement forward. They are unsure of how to change their current situation. I like to use the analogy of being on a train heading to a destination. Every train is on its specific track and heads towards a specific location. There are many tracks and trains. We make a choice on which train we take, knowing that its tracks will take us to the place we seek. But sometimes the destination of that train ticket you are purchasing is going to a horror town called "Frustration," "Pain," or "Anger." When a patient or friend is speaking to me about their day, challenges, or frustration in relationships, putting themselves in the well-known victim mentality, I smile and ask, "How's the ride?" Looking at me with a puzzled look, they ask what I mean by that. And I explain: If you are speaking of what is making you unhappy and voicing all the problems currently in your life, you are greasing the tracks with your mental, emotional, and spiritual energy into physical manifestation. This speeds up the creation of more unwanted reality until, ultimately, it becomes evident to others of higher vibration that you are heading for a train wreck. You are on a 'train of thought' that is going to the same destination you are previously very familiar with, but do not want. Anger or Emotional Pain Town is not the same as town Pleasantville or Happy Land. That ticket was available, but you chose to get on the train that takes you to where you have been before and are comfortably familiar with. Some of the same people you are friends with are possibly on this train with you, or types of lovers as well. It's so comfortable on this train that you may know nothing else than this. You may have ridden this ride so many times you are so familiar with the crew and captain that you're on first name basis. However, if this is the case and you want to be heading to another destination with better vibration, experiences, and outcome, then you must do the uncomfortable thing and say goodbye to this train and its travelers. Stop immediately by becoming 'aware' of what train you are on and get off immediately! Do not talk, think, or share any stories of your experiences with that old train and its problems or issues. Believe it never even existed. Jump on board the positive train of thought that will take you to the destination you desire, not the one you're so familiar with that is making your soul unhappy. Your thoughts and emotions, as well as the thoughts and emotions of those around you, are significant clues as to where you are going and who you are riding with in life.

20.10 Rejection Isn't Personal; It's a Process

How many times are you willing to stand the rejection of your ideas and plans? This is going to happen, as the law of opposites states it to be so. Once you claim what you want, the Universe tests you by sending you everything that is in contrast to what you want until what you want manifests. Don't quit! Learn the laws and understand that this is a natural process. Rejection is not personal; it's part of the process. Your success will lie in your willingness to apply persistent effort. Without failing, you cannot learn from the mistakes to improve your current situation.

20.11 Get Up Like a Winner

So let's say you wake up and you're not in a good mood. If you continue to feel bad, your day will continue to be that way. A common mistake most people make when they're trying to feel the abundance is that they do not recognize the point where their frequency changes. When you're always running a program and you are very comfortable in running that specific program, you tend to ignore when vibrations change. A vital key to vibrating higher throughout your day is the awareness that your vibration has become low and needs to change for the better. If you can start your day on a positive note, you can keep your vibration high and not have to succumb to the lower vibrations.

Over the years, I struggled with this. If I didn't have a good night sleep I would wake up really cranky and the rest of my day would go like so. So I decided if I want to have a great day and keep it that way, I needed something significant to keep my vibration from changing. I searched for a few easy words I could remember when I woke up. And when I found my four magical words I started repeating them every day I woke up and things changed quickly! Those four action words are: **I Make It Happen!** Yell those four action words out loud next time you can't get out of bed and feel the energy surge you right up! Follow up with: **I'm Happy, Healthy, Wealthy, and Sexy!**

"A lion lives in the heart of every brave man."
~ Turkish proverb

20.12 Starting and Ending Your Day

Upon waking (entering the physical realm) and prior to sleeping (entering the astral realm) you must set your intention so that you are creating deliberately. Otherwise you will be swaying in the currents of the cosmic ocean at the mercy of events and thoughts that have been set out by others among your own. You may be surprised to know that your day's events are good or bad according to how you have created them using your mind prior to starting your day. It is important then after you set your intention to continue that same frequency of intention so that your day proceeds in the same manner; joyful and inspirational rather than feeling like a victim of fate or 'bad luck' as so many believe life to be. It's not luck at all. Coincidences are not weird or odd, they are exactly the moment preparedness has met opportunity and they unfold as special moments of 'A-HA' or synchronicity. Transcending all customs and traditions is the ritualistic act of prayer or meditation. Start your day off right away with meditation and a prayer that feels good to you.

20.13 Apply a New Routine

Get up early. An early start will often help you feel more motivated. This wakes up a tired brain and makes you feel like you've accomplished a lot more than you would in a typical day. Switching from your normal routine can often be enough to energize and inspire you. Change life up! Take a vacation, approach and befriend a stranger, give words of praise to co-workers, volunteer in a shelter or a support group, hit the beach during your lunch break, take an afternoon run before dinner, or take a bike ride. Just get out of that routine!

20.14 Come On, Laugh a Little

Add laughter everywhere! Anything serious requires immediate laughter to liven the mood and raise the frequency. Look at children and how much fun they have as they laugh and play. You would be wise to do the same. What are you here on Earth for? To stress and pay bills? NO! You are here to create and enjoy your life, but, most importantly, to have fun! No matter the situation, you can diffuse it with laughter and humor. Even funerals are fun if you focus on the good times that person had with you, or tell a joke or funny story you shared with the departed that made you feel good. Laughter neutralizes fear and low energy. Is the big bad boogeyman in the closet? No sweat - just envision him with a shrunken head and big red oversized shoes, talking like a chipmunk and shrink him down to about 2 feet tall. Suddenly, he's not so threatening anymore is he?

20.15 Twenty Minutes to Changing the 'Real'

Why must you continue to believe that your current circumstances are real and unchangeable? Why do you have to be 'realistic?' If you continue to focus on the current unfavorable circumstances in front of you, you will only continue to get more of the same. The law of attraction works both in a negative fashion as well as a positive one depending on how you use it. If you insist on being realistic, all you do is bring yourself more of the same bad things according to your current 'realistic' thought patterns. A simple 20 minute meditation bringing closure to the events of the day just before you sleep, and a 20 minute meditation upon awaking to set the day's intention, will do wonders for your health and well-being. When meditating, be unrealistic and soar your imagination to new heights of what is possible on the flip side of your current situation. Certainly the astronauts were not being realistic when they bounced around on the moon, nor were our young presidents being realistic when they thought they had a chance at being the most powerful person in the United States of America. So truth be told, being 'realistic' in your mind won't let you grow further than where you currently are. Be UN- realistic and go for the best of all things. Of course exercise common sense while you pursue your goals. Being 'realistic' is not for big winners like you; that's for the average folk.

20.16 Free Will and Choosing Not to See

"Hear now this, O foolish people, and without understanding; which have eyes, and see not; which have ears, and hear not."
~ Jer. 5:21

We are on the cusp of a great enlightenment as our planet goes through massive changes, the likes of which we've never seen before. As we evolve our spiritual selves and remove our negative suppression, we become attuned to and aware of what we are really capable of as human beings. We are realizing that we are not supposed to look for enlightenment but rather to see that enlightenment is already inside us, and all we need to do is allow it to shine forth. Our enlightenment has never left us; we're in a blissful ignorance, kept down by our own insecurity and lowered self-esteem so as to not remind ourselves of the responsibility we have with our power.

Prisons of the mind that keep us from knowing our supremacy can be religion, ethnic prejudice, class wars, etc. that are all illusions meant to separate and conquer us, when in truth there is only love and unity, the uniformity that each of our uniqueness's express. We are here all here to break the spell of the human limitation that previous centuries have instilled in our ancient DNA.

Protesting is limiting and has very little effect on changing things around us. Our banners and marching in the streets has no power as the focus is still on the problem, not the solution. The solution comes when we all band together and love each other without prejudice or fear. When we believe we are better or less than others that is the true evil to our freedom and our personal justice. Change only happens when the public bands together to speak out against injustice. Silence and avoiding personal action when we know better is unforgivable.

20.17 The Importance of Judging and Timing

As I dug deeper into this work over the years I found out that one of the key elements of success to arrive at anything worthwhile was 'timing.' It did not matter how much I wanted to be financially secure at 18, have the nice car, the gorgeous model girlfriends, or anything else a young man in his early 20's dreams of - it just wasn't the right timing for me. I was preparing for my journey and the road I took at that time was the one of the student. When others at 26 were making millions of dollars in the dot com internet boom, I was sweating profusely studying for tests, class finals, and raking up hundreds of thousands in school debt. Call it my father's programming still in motion (get a diploma, a secure job, etc.), call it my low level of understanding of how the system worked at that time (aka. my Ignorance in spiritual growth), or call it fate - I was always responsible for the outcome. To each their own; the soul has lessons to learn and it will learn them at its own pace, no matter how much the conscious physical self kicks and screams.

Unless each soul's mission statement is examined under the microscope 'per say,' you shouldn't judge the path of that soul's greatness unless you walked a millennia in its shoes. One soul should not be compared to another. Each is at a different period of growth or level of expansion, so only God can judge you based on your own level of soul achievement. And your life is not right or wrong, it just is. We cannot put human perceptions or limits to what God thinks of us or anything else for that matter, as our understanding limits us unless we think like God. Reading all the positive self-help books in the world is not going to do you any good unless the information is absorbed and acted upon. We've heard the phrase, "Knowledge is power," though I have always claimed that is an incomplete statement, and instead believe that, "Applied knowledge is possible power and unapplied knowledge is truly a sin."

20.18 Living Longer – The Secret to Anti-Aging

How long do you have to fulfill your incarnation's purpose on this Earth? The answer is straightforward - just 27,375 days, but only if you do everything 'right.' The average American life span is only 75 and 80 years for men and women respectively. Women tend to live longer, as they take fewer risks than men and are less likely to repress their negative feelings. Living past 75 or higher, you are considered to have done 'really well,' and if you actually hit 100, you're a phenomenon. But what if you want to go way past 100 years? What if we choose to retire at 65 and believe that we're old and 'finished?' We lose purpose. In other cultures, retirement is non-existent. If you do not have a purpose when you wake up then there is no reason to be here and the soul then moves on. Retirees often die a few years after they retire. Why? They get bored, lose their drive and purpose, and slowly but steadily start to degenerate and mentally disintegrate their body so that the soul can exit. Inflammatory response is triggered each time you are stressed out beyond healthy limits. Lessening that stress through meditation and adapting the tips in this book will help you reverse the degeneration and help you live a longer and healthier life. But, there is nothing to fear, as there is no destructive death of the actual spirit. We only leave the physical body when we depart this plane. We are eternal beings so we do not really die; only physically transform planes of existence. However, there are many things we can do to stay here if we seek to extend our life and life's quality. Read *OF MAXIMUM HEALING* to unlock the secrets of better health.

20.19 Tips on Living Longer, Healthier, and Abundantly

- ✓ **Walk more on Earth**. The human body was made to move naturally. The convenience of a car deprives you of natural human movement needed daily that could cut your exercise time at the gym. We were not meant to sit in a car seat or chair for hours on end. Walk barefoot on the beach or through the grass at the park early in the morning. Earth energy is needed by your body and its energy channels for continued health.

- ✓ **Know what your purpose is; especially in career**. Knowing your purpose gives you the roadmap to life's experiences and allows you to experience that which you are here for - service.

A quick note on Career purpose…

The reason for existing in this world should not be laid upon a job title or mundane labor, but more importantly in your joy, happiness, and love for others. When you seek joy through serving, you will draw upon you the 'jobs' or 'career' that makes you very happy. And this would change naturally as your thoughts on what make you happy will change throughout your journey. "What do you do for a living?" is a question that we all get asked at some point. We justify our worth through the job title, label, or money made rather than the joy of feeling our happiness for the sake of serving. Looking for prestige in a job title or office location is 'lack' thinking. In order to feel fulfillment in your life's work, you must look to your abilities and talents and decide to do that which you find joy in and grow those to a point where they blossom also for others. Chasing the money rather than the joy first almost always produces an inner empty void and lack of life purpose. Your spirit cannot enter your body every morning and go to work to do a mundane, unfulfilling job for too long, when it is also yelling for fun and freedom. It is not the paper money that shows you are successful in life but the joy and happiness that makes the money materialize from an abundance mentality. You must feel good about what you do, share this joy with others, and help others find their joy. The more people you reach and help in joyful service, the more opportunity, growth, and prosperity will follow you.

- ✓ **Slow it all down.** Always having the 'On' button pressed causes inflammation related to every stressful, age-related dis-ease. To reverse inflammation, we must make time in our day to rest/nap, meditate, pray, or do nothing at all.

- ✓ **Take 25-50% off.** Everything you do that you feel is in excess, do 25% less of and allow that extra time you save to overflow to other, more meaningful activities. If you watch a lot of television, say 10 hours a week, put 25% of that to activities in self-growth, like reading your favorite book or spending it with friends or family. Eventually, remove 100% of anything that does not contribute to your prosperity.

- ✓ **Please pass the Greek coffee and wine.** On the island of Ikaria, Greece, most coffee drinkers average a life span of 90 years and higher. Wine drinkers historically live longer due to the positive effects of grapes (contain resveratrol). Just 1 or 2 glasses a day with a healthy plant-based meal will do the trick.

- ✓ **It's family time.** A positive happy family expands the life expectancy when invested in children, a monogamous relationship, and helping out aging parents.

- ✓ **Choose plant-based first.** Eat small but quality meals often with a plant-based diet emphasizing beans, green plants, and nuts. Meat should be eaten in smaller portions and twice or less a week.

- ✓ **Spiritual community helps you thrive.** It does not matter what faith you are, studies show that if you congregate with others of positive similar thought, you may live longer.

- ✓ **Pick the right friends; your tribe.** Possibly the most important factor for long life expectancy is picking people who help you stay away from the wrong things. A teenager with friends who do drugs will see a far shorter life expectancy than associating with friends who play recreational sports. Expand your social circle to only include well-minded, supportive, and inspiring individuals free of negativity and self-pity. Avoid negativity at all costs. Avoid it like the plague. Avoid negative people, places, things, and ideas. If you are confronted by negativity, you will feel it as "negative" because you will feel an immediate downward change in your energy pattern, instead of an amplification of your current good feeling. You will repel or start to move away from the trigger. Respect this feeling and do not engage the issue. Do not react to the situation; rather, neutralize it through killing it with kindness.

- ✓ **Truly love thyself.** Those who have an unconditional, healthy, non-egotistical or conceited love for themselves do things necessary to keep themselves growing in healthy ways. They know when they need to say, "No," and take care of themselves, and they know what is in the best interest of all. But most importantly, these people respect themselves enough to do what's right for themselves. An excellent way to know unconditional love is to think about all that unconditional love your pet has for you when they greet you at your door. If they know you're worth it, so should you!

✓ **Get holistic healing regularly.** Life-giving treatments like chiropractic, acupuncture, and reiki all raise and balance precious chi, recharging the body and calming the nervous system.

20.20 Remaining Young with Natural Aging

Aging happens as we move through our perception of time. Our perception of our outward physical looks or feelings of age are based on the experiences of change and accumulation of our life's feelings. We actually co-create our aging process with those around us. One person's thoughts of aging and dying are drastically different from another's, as is their end result. One could grow up thinking they are genetically programmed to have various diseases, while another can live healthy, and look and feel 40 when they are physically 65. As our older relatives die and we attend their funerals, hear on the news which celebrity has died, or visit our aging grandmother who is always telling us, "Aging sucks," we co-create the experience of what aging and dying means to us. If people believe there is decline in their physical and mental abilities with age, then there will be. Do not give your thoughts to those who believe their reality is exactly what you do not want to create for you. Although you may be 40 years old in physical time, it does not mean your cells need to degenerate towards dis-ease. Age is not correlated to how well you should feel. There is no meter that says, "Jim is 50; he should feel stiff or it's time for him to have diabetes," and "Janet is 30, so she should feel young and agile." There are people in this world that are 100+ years old, still moving around well without mental problems; yes it is possible. Do some research on "blue zones" and locations such as Ikaria, Sardinia, Okinawa, Costa Rica, and Loma Linda in California, which break our outdated limiting beliefs on aging.

Envision Youth Exercise

Living a long healthy life doesn't have to be a secret. Feeling alive and abundant can be as much a reality for someone at 80 as it is for someone at 20. If everyone thought differently about aging - that it is not bad, or negative, then that would change the collective consciousness and we would all live longer. If you change the way you see things, the things you see will change. Thought is powerful, and if united by many - it is unstoppable. Since your mind creates your present reality and what you place in your mind is what you will experience, this exercise will help keep you young. Place a photo of yourself in a highly visible area. Your wallet, your purse, your bathroom mirrors, refrigerator, etc. Get a photo from a time you remembered that you loved yourself unconditionally. You may have been thinner, in shape, had better skin, more hair, sexier, or felt much happier. Make sure it's a photo that shows you in a great happy mood and at the age you felt your best. I recommend a 10 year time reversal. If you are 60, I do not recommend a photo of you at 21 but rather one at apx 45-50 that you can better relate to visually and can actually remember more vividly. If you insist on using a drastically different age from your current one, it can still work depending on the attributes you are seeking. Say if you lost your joy at 60 and you seek to remind yourself to be as joyful as you were in your teens or twenties, then that would be an excellent photo to use. If you are 60 and decide you want to look exactly like you did at 21, that may be a more challenging idea to you at this early of your mind training and you may want to pick something that is more around 40 or 30. As you hold this photo with you in your presence, it transcends your reality of 'time.' It is important to also note that what you feel, think, and say out loud to yourself as you view the image will have a great importance to its effects. The photo will input into your mind the trigger each time you view it that you are that which you see. Your conscious mind may fight you, saying to you that you don't look like that anymore, or your negative programming may tell you that WAS you, but now you're fat, ugly, etc.

Tell your conscious mind, "Perhaps yes, I was at one time, but am eternally what I choose to be and I choose to be like 'this,' and I am moving toward a new me now." Reprimand your conscious programmed mind with this instruction each time you have a hindering thought so and you can input positive reinforcement. Patients come back to me almost immediately and tell me the compliments they receive. If they themselves don't immediately notice the changes that start to occur, their friends and family usually do. Patients act with more energy, more passion for life, they do things they didn't try before, and even their love lives rekindle their lost zest. As your mind is reprogrammed your spinal antennae will transmit out the images projected from your aura to others and it will match the best parts of their programming and bring what it is in them closer to what you are. Like truly attracts like. You will start to meet younger people also. One of my senior patients would comment to me that before he would hang out with negative colleagues of his and all the conversations would consist of what new doctor they were seeing, what new drug they are now on, or how they moved closer to a hospital 'just in case.' He said, "It was horrifying to see everyone dying around me when I wanted to do the opposite and live!" After incorporating this method, my patient not only attracted keeping most of his hair, but also made friends with people 20 years younger that are a much more youthful equal to his new energy vibe. He enjoys the energy, the conversation, and the life that his new friends share. In turn, their energy vibration is his new lifeline that keeps him forever young!

20.21 Live Fully By Leaving Earth Without Regrets

I have always wondered why we don't give more respect to those who have more life experience - our elderly. In other cultures and especially in African tribes, the elderly are not 'cast off' like they are in America after age 65. Through the years in my practice, I've been given the chance to learn from my older patients and get some of the invaluable wisdom they had to share. I asked them some great questions, and I am glad I listened. I asked senior patients in their 70's and 80's what they liked and what they did not like about their life thus far, what they would do differently, and what they would keep the same. These are the most moving statements I heard repeated, time and time again, regarding living life here on Earth:

- **Live a more daring and less 'cautious' life. Take more risks.** By putting your trust in God, the source of all energy; you know that you are taken care of. Whatever comes your way is meant to come your way, and you should accept the energy flow and move with it. No matter the challenge, you will rise up to meet it.

- **Don't listen to others' expectations of you. Listen to your own gut.** Put God first, yourself second, and everyone else third. Own your own happiness and take responsibility for nurturing it daily.

- **Make more time for family and friends. Relax more. Don't work so hard; work smart.** If you want to avoid this pitfall in life, work smarter, not harder, and know that 'success' (as society sees it) will never replace good health, good family, and a good life. Balance your time with work and play; you need both equally. Never put the love of money above everything else, as that is against God's teachings of true life prosperity.

- **Get all your feelings off of your chest. Don't let negativity build.** Unhealthy holding of emotions can lead to dis-ease, as has been discussed in previous chapters. Share your energy with others, but do not lower your vibrations to bitterness or anger.

- **Wait as long as possible to get married. Focus on self-development first so you can share a better 'you' with someone as deserving.** Racing to find a mate, any mate, will not fulfill your soul or match your vibrational frequency. Don't compete, complement. See yourself as deserving of a partner who complements you, and who values you.

- **Choose to be happy no matter what.** You can be happy in any situation. Challenge your own story by deleting the past – change your perspective of the past and learn from mistakes to help in future obstacles.

- **Travel a lot and make as many fulfilling relationships as possible around the world.** You're no bigger than the relationships you make real. If you want only success, your only relationship will be what you think makes you successful. If you create and grow personal relationships, you will exponentially bless your network of influence. Enjoy the journey of discovery with others; don't only seek the destination.

- **Treat all people well and with lots of respect.** Everyone has a different reality; there are over 7 billion realities, one per person and each are held as one's own truth. Focus on yours without feeling you must sway others to yours to be 'right.'

Remember that change is not based on outside events. Only by changing energy states and beliefs within you and shaping your inner world for a period of time can you reflect the changes you seek in your physical world. You must smile in the mirror to see the mirror reflect back your smile. If you wait for the mirror to smile first, you will wait forever. Change yourself first to see the change in the world.

Choose now to not have to look back on life with any regrets. Choose to look back and say, "It was an amazing life! So full of love and amazing moments! I am glad I did it the way I did it – I'd change nothing." That's when your soul will really rest in peace (R.I.P.).

20.22 Materialism

It's true, we enslave ourselves with attachments. Every attachment is a heavy ironclad chain reinforced by the last one carried. We end up becoming our own slave drivers working ourselves harder and harder to buy and consume more unnecessary products, growing ever deeper in debt, and drowning in accumulated interest to banks. Not serving soul purpose, but the false idea of what happiness 'is supposed to be,' keeps the people ignorant of their power. Before we realize what we have done and become aware of the illusion, it's usually too late to get out of the grave we dug ourselves into; like a hamster in its wheel, unknowingly exhausting itself to death.

When one looks deep inside themselves, they get the answers to all things. Your power does not stem from things you see with your physical eyes, but sources itself from the deep spiritual information you know subconsciously.

What you see, hear, or touch is a vibration, translated into what you experience in this life. You are vibration. What is sound? It is vibration on your tympanic membrane, causing sound waves that you translate to words, music, etc. Vision and light vibration, are also frequencies our eyes tune into. You are a vibratory creation of many energetic wavelengths. You also create with your thoughts, causing emotion, causing actions which lead to manifestation. This in turn, creates the material reality around you. You are continuously creating the future. Every choice you make through your God-given free will draws upon the universal laws to bring you what you think, feel, and act upon.

Just 15-20 seconds of deep focus on something, is all you need to start a strong magnetizing vibration. Multiply the 20 seconds three times and you have a minute of thought, focused on a positive vibration. This will start the process or materializing ideas. Don't start large, make it in steps. Do 20 seconds, then 40, then 60. Build, stack and repeat. You should only observe the right now, and as you do you will create later. If you see your current situation as good, you bring the better. If you are looking at it as bad, you will build worse for the future. The past only dictates the future if you focus on it now. The past only has meaning if you give it meaning, otherwise it is forever lost without further use to you like a deleted spreadsheet you never want to look at again and shred to forever gone.

Can Materialism Be Spiritual?

"Some people are so poor, all they have is money."
~ Patrick Meagher

A well dressed, affluent looking middle aged woman approach me one day at a seminar and said, "My husband is so materialistic; he's always talking about money and cares only about business. I don't like that he's not here with me at the seminar. He doesn't do self-empowerment programs like I do. He isn't spiritual at all." I quietly pondered for a moment her dilemma and saw she was coming from a strong lack mentality and distorted perception that allowed her ego a reason to hide behind the real issue - the fact that she had no real intimacy with her husband.

I asked her, "Does your husband by any chance own a business or corporation?"

"Yes," she said. "Does he employ many people, possibly hundreds or thousands, across the world?" I continued. "He does," she said surprised. "Do those families depend on this monetary energy to feed and clothe their children and put a roof over their heads?" "Yes I suppose so," she said. I further asked, "Does he provide the food for your family, jewelry you're currently wearing, and money to travel all over the world and go on spiritual outings, retreats, and seminars?" With a slightly flushed face and embarrassment in her voice she said, "Yes he does." I replied, "Then your husband may just be the most spiritually enlightened one in your family because he is serving and providing people with his talents and abilities as his Creator asks. He may not be doing it in a way you are familiar with, but spirit works in many ways and his contribution is loved by the Creator just as much as yours is. We should not belittle or judge anyone's connection to what makes them feel good as they serve others. This judgement does not serve anyone, least of all you." Materials and materialism have no meaning on their own, but will take whatever form the observer gives it.

20.23 Claiming It and Seeing It

Daily meditation, and the ability to clean out the noise of daily life, will provide you with the peace of mind and clarity to the questions you seek. When you consistently work on yourself, your tuning fork vibrates into a better, higher range. You start to become very good at summoning frequencies for deliberate creation. However, be aware that even then you may be able to create an opposite intention at times.

Have you ever lost your keys, remote, or credit card and said, "It's lost, I can't find it?" Well if you have, then you should know that in that very moment, you are claiming that you can't find it, and you never will. Your verbal statement and energy vibration creates a factual belief making you unable to find what you are looking for. The law of expectation will work with the law of attraction to keep you from what you are looking for, even if it is under your very own nose. Try saying, "I found it!" with excitement and feel how good it feels that you found the lost item. Try it next time an item goes missing and see what happens.

20.24 Develop Your Board of Directors

Who do you go to when you need to form a decision or make a choice on important matters? Large corporations have weekly board meetings, or 'think tanks,' where they discuss the best options for the course of their company's success. The saying, "Two heads are better than one," has merit when problem solving and solutions are needed. So who is on your personal Board of Directors? As the C.E.O. of your mind, during meditation you can hire anyone you wish! Do you want to put Albert Einstein at the table along with Abe Lincoln? Done! Do you want to add some love and humility by inviting Jesus or Buddha to sit alongside the group? Sure, why not. Your Board of Directors is anyone you wish them to be, as you run your ideas through them and allow them to whisper ideas and thoughts to you, telling you what they would do in your situation. You can envision yourself going one-by-one around the table as you ask each their opinion on a topic, and then you can make a decision on your course of action. You can always add or remove anyone you wish from your table as you grow.

20.25 How Do We Clean This Planet Up?

"Strength does not come from physical capacity. It comes from an indomitable will."
~ Mahatma Gandhi

What is right not only for me or you, but what is right for *us*? If we want no war in the world, we must not harbor anger in our own relationships. If we want kindness from other nations, we can't be hostile to the panhandler in our backyard. If we want love we cannot hate a brother or sister we call our blood. We cannot be hypocrites with banners and signs marching in streets for a greater cause for those globally when we can't even give compassionate care to those closest to us in our town. The answer to global peace and love starts not only in our own back yards, but deep in each of our own selves. *Luke 6:42* states this beautifully, "how canst thou say to thy brother, Brother, let me pull out the mote that is in thine eye, when thou thyself beholdest not the beam that is in thine own eye? Thou hypocrite, cast out first the beam out of thine own eye, and then shalt thou see clearly to pull out the mote that is in thy brother's eye." The path to world peace starts with each of us.

Chapter 21:
Conclusion

"One thing I know is that I don't know anything."
~ Socrates

21.1 A Gift of Visions

Socrates' wisdom is paramount when working with psychic energy. Our ego mind's ignorance amongst a vast multi-universe of information surely has its limitations. I share the next piece of events, understanding that some will believe and most will doubt. What is important is that I share what I know to be the truth, and that what I've learned from these visions helps you understand that the Creator does indeed know you, and will share with you great truths, should you ask for them.

Taking a Walk with the Father

A few years ago, I was gifted with two separate visions which are etched in my brain so vividly; I cannot forget them even if I tried. At the time, I had been asking myself (and God) questions that I didn't necessarily know how to put into words. One night, I fell asleep, and walked right into what I thought was a dream. I now understand this to have been a vision, and a message from the Creator which felt as real as this world we all experience day to day. I saw myself walking in an environment without shape or distinct color; it was like everything was in molecular deconstruction. The walls would disassemble themselves, and in a blink of an eye, they would reconstruct into what seemed a solid structure. I somehow inherently knew that intention mixed with my thought was the decree that builds worlds. Intention and thought lived in all that was created and flowed in the air around me. Suddenly, I felt sick to my stomach and felt the need to use the bathroom, so I began looking. In front of me were many hallways to bathrooms and it seemed as the Universe was opening up to my request, showing me all possibilities I could use, so I chose and followed a path. When I found the bathroom, I felt the need to vomit, and when I did, this terrible black bile spewed from my body, landing in the porcelain sink. As it drained down the sink hole, it formed a skull and cross bones. I felt immense relief once it was emptied from me. "What is that?" I asked internally to myself, and a voice spoke as if it was thunder vibrating all of my being: "It's all negativity leaving your body."

Then, I felt a hand take my shoulder, and immediately felt a kindly, almost grandfatherly presence. This force - energy - was everything and everyone. It was too grand for words and I was in awe. I was comforted, and knew I was with someone who deeply loved me. We began walking, and as we did, the disassociated environment I had been venturing through began to solidify, but not into individual forms. It was as if those pixels from different forms in this vision's world were combining into a bright blue background as they took the form of sacred geometric shapes. The energy was everywhere and it was in everything. The shapes formed this glitter-like blue flower pattern full of illuminated energy, and it was breathtakingly beautiful and in everything.

"What is that?" I asked again, and the voice vibrated its reply throughout my entire body: "This is the energy of life." I stared at this flower (I later learned that what I saw was witnessing was the famous sacred geometry known as the "flower of life") and then realized there were many people around us. They were faceless beings with vivid light bodies and I felt them; almost knew them without knowing them. As I focused on their faces, each began to quickly change into another face. White, African, Asian, Indian, female, male, young, old - the faces of these energy forms kept changing the more I focused and tried to identify them. I asked, "What is going on with their faces?" to which the reply was, "Those are the masks they chose to wear throughout their lifetimes." A feeling of awe that washed over me, and the knowledge of what he meant by that was like nothing I'd ever experienced. I found myself thinking of so many other questions and shouted, "I want to go back and be like Jesus. I want to heal people." The voice that responded inside my own head and permeated all my being spoke sternly, as if waves and thunder had crashed together: "You already do. I only ask that you love people." Like a bratty child wanting special attention, I exclaimed: "I already do love people! I'm kind to others and I help them!" But then the voice showed me the vision of a leper, covered in boils and warts a few feet from me, reaching out to touch me, and I couldn't help it - I jumped back in disgust. I was immediately ashamed, but the voice calmly stated: "I want you to love even the leper as you would love yourself. Love all like this." Then, in contrast to what I felt love was, the feeling of love the Creator wanted me to have started to fill/expand my chest and the 'perfect' love I thought I had in me already was nothing in comparison to what was filling my heart at that moment. I instantly knew that his love was larger than any feeling I had felt before, and that my capability to feel and share love was deeper than I ever knew. "What else would you like to know?" The voice asked me, unprompted. By this time I felt 'eternity' was getting too tiring to my body; I felt so overwhelmed by what I was seeing and experiencing around me that I felt drained and felt like I was unable to retain all of it in my body. "I feel tired and want to go to sleep," I said. The voice chuckled, much like a grandfather would, and replied: "My son, there is no such thing as sleep." I knew in that moment that the life we live on Earth is an illusion, merely a dream for a period of time, and that where I currently was - right there, walking with the Creator of ALL – this, THIS was the true reality. Gasping with this newfound awareness, I saw a flash of light.

Upon waking up my mind was unstoppable. I felt as if I had downloaded libraries of information and all anxiety in my life that I had prior to this, had faded to zero. I suddenly had a feeling of eternal peace and understanding which no teacher, parent, or priest could offer me. I kept praying and meditating with my questions. I wanted to see more. I wanted to learn more. My prayers were answered again.

A Gift of Knowledge From an Unsympathetic Place

About three months later I had another vision, but this one was entirely different from the first. In a similar shapeless, drifting environment, I began walking towards a room. I opened the door to the room, peered behind me to check that all was well, and then entered the room and shut the door. Something told me to open the door and look back outside again. When I did, it was like the place I was before had disappeared, and the door opened to a huge, empty void, like being at the top of island floating in the middle of nowhere; I was not where I wanted to be and felt an overwhelming sense of doom come upon me. I slammed the door shut, the room started to close in and become damp. I began to feel an intense thirst, like nothing I'd ever experienced. I also began to hear voices speaking out to me, offering me 'deals.' I ran for the sink in this room, which turned out to look like a bathroom, similar to the one I was in my prior vision. I drank as much water as I could get in my mouth. As I drank, the voices got louder and my thirst got worse. I looked around and realized the voices were coming from the walls - and the walls were moving. Faces pressed through the paint, like people trying to come through a portal – I was terrified. "Where am I?" I shouted even though my throat was on fire. A golden book appeared before me like a hologram, with gold lettering that burned onto the page. It read: "In this place of torment, thirst will never be quenched." I immediately recognized the book as the Bible, and I knew it was referring to Hell. But there was no fire, no brimstone at this vibratory frequency that I was experiencing. And worst of all, there was no sense of time as we know it here on Earth. I felt I and the place I was in were never-ending - eternal. I was just in a room, with a burning throat, and terrible noises pressing at me from all sides - this is not what I pictured Hell to be, but it was exactly that - a dimension of Hell. I shouted and banged on the door, knowing nobody would help me. I couldn't even fathom the identity of the person who could help me. I had lost all perception of my Creator - I was utterly alone and disconnected. Pain, darkness, continuous suffering is all I felt. I remember how much I wanted just a drop, even a half of a drop of water to relieve this feeling of death. After what seemed like a millennia of this torture, the whole floor turned into maggots, and they began to chew at my legs. As soon as the worms ate my flesh on my hands and legs, the skin, muscle and bone immediately regrew and the worms ate it again. I felt unexplainable pain again and again. Soon, the worms were all over and inside me; the pain was so intense that I wished death upon myself. I screamed, "I wouldn't wish this torment on my worst enemy!" and then the golden book reappeared in front of me. This time, it read: "In this place of torment, the soul will seek death and death will escape it," and then it was gone. I knew in that moment that this was eternity, and I was never getting out. It was chillingly real. I felt no hope, so lost, disconnected from life and I felt as if I was going to stay that way forever.

Then, out of nowhere, came that same voice from my first vision. It boomed: "What do you want?" and although my throat was in excruciating pain, like nothing I could ever imagine, I shouted back with my thoughts and mind: "I don't know! I don't know! I don't know!" I ran to the door, threw it open, and still saw only that abyss. The thirst was intolerable, the voices were louder than before, and the fear gripped me even stronger. It was the worst "Groundhog Day" ever; the repetition was enough to make me want to die. Then, the pain began to subside, just a small bit to allow me some awareness. All of a sudden, the idea of God came to me. I remembered Him! I shouted: "Jesus Christ, Son of God, help me! Get me out of this place!" Then, instantly the worms were gone, the thirst was quenched and when I opened the door; I wasn't in the abyss anymore. I was in a house, and I ran down the hall of white light, as I opened my eyes to find myself back on my bed.

While I have no doubt that I was shown these visions by our Creator Himself, I know that others who read my testimony will doubt these claims and pass them as 'fairytale' ideas. I do not wish to convince you of believing anything said in this book. *I only wish to openly share my personal experiences and whole-heartedly urge you to have your own witness and connection with the Divine.* I wish for you to come to your own understanding of the Almighty, for I know if you ask with pure intent, it will all be shown to you. What these visions have shown me is that **we are all creators like the power who made us; the soul asks that we instruct our creation. We must not imprison our minds with indecisiveness or ill creation, as these both lead to personal ruin.** What I have come to understand is that we damn our soul when we prevent it from creating, and when we do not ask for help from God, our one ALL Source. I felt what the soul feels when it doesn't create in a positive manner; I know it felt like Hell. I was also shown the absolute beauty of positive creation, and the beauty in the energy of all things.

I believe I was shown this because I had been asking God to show me, to teach me how to lead people. These were His messages to me. What I know now, without doubt, is that **we should love each other, more than we even know we're capable of. We change the dynamic and structure of everything and everyone when we love. We must create in order to give thanks to our Creator and to fully embrace our divine energy. We are truly made in the image and likeness of our Creator. Thus, we must create and create well.**

21.2 Closing Thoughts

The information in this book herein is the truth as I know it in this moment in time, and I share it lovingly "As Is." I do not expect you, the reader, to believe any of it to the degree I do, nor do I ask that of you. This information will change and reform as I gather new data and experiences in my own life. I urge you to filter the data you have read and put it into good use for you now in your life as you wish to grow. Truthful concepts and ideas will ring loudly for you in your heart when they are heard, read or felt. I hope this has been the case for you and that you share it with those who are in need. There is no expiration date on truth. Re-read necessary sections to reinforce what you know or feel to be real for you. Re-read anything that inspires or uplifts you. The sweetest gift I can give you is this message of prosperous thinking, for if you use this information correctly, you will never lack any good thing ever again.

To the doubters and cynics of the spiritual energy methods, practices, or information described in this book, I say it is perfect that you doubt, as it is perfect when you decide to believe. The amount of love, abundance, health, and wealth that exists for the believer exists also for the non-believer. Duality is such that we can believe or not believe, experience or not experience, see or not see. There is no judgment in the choice. Therefore, let us respect the duality of each, and respect what each one of us chooses. The same number of angelic energies that care for the system of creation exist for all believers and non-believers alike, just as the rain falls on all people, no matter their belief system. However, would you not base your beliefs on the system of energy that animates you and keeps you alive at this very moment? When we both agree that there is no separatism in this, we all know what we all are - simply Divine in nature.

Let me finish with a sweet little story I share with my patients. It is one of my favorites on personal power that has stuck with me a long time; told to me by an inspiring teacher in grade school.

It was a busy day in Heaven as creation of the earth had just been completed, and Man was about to be created as well. All of a sudden, trumpets blazed and angels sang hymns of attention. A big meeting was being called by God to attend to a certain matter that was troubling Him. As the meeting was called to the grand Holy table, all the angels rounded together in anxious excitement to hear what was on God's mind; causing Him to be so frustrated.

The Lord said, "I am at a dilemma, loved ones, as I am about to create the most awesome being ever imagined to roam free on this new land. I shall give him all the power I have; as he will be made in my image. I will give him free will, and this I will never take from him, as this is true God Force. He will truly be as his Creator intends him to be, and able to create as I do. However, I know that this great power that I give him - the ability to move mountains, calm storms, and create anything his heart desires - could be used both for great things, or misused to destroy himself and others. Where should this God Force be put on this land, so that man can seek it, attain it, and appreciate it fully?"

The angels saw the great dilemma and the important matter at hand. Their wings fluttered in excitement, each one wanting to be the one to offer the solution to the massive problem. The silence was eventually broken when a great archangel exclaimed, "Lord I know! Give it to me and I shall fly the God Force to the highest mountain range and put it there, that way man will take long to find it, and when he does, he shall appreciate this grand gift." God stroked his beard and thought for a while before saying, "No, it would not be right as the human is an adventurer, able to climb all heights and will surely be there quickly."

The angels continued brainstorming and talking amongst themselves when a few seconds later an angel exclaimed, "Lord give it to me and I will fly it down to the most darkest, deepest reaches of the sea and leave it there. Surely the human will take a long time to find the precious gift!"

"No, no," said the Lord, "The human is curious and expansive; all lands above and below the sea will easily be found by the human."

A little longer time passed, and a little cherub angel, timid, but sure he had the answer, pops through the ranks and, with excitement, appeals with a tender voice, "My Lord! I know! **Put it inside their chests, at the deepest reaches of their hearts. Man will be too busy looking elsewhere outside themselves and never think of looking there first.**"

"It is done," said the Lord.

In the next several decades there will surely be grand discoveries in the fields of the mind, human potential, free energy, multi-dimensional reality, robotics, and quantum physics. Groundbreaking inventions are just around the corner, which may allow us to see and measure quantum energy using plasma and kryo-energetics. Computer technology and humans may merge, creating bio-energetic chips in medicine and healing which could eradicate disease. For these amazing next steps in human evolution to occur, so that we can use the technology for our common good instead of our demise, the personal vibration of each and every human being must evolve to more than what it is today.

I pray the content herein will give you a glimpse into your mind potentials as you work spiritually on yourself here on Earth, and move away from relying on written accounts of experiences and instead activate the Divine ability within you. In turn, together we bring about the intuition age, where the availability of and connection to all information desired is unlimited. May we open our hearts and minds towards understanding the vast information pouring in to us from the areas of energy healing. It is important to keep a healthy skepticism and an open mind, asking for more data, as opposed to cynicism (arrogance mixed with ignorance). Think and feel for yourself.

I pray that the information and exercises provided to you in this book will aid in your path to further enlightenment. Ask God. Be open. Allow and receive.

"We cannot teach people anything; we can only help them discover it within themselves."
~ Galileo Galilei

See you at the seminars!
In the highest vibration of love and light - God bless,

Theodoros Kousouli D.C., CHt.

About the Author

A holistic health care advisor, teacher, speaker, mentor and author who is featured on major networks, Theodoros Kousouli D.C., CHt., is Los Angeles' premier holistic metaphysical energy healer. He is recognized and trusted for effective quick drug-free results, and his remarkable natural, pain-free, holistic healing system, the Kousouli® Method, focuses on getting patients to their top performance levels by unblocking pathways using the body's own repair mechanisms.

His desire to help others stems from his personal journey recovering from semi-paralysis and major heart surgeries, and includes everything he's learned about the optimum wellness techniques that define his practice.

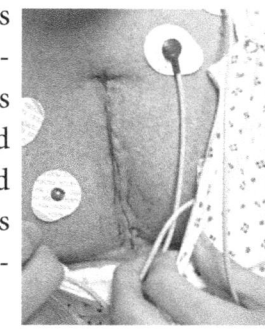 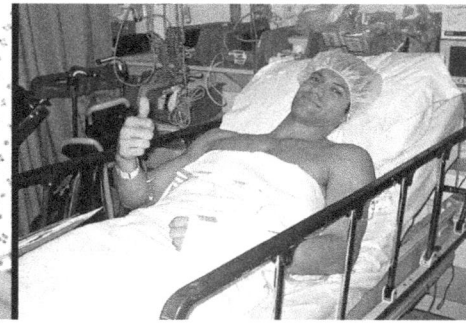

Dr. Theo Kousouli is the author of seven previous books, including *BE A MASTER® of SEX ENERGY* and *BE A MASTER® of MAXIMUM HEALING*. (www.BeAMaster.com). A personal coach and advisor to entertainers, business leaders, energy healers, and spiritual seekers of all varieties, Dr. Kousouli holds seminars teaching people how to tap into their inner healing and higher level abilities through the use of their nervous systems. Visit **www.KousouliMethod.com** for more information on developing your intuition and personal power to live a more purpose-filled, meaningful, and healthy life. Dr. Kousouli is the ideal speaker for your next event.

To Schedule Dr. Theo Kousouli To Speak At Your Event:
www.DrKousouli.com

Be a Master® of Psychic Energy

Life Changing Products · Books · Seminars · Empowerment Audios · Get on the Newsletter!
Connect with Dr. Kousouli, www.DrKousouli.com and on all Social Media Platforms
@DrKousouli #DrKousouli #KousouliMethod
You Will Also Enjoy Dr. Kousouli's Other Published Works Available Now from Major Retailers:

BE A MASTER® OF MAXIMUM HEALING
How to Lead a Healthy Life Without Limits
- Holistic Solutions for over 60 Diseases to Help You and Your Loved Ones Heal!

BE A MASTER® OF SEX ENERGY
Hypnotize Your Partner for Love and Great Sex
- Build a Stronger Bond with Your Lover(s) Using Subconscious Science!

BE A MASTER® OF SUCCESS
Dr. Kousouli's 33 Master Secrets to Achieving Your Dreams
- Solid Success Principles You can Apply Right Now to Empower Your Life!

BE A MASTER® OF SELF IMAGE
Dr. Kousouli's 33 Master Secrets to Living Healthier, Happier and Hotter
- Simple Holistic Tips & Tricks for More Weight Loss and Body Benefit to You!

BE A MASTER® OF SELF LOVE
Dr. Kousouli's 33 Master Secrets to Loving Your Extraordinary Life
- Overcome Bullying, Abuse, Depression and Build Massive Self-Esteem & Self-Love!

BE A MASTER® OF YOUR REALITY
Authentically Manifest Your Desires
- Use the Law of Attraction to Radically Transform Your Life!

If you would like to share your story of how Dr. Kousouli's books, audios or seminars have impacted your life for the better, we would love to hear from you! (Messages are screened by staff and forwarded when appropriate.)

For A Free Gift from Dr. Theo Kousouli visit www.FreeGiftFromDrTheo.com

References

Akhilesh. (2011). 51 ways to get motivated now. Retrieved from http://www.thinkwellplanwell.com/51-ways-to-get-motivated-now/.

Alcock, J. E. (1981). *Parapsychology: science or magic? A psychological perspective.* Oxford, England: Pergamon.

Alcock, J. E. (1991). On the importance of methodological skepticism. *New Ideas in Psychology, 9*(2), 151-155.

Alexander, S. (2000). *Rhinoceros success.* Franklin, TN: Spot Light Publishers.

All that is. (2011). Retrieved from http://twocrows1023.wordpress.com/.

American Psychiatric Association. (2000). *Diagnostic and statistical manual of mental disorders (DSM-IV-TR).* Washington, D.C.: American Psychiatric Association.

Anka, D. (n. d.).The teachings of Bashar. Retrieved from www.Bashar.org.

Ansari, M. (1991). *Modern hypnosis: Theory and practice.* Washington, D.C.: Mas-Press.

Antony, M., & Rowa, K. (2005). Psychological treatments for social phobia. *The Canadian Journal of Psychiatry, 50*(6), 308-316.

Aquinas, T. (2009). *The summa theologica of St. Thomas Aquinas.* Charleston, SC: BiblioLife.

Arias, A., Banga, A., Steinberg, K., & Trestman, R. (2006). Systematic review of the efficacy of meditation techniques as treatments for checkup illness. *Journal of Alternative and Complementary Medicine, 12*(8), 817-832.

Atwal, S. (2013). Indian psychology: The connection between mind, body, and the universe. Retrieved from http://antia-messages.blogspot.com

Au, P., & Weinstein, E. (1991). Use of hypnosis before and during angioplasty. *American Journal of Clinical Hypnosis, 34*(1), 29-37.

Auerbach, S., Gramling, S., & Rausch, S. (2006). Effects of a single session of large group meditation and progressive muscle relaxation training on stress reduction, reactivity, and recovery. *International Journal of Stress Management, 13*(3), 273- 290.

Averill, P., Beck, J., Diefenbach, G., Hopko, D., Novy, D., Stanley, M., & Swann, A. (2003). Cognitive-behavioral treatment of late-life generalized anxiety disorder. *Journal of Consulting and Clinical Psychology, 71*(2), 309-319.

Ayers, C., Sorrell, J., Thorp, S., & Wetherell, J. (2007). Evidence-based psychological treatments for late-life anxiety. *Psychology and Aging, 22*(1), 8-17.

Baker, H. (2001). Hypnosis for anxiety reduction and ego-enhancement. *Australian Journal of Clinical and Experimental Hypnosis, 29*(2), 147-151.

Balon, R. (Ed). (1998). *Practical management of the side effects of psychotropic drugs.* New York: Marcel Dekker.

Banerjee, K., & Singh, A. (2002). Treating panic attack with hypnosis in combination with rational emotive therapy. *Journal of Projective Psychology & Mental Health, 9*(2), 105-108.

Barabasz, A., Barabasz, M., & Smith, J. (1996). Comparison of hypnosis and distraction in severely ill children undergoing painful medical procedures. *Journal of Counseling Psychology, 43*(2), 187-195.

Barnard, S. (2002). Hypnosis, trauma, and anxiety. *Australian Journal of Clinical and Experimental Hypnosis, 30*(1), 78-91.

Barrowclough, C., Colville, J., & King, P. (2001). A randomized trial of the effectiveness of cognitive-behavioral therapy and supportive counseling for anxiety symptoms in older adults. *Journal of Consulting and Clinical Psychology, 69*(5), 756-762.

Baynes, H. G., & Jung, C. (1928). Two essays on analytical psychology. London, England: Bailliere, Tindall, & Cox.

Beck, A., Brown, G., Epstein, N., & Steer, R. (1988). An inventory for measuring clinical anxiety: Psychometric properties. *Journal of Consulting and Clinical Psychology, 56*(6), 893-897.

Beck, G., Diefenbach, G., Novy, D., Stanley, M., & Swann, A. (2003). Differentiating anxiety and depression in older adults with generalized anxiety disorder. *Psychological Assessment, 15*(2), 184-192.

Belanger, M. (2007). *The psychic energy codex. Awakening your subtle senses.* San Francisco, CA: Weiser Books.

Bell, C. (2013). *Poll: Americans love the Bible but don't read it much.* Retrieved from http://www.religionnews.com/2013/04/04/poll-americans-love-the-bible-but-dont-read-it-much/

Bertoldi, C. (2012). *Inside the other side.* New York, NY: William Morrow.

Bible teachings on angels. (n.d.). Retrieved from http://wisaac3rd.com/id94.html

Blackmore, S. (1990). The lure of the paranormal. *New Scientist, 127* (1735), 62-65.

Boehme, J. (2010). *Signature of all things; of the supersensual life; of heaven and hell; discourse between two souls.* Whitefish, MT: Kessinger Publishing

Boutin, G., & Tosi, D. (1983). Modification of irrational ideas and test anxiety through rational stage directed hypnotherapy (RSDH). *Journal of Clinical Psychology, 39*(3), 382-391.

Breakthrough discovery! Iron mountain mine catalyst breaks down pesticide, herbicide, & fungicide residues in soil. (n.d.). Retrieved from http://www.ironmountainmine.com/ARMAN_part4.htm

Brennan, B. (1987). *Hands of Light.* New York, NY: Bantam Books.

Browne, S. (2006). *The Mystical Life of Jesus*, New York, NY: Dutton Penguin Group.

Bryant, R., Guthrie, R., Moulds, M., & Nixon, R. (2005). The additive benefit of hypnosis and cognitive-behavioral therapy in treating acute stress disorder. *Journal of Consulting and Clinical Psychology, 73*(2), 334-340.

Burns, G., Everett, J., Marvin, J., & Patterson, D. (1992). Hypnosis for the treatment of burn pain. *Journal of Consulting and Clinical Psychology, 60*(5), 713-717.

Butterworth, E. (1983). *Spiritual economics.* Unity Village, MO: Unity School of Christianity.

Byron, D. (2002). The use of hypnosis to help an anxious student with a social communication disorder to attend school. *Contemporary Hypnosis, 19*(3), 125- 132.

Carroll, L. (n. d.). The teachings of Kryon. Available on www.Kryon.com.

Chambless, D., & Siev, J. (2007). Specificity of treatment effects: Cognitive therapy and relaxation for generalized anxiety and panic disorders. *Journal of Consulting and Clinical Psychology, 75*(4), 513-522.

Chambless, D. L., Dowdall, D., & Fydrich, T. (1992). Reliability and validity of the beck anxiety inventory. *Journal of Anxiety Disorders, 6*, 55-61.

Charney, D., Garakani, A., & Mathew, S. (2006). Neurobiology of anxiety disorders and implications for treatment. *The Mount Sinai Journal of Medicine, 73*(7), 941-949.

Chaves, F. (2000). Hypnosis in the management of anxiety associated with medical conditions and their treatment. *In the management of stress and anxiety in medical disorders* (pp. 119-142). Needham Heights, MA: Allyn & Bacon.

Chiropractic. (n.d.). Retrieved from http://www.tuquiropracticopr.com/index.php?p=77349

Clark, D., Ehlers, A., Fennell, M., Grey, N., Hackmann, A., McManus, F., …& Wild, J. (2006). Cognitive therapy versus exposure and applied relaxation in social phobia: A randomized controlled trial. *Journal of Consulting and Clinical Psychology, 74*(3), 568-578.

Clark, G. *The man who tapped the secrets of the universe.* Mansfield Centre, CT: Martino Publishing.

Clark, H. (1995). *The cure for all diseases*. Chula Vista, CA: New Century Press.

Cohen, J. (1988). *Statistical power analysis for the behavioral sciences* (2nd ed.). Hillside, NJ: Lawerence Erlbaum.

Cohen, R.J., & Swerdlik, M.E. (2002). *Psychological testing and assessment: An introduction to test and measurement* (5th ed.). Boston, MA: McGraw-Hill.

Collins COBUILD English Language Dictionary. (1987). London, England: Collins.

Collins, H. M. & Pinch, T. J. (1979). The construction of the paranormal: Nothing unscientific is happening. In Roy Wallis (Ed.), On the margins of science: The social construction of rejected knowledge (pp. 237-269). *Sociological Review Monograph, 27*.

Coman, G., & Evans, B. (2003). Hypnosis with treatment for the anxiety disorders. *Australian Journal of Clinical and Experimental Hypnosis, 31*(1), 1-31.

Coomaraswamy, A. (2005). Who is Satan and where is hell? Retrieved from http://elkorg-projects.blogspot.com/2005/05/ananda-k-coomaraswamy-who-is-satan-and.html

Corrective care: Getting to the root of the problem. (n.d.). Retrieved from http://www.woudsmachiropractic.com/CORRECTIVE-CARE.aspx

Cranton, E. (2012). Chelation therapy: New hope for victims of cardiovascular and age-associated diseases. Retrieved from http://www.drcranton.com/newhope.htm.

Davies, B. (2000). *The 7 Healing Chakras*. Berkeley, CA: Ulysses Press.

Davies, S., Davies, T., & Wickramasekera, I. (1996). Applied psychophysiology: A bridge between the biomedical model and biopsychosocial model in family medicine. *Professional Psychology: Research and Practice, 27*(3), 221-233.

Davidson, F. (n.d.). For the Energetically Sensitive. Retrieved from http://www.psychicandenergywork.com.au/For-the-Energetically-Sensitive.php

Davidson, F. (1999). Life in a world of atoms. *Well Being Magazine,* (77).

DeBerry, S., & Reinhard, K. (1989). A comparison of meditation-relaxation and cognitive-behavioral techniques for reducing anxiety and depression in a geriatric population. *Journal of Geriatric Psychiatry, 22*(2), 231-247.

Degun-Mather, M. (2001). The value of hypnosis in the treatment of chronic PTSD with dissociative fugues in a war veteran. *Contemporary Hypnosis, 18*(1), 4-13.

Dervin, B. (1983). An overview of sense-making research: concepts, methods, and results to date. Paper presented at the *International Communication Association Annual Meeting*. Dallas, TX.

Dervin, B. (1992). From the mind's eye of the user: the sense-making qualitative-quantitative methodology. In Jack D. Glazier & Ronald R. Powell (Eds.), *Qualitative research in information management* (pp. 61-84) . Englewood, NJ: Libraries Unlimited.

Detering, N. (2005). Anxiety, memory enhancement, and hypnosis. *Australian Journal of Clinical and Experimental Hypnosis, 33*(1), 64-73.

Dugas, M., Freeston, M., Ladouceur, R., Langlois, F., Leger, E., & Provencher, M. (2003). Group cognitive-behavioral therapy for generalized anxiety disorder: Treatment outcome and long-term follow-up. *Journal of Consulting and Clinical Psychology, 71*(4), 821-825.

Edmunds, S. (1969). *Hypnotism and the supernormal*. Hollywood, CA: Wilshire Book Company.

Edwards, J. (2010). *After life*. New York, NY: Sterling Publishing

Efthimiou, M. (n.d.). How old is the orthodox faith? Retrieved from http://www.orthodoxphotos.com/history.shtml.

Elder Paisios of Mount Athos. (2010). *Spiritual struggle, volume III*. Montreal: Alexander Press.

Ellsmore, W. (2001). Hypnosis in the multi-modal treatment of chronic anxiety. *Australian Journal of Clinical and Experimental Hypnosis, 29*(2), 122-130.

Environmental toxicity: An alternative way of assessing heavy metals? (n.d.). Retrieved from http://www.lightparty.com/Health/HealingRegeneration/PDF/EnvironmentalToxicity.htm

Erdelez, S. (1997). Information encountering: a conceptual framework for accidental information discovery. In Vakkari, P., Savolainen, R., & Dervin, B (Eds.), *Information seeking in context*. London, England: Taylor Graham.

Etemad, B., Garcia, F., Khalid, S., Rickels, K., & Rynn, M. (2006). Early response and 8-week treatment outcome in GAD. *Depression and Anxiety, 23*(1), 461-465.

Evans, B. (2003). Hypnosis for post-traumatic stress disorders. *Australian Journal of Clinical and Experimental Hypnosis, 31*(1), 54-73.

Exploring consciousness more closely. (n.d.). Retrieved from http://www.umsonline.org/consciousness.htm

Eymann, P. &, Bechtle, J. (n.d.). Angels. Retrieved from http://www.rapturenotes.com/angels.html

Fabian, G., & Fabian, T. (1998). Stress of life, stress of death: Anxiety in dentistry from the viewpoint of hypnotherapy. In *Stress of life: From molecules to man*. New York, NY: New York Academy of Sciences.

Fromm, E., & Nash, M. (Eds). (1992). *Contemporary hypnosis research*. New York, NY: Guilford Press.

Gabbard, G. (Ed.). (2009). *Textbook of psychotherapeutic treatments.* Arlington: American Psychiatric Publishing, Inc.

Gale Reference Team. (2001). *The Gale encyclopedia of psychology: Charcot, Jean Martin (1825-1893)* (2nd ed.). Farmington Hills, MI: Thomson Gale.

Gantt, L., & Tinnin, L. (2007). Intensive trauma therapy of PTSD and dissociation: An outcome study. *The Arts in Psychotherapy, 34*(1), 69-80.

Gearan, P., Kirsch, I., Montgomery, G., Pastyrnak, S., & Schoenberger, N. (1997). Hypnotic enhancement of a cognitive-behavioral treatment for public speaking anxiety. *Behavior Therapy, 28*(1), 127-140.

German, E. (2004). Hypnosis and CBT with depression and anxiety. *Australian Journal of Clinical and Experimental Hypnosis, 32*(1), 71-85.

Gorenstein, E., Kleber, M., & Mohlman, J. (2005). Cognitive-behavioral therapy for management of anxiety and medication taper in older adults. *American Journal of Geriatric Psychiatry, 13*(10), 901-909.

Gow, M. (2006). Hypnosis with a 31-year-old female with dental phobia requiring an emergency extraction. *Contemporary Hypnosis, 23*(2), 83-91; 92-100.

Green. L. liveyourdreamsmentor (Poster). (2010, Oct. 18). The law of vibration universal law – check your vibes - trust your vibes! [Video] Retrieved from http://www.youtube.com/watch?v=rqhAMnUsbr0.

Green, M. (1982). *The day death died.* Leicester, England: Inter-Varsity Press.

Green, T.S. (1976). *Greek-English lexicon of the New Testament.* London, England: Samuel Bagster & Sons.

Grube, G. M. A., & Reeve, C. D. C. (1992). *Plato: Republic* (2nd ed.). Indianapolis, IN: Hackett Publishing.

Hall, M. P. (2003). *Secret teachings of all ages (reader's edition).* New York, NY: Tarcher.

Halpern, D., & Nilan, M. S. (1988). A step toward shifting the research emphasis in information science from the system to the user: an empirical investigation of source-evaluation behavior information seeking and use. In Borgman, C. L., & Pai, E. Y. H. (Eds.), *ASIS '88: Proceedings of the 51st annual meeting of ASIS* (pp. 169-176). Medford, OR: ASIS.

Heino, H. (1994). *Lukijalle.* (O. Aho, Trans.). Helsinki, Finland: Kirjaneliö.

Hewitt, W. W. (1997). *Hypnosis for beginners.* St. Paul, MN: Llewellyn Publications.

Hiatt, M. (2006). *Mind magic*. Woodbury, MN: Llewellyn Publishing.

Hilgard, E. (1967). The use of pain-state reports in the study of hypnotic analgesia to the pain of ice water. *Journal of Nervous and Mental Disease, 144*(6), 506-513.

Hicks, E., & Hicks, J. (2007). *The astonishing power of emotions*. Carlsbad, CA: Hay House Publishing.

Hilgard, E., Knox, V., & Morgan, A. (1974). Pain and suffering in ischemia: The paradox of hypnotically suggested anesthesia as contradicted by reports from the hidden observer. *Archives of General Psychiatry, 30*(6), 840-847.

Hill, N. (2011). *Outwitting the Devil*. New York, NY: Sterling Publishing.

Hill, R. (2005). The use of hypnosis in the treatment of driving phobia. *Contemporary Hypnosis, 22*(2), 99-103.

Hobhouse, S., & Law, W. (2005). The spirit of love. Whitefish, MT: Kessinger Publishing

Hobhouse, S. William (1927). *William Law and eighteenth century Quakerism; including some unpublished letters and fragments of William Law and John Byrom*. London, England: George Allen & Unwin.

Hoffman, F. (2000). Relativity: Spiritual vs. physical. Retrieved from http://www.all-creatures.org/sermons98/s30jan2000.html

Horowitz, S. (1970). Strategies within hypnosis for reducing phobic behavior. *Journal of Abnormal Psychology, 75*(1), 104-112.

Hosford, R. (1969). Behavioral counseling: A contemporary overview. The *Counseling Psychologist, 1*(4), 1-33.

How do emotions affect my health? (n.d.). Retrieved from http://www.kinesiologyhealthpractice.com.au/page/how_does_emotions_affect_our_life.html

Hoy, T. (2009). Aura psychic reading: How your aura can reveal your personality.Retrieved from http://ezinearticles.com/ ?Aura-Psychic-Reading---How-Your-Aura-Can-Reveal-Your-Personality&id=3336390.

Iglesias, A., & Iglesias, A. (2005). Awake-alert hypnosis in the treatment of panic disorder: A case report. *American Journal of Clinical Hypnosis, 47*(4), 249-257.

Injured on the job? Speed your recovery. (2013) Retrieved from http://absolutehealthmn.blogspot.com/

Jackson, D. (1999). You will feel no pain. *Smithsonian, 29*, 126-140.

James, W. (1982). *The varieties of religious experience: A study in human nature.* New York, NY: Penguin Classics

Jensen, M., & Patterson, D. (2003). Hypnosis and clinical pain. *Psychological Bulletin, 129*(4), 495-521.

Johnson, D., & Soloman, S. (2002). Psychosocial treatment of post-traumatic stress disorder: A practice-friendly review of outcome research. *Journal of Clinical Psychology, 58*(8), 947-959.

Johnston, D. *Lessons for Living Lesson Eight: "The Four Levels of Healing."* Retrieved from http://www.lessons4living.com/wmaz8.htm

Jung, C. (1935). *The integration of personality.* London, England: Routledge & Kegan Paul Ltd.

Kaleshwar, S. (2010). *The real life and teachings of Jesus Christ.* Andhra Pradesh, India: S. Kaleshwar Publications.

Kari, Jarkko (1996). Paranormal information seeking in everyday life – Part I: A survey on paranormal information needs and seeking in the framework of everyday life information seeking]. (Unpublished master's thesis). University of Tampere, Finland.

Katz, D. L. (2004). *You are psychic.* Woodbury, MN: Llewellyn Publishing.

Katz, D. L. (2009). *Freeing the genie within.* Woodbury, MN: Llewellyn Publishing.

Keith, S., Rickard, H., & Scogin, F. (1992). Progressive and imaginal relaxation training for elderly persons with subjective anxiety. *Psychology and Aging, 7*(3), 419- 424.

Kessler, R., & Whalen, T. (1999). Hypnotic preparation in anesthesia and surgery. In Temes, R. (Ed.), *Medical hypnosis: An introduction and clinical guide. medical guides to complementary and alternative medicine* (pp. 43-57). New York, NY: Churchill Livingstone

Kousouli, T. (2014). *Dirty Little Secrets of the Healthcare Industry: What Every Patient Should Know.* Indianapolis, IN: Dog Ear Publishing.

Kreeft, P., & Tecelli, R. K. (2003). *Pocket handbook of Christian apologetics.* Downers Grove, IL: InterVarsity Press.

Krikelas, J. (1983). Information-seeking behavior: patterns and concepts. *Drexel Library Quarterly, 19* (2), 5 20.

Kuningas, T. (1995). Need for information is growing. *Ultra , 24* (11), 3.

Kurtz, P. (1985). Is parapsychology a science? In Paul Kurtz (Ed.), *A skeptic's handbook of parapsychology* (pp. 503-518). Buffalo, NY: Prometheus.

Lansky, A. (n.d.). Consciousness as an active force. Retrieved from http://homepages.ihug.co.nz/~sai/consciousness.html

Lewis, C. S. (1941). The weight of glory. (Reprinted from *Theology, November 1941)*. Retrieved from http://www.ucs.louisiana.edu/~ras2777/spirituality/lewis.htm

Lewis, C. S. (1980). *The weight of glory and other addresses.* New York, NY: Collier Books.

Lippmann, W. (1922). *Public opinion.* New York, NY: Harcourt, Brace, and Company.

Looking at guided meditation as a tool for daily living. (2013). Retrieved from http://alternative-medicinesresources.com/category/natural-heading/meditation/.

Macdonald, D. B. (1934). *The Hebrew philosophical genius.* Princeton, NJ: Princeton University Press.

Marsh, C. (2008). *The mentalist's handbook.* San Francisco, CA: Weiser Books.

McKay, B., & McKay, K. (2011). Becoming superhuman in 2011. Retrieved from http://artofmanliness.com/2011/01/02/becoming-superhuman-in-2011/.

Meredith, R. (n.d.). Restoring original Christianity. Retrieved from http://www.tomorrowsworld.org/node/5783.

Millman, D. (1995). *The laws of spirit.* Tiburon, CA: HJ Kramer.

Mind control theories and techniques used by mass media. (2010). Retrieved from http://veracityvoice.com/?p=8136.

Mondithoka, S. (n.d.) Life after death: reincarnation or resurrection? Retrieved from http://mondithokas.com/docs/Life_after_Death_Reincarnation_or_Resurrection_2.doc

Nicene-Constantinopolitan Creed. (n. d.). Retrieved October 22, 2012 from the Orthodox Wiki: http://orthodoxwiki.org/Nicene-Constantinopolitan_Creed

Our desires. (2009). Retrieved from http://www.douban.com/note/47005404/

Organization of the nervous system: An introduction for students in the human anatomy course. (n.d.). Retrieved from http://www.emory.edu/ANATOMY/AnatomyManual/nervous_system.html

Parsons, K. M. (1992). The study of pseudoscience and the paranormal in the university curriculum. *Electronic Newsletter of the Georgia Skeptics, 5* (5).

Peirce, P. (2009). *Frequency: The power of personal vibration.* Hillsboro, OR: Atria Books

Perttula, S. (1994). On studying information action as a process. *Library and Information Science, 13* (2), 38-47.

Pfeiffer, F. (1992). *Works of Meister Eckhart.* Whitefish, MT: Kessinger Publishing.

Prayer. (n. d.). Retrieved October 22, 2012 from the Orthodox Wiki: http://orthodoxwiki.org/Prayer

Robbins, J. (1996). Health care a look beyond. Excerpted from *Reclaiming our health: Exploding the medical myth and embracing the source of true health.* Retrieved from http://lightparty.com/Health/HealthCare.html

Roman, S., & Packer, D. (1987). *Opening to channel.* Tiburon, CA: HJ Kramer.

Roman, S., & Packer, D. (2008). *Creating money.* Novato, CA: HJ Kramer.

Rozsa, M. (2014). *7 things Americans think are more plausible than global warming.* Retrieved from http://www.salon.com/2014/12/20/7_things_americans_think_are_more_plausible_than_global_warming_partner/

Sanford, A. (1971). *The healing light: The art and method of spiritual healing.* Edina, MN: Macalester Park Publishing. Retrieved from http://self-improvement-ebooks.com/books/sanford2.php

Sanford, A. (n.d.). Retrieved March 28, 2013 from http://en.wikipedia.org/wiki/Agnes_Sanford

Sanford, A. (1897-1982). World-renowned spiritual healer. Retrieved from http://agnessanford.wwwhubs.com/

Scheib, A. (n.d.) Pikuach Nefesh. Jewish Virtual Library. Retrieved from http://www.jewishvirtuallibrary.org/jsource/Judaism/pikuach_nefesh.html)Schumaker, J. F. (1987). Mental health, belief deficit compensation, and paranormal beliefs. *Journal of Psychology, 121* (5), 451-457.

Schwartz, D. J. (1987). *The magic of thinking big.* New York, NY: Simon & Schuster.

Silver, J. (2009).Negative and Fixed Mindset Patterns. Retrieved from http://www.holistic-mind-body-healing.com/fixed-mindset.html

Snyder, J. (1984). *Reincarnation vs. resurrection.* Chicago, IL: Moody Press.

Sparks, G. G., Sparks, C. W., & Gray, K. (1995). Media impact on fright reactions and belief in UFOs: the potential role of mental imagery. *Communication Research, 22* (1), 3 23.

Stevenson, I. (1966). *Twenty cases suggestive of reincarnation.* New York, NY: American Society for Psychical Research.

Stratton, E. (2012). Awakening the healer within - empowering spiritual healing. Reprinted from

The International Journal of Healing and Caring, September, 2001). Retrieved from http://www.touchingspirit.org/awakening.htm

Sullivan, H. S. (1938). Introduction to the study of interpersonal relations. *Psychiatry*, 1.

Taylor, S. (2015). *List of archangels: Archangel names.* Retrieved from http://www.angelsbysharae.com/ArchangelsList.html

Tobacyk, J., & Milford, G. (1983). Belief in paranormal phenomena: assessment instrument development and implications for personality functioning. *Journal of Personality and Social Psychology, 44* (5), 1029 1037.

Ward, S. A. (1983). Epilogue: outline of a research agenda. In Ward, S., & Reed, L. J. (Eds.) *Knowledge structure and use: Implications for synthesis and interpretation* (pp. 671-681). Philadelphia, PA: Temple University.

Wersig, G., & Windel, G. (1985). Information science needs a theory of "information actions." *Social Science Information Studies*, (5), 11-23.

Walsch, N. D. (1995). *Conversations with God.* New York, NY: G.P. Putnam.

What does the Bible teach about angels? (n.d.). Retrieved from http://christiananswers.net/q-acb/acb-t005.html

What is detoxification? (n.d.). Retrieved from http://www.lightparty.com/Health/HealingRegeneration/html/WhatIsDetoxification.html

What is remote viewing? (n.d.). Retrieved from http://www.remoteviewed.com/about_remote_viewing.htm

What on earth am I here for? (2006). Retrieved from http://www.grenoblechurch.org/Main/WhatOnEarthAmIHereFor

Wikia. *How many different gods in religion.* Retrieved April 2, 2013 from Wikia: http://answers.wikia.com/wiki/How_many_different_gods_in_religion.

Wilson, P. (1977). *Public knowledge, private ignorance: toward a library and information policy* (Contributions in librarianship and information science no. 10). Westport, CT: Greenwood.

Wilson, T.D. (1981). On user studies and information needs. *Journal of Documentation, 37*(1), 3-15.

Wynne, G.T. (1991). *History of the occult.* London, England: Grange Books.

www.ingramcontent.com/pod-product-compliance
Lightning Source LLC
Chambersburg PA
CBHW080919180426

43192CB00040B/2474